PEARSON CUSTOM LIBRARY
POLITICAL SCIENCE

A CUSTOMIZED POLITICAL SCIENCE READER
GENERAL EDITOR GREGORY M. SCOTT
UNIVERSITY OF CENTRAL OKLAHOMA

THE AMERICAN NATIONAL GOVERNMENT
POLITICAL SCIENCE 201
DALEY COLLEGE

PEARSON

ISBN 10: 1-269-11583-9
ISBN 13: 978-1-269-11583-4

ACKNOWLEDGEMENTS

The collection of more than 450 readings from journals, newspapers and primary source material was selected by an editorial board of experts. Special thanks to our general editor, Gregory M. Scott, *University of Central Oklahoma*, whose proficient knowledge of the subject matter helped to shape our article offerings and their pedagogical support. We also wish to thank our contributing editors, Robert P. Watson, *Florida Atlantic University*, and Terence M. Garrett, *The University of Texas at Brownsville*, for their assistance in strengthening the content which falls within their specialty. Lastly, we'd like to recognize Pearson Arts & Science for allowing us to include their best-selling textbook content within this program. Their high publishing standards complement what we demand of our article selection.

The articles presented in *Choices* also undergo review from experts in the field of political science. These reviewers have influenced our decisions about the development of *Choices* as a classroom resource. With sincere thanks, we acknowledge:

Timothy Ballard, *Imperial Valley College*; Brian Bearry, *University of Texas, Dallas*; Amy Black, *Wheaton College*; Ted Blair, *Las Positas College*; Angela Bos, *University of Minnesota, Morris*; Corey Cook, *San Francisco State University*; Michael Deaver, *Sierra College*; Bryan M. Dubin, *Oakland Community College*; Michael Ebeid, *Boston University*; James Hanley, *Adrian College*; Kay Hofer, *Texas State University-San Marcos*; Richard Holtzman, *Texas State University-San Marcos*; W.V. Hood III, *University of Georgia*; Alice M. Jackson, *Morgan State University*; Dr. Scott P. Johnson, *Frostburg State University*; Ken Kollman, *University of Michigan*; Douglas Koopman, *Hope College*; Gary Lee Malecha, *University of Portland*; Dr. Lee March, *Young Harris College*; Nathan Melton, *Utah Valley State College*; Ted Ritter, *University of Oklahoma*; Carroll G. Robinson, *Texas Southern University*; Debra Salazar, *Western Washington University*; Jason Vitaich, *American River College*; Heather Wyatt-Nichol, *Stephen F. Austin State University*.

Table of Contents

American Government: Roots, Context, and Culture

From Chapter 1 of *Essentials of American Government: Roots and Reform,* 2012 Election Edition. Karen O'Connor. Copyright © 2014 by Pearson Education, Inc. Published by Pearson Education, Inc. All rights reserved.

American Government: Roots, Context, and Culture

I n December 1606, three ships—the *Susan Constant*, the *Godspeed*, and the *Discovery*—set sail from Blackwall, England, to America. These ships held 104 men and boys seeking their fortunes, for the New World was reputed to offer tremendous riches. However, this sorry mix lacked the skills necessary to sustain a colony in the harsh terrain and conditions they were to encounter.

The London Company, a joint stock company that was created to attract much-needed capital to aid British colonization of the New World, financed the colonists. Joint stock companies allowed potential investors to purchase shares of stock in companies anticipating large payoffs for their investments several years down the road. Enthusiasm for this new business model led thousands of English citizens to invest in the London Company. The company was issued the first Virginia Charter in April 1606, legally allowing it to settle a region extending from present-day Cape Fear, North Carolina, to the Long Island Sound. The settlers were under the direction of Sir Thomas Smith, reputed to be one of London's wealthiest financiers, lending further credibility to the venture.

1	**2**	**3**	**4**	**5**	**6**	**7**
Trace the origins of American government.	Evaluate the different types of governments countries may employ.	Explain the functions of American government.	Describe American political culture, and identify the basic tenets of American democracy.	Analyze the changing characteristics of the American public.	Assess the role of political ideology in shaping American politics.	Characterize changes in Americans' attitudes toward and expectations of government.

THE U.S. POPULATION IS CHANGING Above, an artist's rendition of the first English settlement, Jamestown, in what is today Virginia. Below, Manhattan Island, New York City.

MyPoliSciLab Videos

 Watch on **MyPoliS**

The Big Picture Is it really possible for anyone born in the United States to become president? Author Karen O'Connor describes how the political landscape in America has radically changed over time due to shifting demographics, and explains why these changes are going to affect policy decisions in the future.

The Basics What function does government serve? In this video, you will analyze this question and explore the core values that shape our political system and how the growing diversity of our population is changing—and reaffirming—the definition of what it means to be American.

Who are Americans?

In Context Discuss the importance of American exceptionalism in American political culture. In this video, University of Oklahoma political scientist Allyson Shortle examines the core values that make up American political culture. She also discusses how these values gave rise to the American Dream.

Think Like a Political Scientist Find out how and why research on American politics has shifted. Boston University political scientist Neta C. Crawford discusses how scholars who once focused on voters and institutions are now looking at deliberation as the primary indicator of the health of a democratic system.

In the Real World What is the government's function in everyday life? Real people share their opinions on how involved the federal government should be in education by evaluating the effectiveness of the No Child Left Behind Act, which encourages standardized testing.

So What? What is your government doing for you? Author Karen O'Connor lays out the most pressing issues that America faces today—including student loans and Social Security—and argues that students must understand how the government works in order to be taken care of later on.

Although Smith directed the expedition, he chose to remain in England when the ships set sail for the New World. The colonists settled in a swampy area 30 miles from the mouth of the James River, creating Jamestown, Virginia—the first permanent settlement in America—in 1607. Immediately, dismal conditions prevailed. Insufficient numbers of settlers opted to pursue agricultural ventures, and people began to starve. Settlers died of hunger, Indian attacks, lack of proper supplies, and disease.

One major problem with the settlement was a lack of strong leadership. This situation improved with the election of Captain John Smith as the colony's third president. Smith instituted improvements, forcing all colonists to work and attempting to negotiate food trade with local Indians. These efforts succeeded for a short time, but eventually failed, and the harsh winter of 1609–1610 was deemed "The Starving Time." The conditions reached such dire proportions that a few settlers resorted to cannibalism.

The introduction of tobacco as a cash crop in 1612 improved the economic status of the settlement, but living conditions remained grim. One resident called the area "an unhealthy place, a nest of Rogues, whores, desolate, and rooking persons; a place of intolerable labour, bad usage, and a hard Diet."[1] While eventually life in the settlement improved, it is important to remember the sacrifices of early colonists and the trials other waves of immigrants faced to be part of the American dream.

• • •

In this text, we explore the American political system through a historical lens. This perspective allows us to analyze the ways that ideas and actions of a host of different Americans—from Indians, to colonists, to the Framers of the Constitution and beyond—have affected how our **government**—the formal vehicle through which policies are made and affairs of state are conducted—works. Much has changed since the days of the Jamestown Colony, and the people who live in America today differ greatly from those early settlers. The experiences and values of those settlers, however, continue to influence politics. This chapter explores the political process, placing people at its center.

government
The formal vehicle through which policies are made and affairs of state are conducted.

Roots of American Government: We the People

1   Trace the origins of American government.

The Preamble to the U.S. Constitution begins with the phrase "We the People." But, who are "the People"? In this section, we explore that question by looking at the earliest inhabitants of the Americas, their initial and ongoing interactions with European colonists, and how Americans continually built on the experiences of the past to create a new future.

☐ The Earliest Inhabitants of the Americas

By the time the first colonists arrived in what is now known as the United States, indigenous peoples had been living in the area for more than 30,000 years. Most historians and archaeologists believe that these peoples migrated from present-day Russia through the Bering Strait into North America and then dispersed throughout the American continents.

The indigenous peoples were not a homogeneous group; their cultures, customs, and values varied widely, as did their political systems. The number of these indigenous peoples, who lived in all parts of what is now the United States, is impossible to know for certain. Estimates, however, have ranged as high as 100 million people, a number that quickly diminished as colonists brought with them to the New World a range of diseases to which the indigenous peoples had not been exposed. In addition, warfare

★
The Living Constitution

> *We the People of the United States, in Order to form a more perfect Union, establish Justice, insure domestic Tranquility, provide for the common defence, promote the general Welfare, and secure the Blessings of Liberty to ourselves and our Posterity, do ordain and establish this Constitution for the United States of America.* — PREAMBLE

The Preamble to the United States Constitution is little more than a declaration of intent; it carries no legal weight. But, its language has steered the American government, politics, institutions, and people for over 200 years. While the language of the Preamble has not changed since the Constitution was written, its meaning in practice has evolved significantly; this is what we mean by a living constitution. For example, the phrases "We the People" and "ourselves" included a much smaller group of citizens in 1787 than they do today. Voting was largely limited to property-owning white males. Indians, slaves, and women could not vote. Today, through the expansion of the right to vote, the phrase "the People" encompasses men and women of all races, ethnic origins, and social and economic statuses. This has changed the demands that Americans place on government, as well as expectations about the role of government in people's lives.

Many citizens today question how well the U.S. government can deliver on the goals set out in the Preamble. Few Americans classify the union as "perfect," and many feel excluded from "Justice" and the "Blessings of Liberty." Even our leaders do not believe that our domestic situation is particularly tranquil, as evidenced by the continuing debates about the best means to protect America. Still, in appraising how well government functions, it is imperative to look at not only the roots of the political system, but also how it has been reformed over time through amendment, legislation, common usage, and changing social mores.

CRITICAL THINKING QUESTIONS

1. How do you think the Framers would respond to the broad interpretation of the Preamble's intent embraced by many modern political leaders?
2. How have ideas such as promoting "the general Welfare" evolved over time? How has this affected the role and power of American government?

---

with the European settlers as well as within tribes not only killed many American Indians but also disrupted previously established ways of life. Furthermore, the European settlers displaced Indians, repeatedly pushing them westward as they created settlements and, later, colonies.

☐ The First Colonists

Colonists journeyed to North America for a variety of reasons. Many wealthy Englishmen and other Europeans left home seeking to enhance their fortunes. With them came a host of laborers who hoped to find their own opportunities for riches. In fact, commerce was the most common initial reason for settlement in North America.

In addition to the English commercial settlements in Virginia, in 1609 the Dutch New Netherlands Company settled along the Hudson and lower Delaware Rivers, calling the area New Netherlands. Later, the Dutch West India Company established trading posts on the Hudson River. Both Fort Orange, in what is now Albany, New York, and New Amsterdam, New York City's Manhattan Island, were populated not by colonists but by salaried employees. Among those who flocked to New Amsterdam (renamed New York in 1664) were settlers from Finland, Germany, and Sweden. The varied immigrants also included free blacks. This ethnic and racial mix created its own system of cultural inclusiveness that continues to make New York City and its citizenry unique today (see Figure 1).

A RELIGIOUS TRADITION TAKES ROOT In 1620, a group of Protestants known as Puritans left Europe aboard the *Mayflower.* Destined for Virginia, they found themselves

FIGURE 1 WHAT DID COLONIAL SETTLEMENT LOOK LIKE BEFORE 1700?

Prior to 1700, pockets of colonial settlement existed along the East Coast of what became the United States, from present-day Virginia to what is now Maine. These settlements were divided among a number of colonial powers, including the English in the Northeast and around the Chesapeake Bay, the Dutch in what is present-day New York, and the Swedes, largely in present-day Delaware.

off course and landed instead in Plymouth, in what is now Massachusetts. These new settlers differed from those in Virginia and New York, who saw their settlements as commercial ventures. Adhering to Calvinistic beliefs, the Puritans came instead as families bound together by a common belief in the powerful role of religion in their lives.

Soon, the ideas at the core of these strict puritanical values faced challenges. In 1631, Roger Williams arrived in Boston, Massachusetts. He preached extreme separation from the Church of England and even questioned the right of Europeans to settle on Indian lands. He believed that the Puritans went too far when they punished settlers who deviated from their strict code of morality, arguing that it was God, not people, who should punish individuals for their moral shortcomings. These "heretical views" prompted local magistrates to banish him from the colony. Williams then helped to establish Providence, a village in present-day Rhode Island.

A later challenge to the Puritans' religious beliefs came from midwife Anne Hutchinson. She began to share her view that the churches established in Massachusetts had lost touch with the Holy Spirit. Many of her followers were women who were attracted to her progressive ideas on the importance of religious tolerance, as well as on the equality and rights of women. Authorities in Massachusetts tried Hutchinson for blasphemy for her views and banished her from the colony. She and her followers eventually settled in Portsmouth, Rhode Island, which became a beacon for those seeking religious toleration and popular—as opposed to religious—sovereignty.

Thomas Hooker, too, soon found himself at odds with the Calvinist Puritans in the Massachusetts Bay Colony. Hooker believed they were too narrow-minded; in his view all men should have the right to vote regardless of religious views or property qualifications. He and his supporters thus relocated to Connecticut, where they developed a settlement at Hartford.

Later colonies in the New World were established with religious tolerance in mind. In 1632, King Charles I granted a well-known English Catholic, George Calvert, the first Lord Baltimore, a charter to establish a Catholic colony in the New World. This area eventually became known as Maryland after Mary, the mother of Jesus.

In 1681, King Charles II bestowed upon William Penn a charter giving him sole ownership of a vast area of land just north of Maryland. The king called the land Pennsylvania, or Penn's Woods. Penn, a Quaker, eventually also purchased the land that is present-day Delaware. In this area, Penn launched what he called "the holy experiment," attracting other persecuted Europeans, including German Mennonites and Lutherans and French Huguenots.

monarchy

A form of government in which power is vested in hereditary kings and queens who govern in the interest of all.

totalitarianism

A form of government in which power resides in a leader who rules according to self-interest and without regard for individual rights and liberties.

Types of Government

| 2 | Evaluate the different types of governments countries may employ. |

Early Greek theorists such as Plato and Aristotle tried to categorize governments by who participates, who governs, and how much authority those who govern enjoy. As Table 1 shows, a **monarchy,** the form of government in England from which the colonists fled, is defined by the rule of one hereditary king or queen in the interest of all of his or her subjects. Another form, an aristocracy, is government by the few in the service of the many.

Totalitarianism is a type of government that Aristotle considered rule by "tyranny." Tyrants rule their countries to benefit themselves. This is the case in North Korea under Kim Jong-Un. In tyrannical or totalitarian systems, the leader exercises unlimited power, and individuals have no personal rights or liberties. Generally, the rule of these systems tends to be based on a particular religion or orthodoxy, an ideology, or a personality cult organized around a supreme leader.

oligarchy

A form of government in which the right to participate depends on the possession of wealth, social status, military position, or achievement.

democracy

A system of government that gives power to the people, whether directly or through elected representatives.

direct democracy

A system of government in which members of the polity meet to discuss all policy decisions and then agree to abide by majority rule.

indirect democracy

A system of government that gives citizens the opportunity to vote for representatives who work on their behalf.

republic

A government rooted in the consent of the governed; a representative or indirect democracy.

TABLE 1 HOW DID ARISTOTLE CLASSIFY THE TYPES OF GOVERNMENTS?

Rule by	In Whose Interest	
	Public	Self
One	Monarchy	Tyranny
The Few	Aristocracy	Oligarchy
The Many	Polity	Democracy

SOURCE: Aristotle, *Politics* 3, 7.

An **oligarchy** occurs when a few people rule in their own interest. In an oligarchy, wealth, social status, military position, or achievement dictates participation in government. China and Russia are countries that have governments with oligarchic tendencies.

Aristotle called rule of the many for the benefit of all citizens a "polity" and rule of the many to benefit themselves a "democracy." The term **democracy** derives from the Greek words *demos* ("the people") and *kratia* ("power" or "authority") and may apply to any system of government that gives power to the people, either directly, or indirectly through elected representatives. Most governments worldwide are democracies.

☐ Devising a National Government in the American Colonies

American colonists rejected a system with a strong ruler, such as the British monarchy, when they declared their independence. The colonists also feared replicating the landed and titled system of the British aristocracy. They viewed the formation of a republican form of government as far more in keeping with their values.

The Framers wanted to create a political system with the people at the center of power. Due to the vast size of the new nation, **direct democracy** was unworkable. As more and more settlers came to the New World, many town meetings were replaced by a system of **indirect democracy,** in which people vote for representatives who work on their behalf.

Many citizens were uncomfortable with the term democracy because it conjured up fears of the people and mob rule. Instead, they preferred the term **republic,** which implied a system of government in which the interests of the people were represented by more educated or wealthier citizens who were responsible to those who elected them. Today, representative democracies are more commonly called republics, and the words democracy and republic often are used interchangeably. Yet, in the United States, we still pledge allegiance to our "republic," not our democracy.

Functions of American Government

3 Explain the functions of American government.

I n attempting "to form a more perfect Union," the Framers, through the Constitution, set forth several key functions of American government, as well as governmental guarantees to the people, which have continuing relevance today. These principal functions of government and the guarantees they provide to citizens permeate our lives.

☐ Establishing Justice

One of the first tasks expected of any government is the creation of a system of laws allowing individuals to abide by a common set of principles. Societies adhering to the rule of law allow for the rational dispensing of justice by acknowledged legal authorities. Thus, the Constitution authorized Congress to create a federal judicial system to dispense justice. The Bill of Rights also entitles people to a trial by jury, to be informed of the charges against them, and to be tried in a courtroom presided over by an impartial judge.

political culture
Commonly shared attitudes, beliefs, and core values about how government should operate.

☐ Ensuring Domestic Tranquility

The role of governments in ensuring domestic tranquility is a subject of much debate and has been since the period of the 1600s and 1700s known as the Enlightenment. In crises, such as the terrorist attacks of September 11, 2001, the federal government, as well as state and local governments, can take extraordinary measures to contain the threat of terrorism from abroad as well as within the United States. Local governments have police forces, states have national guards, and the federal government has both the armed services and the ability to call up state militias to quell any threats to order.

☐ Providing for the Common Defense

The Framers recognized that a major purpose of government is to provide defense for its citizens against threats of foreign aggression. Thus, the Constitution calls for the president to be commander in chief of the armed forces, and Congress has the authority to raise an army. The defense budget continues to be a considerable and often controversial proportion of all federal outlays.

☐ Promoting the General Welfare

When the Framers added "promoting the general Welfare" to their list of key governmental functions, they never envisioned how governmental involvement at all levels would expand so tremendously. In fact, promoting the general welfare was more of an ideal than a mandate for the new national government. Over time, though, our notions of what governments should do have expanded along with governmental size. However, universal agreement on the scope of what governments should do is absent.

☐ Securing the Blessings of Liberty

Americans enjoy a wide range of liberties and opportunities to prosper. They are able to criticize the government and to petition it when they disagree with its policies or have a grievance. This freedom to criticize and to petition is perhaps the best way to "secure the Blessings of Liberty."

American Political Culture and the Basic Tenets of American Democracy

4 Describe American political culture, and identify the basic tenets of American democracy.

We can define **political culture** as commonly shared attitudes, beliefs, and core values about how government should operate. American political culture emphasizes the values of liberty and equality; popular consent, majority rule, and popular sovereignty; individualism; and religious faith and freedom.

How Do You Measure Freedom?

Two indicators are used to measure freedom in any given country: the right to free speech and the right to privacy. History has shown us that defense of these rights becomes even more important in the face of a foreign threat. Examine the data below, which shows how committed Americans are to these two ideals of freedom.

Free Speech Strengthens in the United States

Between 1980 and 2010, more Americans support free speech for more groups. The exceptions are racists and radical Muslims.

Homosexual
66% in 1980
85% in 2010

Atheist
66% in 1980
76% in 2010

Militarist
57% in 1980
68% in 2010

Communist
55% in 1980
64% in 2010

Racist
62% in 1980
57% in 2010

Radical Muslim Cleric
not asked
41% in 2010

SOURCE: Data from General Social Survey, 1980, 2006, and 2010

Right to Privacy Weaken in the United States

If the government suspects that a terrorist act is about to happen, do you think the authorities should have the right to ...

... detain people for as long as they want without putting them on trial?
55% YES
43.5% NO

... tap people's telephone conversations?
55.9% YES
43.9% NO

... stop and search people in the street at random?
41.3% YES
58.1% NO

Investigate Further

Concept How does support for free speech and individual privacy measure freedom? Protecting free speech ensures that all ideas can be expressed and debated, even if they are unpopular. Likewise, protecting the privacy rights of everyone, even those who appear to be threatening, ensures equal treatment for all.

Connection How has Americans' support for free speech changed between 1980 and 2010? Overall, Americans are more tolerant of speech from "controversial" groups. More Americans support free speech for people who were previously marginalized, particularly atheists and homosexuals. Fewer Americans are willing to tolerate racist speech.

Cause How did the threat of terrorism change freedom in America? Most Americans will still not tolerate random searches. But after 9/11, Americans don't support speech by radical Muslim clerics and they are willing to detain potential terrorists indefinitely and wiretap suspects' phones.

Liberty and Equality

Liberty and equality are the most important characteristics of the American republican form of government. The Framers wrote the Constitution itself to ensure life and liberty. Over the years, however, our concepts of **personal liberty** have changed and evolved from freedom *from* to freedom *to*. The Framers intended Americans to be free from governmental infringements on freedom of religion and speech, from unreasonable searches and seizures, and so on. The addition of the Fourteenth Amendment to the Constitution and its emphasis on due process and on equal protection of the laws, as well as the subsequent passage of laws guaranteeing civil rights and liberties, however, expanded Americans' concept of liberty to include demands for freedom to work or go to school free from discrimination.

Another key feature of our democracy is **political equality,** the principle that all citizens are the same in the eyes of the law. Notions of political equality have changed dramatically from the founding era. The U.S. Constitution once regarded a slave as equal to only three-fifths of a white person for purposes of assessing state population. No one then could have imagined that in 2008 and 2012, Barack Obama would be elected president by large margins.

Popular Consent, Majority Rule, and Popular Sovereignty

Popular consent, the principle that governments must draw their powers from the consent of the governed, is another distinguishing trait of American democracy. Derived from English political philosopher John Locke's social contract theory, the notion of popular consent was central to the Declaration of Independence. Today, a citizen's willingness to vote represents his or her consent to be governed and is thus an essential premise of democracy.

Majority rule, another core political value, means that election of officials and transformation of policies into law will take place only if the majority (normally 50 percent of the total votes cast plus one) of citizens in any political unit support such changes. This principle holds for both voters and their elected representatives. Yet, the American system also stresses preservation of minority rights, as evidenced by myriad protections of individual rights and liberties found in the Bill of Rights.

Popular sovereignty, or the notion that the ultimate authority in society rests with the people, has its basis in **natural law,** a doctrine that certain ethical principles are part of nature and, as such, can be understood by reason. Ultimately, political authority rests with the people, who can create, abolish, or alter their governments. The idea that all governments derive their power from the people is found in the Declaration of Independence and the U.S. Constitution, but the term popular sovereignty did not come into wide use until pre–Civil War debates over slavery. At that time, supporters of popular sovereignty argued that citizens of new states seeking admission to the union should be able to decide whether or not their states would allow slavery within their borders.

Individualism

Although many core political tenets focus on protecting the rights of all people, American democracy places heavy importance on the individual, an idea that may be traced back to the Puritans. This emphasis on individualism makes Americans quite different from citizens of other democracies such as Canada, which practices a group approach to governance. Group-focused societies reject the American emphasis on individuals and try to improve the lives of their citizens by making services and rights available on a group or universal basis. In contrast, in the U.S. system, all individuals are deemed rational and fair and endowed, as proclaimed in the Declaration of Independence, "with certain unalienable rights."

personal liberty
A key characteristic of U.S. democracy. Initially meaning freedom *from* governmental interference, today it includes demands for freedom *to* engage in a variety of practices without governmental interference or discrimination.

political equality
The principle that all citizens are the same in the eyes of the law.

popular consent
The principle that governments must draw their powers from the consent of the governed.

majority rule
The central premise of direct democracy in which only policies that collectively garner the support of a majority of voters will be made into law.

popular sovereignty
The notion that the ultimate authority in society rests with the people.

natural law
A doctrine that society should be governed by certain ethical principles that are part of nature and, as such, can be understood by reason.

☐ Religious Faith and Religious Freedom

Religious conflicts in Europe brought many settlers to the New World. Seeking an opportunity to practice their religious faith, men, women, and their families initially settled large sections of the East Coast. However, that faith did not always imply religious tolerance. The clashes that occurred within settlements, as well as colonies, led the Framers to agree universally that notions of religious freedom must form the foundation of the new nation. Religious tolerance, however, has often proved to be more of an ideal than a reality. For example, as the nation waged war in Iraq and Afghanistan and attempted to export democracy, large numbers of Americans considered Islam "a religion that encourages violence" and did not view Islam as having much in common with their own religion.[2]

The Changing American Public

5 Analyze the changing characteristics of the American public.

Explore on
MyPoliSciLab
Simulation: You Are a
City Council Member

One year after ratification of the U.S. Constitution, fewer than 4 million people lived in the thirteen states. Most of those people shared a single language and a Protestant-Christian heritage, and those who voted were white male property owners. The Constitution mandated that the number of members of the House of Representatives should not exceed one for every 30,000 people and set the size of the first House at sixty-five members.

As the nation grew westward, hundreds of thousands of new immigrants came to America, often in waves, fleeing war or famine or simply in search of a better life. Although the geographic size of the United States has remained stable since the addition of Alaska and Hawaii as states in 1959, in 2013 more than 314 million Americans populated the country. As a result of this population growth, most citizens today feel far removed from the national government and their elected representatives (see Figure 2).

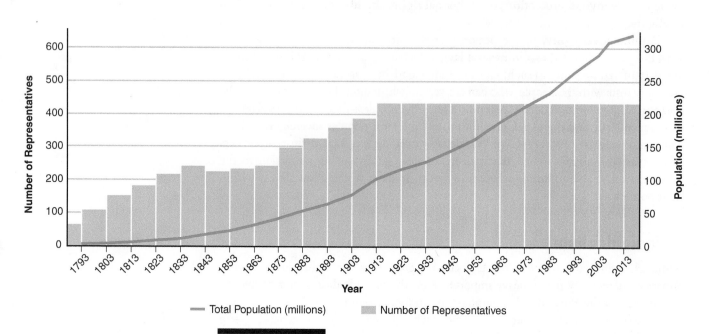

— Total Population (millions)   ▢ Number of Representatives

FIGURE 2 HOW DOES POPULATION AFFECT REPRESENTATION?

The population of the United States has grown dramatically since the nation's founding. Larger geographic area, immigration, and living longer have contributed to this trend. The size of the House of Representatives, however, has not kept pace with this expansion.

SOURCE: U.S. Census Bureau Population Projections, www.census.gov.

☐ Racial and Ethnic Composition

The American population has changed constantly by the arrival of immigrants from various regions—Western Europeans fleeing religious persecution in the 1600s to early 1700s; slaves brought in chains from Africa in the late 1700s; Chinese laborers arriving to work on the railroads following the Gold Rush in 1848; Irish Catholics escaping the potato famine in the 1850s; Northern and Eastern Europeans from the 1880s to 1910s; and, most recently, South and Southeast Asians, Cubans, and Mexicans, among others.

Today, nearly 40 million people in the United States can be classified as immigrants, and most of them are Hispanic.* Unlike other groups that have come before, many Hispanics have resisted American cultural assimilation. Language appears to be a particularly difficult and sometimes controversial policy issue. In some sections of the country, Spanish-speaking citizens have necessitated changes in the way governments do business. Many government agencies print official documents in both English and Spanish. This action has raised a debate over whether all Americans should speak English or if the nation should move toward a more bilingual society such as Canada, where English and French are the official languages.

Immigration has led to significant alterations in American racial and ethnic composition. The balance in America has changed dramatically over the past fifty years, with the proportion of Hispanics overtaking African Americans as the second most common racial or ethnic group. The Asian American population, moreover, is now the fastest growing minority group in the United States. This means that the majority of babies born in the United States are now members of a minority group, a fact that will have a significant impact not only on the demographics of the American polity but also on how America "looks." In a generation, minorities may be the majority in America, as they are in nine states in 2013.

☐ Aging

Just as the racial and ethnic composition of the American population is shifting, so, too, is the average age. "For decades, the U.S. was described as a nation of the young because the number of persons under the age of twenty greatly outnumber[ed] those sixty-five and older," but this is no longer the case.[3] Because of changes in patterns of fertility, life expectancy, and immigration, the nation's age profile has altered drastically. At the founding of the United States, the average life expectancy was thirty-five years; by 2010, it was more than seventy-eight years.

An aging population places a host of costly demands on the government. In 2008, the first of the Baby Boomers (the 76.8 million people who were born between 1946 and 1964) reached age sixty-two and qualified for Social Security benefits; in 2011, they reached sixty-five and qualified for Medicare.[4] An aging America also imposes a great financial burden on working Americans, whose proportion in the population is rapidly declining.

☐ Religious Beliefs

As we have discussed throughout this chapter, many of the first settlers came to America to pursue their religious beliefs free from governmental intervention. Although these early immigrants were members of a number of different churches, all identified with Christian sects. Moreover, they viewed the Indians' belief systems,

---

*In this text, we have made the decision to refer to those of Spanish, Latin American, Mexican, Cuban, and Puerto Rican descent as Hispanic instead of Latino/a. Although this label is not accepted universally by the community it describes, Hispanic is the term used by the U.S. government when reporting federal data. In addition, a 2008 survey sponsored by the Pew Charitable Trusts found that 36 percent of those who responded preferred the term Hispanic, 21 percent preferred the term Latino, and the remainder had no preference. See www.pewhispanic.org.

Explore Your World

Immigration is a contentious issue in many countries around the world. States struggle to create immigration policies that balance having an open door with protecting their security and political culture. Many states screen their immigrants before allowing them to enter the country, placing them in detention facilities such as those seen below and requiring them to undergo mandatory health and background checks.

Female detainees are held in the Willacy Detention Center in Raymondville, Texas, United States. The facility, which was constructed in 2006 by the Department of Homeland Security, can house up to 2,000 suspected illegal immigrants in ten giant tents.

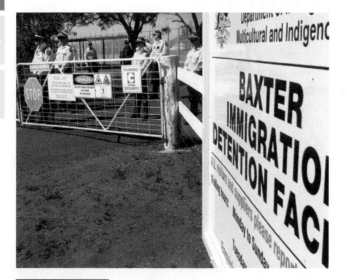

Multiple fences and guards limit exit and entry at the Baxter Detention Facility in Port Augusta, Australia. Note, especially, the height of the second fence and the barren terrain.

Migrants seeking refuge in Europe are held at this detention center on the island of Lampedusa, located in the Mediterranean Sea between Tunisia and Italy. The center can only be used during the winter months, as warmer weather and calm waters encourage many detainees to attempt to escape and make the trip to the nearby island of Sicily.

CRITICAL THINKING QUESTIONS

1. What role does national identity play in the creation of these policies? Do countries have an interest in screening immigrants before they are allowed to enter or remain in a country?

2. How do policies around the world compare to the immigration and detention policies used in the United States, both historically and in modern times?

3. Are the screening and detention practices depicted here acceptable in the name of national security? Do they violate basic human rights?

which included multiple gods, to be savage and unholy. Their Christian values still permeate American social and political systems.

While many people still view the United States as a Christian nation, a great number of religious groups—including Jews, Buddhists, Hindus, and Muslims—have established roots in the country. With this growth have come different political and social demands. For example, evangelical Christians regularly request school boards adopt textbooks with particular viewpoints. Likewise, American Jews continually work to ensure that America's policies in the Middle East favor Israel, while Muslims demand more support for a Palestinian state.

☐ Regional Growth and Expansion

Regional sectionalism emerged almost immediately in the United States. Settlers from the Virginia colony southward largely focused on commerce. Those seeking various forms of religious freedom populated many of the settlements to the North. That search for religious freedom also came with puritanical values, so that New England evolved differently from the South in many aspects of culture.

One of the most long-standing and dramatic regional differences in the United States is that between the South and the North. During the Constitutional Convention, most Southerners staunchly advocated a weak national government. The Civil War was later fought in part because of basic philosophical differences about government as well as slavery, which many Northerners opposed. As we know from modern political polling, the South continues to lag behind the rest of the nation in supporting civil rights, while still favoring return of power to the states and downsizing the national government.

The West, too, has always appeared unique compared with the rest of the United States. Populated first by those seeking free land and then by many chasing dreams of gold, the American West has often been characterized as "wild." Its population today is a study in contrasts. Some people have moved there to avoid city life and have an anti-government bias. Other Westerners are interested in water rights and seek governmental solutions to their problems.

Significant differences in attitude also arise in rural versus urban areas. Those in rural areas are much more conservative than those in large cities.[5] One need only look at a map of the vote distribution in the 2012 presidential election to see stark differences in candidate appeal. Barack Obama carried almost every large city in America; Mitt Romney carried 60 percent of the rural voters as well as most of America's heartland.[6] Republicans won the South, the West, and much of the Midwest; Democrats carried the Northeast and West Coast.

☐ Family and Family Size

In the past, familial gender roles were clearly defined. Women did housework and men worked in the fields. Large families were imperative; children were a source of cheap farm labor. Industrialization and knowledge of birth control methods, however, began to put a dent in the size of American families by the early 1900s. No longer needing children to work for survival of the household, couples began to limit family size.

In 1949, 49 percent of those polled thought that four or more children constituted the "ideal" family size; by 2011, 58 percent responded that no children to two children was "best" and only 33 percent preferred to have more than three children.[7] In 1940, nine of ten households were traditional family households. By 2010, just 69 percent of children under eighteen lived with both parents. In fact, over 25 percent of children under eighteen lived with just one of their parents; the majority of those lived with their mother. Moreover, by 2010, more than 31 percent of all households consisted of a single person, a trend that reflects, in part, the aging American population and declining marriage rate.[8]

Political Ideology

political ideology
The coherent set of values and beliefs about the purpose and scope of government held by groups and individuals.

6 Assess the role of political ideology in shaping American politics.

Political ideologies are sets or systems of beliefs that shape the thinking of individuals and how they view the world, especially in regard to issues of "race, nationality, the role and function of government, the relations between men and women, human responsibility for the natural environment, and many other matters."[9] Observers increasingly have recognized these beliefs as a potent political force. Isaiah Berlin, a noted historian and philosopher, stated that two factors above all others shaped human history in the twentieth century: "one is science and technology; the other is ideological battles—totalitarian tyrannies of both right and left and the explosions of nationalism, racism, and religious bigotry that the most perceptive social thinkers of the nineteenth century failed to predict."[10]

It is easier to understand how ideas turn into action when we examine the four functions political scientists attribute to ideologies. These include:

1. *Explanation.* Ideologies can offer reasons why social and political conditions are the way they are, especially in time of crisis.
2. *Evaluation.* Ideologies can provide standards for evaluating social conditions and political institutions and events.
3. *Orientation.* Much like a compass, ideologies provide individuals with an orientation toward issues and a position within the world.
4. *Political Program.* Ideologies help people make political choices and guide their political actions.

☐ Finding Your Political Ideology

The four functions of ideology discussed above clearly have real-world implications. Religious, philosophical, and cultural beliefs can become cohesive ideologies that create natural groups within society and lead to political conflict. In America, we often hear about conservative, liberal, and moderate political ideologies (see Figure 3).

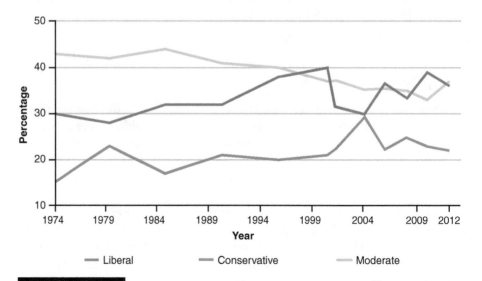

FIGURE 3 WHAT ARE AMERICANS' POLITICAL IDEOLOGIES?

Americans' political ideologies have shifted dramatically over time. What was once a largely moderate nation has today become much more closely divided between liberals, conservatives, and moderates. These divisions can make governing particularly challenging and lead to gridlock in our political institutions.

SOURCE: Roper Center for Public Opinion Research and Pew Research Center 2012 Values Survey.

CONSERVATIVES **Conservatives** tend to believe that limited government is best, especially in terms of regulating the economy. Conservatives favor local and state action over federal intervention, and they emphasize fiscal responsibility, most notably in the form of balanced budgets. Conservatives are also likely to believe that the private sector is better equipped than the government to address domestic problems such as homelessness, poverty, and discrimination.

Since the 1970s, a growing number of **social conservative** voters (many with religious ties to the evangelical or Religious Right) increasingly have affected politics and policies in the United States. Social conservatives believe that moral decay must be stemmed and that government should support and further traditional moral teachings. These voters favor government intervention to regulate sexual and social behavior and have mounted effective efforts to restrict contraceptives, abortion, and same-sex marriage. While a majority of social conservatives are evangelical Protestants, Mormons, and Roman Catholics, some Jews and many Muslims are also social conservatives. Others are not affiliated with a traditional religion.

LIBERALS A **liberal** is one who seeks to use the government to change the political, economic, and social status quo and foster the development of equality and the well-being of individuals.[11] The meaning of the word "liberal" has changed over time, but in the modern United States, liberals generally value equality over other aspects of shared political culture. They support well-funded government social welfare programs that seek to protect individuals from economic disadvantages or to correct past injustices, and they generally oppose government efforts to regulate private behavior or infringe on civil rights and liberties.

MODERATES In general, a **moderate** takes a relatively centrist view on most political issues. Aristotle actually favored moderate politics, believing that domination in the center was better than any extremes, whether dealing with issues of wealth, poverty, or the role of government. Approximately 35 percent of the population today consider themselves political moderates.

☐ Problems with Ideological Labels

In a perfect world, liberals would be liberal and conservatives would be conservative. Studies reveal, however, that many people who call themselves conservative actually take fairly liberal positions on many policy issues. In fact, anywhere from 20 percent to 60 percent of people will hold a traditionally conservative view on one issue and a traditionally liberal view on another.[12]

Some critics also charge that a simple left-to-right continuum cannot capture the full complexity of most citizens' political ideologies. They suggest that the ideologies of most people are better represented by a spectrum measuring individuals' viewpoints on government interference in both economic and personal liberties. This spectrum includes not only liberal, conservative, and moderate ideologies but also other perspectives such as **statist** (pro-governmental interference) and **libertarian** (anti-governmental interference).

conservative
One who favors limited government intervention, particularly in economic affairs.

social conservative
One who believes that the government should support and further traditional moral teachings.

liberal
One who favors greater government intervention, particularly in economic affairs and in the provision of social services.

moderate
A person who takes a relatively centrist or middle-of-the-road view on most political issues.

statist
One who believes in extensive government control of personal and economic liberties.

libertarian
One who believes in limited government interference in personal and economic liberties.

politics
The study of who gets what, when, and how—or how policy decisions are made.

Toward Reform: People and Politics

7 Characterize changes in Americans' attitudes toward and expectations of government.

As the American population has changed over time, so has the American political process. **Politics** is the study of who gets what, when, and how—the process by which policy decisions are made. The evolving nature of the American citizenry deeply affects this process. Competing demands often

Take a Closer Look

The Nolan Chart, created by Libertarian Party leader David Nolan, is a political ideology chart that helps to classify citizens' political beliefs on two key dimensions—economic and personal freedom. Out of the intersection of citizens' views toward government intervention in each of these areas, Nolan identified five key political ideologies: liberal, moderate, conservative, libertarian, and statist.

Libertarians believe in limited government interference in personal and economic affairs.

Conservatives favor limited government intervention, particularly in economic affairs. In the modern American context, they are associated closely with the Republican Party.

Moderates take middle-of-the-road viewpoints on government intervention in most issue areas.

Liberals favor greater government intervention, particularly in economic affairs. In the modern American context, they are associated closely with the Democratic Party.

Statists believe in extensive government control of personal and economic liberties.

A score of 100 means a respondent supports absolute freedom and 0 means a respondent supports complete government control.

SOURCE: Advocates for Self Government.

CRITICAL THINKING QUESTIONS

1. How does reducing political ideology to two dimensions—economic and personal freedom—help to simplify our understandings of politics? What information does it leave out?

2. What famous (or notorious) political leaders can you think of to exemplify each of these political ideologies?

3. What is your political ideology? Take an online ideology quiz such as the "World's Smallest Political Quiz" to determine where you stand.

lead to political struggles, which create winners and losers within the system. A loser today, however, may be a winner tomorrow in the ever-changing world of politics. The political ideologies of those in control of Congress, the executive, and state houses also have a huge impact on who gets what, when, and how.

Nevertheless, American political culture continues to bind citizens together. Many Americans also share the common goal of achieving the **American dream**—an American ideal of a happy and successful life, which often includes wealth, a house, a better life for one's children, and, for some, the opportunity to grow up to be president.

American dream

An American ideal of a happy, successful life, which often includes wealth, a house, a better life for one's children, and, for some, the opportunity to grow up to be president.

☐ Redefining Our Expectations

In roughly the first 150 years of our nation's history, the federal government had few responsibilities, and citizens had few expectations of it beyond national defense, printing money, and collecting tariffs and taxes. The state governments were generally far more powerful than the federal government in matters affecting the everyday lives of Americans.

As the nation and its economy grew in size and complexity, the federal government took on more responsibilities, such as regulating some businesses, providing poverty relief, and inspecting food. With these new roles come greater demands on government.

Today, many Americans lack faith in the country's institutions (see Figure 4). And, a 2012 poll revealed that more than seven in ten Americans think the country is headed in the wrong direction.[13] These concerns make it even easier for citizens to blame the government for all kinds of woes—personal as well as societal—or to fail to credit it for those things it does well. Many Americans, for example, enjoy a remarkably high standard of living, and much of it is due to governmental programs and protections.

Even in the short time between when you get up in the morning and when you leave for classes or work, the government—its rulings or regulations—pervades your life. National or state governments, for example, set the standards for whether you wake up on Eastern, Central, Mountain, or Pacific time. The national government regulates the airwaves and licenses the radio and TV broadcasts you might listen to as you eat and get dressed. States, too, regulate and tax telecommunications. Whether the water you use to brush your teeth contains fluoride is a state or local governmental issue. The federal Food and Drug Administration inspects your breakfast meat

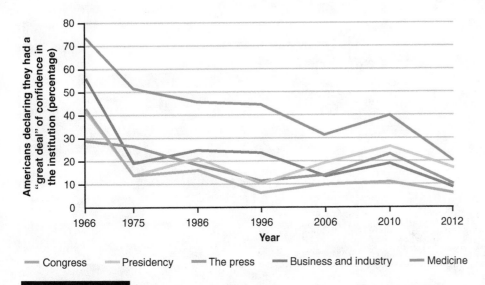

FIGURE 4 DO AMERICANS HAVE CONFIDENCE IN POLITICAL INSTITUTIONS?

The line graph below shows the percentages of Americans declaring they had a "great deal" of confidence in American institutions. Note the declining trend of trust in all political institutions, as well as Americans' record low levels of trust in institutions such as Congress and the press.

SOURCE: *Newsweek* (January 8, 1996):32; *Public Perspective* 8 (February/March 1994): 4; Lexis-Nexis RPOLL; *Washington Post* (June 13, 2006): A2; www.pollingreport.com; www.gallup.com/poll/1597/confidence-institutions.aspx.

Is the American Dream a Reality?

The American Dream has long been the aspirational goal of many American people. Traditionally, this dream included visions of home ownership and a life better than that of previous generations. Examine the visual below to consider how understandings of the American Dream are changing in our modern world.

THE AMERICAN DREAM IS MORE IMPORTANT TO YOUNGER GENERATIONS

How important is it to you to achieve the American Dream in your lifetime?

	Not at all important
	Not very important
	Somewhat important
	Very important

SILENT GENERATION: 15%, 35%, 36%, 14%

BABY BOOMERS: 3%, 17%, 47%, 33%

GENERATION X: 2%, 12%, 44%, 42%

GENERATION Y: 1%, 10%, 34%, 55%

TRADITIONAL MILESTONES ARE NOT ESSENTIAL

Is it possible to achieve the American Dream without...

PERCENTAGE OF ALL RESPONDENTS WHO SAID "YES"

A POSTGRADUATE DREGREE?	76%
BEING MARRIED?	71%
HAVING CHILDREN?	70%
BEING WEALTHY?	70%
A COLLEGE EDUCATION?	65%
OWNING YOUR OWN HOME?	59%

FRIENDS AND FAMILY ARE MOST IMPORTANT TO YOUNG PEOPLE

In the current economic climate, which of the following is more important to you?

PERCENTAGE OF GENERATION Y RESPONDENTS

33%	CLOSE FRIENDS AND FAMILY
23%	HAVING A ROOF OVER YOUR HEAD

AMERICANS VALUE PERSONAL FULFILLMENT OVER MONEY

What is the key to achieving the American Dream?

PERCENTAGE OF ALL RESPONDENTS

FEELING A SENSE OF PERSONAL FULFILLMENT IN YOUR LIFE	34%
HAVING ENOUGH MONEY TO LIVE THE WAY YOU WANT	27%
PROVIDING SECURITY FOR YOUR CHILDREN	18%
INCOME AND FINANCIAL SUCCESS	12%

HALF OF ALL YOUNG AMERICANS SAY THEY WORK HARDER THAN THEIR PARENTS

Do you think you're working as hard, harder, or less hard than your parents when they were your age?

PERCENTAGE OF GENERATION Y RESPONDENTS

16% LESS HARD
50% HARDER
34% SAME

AND MAKE MORE OF AN EFFORT TO BE SUCCESSFUL

Which of the following would you be willing to do to achieve the American Dream?

| | Silent Generation | | Generation X |
| | Baby Boomers | | Generation Y |

TAKE A JOB FOR WHICH YOU ARE OVERQUALIFIED: 12%, 27%, 39%, 45%

GET ADDITIONAL JOB TRAINING: 6%, 23%, 41%, 48%

RELOCATE TO ANOTHER CITY/STATE: 10%, 27%, 34%, 40%

GO BACK TO SCHOOL: 5%, 18%, 37%, 45%

START YOUR OWN BUSINESS: 9%, 20%, 34%, 30%

CHANGE INDUSTRIES: 3%, 21%, 35%, 26%

CRITICAL THINKING QUESTIONS

1. What, according to this visual, is the modern American Dream?

2. How do visions of the American Dream differ across generations? Why might these differences exist?

3. How might the trends you observe in this visual affect the demands that citizens place on their government? How might they affect politics?

and sets standards for the advertising on your cereal box, orange juice carton, and other food packaging.

The current frustration and dissatisfaction with politics and government may be just another phase, as the changing American body politic seeks to redefine its ideas about and expectations of government and how to reform it. This process is likely to define politics well into the future, but the individualistic nature of the American system will have long-lasting effects on how to accomplish that redefinition. Many Americans say they want less government, but as they get older, they don't want less Social Security. They want lower taxes and better roads, but they don't want to pay road tolls.

In this text, we present you with the tools needed to understand how our political system has evolved and to understand changes yet to come. Approaching the study of American government and politics with an open mind should help you become a better citizen. We hope that you learn to ask questions, to comprehend how various issues have come to be important, and to see why a particular law was enacted, how it was implemented, and if it needs reform. We further hope that you will learn not to accept at face value everything you see on the TV news, hear on the radio, or read in the newspaper and on the Internet, especially in the blogosphere. Work to understand your government, and use your vote and other forms of participation to help ensure that your government works for you.

On MyPoliSciLab

Review the Chapter

 Listen to **Chapter** on **MyPoliSciLab**

Roots of American Government: We the People

1 Trace the origins of American government.

American government is rooted in the cultures and experiences of early European colonists as well as interactions with the indigenous populations of the New World. The first colonists sought wealth. Later pilgrims came for religious freedom. The colonies set up systems of government that differed widely in terms of form, role, and function. As they developed, they sought more independence from the British monarchy.

Types of Government

2 Evaluate the different types of governments countries may employ.

Aristotle classifies the types of governments according to who rules, and in whose interest. Types of governments include monarchy, totalitarianism, aristocracy, oligarchy, polity, and democracy. Fears about mob rule and the vast size of the United States led the Framers to create a republican democracy that relies on the role of representatives to filter citizens' viewpoints.

Functions of American Government

3 Explain the functions of American government.

The functions of American government include establishing justice, ensuring domestic tranquility, providing for the common defense, promoting the general welfare, and securing the blessings of liberty.

American Political Culture and the Basic Tenets of American Democracy

4 Describe American political culture, and identify the basic tenets of American democracy.

Political culture is a group's commonly shared attitudes, beliefs, and core values about how government should operate. Key tenets of Americans' shared political culture are liberty and equality; popular consent, majority rule and popular sovereignty; individualism; and religious freedom.

The Changing American Public

5 Analyze the changing characteristics of the American public.

Several characteristics of the American electorate can help us understand how the system continues to evolve and change. Among these are changes in size and population, racial and ethnic composition, age, religious beliefs, regional growth and expansion, and family and family size.

Political Ideology

6 Assess the role of political ideology in shaping American politics.

Ideologies, the belief systems that shape the thinking of individuals and how they view the world, affect people's ideas about government. The major categories of political ideology in America are conservative, liberal, and moderate.

Toward Reform: People and Politics

7 Characterize changes in Americans' attitudes toward and expectations of government.

Shifts in population have created controversy in the American electorate throughout America's history. Americans have high and often unrealistic expectations of government, yet often fail to appreciate how much their government actually does for them. Americans' failing trust in institutions also explains some of the apathy among the American electorate.

Learn the Terms

 Study and **Review** the **Flashcards**

American dream
conservative
democracy
direct democracy
government
indirect democracy
liberal
libertarian

majority rule
moderate
monarchy
natural law
oligarchy
personal liberty
political culture
political equality

political ideology
politics
popular consent
popular sovereignty
republic
social conservative
statist
totalitarianism

Test Yourself

 Study and **Review** the **Practice Tests**

1. Before the Pilgrims traveled to the New World on the *Mayflower*, the most common reason for settlement in North America was

a. religious freedom.
b. fatal diseases in their homeland.
c. commerce.
d. independence from the crown.
e. to create "a city on a hill."

2. Which of the following settlements was not founded for primarily religious reasons?

a. Connecticut
b. Portsmouth
c. Jamestown
d. Massachusetts Bay Colony
e. Boston

3. As the population of the New World increased, the town meeting form of government was gradually replaced with an indirect democratic system colonists called a(n)

a. direct democracy.
b. monarchy.
c. oligarchy.
d. republic.
e. democracy.

4. Which of the following is NOT a function of American government listed in the Preamble?

a. Establish justice
b. Promote equality
c. Provide for the common defense
d. Secure the blessings of liberty
e. Ensure domestic tranquility

5. Which American ideal, central to the Declaration of Independence, was derived from the social contract theory?

a. Majority rule

b. Popular consent

c. Religious freedom

d. Natural law

e. Political equality

6. Which of these is a major contributor to American population growth since 1940?

a. Longer life expectancy

b. Western European immigration

c. Industrial growth

d. New states added to the United States

e. Higher birthrates

7. Which of the following statements best describes recent demographic trends in the United States?

a. Population has grown largely in Midwestern and Mid-Atlantic states.

b. African Americans have consistently composed the second largest minority group.

c. Couples favor having more children than in the mid-twentieth century.

d. The average age of Americans has increased.

e. More than 50 percent of American children today live with only one parent.

8. According to political scientists, which of the following is NOT considered a function of political ideologies?

a. Political program

b. Evaluation

c. Orientation

d. Explanation

e. Partisanship

9. Which political ideology is most associated with a limited role of government in personal and economic affairs?

a. Liberal

b. Conservative

c. Moderate

d. Libertarian

e. Statist

10. For most Americans, the definition of achieving the American Dream includes obtaining

a. incredible wealth.

b. a job in business.

c. a job in government.

d. a happy and successful life.

e. children.

Explore Further

Ball, Terence, and Richard Dagger. *Political Ideologies and the Democratic Ideal,* 8th ed. New York: Longman, 2010.

Dahl, Robert A. *Polyarchy: Participation and Opposition.* New Haven, CT: Yale University Press, 1972.

Estlund, David M. *Democratic Authority: A Philosophical Framework.* Princeton, NJ: Princeton University Press, 2012.

Fiorina, Morris P., Samuel J. Abrams, and Jeremy C. Pope. *Culture War? The Myth of a Polarized America,* 3rd ed. New York: Longman, 2010.

Ghosh, Cyril. *The Politics of the American Dream: Democratic Inclusion in Contemporary American Political Culture.* New York: Palgrave Macmillan, 2013.

Hobbes, Thomas. *Leviathan.* Ed. Richard Tuck. New York: Cambridge University Press, 1996.

Jamieson, Kathleen Hall. *Everything You Think You Know About Politics . . . and Why You're Wrong.* New York: Basic Books, 2000.

Kazin, Michael. *American Dreamers: How the Left Changed a Nation.* New York: Vintage, 2012.

Locke, John. *Two Treatises of Government.* Ed. Peter Lasleti. New York: Cambridge University Press, 1988.

Nye, Joseph S., Jr. *The Paradox of American Power: Why the World's Superpower Can't Go It Alone.* New York: Oxford University Press, 2002.

Putnam, Robert D., and David E. Campbell. *American Grace: How Religion Divides Us and Unites Us.* New York: Simon and Schuster, 2010.

Rosenfeld, Michael J. *The Age of Independence: Interracial Unions, Same Sex Unions, and the Changing American Family.* Cambridge, MA: Harvard University Press, 2009.

Smith, Hedrick. *Who Stole the American Dream? Can We Get it Back?* New York: Random House, 2012.

Verba, Sidney, Kay Schlozman, and Henry Brady. *Voice and Equality: Civic Volunteerism in American Politics,* 2nd ed. Cambridge, MA: Harvard University Press, 2002.

Wolfe, Alan, and Ira Katznelson, eds. *Religion and Democracy in the United States: Danger or Opportunity?* Princeton, NJ: Princeton University Press, 2012.

To learn more about shifts in the American population, go to the U.S. Census Bureau at **www.census.gov.**

To learn more about Americans' attitudes and expectations of government, go to the Pew Research Center at **www.pewresearch.org.**

To learn about the policy positions and attitudes of American conservatives, go to the American Conservative Union at **www.conservative.org.**

To learn more about the policy positions and attitudes of American liberals, go to the Liberal Oasis at **www.liberaloasis.com.**

Credits

Credits are listed in order of appearance.

Answer Key

1. c; 2. c; 3. d; 4. b; 5. b; 6. a; 7. d; 8. e; 9. d; 10. d

Notes

1. John Hammond, *Leah and Rachael, or the Two Fruitful Sisters, Virginia and Maryland; their Present Condition Impartially Stated and Related* (London: Force Tracts, 1656).
2. Pew Forum on Religion and Public Life, "Growing Number of Americans Say Islam Encourages Violence" (July 24, 2003): www.pewforum.org.
3. Susan A. MacManus, *Young v. Old. Generational Combat in the 21st Century* (Boulder, CO: Westview, 1995), 3.
4. Dennis Cauchon, "Who Will Take Care of an Older Population?" *USA Today* (October 25, 2005): 1–2B.
5. James B. Gimpel and Kimberly A. Karnes, "The Rural Side of the Urban-Rural Gap," *PS: Political Science and Politics* (July 2006): 467–72.
6. CNN Exit Polls, http://www.cnn.com/election/2012/results/race/president?hpt=po_t1#exit-polls.
7. "Americans' Preference for Smaller Families Edges Higher," Gallup Poll (June 30, 2011): http://www.gallup.com/poll/148355/Americans-Preferences-Smaller-Families-Edges-Higher.aspx.
8. U.S. Census Bureau, *2012 Statistical Abstract of the United States.*
9. Terence Ball and Richard Dagger, *Political Ideologies and the Democratic Ideal* (New York: Pearson, 2006): 2.
10. Isaiah Berlin, *The Crooked Timber of Humanity: Chapters in the History of Ideas* (New York: Vintage, 1992), 1.
11. Jack C. Plano and Milton Greenberg, *The American Political Dictionary,* 9th ed. (Fort Worth, TX: Harcourt Brace, 1993), 16.
12. Philip E. Converse, "The Nature of Belief Systems in Mass Publics," in David E. Apter, ed., *Ideology and Discontent* (New York: Free Press, 1964), 206–21.
13. Rasmussen Reports, "Right Direction or Wrong Track" (June 27, 2012): http://www.rasmussenreports.com/public_content/politics/mood_of_america/right_direction_or_wrong_track/.

The Constitution

The Constitution

t age eighteen, all American citizens are eligible to vote in state and national elections. This has not always been the case. It took an amendment to the U.S. Constitution—one of only seventeen that have been added since ratification of the Bill of Rights in 1791—to guarantee the vote in national elections to those younger than twenty-one years of age.

In 1942, during World War II, Representative Jennings Randolph (D–WV) proposed a constitutional amendment that would lower the voting age to eighteen, believing that since young men were old enough to be drafted, to go to war, and to fight and die for their country, they also should have the right to vote. He continued to reintroduce his proposal during every session of Congress, and in 1954, President Dwight D. Eisenhower endorsed the idea in his State of the Union Address. Presidents Lyndon B. Johnson and Richard M. Nixon—men who had also called upon the nation's young men to fight on foreign shores—echoed his appeal.[1]

During the 1960s, the campaign to lower the voting age took on a new sense of urgency as the draft sent hundreds of thousands of young men to fight in the unpopular war in Vietnam, and thousands of men and women were killed in action. "Old Enough to Fight, Old Enough to Vote" was one popular slogan of the day. By 1970, four states—the U.S. Constitution allows states to set the eligibility requirements for their voters—had lowered their voting ages to eighteen. Later that year, Congress passed legislation that designated eighteen as the voting age in national, state, and local elections.

The state of Oregon, however, challenged the constitutionality of the law in court, arguing that the Constitution did not give Congress the authority to establish a uniform voting age in state and local government elections. The U.S. Supreme Court agreed.[2] The decision from the divided Court meant that those under age twenty-one could vote in national elections but that the states were free to prohibit them from voting in state and local elections. The decision presented the

1	2	3	4	5	6
Trace the historical developments that led to the colonists' break with Great Britain and the emergence of the new American nation.	Identify the key components of the Articles of Confederation and the reasons why it failed.	Outline the issues and compromises that were central to the writing of the U.S. Constitution.	Analyze the underlying principles of the U.S. Constitution.	Explain the conflicts that characterized the drive for ratification of the U.S. Constitution.	Distinguish between the methods for proposing and ratifying amendments to the U.S. Constitution.

MANY CONSTITUTIONAL AMENDMENTS HAVE ADDRESSED VOTING RIGHTS Above, women cast a ballot after the ratification of the Nineteenth Amendment in 1920. Below, a young voter uses an electronic voting machine in a recent election.

MyPoliSciLab Videos

The Big Picture Discover why what the Constitution does not say is just as important as what it does say. Author Alixandra B. Yanus considers how the government refers to the Constitution for answers to current questions that it does not explicitly address, thereby leaving plenty of room for interpretation.

The Basics What is the purpose of a constitution? In this video, you will discover the reasons why the Framers wrote the Constitution and how the Constitution sets up checks and balances, the protection of liberties, and the framework we need for a functioning democracy.

How does the Constitution change?

In Context Why is it unusual that the U.S. Constitution has governed so long in its present form? Fordham University political scientist Costas Panagopolos explains why the Constitution is such a rarity and how it has succeeded in an evolving American society.

Thinking Like a Political Scientist How do the institutions created by the U.S. Constitution operate and how has their role changed over time? Fordham University political scientist Costas Panagopolos examines this and other emerging issues in the research and in the study of the Constitution.

In the Real World How well does the system of checks and balances in the United States work, and is it actually fair? Real people voice their opinions on whether or not they believe it is constitutional for Congress to check the power of the president—and vice versa.

So What? The United States has changed a lot in the past two hundred years; so why have we always been governed by the same document? In this video, author Alixandra B. Yanus explains the unique features of the U.S. Constitution that have allowed it to remain effective for so long.

states with a logistical nightmare. Setting the voting age at twenty-one would force states to keep two sets of registration books: one for voters twenty-one and over and one for voters under twenty-one.

Jennings Randolph, by then a senator from West Virginia, reintroduced his proposed amendment to lower the national voting age to eighteen.[3] Within three months of the Supreme Court's decision, Congress sent the proposed Twenty-Sixth Amendment to the states for ratification. The required three-fourths of the states approved the amendment within three months—making its adoption on June 30, 1971, the quickest in the history of the constitutional amending process.

While young people have not traditionally exercised their Twenty-Sixth Amendment rights in large numbers, voter turnout among those 18 to 29 does seem to be on the rise. Record numbers of young voters went to the polls in the 2012 presidential election; many credited discussions on Facebook and other social networking sites for their political interest and activism. The votes of young people played a decisive role in electing Barack Obama. Young people not only made up 19 percent of all voters—a higher percentage than those age 65 and older—but 60 percent of those age 18 to 29 also voted for Obama.

●●●

The Framers never intended the U.S. Constitution to be easily changed. They made the amendment process time consuming and difficult. Over the years, thousands of amendments—including those to prohibit child labor, provide equal rights for women, grant statehood to the District of Columbia, balance the federal budget, and ban flag burning—have been debated or sent to the states for approval, only to die slow deaths. Only twenty-seven amendments have made their way into the Constitution. What the Framers wrote in Philadelphia has continued to work, in spite of increasing demands on and dissatisfaction with our national government. Although Americans often clamor for reform, perhaps they are happier with the system of government created by the Framers than they realize. The ideas that went into the making of the Constitution and the ways that it has evolved to address the problems of a growing and changing nation form the core of our discussion in this chapter.

Roots of the New American Nation

1 Trace the historical developments that led to the colonists' break with Great Britain and the emergence of the new American nation.

Beginning in the early seventeenth century, colonists came to the New World for a variety of reasons. Often they wished to escape religious persecution. Others sought a new start on a continent where land was plentiful or saw business opportunities to be gained in the New World. The independence and diversity of the settlers in the New World complicated the question of how best to rule the new colonies. More than merely an ocean separated Great Britain from the colonies; the colonists were independent people, and it soon became clear that the crown could not govern its subjects in the colonies with the same close rein used at home. King James I thus allowed some local participation in decision making through arrangements such as the first elected colonial assembly, the Virginia House of Burgesses, formed in 1619, and the elected General Court that governed the Massachusetts Bay Colony after 1629. Almost all of the colonists agreed that the king ruled by divine right, but British monarchs allowed the colonists significant liberties in terms of self-government, religious practices, and economic organization. For 140 years, this system worked fairly well.[4]

By the early 1760s, however, a century and a half of physical separation, development of colonial industry, and relative self-governance by the colonies led to

mercantilism
An economic theory designed to increase a nation's wealth through the development of commercial industry and a favorable balance of trade.

Stamp Act Congress
Meeting of representatives of nine of the thirteen colonies held in New York City in 1765, during which representatives drafted a document to send to the king that listed how their rights had been violated.

weakening ties with—and loyalties to—the crown. By this time, each of the thirteen colonies had drafted its own constitution, which provided the fundamental rules or laws by which it operated. Moreover, many of the most oppressive British traditions—feudalism, a rigid class system, and the absolute authority of the king—were absent in the colonies. Land was abundant. The guild and craft systems that severely limited entry into many skilled professions in Great Britain were not part of life in the colonies. And, although religion was central to the lives of most colonists, no single state church existed, so the colonists did not follow the British practice of compulsory tithing (giving a fixed percentage of one's earnings to the state-sanctioned and -supported church).

☐ Trade and Taxation

Mercantilism, an economic theory designed to increase a nation's wealth through the development of commercial industry and a favorable balance of trade, justified Britain's maintenance of strict import/export controls on the colonies. After 1650, for example, the British Parliament passed a series of navigation acts to prevent its chief rival, Holland, from trading with the British colonies. From 1650 until well into the 1700s, Britain tried to control colonial imports and exports, believing it critical to export more goods than it imported as a way of increasing the gold and silver in its treasury. Britain found it difficult to enforce these policies, however, and the colonists, seeing little self-benefit in their operation, widely ignored them. Thus, for years, an unwritten agreement existed. The colonists relinquished to the crown and the British Parliament the authority to regulate trade and conduct international affairs, but they retained the right to levy their own taxes.

This fragile agreement was soon put to the test. The French and Indian War, fought from 1756 to 1763 on the western frontier of the colonies and in Canada, was part of a global war initiated by the British, then the greatest power in the world. This American phase of what was called the Seven Years War was fought between Britain and France with Indian allies. To raise money to pay for the war as well as the expenses of administering the colonies, Parliament enacted the Sugar Act in 1764. This act placed taxes on sugar, wine, coffee, and other products commonly exported to the colonies. A postwar colonial depression heightened resentment of the tax. Major protest, however, failed to materialize until imposition of the Stamp Act by the British Parliament in 1765. This law required that all paper items, from playing cards to books, bought and sold in the colonies carry a stamp mandated by the crown. The colonists did not find the tax itself offensive. However, they feared this act would establish a precedent for the British Parliament not only to control commerce in the colonies but also to raise revenues from the colonists without approval of the colonial governments. The political cry "no taxation without representation" rang out across the colonies.

Colonists were outraged. Men throughout the colonies organized the Sons of Liberty, under the leadership of Samuel Adams and Patrick Henry. Women formed the Daughters of Liberty. Protests against the Stamp Act were violent and loud. Riots, often led by the Sons of Liberty, broke out. These were especially violent in Boston, where an angry mob burned the colonial governor's home and protesters threatened British stamp agents charged with collecting the tax. The outraged colonists also organized a boycott of goods needing the stamps, as well as of British imports.

☐ First Steps Toward Independence

In 1765, at the urging of Samuel Adams, nine of the thirteen colonies sent representatives to a meeting in New York City, where they drafted a detailed list of crown violations of the colonists' fundamental rights. Known as the **Stamp Act Congress,** this gathering was the first official meeting of the colonies and the first step toward creating a unified nation. Attendees defined what they thought to be the proper relationship between colonial governments and the British Parliament; they ardently believed

Parliament had no authority to tax them without colonial representation in that body, yet they still remained loyal to the king. In contrast, the British believed that direct representation of the colonists was impractical and that members of Parliament represented the best interests of all the British, including the colonists.

The Stamp Act Congress and its petitions to the crown did little to stop the onslaught of taxing measures. Parliament did, however, repeal the Stamp Act and revise the Sugar Act in 1766, largely because of the uproar made by British merchants who were losing large sums of money as a result of the boycotts. Rather than appeasing the colonists, however, these actions emboldened them to increase their resistance. In 1767, Parliament enacted the Townshend Acts, which imposed duties on all kinds of colonial imports, including tea. Responses from the Sons and Daughters of Liberty came immediately. Protesters announced another boycott of tea, and almost all colonists gave up their favorite drink in a united show of resistance to the tax and British authority.[5] Tensions continued to run high, especially after the British sent 4,000 troops to Boston. On March 5, 1770, British troops opened fire on an unruly mob that included disgruntled dockworkers, whose jobs had been taken by British soldiers, and members of the Sons of Liberty, who were taunting the soldiers and throwing objects at British sentries stationed in front of the Boston Customs House.

WHAT REALLY HAPPENED AT THE BOSTON MASSACRE?

Paul Revere's famous engraving of the Boston Massacre played fast and loose with the facts. While the event occurred on a cold winter's night, the engraving features a clear sky and no ice or snow. Crispus Attucks, the Revolution's first martyr, was African American, although the engraving depicts him as a white man. Popular propaganda such as this engraving—and even dubbing the incident a "massacre"—did much to stoke anti-British sentiment in the years leading up to the Revolutionary War.

Committees of Correspondence
Organizations in each of the American colonies created to keep colonists abreast of developments with the British; served as powerful molders of public opinion against the British.

First Continental Congress
Meeting held in Philadelphia from September 5 to October 26, 1774, in which fifty-six delegates (from every colony except Georgia) adopted a resolution in opposition to the Coercive Acts.

Second Continental Congress
Meeting that convened in Philadelphia on May 10, 1775, at which it was decided that an army should be raised and George Washington of Virginia was named commander in chief.

The troops killed five colonists in what became known as the Boston Massacre. Following this confrontation, Parliament lifted all duties except those on tea. The tea tax, however, continued to be a symbolic irritant. In 1772, at the suggestion of Samuel Adams, colonists created **Committees of Correspondence** to keep each other abreast of developments with the British. These committees also served as powerful molders of public opinion against the British.

Meanwhile, despite dissent in Britain over treatment of the colonies, Parliament passed another tea tax designed to shore up the sagging sales of the East India Company, a British exporter of tea. The colonists' boycott had left that trading company with more than 18 million pounds of tea in its warehouses. To rescue British merchants from disaster, in 1773, Parliament passed the Tea Act, granting a monopoly to the financially strapped East India Company to sell tea imported from Britain. This act allowed the company to funnel business to American merchants loyal to the crown, thereby undercutting dissident colonial merchants, who could sell only tea imported from other nations. This practice drove down the price of tea and hurt colonial merchants, who were forced to buy tea at higher prices from other sources.

When the next shipment of tea arrived in Boston from Great Britain, the colonists responded by throwing the Boston Tea Party; other colonies held similar tea parties. When the news reached King George III, he flew into a rage against the actions of his disloyal subjects. "The die is now cast," the king told his prime minister. "The colonies must either submit or triumph."

King George's first act of retaliation was to persuade Parliament to pass the Coercive Acts of 1774. Known in the colonies as the Intolerable Acts, they contained a key provision calling for a total blockade of Boston Harbor, cutting off Bostonians' access to many foodstuffs, until restitution was made for the tea. Another provision reinforced the Quartering Act. It gave royal governors the authority to house British soldiers in the homes of local Boston citizens, allowing Britain to send an additional 4,000 soldiers to patrol Boston.

☐ The Continental Congresses

The British could never have guessed how the cumulative impact of these actions would unite the colonists. Samuel Adams's Committees of Correspondence spread the word, and the people of Boston received food and money from all over the thirteen colonies. The tax itself was no longer the key issue; now the extent of British authority over the colonies presented the far more important question. At the request of the colonial assemblies of Massachusetts and Virginia, all but Georgia's colonial assembly agreed to select a group of delegates to attend a continental congress authorized to communicate with the king on behalf of the now-united colonies.

The **First Continental Congress,** comprising fifty-six delegates, met in Philadelphia from September 5 to October 26, 1774. The colonists had yet to think of breaking with Great Britain; at this point, they simply wanted to iron out their differences with the king. By October, they had agreed on a series of resolutions to oppose the Coercive Acts and to establish a formal organization to boycott British goods. The Congress also drafted a Declaration of Rights and Resolves, which called for colonial rights of petition and assembly, trial by peers, freedom from a standing army, and the selection of representative councils to levy taxes.

King George III refused to yield, tensions continued to rise, and a **Second Continental Congress** was deemed necessary. Before it could meet, fighting broke out in the early morning of April 19, 1775, at Lexington and Concord, Massachusetts, with what American writer and philosopher Ralph Waldo Emerson later called "the shot heard 'round the world." Eight colonial soldiers, called Minutemen, were killed, and 16,000 British troops besieged Boston.

When the Second Continental Congress convened in Philadelphia on May 10, 1775, delegates were united by their increased hostility to Great Britain. In a final attempt to avert conflict, the Second Continental Congress adopted the Olive Branch Petition on July 5, 1775, asking the king to end hostilities. King George III rejected the petition and sent an additional 20,000 troops to quell the rebellion.

□ The Declaration of Independence

In January 1776, Thomas Paine, with the support and encouragement of Benjamin Franklin, issued (at first anonymously) *Common Sense*, a pamphlet forcefully arguing for independence from Great Britain. *Common Sense* galvanized the American public against reconciliation with Great Britain. On May 15, 1776, Virginia became the first colony to call for independence, instructing one of its delegates to the Second Continental Congress to introduce a resolution to that effect. On June 7, 1776, Richard Henry Lee of Virginia rose to move "that these United Colonies are, and of right ought to be, free and independent States, and that all connection between them and the State of Great Britain is, and ought to be, dissolved." His three-part resolution—which called for independence, the formation of foreign alliances, and preparation of a plan of confederation—triggered hot debate among the delegates. A proclamation of independence from Great Britain constituted treason, a crime punishable by death. Although six of the thirteen colonies had already instructed their delegates to vote for independence, the Second Continental Congress was suspended to allow its delegates to return home to their respective colonial legislatures for final instructions. Independence was not a move the colonists would take lightly.

The Congress set up committees to consider each point of Richard Henry Lee's proposal. The Committee of Five began work on the **Declaration of Independence.** Committee members included Benjamin Franklin of Pennsylvania, John Adams of Massachusetts, Robert Livingston of New York, and Roger Sherman of Connecticut. Adams lobbied hard for the addition of Thomas Jefferson, a Southerner, to add balance. Jefferson's writings, which revealed a "peculiar felicity of expression," had also impressed Adams. Thus, the Congress chose Jefferson of Virginia as chair.

On July 2, 1776, twelve of the thirteen colonies (with New York abstaining) voted for independence. Two days later, the Second Continental Congress voted to adopt the Declaration of Independence, largely penned by Jefferson. On July 9, 1776, the Declaration, now with the approval of New York, was read aloud in Philadelphia.[6]

In simple but eloquent language, the Declaration set out the reasons for separation of the colonies from Great Britain. Most of its stirring rhetoric drew heavily on the works of seventeenth- and eighteenth-century political philosophers, particularly the English philosopher John Locke, who argued that governments exist based on the consent of the governed.

Thus, in stirring language, the Declaration of Independence proclaims:

> We hold these truths to be self-evident, that all men are created equal, that they are endowed by their Creator with certain unalienable Rights, that among these are Life, Liberty and the pursuit of Happiness.

Jefferson and others in attendance at the Second Continental Congress wanted to have a document that would stand for all time, justifying their break with Great Britain and clarifying their notions of the proper form of government. So, the Declaration continued:

> That to secure these rights, Governments are instituted among Men, deriving their just powers from the consent of the governed. That whenever any Form of Government becomes destructive of these ends, it is the Right of the People to alter or abolish it, and to institute new Government, laying its foundation on such Principles and organizing its Powers in such form, as to them shall seem most likely to effect their Safety and Happiness.

After this stirring preamble, the Declaration enumerates the wrongs suffered by the colonists under British rule. After the Congress signed and transmitted the Declaration to the king, the Revolutionary War raged on while the Continental Congress struggled to fashion a new united government.

Declaration of Independence
Document drafted largely by Thomas Jefferson in 1776 that proclaimed the right of the American colonies to separate from Great Britain.

Take a Closer Look

The Declaration of Independence is arguably one of the most sacred American documents. In clear, concise prose, Thomas Jefferson states the colonists' rationale for their split from Great Britain. But, the document was not always as articulate and powerful as it is today. After Thomas Jefferson submitted his "Rough Draught" to the Committee of Five, other members, including John Adams and Benjamin Franklin, made significant revisions to the document.

The Declaration originally began:

> When in the course of human events it becomes necessary for a people to advance that subordination in which they have hitherto remained, and to assume among the powers of the earth the equal and independant station to which the laws of nature and of nature's god entitle them, a decent respect to the opinions of mankind requires that they should declare the causes which impel them to the change.

The committee changed this to state:

> When in the Course of human events, it becomes necessary for one people to dissolve the political bands which have connected them with another, and to assume among the powers of the earth, the separate and equal station to which the Laws of Nature and of Nature's God entitle them, a decent respect to the opinions of mankind requires that they should declare the causes which impel them to the separation.

Here, Jefferson's phrase "sacred and undeniable" became "self-evident."

The original draft stated that

> ...all men are created equal and independant, that from that equal creation they derive rights inherent and inalienable, among which are the preservation of life, and liberty, and the pursuit of happiness.

In the final draft, however, Jefferson stated,

> that they are endowed by their Creator with certain unalienable Rights, that among these are Life, Liberty and the pursuit of Happiness.

CRITICAL THINKING QUESTIONS

1. Why do you think committee members made revisions such as the ones you see here? What factors may have influenced their changes?

2. Are any edits that appear to weaken the document seen here? Why do you prefer the original language? Why do you think it was not ultimately used?

3. Who was the audience for the Declaration? How did this influence the authors' arguments?

The First Attempt at Government: The Articles of Confederation

2 | Identify the key components of the Articles of Confederation and the reasons why it failed.

Articles of Confederation
The compact between the thirteen original colonies that created a loose league of friendship, with the national government drawing its powers from the states.

confederation
Type of government in which the national government derives its powers from the states; a league of independent states.

The British had no written constitution. Delegates to the Second Continental Congress were attempting to codify many arrangements that had never before been expressed in legal terminology. To make matters more complicated, the delegates had to arrive at these decisions in a wartime atmosphere. Nevertheless, in late 1777, the Congress passed the **Articles of Confederation,** creating a loose "league of friendship" between the thirteen sovereign, or independent, colonies (some that even called themselves separate countries), and presented the Articles to the states for ratification.

The Articles, ratified in March 1781, created a type of government called a **confederation** or confederacy. Unlike Great Britain's unitary system, wherein all governmental powers reside in the national government, the national government in a confederation derives all its powers directly from the states. Thus, the national government in a confederacy is weaker than the sum of its parts, and the states often consider themselves independent nation-states linked together only for limited purposes, such as national defense. So, the Articles of Confederation proposed the following:

- A national government with a Congress empowered to make peace, coin money, appoint officers for an army, control the post office, and negotiate with Indian tribes.
- Each state's retention of its independence and sovereignty, or ultimate authority, to govern within its territories.
- One vote in the legislature, the Congress of the Confederation for each state, regardless of size.
- The vote of nine states to pass any measure (a unanimous vote for any amendment).
- The selection and payment of delegates to the Congress by the states.

☐ Problems Under the Articles of Confederation

In 1784, just one year after the Revolutionary Army was disbanded, governing the new nation under the Articles of Confederation proved unworkable.[7] In fact, historians refer to the chaotic period from 1781 to 1789, when the former colonies were governed under the Articles, as the critical period. Congress rarely could assemble the required quorum of nine states to conduct business. Even when it did meet, states found it difficult to agree on any policies. To raise revenue to pay off war debts and run the government, Congress proposed various land, poll, and liquor taxes. But, since it had no specific power to tax, all these proposals were rejected. At one point, Congress was even driven out of Philadelphia (then the capital of the new national government) by its own unpaid army.

Although the national government could coin money, it had no resources to back up the value of its currency. Continental dollars were worth little, and trade between states grew chaotic as some of them began to coin their own money. Another weakness was that the Articles of Confederation did not allow Congress to regulate commerce among the states or with foreign nations. As a result, individual states attempted to enter into agreements with other countries, and foreign nations were suspicious of trade agreements made with the Congress of the Confederation.

The Articles of Confederation, moreover, had no provision for an executive branch or a judicial system to handle the growing number of economic conflicts and boundary

constitution
A document establishing the structure, functions, and limitations of a government.

disputes among the individual states. Several states claimed the same lands to the west, and Pennsylvania and Virginia went to war with each other.

The Articles' greatest weakness, however, was its failure to provide for a strong central government. Although states had operated independently before the war, during the war they acceded to the national government's authority to wage armed conflict. Once the war was over, however, each state resumed its sovereign status and was unwilling to give up rights, such as the power to tax, to an untested national government. Consequently, the government could not force states to abide by the provisions of the second Treaty of Paris, signed in 1783.

A series of bad harvests kept farmers in debt and worsened the crumbling economy. George Washington and Alexander Hamilton, both interested in the questions of trade and frontier expansion, soon saw the need for a stronger national government with the authority to step in and solve some of these problems.

The Miracle at Philadelphia: Writing the U.S. Constitution

3 Outline the issues and compromises that were central to the writing of the U.S. Constitution.

On February 21, 1787, in the throes of economic turmoil and with domestic tranquility gone haywire, the Congress passed an official resolution. It called for a Constitutional Convention in Philadelphia for "the sole and express purpose of revising the Articles of Confederation." However, many delegates who gathered in sweltering Philadelphia on May 25, 1787, were prepared to take potentially treasonous steps to preserve the union. For example, on the first day the convention was in session, Edmund Randolph and James Madison of Virginia proposed fifteen resolutions creating an entirely new government (later known as the Virginia Plan). Their enthusiasm, however, was not universal. Many delegates, including William Paterson of New Jersey, considered these resolutions to be in violation of the convention's charter, and proposed the New Jersey Plan, which took greater steps to preserve the Articles. These proposals met heated debate on the convention's floor.

☐ The Characteristics and Motives of the Framers

The fifty-five delegates who attended the Constitutional Convention labored long and hard that hot summer. Owing to the high stakes of their action, they conducted all of the convention's work behind closed doors. George Washington of Virginia, who was unanimously elected the convention's presiding officer, cautioned delegates not to reveal details of the convention even to family members.

All of the delegates to the Constitutional Convention were men; hence, they often are called the "Founding Fathers." This text generally refers to them as the Framers, because their work provided the framework for the new government of the United States. Most of them were quite young, many in their twenties and thirties, and only one—Franklin at eighty-one—was rather old. Seventeen owned slaves.

The Framers brought with them a vast amount of political, educational, legal, and business experience. Clearly, they were an exceptional lot who ultimately produced a brilliant **constitution,** or document establishing the structure, functions, and limitations of a government.

However, debate about the Framers' motives filled the air during the ratification struggle and has provided grist for the mill of historians and political scientists over the years. In his *Economic Interpretation of the Constitution of the United States* (1913),

Who Were the Framers?

The Framers of the Constitution spent a summer in Philadelphia in nearly complete secrecy, drafting our nation's supreme code of laws. But, who really were these men? They came from varied jobs, cultures, and viewpoints; some men were slaveholders, many were lawyers, and others had little political experience. These differences influenced many of the compromises seen in the final version of the Constitution.

STATE	DELEGATES	PERCENT
Rhode Island	0	0%
New Hampshire	2	3.6%
Connecticut	3	5.4%
New York	3	5.4%
Georgia	4	7.2%
Massachusetts	4	7.2%
South Carolina	4	7.2%
Delaware	5	9.1%
Maryland	5	9.1%
New Jersey	5	9.1%
North Carolina	5	9.1%
Virginia	7	12.7%
Pennsylvania	8	14.6%

* States are drawn in proportion to their representation.

More than just a **name**

OCCUPATION
- 32 58%
- 10 18%
- 5 9%
- 2 4%
- 2 4%
- 2 4%
- 1 2%
- 1 2%

Lawyer / Doctor / Farmer
Merchant / Soldier / Inventor
Politician / Teacher

SLAVEHOLDERS
- 17 31%
- 38 69%

Not Slaveholders
Slaveholders

SIGNED CONSTITUTION
- 16 29%
- 39 71%

Signed
Did not sign

Rhode Island sent
no one.
71%
Only of attendees signed the final document.

CRITICAL THINKING QUESTIONS

1. Analyze the occupations of the Framers. Were they a fair representation of the American population at that time? Should more delegates have come from the working class?

2. Examine the percentages of Framers who owned slaves and those who did not. How might these numbers have shaped constitutional compromises on the issue of slavery?

3. Can the words of these Framers, written more than 225 years ago, continue to serve as a framework for government today, or should the Constitution change alongside the nation? Explain your answer.

Virginia Plan
The first general plan for the Constitution offered in Philadelphia. Its key points were a bicameral legislature, as well as an executive and a judiciary chosen by the national legislature.

New Jersey Plan
A framework for the Constitution proposed by a group of small states. Its key points were a one-house legislature with one vote for each state, a Congress with the ability to raise revenue, and a Supreme Court with members appointed for life.

Charles A. Beard argued that the 1780s were a critical period not for the nation as a whole, but rather for business owners who feared that a weak, decentralized government could harm their economic interests.[8] Beard argued that merchants wanted a strong national government to promote industry and trade, to protect private property, and to ensure payment of the public debt—much of which was owed to them.

By the 1950s, Beard's view had fallen into disfavor when other historians were unable to find direct links between wealth and the Framers' motives for establishing the Constitution. Others faulted Beard's failure to consider the impact of religion and individual views about government.[9] In the 1960s, however, another group of historians began to argue that social and economic factors were, in fact, important motives for supporting the Constitution. In *The Anti-Federalists* (1961), Jackson Turner Main posited that while the Constitution's supporters might not have been the united group of creditors suggested by Beard, they were wealthier, came from higher social strata, and had greater concern for maintaining the prevailing social order than the general public.[10] In 1969, Gordon S. Wood's *The Creation of the American Republic* resurrected this debate. Wood deemphasized economics to argue that major social divisions explained different groups' support for (or opposition to) the new Constitution. He concluded that the Framers were representative of a class that favored order and stability over some of the more radical ideas that had inspired the American Revolutionary War and the break with Britain.[11]

☐ The Virginia and New Jersey Plans

The **Virginia Plan,** proposed by Edmund Randolph and written by James Madison, called for a national system based heavily on the European nation-state model, wherein the national government derives its powers from the people and not from the member states.

Its key features included:

- Creation of a powerful central government with three branches—the legislative, executive, and judicial.
- A two-house legislature with one house elected directly by the people, the other chosen from among persons nominated by the state legislatures.
- A legislature with the power to select the executive and the judiciary.

In general, smaller states such as New Jersey and Connecticut felt comfortable with the arrangements under the Articles of Confederation. These states offered another model of government, the **New Jersey Plan.** Its key features included:

- Strengthening the Articles, not replacing them.
- Creating a one-house legislature with one vote for each state and with representatives chosen by state legislatures.
- Giving Congress the power to raise revenue from duties on imports and from postal service fees.
- Creating a Supreme Court with members appointed for life by the executive.

☐ Constitutional Compromises

A series of compromises shaped the final Constitution; three of these were particularly important. Below, we discuss the Great Compromise, which concerned the form of the new government, the issue of slavery, and the Three-Fifths Compromise, which dealt with representation.

THE GREAT COMPROMISE The most serious disagreement between the Virginia and New Jersey Plans concerned state representation in Congress. When a deadlock loomed, Connecticut offered its own compromise. Representation in the lower house would be determined by population, and each state would have an equal vote in the upper house. Again, a stalemate occurred.

A committee to work out an agreement soon reported back what became known as the **Great Compromise.** Taking ideas from both the Virginia and New Jersey Plans, it recommended:

- A two-house, or bicameral, legislature.

- In one house of the legislature (later called the House of Representatives), representatives would number fifty-six—no more than one representative for every 30,000 inhabitants. The people would directly elect representatives.

- That house would have the power to originate all bills for raising and spending money.

- In the second house of the legislature (later called the Senate), each state would have an equal vote, and state legislatures would select the representatives.

- In dividing power between the national and state governments, national power would be supreme.[12]

The Great Compromise ultimately met with the approval of all states in attendance. The smaller states were pleased because they received equal representation in the Senate; the larger states were satisfied with the proportional representation in the House of Representatives. The small states then would dominate the Senate, while the large states, such as Virginia and Pennsylvania, would control the House. But, because both houses had to pass any legislation, neither body could dominate the other.

THE ISSUE OF SLAVERY The Great Compromise dealt with one major concern of the Framers—how best to address the differences in large and small states—but other problems stemming largely from regional differences remained. Slavery, which formed the basis of much of the southern states' cotton economy, was one of the thorniest issues to tackle. To reach an agreement on the Constitution, the Framers had to craft a compromise that balanced southern commercial interests with comparable northern concerns. Eventually, the Framers agreed that Northerners would support continuation of the slave trade for twenty more years, as well as a twenty-year ban on taxing exports to protect the cotton trade, while Southerners consented to a provision requiring only a majority vote on navigation laws. The Framers also gave the national government the authority to regulate foreign commerce and agreed that the Senate would have the power to ratify treaties by a two-thirds majority, which assuaged the fears of southern states, who made up more than one-third of the nation.

THE THREE-FIFTHS COMPROMISE One major conflict had yet to be resolved: how to determine state population with regard to representation in the House of Representatives. Slaves could not vote, but the southern states wanted them included in the determination of population numbers. After considerable dissension, the delegates decided that population for purposes of representation and the apportionment of direct taxes would be calculated by adding the "whole Number of Free Persons" to "three-fifths of all other Persons." "All other Persons" was the delegates' euphemistic way of referring to slaves. Known as the **Three-Fifths Compromise,** this highly political deal ensured that the South would hold 47 percent of the House—enough to prevent attacks on slavery but not so much as to foster the spread of slavery northward.

☐ Unfinished Business: The Executive Branch

The Framers next turned to fashioning an executive branch. While they agreed on the idea of a one-person executive, they could not settle on the length of the term of office or on the procedure for choosing the chief executive. The delegates feared

Great Compromise
The final decision of the Constitutional Convention to create a two-house legislature, with the lower house elected by the people and with powers divided between the two houses. It also made national law supreme.

Three-Fifths Compromise
Agreement reached at the Constitutional Convention stipulating that each slave was to be counted as three-fifths of a person for purposes of determining population for representation in the U.S. House of Representatives.

separation of powers

A way of dividing the power of government among the legislative, executive, and judicial branches, each staffed separately, with equality and independence of each branch ensured by the Constitution.

checks and balances

A constitutionally mandated structure that gives each of the three branches of government some degree of oversight and control over the actions of the others.

putting too much power, including selection of a president, into the hands of the lower classes. At the same time, representatives from the smaller states feared that selection of the chief executive by the legislature would put additional power into the hands of the large states.

Amid these fears, the Committee on Unfinished Portions conducted its sole task: ironing out problems and disagreements concerning the office of chief executive. The committee recommended that the presidential term of office be fixed at four years instead of seven, as had earlier been proposed. The committee also made it possible for a president to serve more than one term.

In addition, the Framers created the Electoral College as a mechanism for selecting the chief executive of the new nation. The Electoral College system gave individual states a key role, because each state would choose electors equal to the number of representatives it had in the House and Senate. This step was a vague compromise that removed election of the president and vice president from both the Congress and the people and placed it in the hands of electors whose method of selection would be left to the states.

In drafting the new Constitution, the Framers also took care to provide for removal of the chief executive. The House of Representatives assumed the sole responsibility of investigating and charging a president or vice president with "Treason, Bribery, or other high Crimes and Misdemeanors." A majority vote then would result in issuing articles of impeachment against the president or vice president. In turn, the Senate took on the sole responsibility of trying the president or vice president on the charges issued by the House. To convict and remove the president or vice president from office required a two-thirds vote of the Senate.

The U.S. Constitution

4   Analyze the underlying principles of the U.S. Constitution.

The U.S. Constitution's opening line, "We the People," ended, at least for the time being, the question of the source of the government's power: it came directly from the people. The Constitution then explained the need for the new outline of government: "in Order to form a more perfect Union" indirectly acknowledged the weaknesses of the Articles of Confederation in governing a growing nation. Next, the optimistic goals of the Framers for the new nation were set out: to "establish Justice, insure domestic Tranquility, provide for the common defence, promote the general Welfare, and secure the Blessings of Liberty to ourselves and our Posterity," followed by the formal creation of a new government: "do ordain and establish this Constitution for the United States of America." On September 17, 1787, the delegates approved the Constitution.

☐ The Basic Principles of the Constitution

The structure of the proposed new national government owed much to the writings of the French philosopher Montesquieu (1689–1755), who advocated distinct functions for each branch of government, called **separation of powers,** with a system of **checks and balances** between each branch. The Constitution's concern with the distribution of power between states and the national government also reveals the heavy influence of political philosophers, as well as the colonists' experience under the Articles of Confederation.[13]

FEDERALISM The question before and during the convention concerned how much power states would give up to the national government. Given the nation's

Explore Your World

Written in 1787, the U.S. Constitution is the world's shortest and oldest national constitution still in use. In fact, around the world, the average life span of a constitution written since 1789 is about seventeen years. A lasting, stable constitution may be advantageous for a state, but it may also pose unique challenges; more recent constitutions are able to address modern problems such as civil rights, government bureaucracy, and global trade.

The Constitution of the Kingdom of Norway

(Adopted May 17, 1814)

Section A. Form of Government and Religion

Section B. The Executive Power, the King, and the Royal Family

Section C. Rights of the Citizens and the Legislative Power

Section D. The Judicial Power

Section E. General Provisions

Both constitutions lay out a basic structure of government that includes three branches: executive, legislative, and judicial.

The Norwegian Constitution is the world's second oldest. It created a unitary system of government led by a constitutional monarch. This constitution endures in part because it can easily be amended to add and delete provisions. In 2012, for example, the legislature passed an amendment separating church and state, thereby nullifying part of the Norwegian Constitution's first section.

THE CONSTITUTION OF THE RUSSIAN FEDERATION

(Adopted December 12, 1993)

SECTION ONE

Chapter 1. The Fundamentals of the Constitutional System
Chapter 2. The Rights and Liberties of Man and Citizen
Chapter 3. The Russian Federation
Chapter 4. The President of the Russian Federation
Chapter 5. The Federal Assembly
Chapter 6. The Government of the Russian Federation
Chapter 7. The Judiciary
Chapter 8. Local Self-Government
Chapter 9. Constitutional Amendments and Revisions

SECTION TWO

Concluding and Transitional Provisions

The Russian Constitution, written after the fall of the Soviet Union, creates a federal system of government. Accordingly, the document contains a high level of detail about the role and powers of state and local governments. It also clearly reserved rights to the people, as articulated in its first section.

CRITICAL THINKING QUESTIONS

1. What are the key differences you observe between these two documents? Are these differences likely the result of temporal, cultural, or political differences?

2. Which elements of the Norwegian Constitution may have enabled it to survive for almost 200 years? How do these elements reflect the era in which it was written?

3. Which elements of the Russian Constitution are particularly striking? How do these elements enable the state to thrive in a globalized, modern world?

federal system
System of government in which the national government and state governments share power and derive all authority from the people.

experiences under the Articles of Confederation, the Framers believed that a strong national government was necessary for the new nation's survival. However, they were reluctant to create a powerful government after the model of Great Britain, the country from which they had just won their independence. The colonists did not even consider Great Britain's unitary system. Instead, they fashioned a way (now known as a **federal system**) to divide the power of government between a strong national government and the individual states, with national power being supreme.

SEPARATION OF POWERS Separation of powers is simply a way of parceling out power among the three branches of government. Its three key features are:

- Three distinct branches of government: the legislative, the executive, and the judicial.
- Three separately staffed branches of government to exercise these functions.
- Constitutional equality and independence of each branch.

As illustrated in Figure 1, the Framers carefully created a system in which law-making, law-enforcing, and law-interpreting functions were assigned to independent

Legislative Checks on the Executive
Impeach the president
Reject legislation or funding the president wants
Refuse to confirm nominees or approve treaties*
Override the president's veto by a two-thirds vote

EXECUTIVE BRANCH POWERS
Enforce federal laws and court orders
Propose legislation to Congress
Make foreign treaties
Nominate officers of the U.S. government and federal judges
Serve as commander in chief of the armed forces
Pardon people convicted in federal courts or grant reprieves

Executive Checks on the Legislative
Veto legislation
Call Congress into special session
Implement (or fail to implement) laws passed by Congress

LEGISLATIVE BRANCH POWERS
Pass all federal laws
Pass the federal budget
Declare war
Establish lower federal courts and the number of judges

Judicial Checks on the Legislative
Rule federal and state laws unconstitutional

Judicial Checks on the Executive
Declare executive branch actions unconstitutional
Chief justice presides over impeachment trials

Legislative Checks on the Judicial
Change the number and jurisdiction of federal courts
Impeach federal judges
Propose constitutional amendments to override judicial decisions

JUDICIAL BRANCH POWERS
Interpret federal laws and U.S. Constitution
Review the decisions of lower state and federal courts

Executive Checks on the Judicial
Appoint federal judges
Refuse to implement decisions

*This power belongs to the Senate only.

FIGURE 1 WHAT ARE THE SEPARATION OF POWERS AND HOW DO CHECKS AND BALANCES WORK UNDER THE U.S. CONSTITUTION?
Drawing inspiration from Montesquieu, the Framers crafted a political system of checks and balances and separation of powers. Each of the three branches—executive, legislative, and judicial—has distinct powers, and each branch has powers that intersect with the powers of each of the other branches. This system prevents any one branch from becoming too powerful.

branches of government. Only the legislature has the authority to make laws; the chief executive enforces laws; and the judiciary interprets them. Moreover, initially, members of the House of Representatives, members of the Senate, the president, and members of the federal courts were selected by, and therefore responsible to, different constituencies.

The Framers could not have foreseen the intermingling of governmental functions that has since evolved. In Article I of the Constitution, the legislative power is vested in Congress. But, the president also has a role in the legislative process; in order for a bill to become law, he must sign the legislation. If he disagrees with the content of a bill, he may also veto the legislation, although a two-thirds vote in Congress can override his veto. Judicial interpretation also helps to clarify the language or implementation of legislation enacted through this process.

CHECKS AND BALANCES The separation of powers among the three branches of the national government is not complete. According to Montesquieu and the Framers, the powers of each branch (as well as the powers of the two houses of the national legislature and the powers between the states and the national government) could be used to check those of the other two governmental branches. The power of each branch of government is checked, or limited, and balanced because the legislative, executive, and judicial branches share some authority, and no branch has exclusive domain over any single activity. The creation of this system allowed the Framers to minimize the threat of tyranny from any one branch. Thus, for almost every power granted to one branch, the Framers established an equal control in the other two branches.

☐ The Articles of the Constitution

The document finally signed by the Framers condensed numerous resolutions into a Preamble and seven separate articles remedying many of the deficiencies within the Articles of Confederation (see Table 1). The first three articles established the three branches of government, defined their internal operations, and clarified their relationships with one another. The Framers technically considered all branches of government equal, yet some initially appeared more powerful than others. The order of the articles, as well as the detail contained in the first three, reflects the Framers' concern that these branches of government might abuse their powers. The four remaining articles define the relationships between the states, declare national law to be supreme, and set out methods of amending and ratifying the Constitution.

ARTICLE I: THE LEGISLATIVE BRANCH Article I vests all legislative powers in the Congress and establishes a bicameral legislature, consisting of the Senate and the House of Representatives. It also sets out the qualifications for holding office in each house, the terms of office, the methods of selection of representatives and senators, and the system of apportionment among the states to determine membership in the House of Representatives.

One of the most important sections of Article I is section 8. It carefully lists those powers the Framers wished the new Congress to possess. These specified, or **enumerated, powers** contain many key provisions that had been denied to the Continental Congress under the Articles of Confederation.

After careful enumeration of seventeen powers of Congress in Article I, section 8, a final, general clause authorizing Congress to "make all Laws which shall be necessary and proper for carrying into Execution the foregoing Powers" completes Article I. Often referred to as the elastic clause, the **necessary and proper clause** has been a source of tremendous congressional activity never anticipated by the Framers, including the passage of laws that regulate the environment, welfare programs, education, and communication. The necessary and proper clause is the basis for the **implied powers** that Congress uses to execute its other powers.

ARTICLE II: THE EXECUTIVE BRANCH Article II vests the executive power, that is, the authority to execute the laws of the nation, in a president of the United States.

enumerated powers
The powers of the national government specifically granted to Congress in Article I, section 8 of the Constitution.

necessary and proper clause
The final paragraph of Article I, section 8, of the Constitution, which gives Congress the authority to pass all laws "necessary and proper" to carry out the enumerated powers specified in the Constitution; also called the elastic clause.

implied powers
The powers of the national government derived from the enumerated powers and the necessary and proper clause.

TABLE 1 HOW DO THE ARTICLES OF CONFEDERATION AND THE U.S. CONSTITUTION COMPARE TO ONE ANOTHER?

	Articles of Confederation	Constitution
Formal name of the nation	The United States of America	Not specified, but referred to in the Preamble as "the United States of America"
Legislature	Unicameral, called Congress	Bicameral, called Congress, divided into the House of Representatives and the Senate
Members of Congress	Between two and seven members per state	Two senators per state, representatives apportioned according to population of each state
Voting in Congress	One vote per state	One vote per representative or senator
Appointment of members	All appointed by state legislatures, in the manner each legislature directed	Representatives elected by popular vote; senators appointed by state legislatures
Term of legislative office	One year	Two years for representatives; six for senators
Term limit for legislative office	No more than three of every six years	None
When Congress is not in session	A Committee of States had the full powers of Congress	The president of the United States can call on Congress to assemble
Chair of legislature	President of Congress	Speaker of the House of Representatives; vice president is president of the Senate
Executive	None	President
National judiciary	Maritime judiciary established—other courts left to states	Supreme Court established, as well as other courts Congress deems necessary
Adjudicator of disputes between states	Congress	Supreme Court
New states	Admitted upon agreement of nine states (special exemption provided for Canada)	Admitted upon agreement of majority of Congress
Amendment	When agreed upon by all states	When agreed upon by three-fourths of the states
Navy	Congress authorized to build a navy; states authorized to equip warships to counter piracy	Congress authorized to build a navy; states not allowed to keep ships of war
Army	Congress to decide on size of force and to requisition troops from each state according to population	Congress authorized to raise and support armies
Power to coin money	United States and the states	United States only
Taxes	Apportioned by Congress, collected by the states	Levied and collected by Congress
Ratification	Unanimous consent required	Consent of nine states required

Section 1 sets the president's term of office at four years and explains the Electoral College. It also states the qualifications for office and describes a mechanism to replace the president in case of death, disability, or removal from office. Article II also limits the presidency to natural-born citizens.

The powers and duties of the president are set out in section 3. Among the most important of these are the president's role as commander in chief of the armed forces, the authority to make treaties with the consent of the Senate, and the authority to "appoint Ambassadors, other public Ministers and Consuls, the Judges of the supreme Court, and all other Officers of the United States." Other sections of Article II instruct the president to report directly to Congress "from time to time," in what has come to be known as the State of the Union Address, and to "take Care that the Laws be faithfully executed." Section 4 provides the mechanism for removal of the president, vice president, and other officers of the United States.

ARTICLE III: THE JUDICIAL BRANCH Article III establishes a Supreme Court and defines its jurisdiction. During the Philadelphia meeting, the small and large states differed significantly regarding both the desirability of an independent judiciary and the role of state courts in the national court system. The smaller states feared that a strong unelected judiciary would trample on their liberties. In compromise, the Framers permitted Congress to establish lower national courts but did not require it. Thus, state courts and the national court system would exist side by side with distinct areas of authority. Federal courts had authority to decide cases arising under federal law and the U.S. Constitution. The U.S. Supreme Court also assumed the power to settle disputes between states, or between a state and the national government.

Although some delegates to the convention urged that the president have authority to remove federal judges, ultimately judges received appointments for life, presuming "good behavior." And, like the president's, their salaries cannot be lowered while they hold office, thereby ensuring that the legislature not attempt to punish the Supreme Court or any other judges for unpopular decisions.

ARTICLES IV THROUGH VII The remainder of the articles in the Constitution attempted to anticipate problems that might occur in the operation of the new national government as well as its relations to the states. Article IV begins with what is called the **full faith and credit clause,** which mandates that states honor the laws and judicial proceedings of other states. Article IV also includes the mechanisms for admitting new states to the union.

Article V (discussed in greater detail on MyPoliSciLab) specifies how amendments can be added to the Constitution. The Bill of Rights, which added ten amendments to the Constitution in 1791, was one of the first items of business when the First Congress met in 1789.

Article VI contains the supremacy clause, which asserts the basic primacy of the Constitution and national law over state laws and constitutions. The **supremacy clause** provides that the "Constitution, and the laws of the United States" as well as all treaties are to be the supreme law of the land. All national and state officers and judges are bound by national law and take oaths to support the federal Constitution above any state law or constitution. Because of the supremacy clause, any legitimate exercise of national power supersedes any state laws or action, in a process called preemption.

Article VI also specifies that no religious test shall be required for holding any office. This mandate is strengthened by the separation of church and state guarantee that became part of the Constitution when the First Amendment was ratified. The seventh and final article of the Constitution concerns the procedures for ratifying the new Constitution: nine of the thirteen states would have to agree to, or ratify, its new provisions before it would become the supreme law of the land.

full faith and credit clause
Section of Article IV of the Constitution that ensures judicial decrees and contracts made in one state will be binding and enforceable in any other state.

supremacy clause
Portion of Article VI of the Constitution mandating that national law is supreme to (that is, supersedes) all other laws passed by the states or by any other subdivision of government.

Federalists
Those who favored a stronger national government and supported the proposed U.S. Constitution; later became the first U.S. political party.

The Drive for Ratification of the U.S. Constitution

5   Explain the conflicts that characterized the drive for ratification of the U.S. Constitution.

The Congress of the Confederation immediately accepted the work of the convention and forwarded the proposed Constitution to the states for their vote. It was by no means certain, however, that the states would adopt the new Constitution. From the fall of 1787 to the summer of 1788, debate over the proposed Constitution raged around the nation.

Explore on MyPoliSciLab
Simulation: You Are a Founder

☐ Federalists Versus Anti-Federalists

During the debate over whether to ratify the Constitution, those who favored the new strong national government chose to call themselves **Federalists.** They were well aware

How Long Did It Take to Ratify the Constitution?

A mericans today generally support the principles of the Constitution, but after the Framers adjourned on September 17, 1787, three years passed before all thirteen states approved the document. The ensuing ratification debate was an inherently political game of multiple moves, in which the Constitution was kept alive by relatively narrow majorities, particularly in two strategically located states.

Ratification Timeline

1787

Sep. 17
Constitutional Convention adjourns.
Sep. 28
Congress sends Constitution to the states.

Dec. 7 DE, 30–0
Dec. 12 PA, 46–23
Dec. 18 NJ, 38–0

1788

Jan. 2 GA, 26–0
Jan. 9 CT, 128–40
Feb. 6 MA, 187–168

Mar. 24
Rhode Island rejects in referendum.

Apr. 28 MD, 63–11

May 23 SC, 149–73

Constitution meets ◄········· ratification requirement.

June 21 NH, 57–47
June 25 VA, 89–79
July 26 NY, 30–27

Aug. 2
North Carolina adjourns without ratifying.

Federalist Papers Debate

1789

Apr. 1
Congress achieves quorum.
Apr. 30
Washington sworn in as President.

Sep. 25
Bill of Rights approved, sent to states.

Nov. 21 NC, 194-77

1790

May 29 RI, 34-32

The United States in 1790

NEW YORK was an important center of commerce. Located between New England and the mid-Atlantic states, holding the Republic together would have been difficult without New York.

4% NH
11% MA
10% NY
2% RI
7% CT
9% PA
5% NJ
9% MD
2% DE
21% VA
11% NC
7% SC
2% GA

Half of all Americans were southerners, and two-in-five southerners were **VIRGINIANS**. It was the political and economic center of the South, and the source of the intellectual force behind the Constitution.

* Percents indicate a state's percentage of the national population.

Investigate Further

Concept Why did it take three years for all thirteen states to ratify the Constitution? The first states to ratify the Constitution did so with a strong majority of support for the document. But as those states signed on, opposition in remaining states grew, and the ratification debate intensified.

Connection Which states were most closely divided on ratification? The debate intensified in two strategic states: New York and Virginia. Ratification in those two holdout states was necessary in order to lend legitimacy to the new government.

Cause What were the issues of the debate? Written in support of the new government, *The Federalist Papers* addressed New Yorkers' concerns about federal power. For Virginians, the sticking point was a Bill of Rights, which James Madison promised to introduce in the new Congress.

that many people still generally opposed the notion of a strong national government. They did not want to risk being labeled nationalists, so they tried to get the upper hand in the debate by nicknaming their opponents **Anti-Federalists.** As noted in Table 2, Anti-Federalists argued that they simply wanted to protect state governments from the tyranny of a too powerful national government.[14]

Federalists and Anti-Federalists participated in the mass meetings held in state legislatures to discuss the pros and cons of the new plan. Tempers ran high at these meetings, which played a powerful role in the adoption process.

☐ *The Federalist Papers*

Between October 1787 and May 1788, eighty-five essays written under the pen name "Publius" routinely appeared in newspapers in New York, a state where ratification was in doubt. Alexander Hamilton and James Madison wrote most of them. Hamilton, a young, fiery New Yorker born in the British West Indies, wrote fifty-one; Madison, a Virginian who later served as the fourth president, authored twenty-six; jointly they penned another three. John Jay, also of New York, and later the first chief justice of the United States, wrote five of the pieces. These eighty-five essays became known as *The Federalist Papers* and are perhaps the best explanations of the Framers' intentions as they drafted the new Constitution.

Forced on the defensive, the Anti-Federalists responded to *The Federalist Papers* with their own series of letters written under the pen names "Brutus" and "Cato," two ancient Romans famous for their intolerance of tyranny. These letters (actually essays) undertook a line-by-line critique of the Constitution.

Anti-Federalists argued that a strong central government would render the states powerless.[15] They stressed the strengths granted to the government under the Articles of Confederation and maintained that the Articles, not the proposed Constitution, created a true federal system. Moreover, they believed that the strong national government would tax heavily, that the U.S. Supreme Court would overwhelm the states by invalidating state laws, and that the president eventually would have too much power as commander in chief of a large and powerful army.[16]

In particular, Anti-Federalists feared the power of the national government to run roughshod over the liberties of the people. They proposed that the taxing power of Congress be limited, that the executive be curbed by a council, that the military consist of state militias rather than a national force, and that the jurisdiction of the Supreme Court be limited to prevent it from reviewing and potentially overturning the decisions of state courts. But, their most effective argument concerned the absence of a bill of rights in the Constitution. James Madison answered these criticisms in *Federalist Nos. 10* and *51*. In *Federalist No. 10*, Madison pointed out that the voters

Anti-Federalists
Those who favored strong state governments and a weak national government; opposed ratification of the U.S. Constitution.

The Federalist Papers
A series of eighty-five political essays written by Alexander Hamilton, James Madison, and John Jay in support of ratification of the U.S. Constitution.

TABLE 2 WHAT WERE THE DIFFERENCES BETWEEN THE FEDERALISTS AND THE ANTI-FEDERALISTS?

	Federalists	**Anti-Federalists**
Who were they?	Property owners, landed rich, merchants of Northeast and Mid-Atlantic	Small farmers, shopkeepers, laborers
Political philosophy	Elitist; saw themselves and those of their class as most fit to govern (others were to be governed)	Believed in the decency of "the common man" and in participatory democracy; viewed elites as corrupt; sought greater protection of individual rights
Type of government favored	Powerful central government; two-house legislature; upper house (six-year term) further removed from the people, whom they distrusted	Wanted stronger state governments (closer to the people) at the expense of the powers of the national government; sought smaller electoral districts, frequent elections, referendum and recall, and a large unicameral legislature to provide for greater class and occupational representation
Alliances	Pro-British, anti-French	Anti-British, pro-French

Bill of Rights
The first ten amendments to the U.S. Constitution, which largely guarantee specific rights and liberties.

would not always succeed in electing "enlightened statesmen" as their representatives. The greatest threat to individual liberties would therefore come from factions within the government, who might place narrow interests above broader national interests and the rights of citizens. While recognizing that no form of government could protect the country from unscrupulous politicians, Madison argued that the organization of the new government would minimize the effects of political factions. The great advantage of a federal system, Madison maintained, was that it created the "happy combination" of a national government too large for any single faction to control and several state governments that would be smaller and more responsive to local needs. Moreover, he argued in *Federalist No. 51* that the proposed federal government's separation of powers would prohibit any one branch from either dominating the national government or violating the rights of citizens.

☐ Ratifying the Constitution

Debate continued in the thirteen states as votes were taken from December 1787 to June 1788, in accordance with the ratifying process laid out in Article VII of the proposed Constitution. Three states acted quickly to ratify the new Constitution. Two small states, Delaware and New Jersey, voted to ratify before the large states could rethink the notion of equal representation of the states in the Senate. Pennsylvania, where Federalists were well organized, was also one of the first three states to ratify. Massachusetts assented to the new government but tempered its support by calling for an immediate addition of amendments, including one protecting personal rights. New Hampshire became the crucial ninth state to ratify on June 21, 1788. This action completed the ratification process outlined in Article VII of the Constitution and marked the beginning of a new nation. But, New York and Virginia, which at that time accounted for more than 40 percent of the new nation's population, had not yet ratified the Constitution. Thus, the practical future of the new nation remained in doubt.

Hamilton in New York and Madison in Virginia worked feverishly to convince delegates to their state conventions to vote for the new government. In New York, sentiment against the Constitution ran high. In Albany, fighting broke out over ratification and resulted in injuries and death. When news of Virginia's acceptance of the Constitution reached the New York convention, Hamilton was able to convince a majority of those present to follow suit by a margin of three votes. Both states also recommended the addition of a series of structural amendments and a bill of rights.

☐ The Bill of Rights

Once the Constitution was ratified, elections took place. When Congress convened, it immediately sent a set of amendments to the states for ratification. An amendment authorizing the enlargement of the House of Representatives and another to prevent members of the House from raising their own salaries failed to garner favorable votes in the necessary three-fourths of the states. The remaining ten amendments, known as the **Bill of Rights,** were ratified by 1791 in accordance with the procedures set out in the Constitution. Sought by Anti-Federalists as a protection for individual liberties, they offered numerous specific limitations on the national government's ability to interfere with a wide variety of personal liberties, some of which many state constitutions had already guaranteed. These include freedom of expression, speech, press, religion, and assembly, guaranteed by the First Amendment. The Bill of Rights also contains numerous safeguards for those accused of crimes. The Ninth Amendment notes that these enumerated rights are not inclusive, meaning they are not the only rights to be enjoyed by the people, and the Tenth Amendment states that powers not given to the national government are reserved by the states or the people.

Toward Reform: Methods of Amending the U.S. Constitution

6 Distinguish between the methods for proposing and ratifying amendments to the U.S. Constitution.

The Framers did not want to fashion a government subject to the whims of the people. Therefore, they made the formal amendment process a slow one to guard against impulsive amendment of the Constitution. In keeping with this intent, only seventeen amendments have been added since the Bill of Rights. However, informal amendments, prompted by judicial interpretation, cultural and social change, and technological change, have had a tremendous impact on the Constitution.

☐ Formal Methods of Amending the Constitution

Article V of the Constitution creates a two-stage amendment process: proposal and ratification. The Constitution specifies two ways to accomplish each stage. As illustrated in Figure 2, amendments to the Constitution can be proposed by: (1) a vote of two-thirds of the members in both houses of Congress; or, (2) a vote of two-thirds of the state legislatures specifically requesting Congress to call a national convention to propose amendments.

The second method has never been used. Historically, it has served as a fairly effective threat, forcing Congress to consider amendments it might otherwise never have debated.

The ratification process is fairly straightforward. When Congress votes to propose an amendment, the Constitution specifies that the ratification process must occur in one of two ways: (1) a favorable vote in three-fourths of the state legislatures; or, (2) a favorable vote in specially called ratifying conventions in three-fourths of the states.

The Constitution itself was ratified by the favorable vote of nine states in specially called ratifying conventions. The Framers feared that the power of special interests in state legislatures would prevent a positive vote on the new Constitution. Since ratification of the Constitution, however, only one ratifying convention has been called. The Eighteenth Amendment, which outlawed the sale of alcoholic beverages nationwide, was ratified by the first method—a vote in state legislatures. Millions of people broke the law, others died from drinking homemade liquor, and still others made their fortunes selling bootleg or illegal liquor. After a decade of these problems, Congress

Methods of Proposal

By two-thirds vote in both houses of Congress

OR

By national constitutional convention called by Congress at the request of two-thirds of the state legislatures. (This method never has been used to propose an amendment.)

Usual method

Used once (Twenty-First Amendment)

Methods of Ratification

By legislatures in three-fourths of the states

OR

By conventions in three-fourths of the states

FIGURE 2 HOW CAN THE U.S. CONSTITUTION BE AMENDED?

There are two stages to the amendment process: proposal and ratification. An amendment can be proposed by two-thirds of either both houses of Congress or the state legislatures. It can be ratified by three-fourths of the state legislatures or special ratifying conventions called in each of the states.

WHICH IS THE ONLY CONSTITUTIONAL AMENDMENT TO BE REPEALED?
For all its moral support from groups such as the Women's Christian Temperance Union (WCTU), whose members invaded bars to protest the sale of alcoholic beverages, the Eighteenth (Prohibition) Amendment was a disaster. Among its side effects was the rise of powerful crime organizations responsible for illegal sales of alcoholic beverages. Once proposed, it took only ten months to ratify the Twenty-First Amendment, which repealed the Prohibition Amendment.

decided to act. It proposed an additional amendment—the Twenty-First—to repeal the Eighteenth Amendment. Congress sent the amendment to the states for ratification, but with a call for ratifying conventions, not a vote in state legislatures.[17] Members of Congress correctly predicted that the move to repeal the Eighteenth Amendment would encounter opposition in the state houses, which conservative rural legislators largely controlled. Thus, Congress's decision to use the convention method led to quick approval of the Twenty-First Amendment.

The intensity of efforts to amend the Constitution has varied considerably, depending on the nature of the change proposed. Whereas the Twenty-First Amendment took only ten months to ratify, the Equal Rights Amendment (ERA) was introduced in every session of Congress from 1923 until 1972, when Congress finally voted favorably for it. Even then, years of lobbying by women's groups were insufficient to garner necessary state support. By 1982, the congressionally mandated date for ratification, only thirty-five states—three short of the number required—had voted favorably on the amendment.[18]

☐ Informal Methods of Amending the Constitution

The formal amendment process is not the only way the Constitution has been altered over time. Judicial interpretation, cultural and social change, and the growth of technology also have had a major impact on how the Constitution has evolved.

JUDICIAL INTERPRETATION As early as 1803, the Supreme Court declared in *Marbury* v. *Madison* that federal courts had the power to nullify acts of the nation's government when the courts found such acts to conflict with the Constitution.[19] Over the years, this check on the other branches of government and on the states has increased the authority of the Court and significantly altered the meaning of various provisions of the Constitution. This fact prompted President Woodrow Wilson to call

The Living Constitution

> **The Congress,** *whenever two thirds of both houses shall deem it necessary, shall propose amendments to this Constitution, or, on the application of the legislatures of two thirds of the several states, shall call a convention for proposing amendments, which, in either case, shall be valid to all intents and purposes, as part of this Constitution, when ratified by the legislatures of three fourths of the several states, or by conventions in three fourths thereof, as the one or the other mode of ratification may be proposed by the Congress.* — ARTICLE V

With this article, the Framers acknowledged the potential need to change or amend the Constitution. This article provides for two methods to propose amendments: by a two-thirds vote of both houses of Congress or by a two-thirds vote of the state legislatures. It also specifies two alternative methods of ratification of proposed amendments: by a three-quarters vote of the state legislatures, or by a similar vote in specially called state ratifying conventions.

During the Constitutional Convention in Philadelphia, the Framers were divided as to how frequently or how easily the Constitution was to be amended. The original suggestion was to allow the document to be amended "when soever it shall seem necessary." Some delegates wanted to entrust this authority to the state legislatures; however, others feared that it would give states too much power. James Madison alleviated these fears by suggesting that both Congress and the states have a role in the process.

In the late 1960s and early 1970s, leaders of the new women's rights movement sought passage of the Equal Rights Amendment (ERA). Their efforts were rewarded when the ERA was approved in the House and Senate by overwhelming majorities in 1972 and then sent out to the states for their approval. In spite of tremendous lobbying, a strong anti-ERA movement emerged and the amendment failed to gain approval in three-quarters of the state legislatures.

The failed battles for the ERA as well as other amendments, including one to prohibit child labor and another to grant statehood to the District of Columbia, underscore how difficult it is to amend the Constitution. Thus, unlike the constitutions of individual states or many other nations, the U.S. Constitution rarely has been amended. Still, the ERA has been proposed in every session of Congress since 1923.

CRITICAL THINKING QUESTIONS

1. What would it take to get an equal rights amendment added to the U.S. Constitution?
2. Does your state already have an equal rights amendment? What does it guarantee?

---

the Supreme Court "a constitutional convention in continuous session, a role demonstrated by recent decisions in civil liberties, civil rights, and economic regulation.."

Today, some analysts argue that the original intent of the Framers—as evidenced in *The Federalist Papers,* as well as in private notes taken by James Madison at the Constitutional Convention—should govern judicial interpretation of the Constitution.[20] Others argue that the Framers knew a changing society needed an elastic, flexible document that could adapt to the ages.[21] In all likelihood, the vagueness of the document was purposeful. Those in attendance in Philadelphia recognized that they could not agree on everything and that it was wiser to leave interpretation to future generations.

SOCIAL AND CULTURAL CHANGE Even the most far-sighted of those in attendance at the Constitutional Convention could not have anticipated the vast changes that have occurred in the United States. For example, although many people were uncomfortable with the Three-Fifths Compromise and others hoped for the abolition of slavery, none could have imagined that an African American would one day become president of the United States.

Social change has also caused alterations in the way institutions of government act. As problems such as the Great Depression appeared national in scope, Congress took on more and more power at the expense of states. In fact, Yale law professor Bruce Ackerman argues that extraordinary times call for extraordinary measures such as the New Deal that, in effect, amend the Constitution.

TECHNOLOGICAL CHANGE Technological advances of the twenty-first century bring up new questions concerning privacy and our rights under the Constitution, including regulation of television airwaves and Internet content, as well as the need for security surveillance systems. The development and growth of social media have also redefined free speech in the classroom and the workplace; online posts can be grounds for firing employees or expelling students.

Changes in technology have also led our political institutions to expand into areas never imagined by the Framers. The Constitution, for example, does not explicitly empower Congress to create a Social Security system. But, in an effort to address growing poverty among senior citizens during the Great Depression, Congress created this program in 1935. Today, owing in part to advances in medical technology and greater life expectancies, the program issues $52.5 million per month to retirees, dependents, and the disabled.[22] In spite of such massive modifications, the Constitution survives, changed and ever changing after more than 200 years.

On MyPoliSciLab

Review the Chapter

 Listen to **Chapter** on **MyPoliSciLab**

Roots of the New American Nation

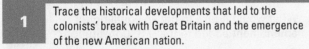

1 Trace the historical developments that led to the colonists' break with Great Britain and the emergence of the new American nation.

Settlers came to the New World for a variety of reasons, but most of these early inhabitants remained loyal to Great Britain and considered themselves subjects of the king. Over the years, as new generations of Americans were born on colonial soil, those ties weakened. A series of taxes levied by the British crown ultimately led colonists to convene the Second Continental Congress and to declare their independence.

The First Attempt at Government: The Articles of Confederation

2 Identify the key components of the Articles of Confederation and the reasons why it failed.

The Articles of Confederation (1781) created a loose league of friendship between the new national government and the states. Numerous weaknesses in the new government quickly became apparent. Among the major flaws were Congress's inability to tax or regulate commerce, the absence of an executive to administer the government, the lack of a strong central government, and no judiciary.

The Miracle at Philadelphia: Writing the U.S. Constitution

3 Outline the issues and compromises that were central to the writing of the U.S. Constitution.

When weaknesses of the Articles of Confederation became apparent, the states called for a meeting to reform them. The Constitutional Convention (1787) threw out the Articles of Confederation and fashioned a new, more workable form of government. The U.S. Constitution resulted from a series of compromises, including those over representation, issues involving large and small states, slavery, and how to determine population. The delegates also made compromises on how members of each branch of government were to be selected. They created the Electoral College to give states a key role in the selection of the president.

The U.S. Constitution

4 Analyze the underlying principles of the U.S. Constitution.

The proposed U.S. Constitution created a federal system that drew heavily on Montesquieu's ideas about separation of powers. These ideas concerned a way of parceling out power among the three branches of government. A system of checks and balances also prevented any one branch from having too much power.

The Drive for Ratification of the U.S. Constitution

 5 Explain the conflicts that characterized the drive for ratification of the U.S. Constitution.

The drive for ratification became a fierce fight between Federalists and Anti-Federalists. Federalists lobbied for the strong national government created by the Constitution; Anti-Federalists favored greater state power.

Toward Reform: Methods of Amending the U.S. Constitution

 6 Distinguish between the methods for proposing and ratifying amendments to the U.S. Constitution.

The Framers did not want the whims of the people to sway the government unduly. Therefore, they designed a deliberate two-stage, formal amendment process that required approval on both federal and state levels; this process has rarely been used. However, informal amendments, prompted by judicial interpretation, cultural and social changes, and technological change, have had a tremendous impact on the Constitution.

Learn the Terms

 Study and **Review** the **Flashcards**

Anti-Federalists
Articles of Confederation
Bill of Rights
checks and balances
Committees of Correspondence
confederation
constitution
Declaration of Independence
enumerated powers

federal system
The Federalist Papers
Federalists
First Continental Congress
full faith and credit clause
Great Compromise
implied powers
mercantilism
necessary and proper clause

New Jersey Plan
Second Continental Congress
separation of powers
Stamp Act Congress
supremacy clause
Three-Fifths Compromise
Virginia Plan

Test Yourself

 Study and **Review** the **Practice Tests**

1. Which organization functioned as a powerful molder of public opinion against the British?

a. Stamp Act Congress
b. Committees of Correspondence
c. First Continental Congress
d. Second Continental Congress
e. The Boston Massacre

2. The first major gathering of the colonies was the

a. Committees of Correspondence
b. First Continental Congress
c. Second Continental Congress
d. Stamp Act Congress
e. Congress of the Confederation

3. The Declaration of Independence was most directly influenced by which political philosopher?

a. John Locke
b. Thomas Hobbes
c. Isaac Newton
d. Montesquieu
e. Jean-Jacques Rousseau

4. Why did the Articles of Confederation create a national system of government whose power was derived from the states?

a. Disagreements in the Continental Congress necessitated a compromise between those who wanted a strong national government and those who supported strong state governments.
b. The Articles formalized the system of government proposed by the Declaration of Independence.
c. The Framers sought to create a system similar to that of other democracies.
d. It was a reaction to Great Britain's unitary system of government.
e. The states wanted to cede power to a stronger national authority.

5. What was the greatest weakness of the Articles of Confederation?

a. Congress had no specific power to tax.
b. Congress was allowed to regulate only international trade.
c. The central government was too strong.
d. There was no provision for a legislative branch.
e. There was no provision for a judicial system.

6. What was the major difference between the Virginia Plan and the New Jersey Plan?

a. The Virginia Plan created a two-house legislature, while the New Jersey Plan created a one-house legislature.

b. The Virginia Plan proposed a new national government deriving its powers from the people, while the New Jersey Plan proposed revising the Articles to maintain a government deriving its power from the states.

c. The Virginia Plan gave the legislature the power to select the executive and the judiciary, and the New Jersey Plan created an elected president and Supreme Court.

d. The Virginia Plan created a unicameral legislature, while the New Jersey Plan created a bicameral legislature.

e. The Virginia Plan created a government that favored small states, while the New Jersey Plan created a government that favored larger states.

7. Which of the following features of American national government was inspired by the political philosophy of Montesquieu?

a. The bicameral legislature

b. Creating a nonpartisan judiciary

c. The separation of powers and checks and balances between the three branches of the national government

d. The division of state and national power under the Articles of Confederation

e. Citizens' role in electing public officials

8. What does Article III of the U.S. Constitution address?

a. The supremacy of the Constitution

b. The executive branch

c. Procedures for ratification

d. The legislative branch

e. The judicial branch

9. Which of the following exemplifies the Anti-Federalists' views?

a. The most elite groups of society are the most fit to govern.

b. A strong central government could strip powers away from the states.

c. Separation of powers will prevent any one group from dominating the national government.

d. The United States should pursue alliances with the French.

e. The U.S. Constitution, in its original form, provided sufficient protections for the citizens.

10. In which of the following ways has the U.S. Constitution NOT been amended?

a. Ratification of an amendment by legislatures in three-fourths of the states

b. Judicial interpretation

c. Social and cultural change

d. Ratification by conventions called in one-fourth of the states

e. Proposal by two-thirds vote in both houses of Congress

Explore Further

Ackerman, Bruce. *The Failure of the Founding Fathers: Jefferson, Marshall, and the Rise of Presidential Democracy*, new ed. Cambridge, MA: Belknap Press, 2007.

Amar, Akhil Reed. *America's Unwritten Constitution: The Precedents and Principles We Live By*. New York: Basic Books, 2012.

Beard, Charles A. *An Economic Interpretation of the Constitution of the United States*, reissue ed. Mineola, NY: Dover, 2004.

Beeman, Richard. *Plain, Honest Men: The Making of the American Constitution*. New York: Random House, 2009.

Bowen, Catherine Drinker. *Miracle at Philadelphia*. Boston: Little, Brown, 1986.

Breyer, Stephen. *Active Liberty: Interpreting Our Democratic Constitution*. New York: Vintage, 2007.

Brinkley, Alan, Nelson W. Polsby, and Kathleen M. Sullivan. *New Federalist Papers: Essays in Defense of the Constitution*. New York: Norton, 1997.

Dahl, Robert A. *How Democratic Is the American Constitution?* 2nd ed. New Haven, CT: Yale University Press, 2004.

Hamilton, Alexander, James Madison, and John Jay. *The Federalist Papers*. New York: Bantam Books, 1989 (first published in 1788).

Main, Jackson Turner. *The Anti-Federalists: Critics of the Constitution, 1781–1788*. Chapel Hill: University of North Carolina Press, 2004.

Sabato, Larry J. *A More Perfect Constitution*. New York: Walker, 2008.

Stewart, David O. *The Summer of 1787: The Men Who Invented the Constitution*. New York: Simon and Schuster, 2007.

Storing, Herbert J. *What the Anti-Federalists Were For*. Chicago: University of Chicago Press, 1981.

Tushnet, Mark V. *Why the Constitution Matters*. New York: Cambridge University Press, 2011.

Wood, Gordon S. *The Creation of the American Republic, 1776–1787*, reissue ed. Chapel Hill: University of North Carolina Press, 1998.

To learn more about the founding of the United States, the Articles of Confederation, and the writing and ratification of the Constitution, go to the educational resources page of the House of Representatives at **www.house.gov/house/Educate.shtml.**

To learn more about the Declaration of Independence, the Constitution, the Bill of Rights, and the Framers, go to the National Archives site at **www.archives.gov/exhibits/charters/charters.html.**

To learn more about the eighteenth-century documents related to the national founding and the Revolutionary War, go to the Avalon Project at Yale Law School at **http://avalon.law.yale.edu/subject_menus/18th.asp.**

To learn more about *The Federalist Papers*, go to the Library of Congress at **thomas.loc.gov.**

Credits

Answer Key

1. b; 2. d; 3. a; 4. d; 5. a; 6. b; 7. c; 8. e; 9. b; 10. d

Notes

1. See Richard B. Bernstein with Jerome Agel, *Amending America* (New York: New York Times Books, 1993), 138–40.
2. *Oregon* v. *Mitchell*, 400 U.S. 112 (1970).
3. Bernstein with Agel, *Amending America*, 139.
4. For an account of the early development of the colonies, see D. W. Meining, *The Shaping of America*, vol. 1: *Atlantic America, 1492–1800* (New Haven, CT: Yale University Press, 1986).
5. For an excellent chronology of the events leading up to the writing of the Declaration of Independence and the colonists' break with Great Britain, see Calvin D. Lonton, ed., *The Bicentennial Almanac* (Nashville, TN: Thomas Nelson, 1975).
6. See Garry Wills, *Inventing America: Jefferson's Declaration of Independence* (New York: Random House, 1978). Wills argues that the Declaration was signed solely to secure foreign aid for the ongoing war effort.
7. For more about the Articles of Confederation, see Merrill Jensen, *The Articles of Confederation* (Madison: University of Wisconsin Press, 1940).
8. Charles A. Beard, *An Economic Interpretation of the Constitution of the United States*, reissue ed. (Mineola, NY: Dover, 2004).
9. John Patrick Diggins, "Power and Authority in American History: The Case of Charles A. Beard and His Critics," *American Historical Review* 86 (October 1981): 701–30; and Robert Brown, *Charles Beard and the Constitution: A Critical Analysis of "An Economic Interpretation of the Constitution"* (Princeton, NJ: Princeton University Press, 1956).
10. Jackson Turner Main, *The Anti-Federalists: Critics of the Constitution, 1781–1788* (Chapel Hill: University of North Carolina, 2004).
11. Gordon S. Wood, *The Creation of the American Republic 1776-1787*, reissue ed. (New York: Norton, 1993).
12. For more on the political nature of compromise at the convention, see Calvin C. Jillson. *Constitution Making: Conflict and Consensus in the Federal Constitution of 1787* (New York: Agathon, 1988).
13. Bernard Bailyn, *The Ideological Origins of the American Revolution* (Cambridge, MA: Belknap Press, 1967).
14. Federal Republicans favored a republican or representative form of government. Do not confuse this term with the modern Republican Party, which came into being in 1854. Ultimately, the word *federal* referred to the form of government embodied in the new Constitution, and *confederation* referred to a "league of states," as under the Articles, and later was applied in the "Confederacy" of 1861–1865 that governed the southern states.
15. See Ralph Ketcham, ed., *The Anti-Federalist Papers and the Constitutional Debates* (New York: New American Library, 1986).
16. See Herbert J. Storing, *What the Anti-Federalists Were For* (Chicago: University of Chicago Press, 1981), for a fuller discussion of Anti-Federalist views.
17. David E. Kyvig, *Repealing National Prohibition* (Chicago: University of Chicago Press, 1978).
18. See Jane J. Mansbridge, *Why We Lost the ERA* (Chicago: University of Chicago Press, 1986).
19. *Marbury* v. *Madison*, 5 U.S. 137 (1803).
20. See, for example, the speech by Attorney General Edwin Meese III before the American Bar Association, July 9, 1985, Washington, DC. See also Antonin Scalia and Amy Gutman, eds., *A Matter of Interpretation: Federal Courts and the Law* (Princeton, NJ: Princeton University Press, 1998).
21. See, for example, the speech by Associate Justice William J. Brennan Jr. at Georgetown University Text and Teaching Symposium, October 10, 1985, Washington, DC.
22. Social Security Administration Office of Retirement and Disability Policy, "Old Age, Survivors, and Disability Insurance." Accessed online at http://www.ssa.gov/policy/docs/statcomps/supplement/2010/5a.html#table5.a4.

The Federal System

From Chapter 3 of *Essentials of American Government: Roots and Reform,* 2012 Election Edition. Karen O'Connor. Copyright © 2014 by Pearson Education, Inc. Published by Pearson Education, Inc. All rights reserved.

The Federal System

The Supreme Court is often called upon to resolve conflicts between the national and state government. During its 2012 term, for example, the Court considered whether states have the authority to enact immigration law that goes above and beyond federal statutes. The case arose out of a law passed by the state of Arizona in 2010. The statue was widely considered the most restrictive immigration law in the land. Intended to discourage the entry and employment of illegal immigrants, the sweeping law authorized a wide range of investigatory powers for local law enforcement. Perhaps most controversially, it permitted police officers to stop and question anyone they suspected to be in the country illegally, and required those who were detained to produce evidence of either citizenship or legal residency.

The cries against the law were loud, even before it was enacted. Hispanic rights advocates, local politicians, and even President Barack Obama spoke out against the legislation. The president's involvement, especially, was unexpected, as the executive branch rarely interferes with state legislative actions. However, President Obama stated that the bill's provisions undermined "basic notions of fairness that we cherish as Americans, as well as the trust between police and our communities that is so crucial to keeping us safe."[1] He also directed his Justice Department to sue to stop enforcement of the law.

Two years later, in 2012, the case of *Arizona* v. *United States* reached the United States Supreme Court. In a controversial and widely discussed decision, the justices decided much of the case in favor of federal power, striking down provisions of the act that made illegal immigration and seeking employment while in the United States unlawfully crimes under state law. They also struck down a third provision authorizing the arrest of suspected illegal immigrants without a warrant. In each of these cases, the Court ruled that the state had come into conflict with existing federal law and, according to the U.S. Constitution, federal law must always be supreme.[2]

However, the Court upheld a fourth provision requiring state and local police to verify the citizenship of illegal immigrants. As a result, many Arizona legislators, as well as Republican Governor Jan Brewer, declared the Court's decision a victory for state powers. Supporters further argued

1	2	3	4	5	6	7
Trace the roots of the federal system and the Constitution's allocation of powers between the national and state governments.	Determine the impact of the Marshall Court on federalism.	Describe the emergence and decline of dual federalism.	Explain how cooperative federalism led to the growth of the national government at the expense of the states.	Describe how the federal budget is used to further influence state and local governments' policies.	Explore the role of the judiciary as arbiter of federal–state conflicts.	Assess the challenges in balancing national and state powers and the consequences for policy making.

IMMIGRATION IS A NATIONAL SECURITY ISSUE Regulating immigration to the United States—and balancing an individual's liberty of movement with the country's security—is a complex issue that requires the cooperation of local, state, national, and international governments. Above, European immigrants are screened for entry at Ellis Island, New York, in the 1890s. Below, Hmong immigrants receive health certifications before immigrating to the United States in the present day.

MyPoliSciLab Videos

The Big Picture What is the source of all power in the United States? The answer may surprise you. Author Karen O'Connor delves into how federalism works, and reveals why the framers chose to use a system that was so different from what the states expected.

The Basics Are you a states-right advocate? This video will help you understand how powers and responsibilities are divided between the national and state governments. You'll also discover how the powers of the national government have expanded and consider whether this is in the best interests of the people.

Should the national government have so much power?

In Context What is the primary mechanism for federalism in the United States? In this video, Barnard College political scientist Scott L. Minkoff explains how the national government tries to force state governments to adopt its policies and how state governments respond.

Thinking Like a Political Scientist Find answers to the most current questions that scholars of federalism are raising in the areas of welfare reform and state rights. Barnard College political scientist Scott L. Minkoff explores the challenges faced by state-rights advocates once they are elected to Congress

In the Real World Should the federal government be allowed to mandate health care reform or should that power belong to the states? Hear supporters and detractors of Obamacare explain their opinions, and learn about the recent Supreme Court decision that handed this power to the federal government.

So What? How is a public school in Arkansas different from a public school in New Hampshire? Author Karen O'Connor discusses why—until recently—there were no national standards for public schools in the United States, and why the system of federalism creates these and other differences between states.

that the experience of local law enforcement makes the state government more equipped to handle modern immigration than the national government. These comments reflected one of the enduring debates in the federal system considered throughout this chapter.

• • •

State and local governments predate the existence of the national government in every one of the original thirteen colonies.

During the Constitutional Convention, many of the Framers believed that, although a national government was necessary, it should have limited powers. As a result, in the federal system created by the Framers, the states reserved significant powers and authority in a wide array of issues from health to education to administering elections. The national government, in contrast, was given power in areas such as conducting foreign affairs, regulating interstate commerce, and coining money. The governments shared power in other areas, creating a system of checks and balances not only between the executive, legislative, and judicial branches of government, but also between the national government and the states. The Framers further stipulated that the people would be the ultimate source of power for both the national and state governments.

Today, the Constitution ultimately binds a diverse array of governments at the national, state, and local levels. The Constitution lays out the duties, obligations, and powers of national and state governments; states establish and charter local governments. Throughout history, however, crises, historical evolution, public opinion, and judicial interpretation have continually reshaped these relationships.

federal system
System of government in which the national government and state governments share power and derive all authority from the people.

unitary system
System of government in which the local and regional governments derive all authority from a strong national government.

enumerated powers
The powers of the national government specifically granted to Congress in Article I, section 8 of the Constitution.

implied powers
The powers of the national government derived from the enumerated powers and the necessary and proper clause.

Roots of the Federal System

1   Trace the roots of the federal system and the Constitution's allocation of powers between the national and state governments.

T he United States became the first country to adopt a **federal system** of government (although the word "federal" never appears in the U.S. Constitution). The Framers designed this system, wherein the national and state governments share power and derive all authority from the people, to remedy many of the problems experienced under the Articles of Confederation.

The new system of government also had to be different from the **unitary system** found in Great Britain, where local and regional governments derived all of their power from a strong national government (see Figure 1). Having been under the rule of English kings, whom they considered tyrants, the Framers feared centralizing power in one government or institution. Therefore, they made both the state and the federal governments accountable to the people. While the governments shared some powers, each government was supreme in some spheres, as described in the following section.

 Explore on **MyPoliSciLab**
Simulation: You Are a Federal Judge

☐ National Powers Under the Constitution

Chief among the **enumerated powers** of the national government are the authorities to coin money, conduct foreign relations, provide for an army and navy, and declare war. In addition, Article I, section 8, contains the necessary and proper clause (also called the elastic clause), which gives Congress the authority to enact laws "necessary and proper" for exercising any of its enumerated powers. These powers derived from enumerated powers and the necessary and proper clause are known as **implied powers.**

The Constitution also clearly set out the federal government's right to collect duties and excises. The Framers wanted to avoid the financial problems experienced by the national government under the Articles of Confederation. If they wished to create a strong new national government, they had to make its power to raise revenue unquestionable. Allowing the new national government to collect tariffs, or taxes on imported

The Federal System

Federal System
National government and states derive authority from the people

Unitary System
Local and regional governments derive authority from the national government

Local and Regional Governments

Confederate System
National government derives authority from states

States   People   National Government

FIGURE 1 WHAT IS THE SOURCE OF GOVERNMENTAL AUTHORITY?

The source of governmental authority varies between federal, unitary, and confederate systems. Having experienced the challenges of both unitary and confederate systems, the Framers of the Constitution chose a federal system, in which the power of both state and national governments derives from the people.

Tenth Amendment
The final part of the Bill of Rights that defines the basic principle of American federalism in stating that the powers not delegated to the national government are reserved to the states or to the people.

goods, was one way to assert this power. And, giving the national government the exclusive power to do so eliminated the financial wars between states that had occurred under the Articles.

Article VI of the federal Constitution underscores the notion that the national government is supreme in situations of conflict between state and national law. It declares that the U.S. Constitution, the laws of the United States, and its treaties are "the supreme Law of the Land; and the Judges in every State shall be bound thereby."

☐ State Powers Under the Constitution

Because states held all the power at the time the Constitution was written, the Framers felt no need, as they did for the new national government, to list and restate all of the powers of the states, although some are specified throughout the Constitution. Article I of the U.S. Constitution not only notes that each state is entitled to two senators; it also leaves to the states the times, places, and manner of elections. Thus, the states may enact their own restrictions on who can and cannot vote. Some states, for example, deny felons the franchise, while other states allow them to retain this right. Article II requires that each state appoint electors to vote for president. And, Article IV guarantees each state a "Republican Form of Government," meaning one that represents the citizens of the state.

Not until the **Tenth Amendment**, the final part of the Bill of Rights, were the states' powers described in greater detail: "The powers not delegated to the United

States by the Constitution, nor prohibited by it to the States, are reserved to the States respectively, or to the people." These powers, often called the states' **reserved powers,** include the ability to legislate for the public health, safety, and morals of their citizens. Today, the states' rights to legislate under their reserved powers provide the rationale for many states' restrictions on abortion, for example. Reserved powers also form the basis for state criminal laws, including those concerning the death penalty.

Concurrent Powers Under the Constitution

As revealed in Figure 2, national and state powers overlap. The area in which the systems overlap represents **concurrent powers**—powers shared by the national and state governments. States already had the power to tax; the Constitution extended this power to the national government as well. Other important concurrent powers include the rights to borrow money, establish courts, charter banks, and spend money for the general welfare.

Powers Denied Under the Constitution

Article I of the Constitution explicitly denies some powers to the national government or states. Congress, for example, is barred from favoring one state over another in regulating commerce, and it cannot lay duties on items exported from any state. Article I also prohibits the national government from granting titles of nobility, and government employees may not accept salaries or gifts from foreign heads of state.

State governments (as well as the national government) are denied the authority to take arbitrary actions affecting constitutional rights and liberties. Neither national nor state governments may pass a **bill of attainder,** a law declaring an act illegal without a judicial trial. The Constitution also bars national and state governments from passing

reserved powers
Powers reserved to the states by the Tenth Amendment that lie at the foundation of a state's right to legislate for the public health and welfare of its citizens.

concurrent powers
Powers shared by the national and state governments.

bill of attainder
A law declaring an act illegal without a judicial trial.

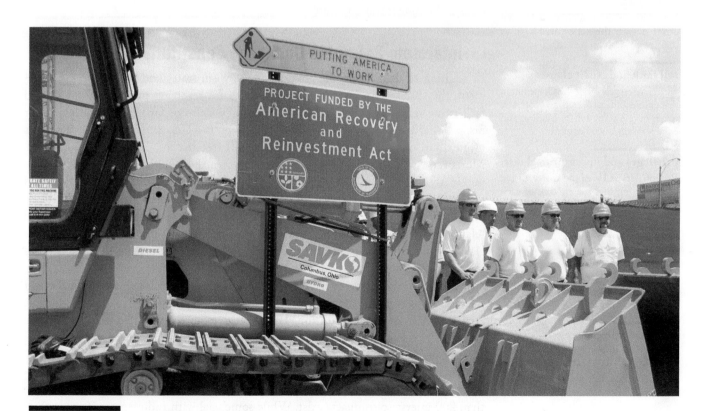

WHEN DO NATIONAL AND STATE GOVERNMENTS WORK TOGETHER?
Intergovernmental cooperation is required to implement many public policies, such as the recent American Recovery and Reinvestment Act, which was enacted as part of the effort to stimulate the economy and create jobs in 2009. Here, work begins on a road construction project jointly funded by the national government and the state of Ohio.

NATIONAL POWERS (ENUMERATED POWERS)	CONCURRENT POWERS	STATE POWERS (RESERVED POWERS)
Collect duties, imposts, and excises Regulate commerce with foreign nations, among the states, and with Indian tribes Establish rules of naturalization Coin money Establish a post office Declare and conduct war Provide for an army and a navy Make laws necessary and proper to carry out Article I powers	Tax Borrow money Establish courts Make and enforce laws Charter banks and corporations Spend money for the general welfare	Set times, places, and manner of elections and appoint electors Ratify amendments to the U.S. Constitution Take measures for public health, safety, and morals Exert powers the Constitution does not delegate to the national government or prohibit the states from using Establish local governments Regulate commerce within a state

FIGURE 2 HOW IS GOVERNMENTAL POWER DISTRIBUTED IN THE FEDERAL SYSTEM?

The Constitution divides power between the national and state governments. It gives the national government a list of enumerated powers, while many state powers are captured in the reserved powers clause of the Tenth Amendment. The national and state governments also share some powers, known as concurrent powers.

ex post facto law
Law that makes an act punishable as a crime even if the action was legal at the time it was committed.

full faith and credit clause
Section of Article IV of the Constitution that ensures judicial decrees and contracts made in one state will be binding and enforceable in any other state.

privileges and immunities clause
Part of Article IV of the Constitution guaranteeing that the citizens of each state are afforded the same rights as citizens of all other states.

extradition clause
Part of Article IV of the Constitution that requires states to extradite, or return, criminals to states where they have been convicted or are to stand trial.

interstate compacts
Contracts between states that carry the force of law; generally now used as a tool to address multistate policy concerns.

ex post facto **laws,** those that make an act punishable as a crime even if the action was legal at the time it was committed.

☐ Interstate Relations Under the Constitution

In addition to delineating the relationship between states and the national government, the Constitution provides a mechanism for resolving interstate disputes and facilitating relations among states. To avoid any sense of favoritism, it arranges for disputes between states to be settled directly by the U.S. Supreme Court under its original jurisdiction as mandated by Article III (see the discussion of the judiciary). Moreover, Article IV requires that each state give "Full Faith and Credit . . . to the public Acts, Records, and judicial Proceedings of every other State." The **full faith and credit clause** ensures that judicial decrees and contracts made in one state will be binding and enforceable in another, thereby facilitating trade and other commercial relationships. Full faith and credit cases continue to make their way through the judicial system. For example, a state's refusal to honor same-sex marriage contracts poses interesting constitutional questions.

Article IV also contains the **privileges and immunities clause,** guaranteeing that the citizens of each state have the same rights as citizens of all other states. In addition, Article IV includes the **extradition clause,** which requires states to extradite, or return, criminals to states where they have been convicted or are to stand trial.

To facilitate relations among states, Article I, section 10, clause 3, of the U.S. Constitution sets the legal foundation for interstate cooperation in the form of **interstate compacts,** contracts between states that carry the force of law. Currently, more than 200 interstate compacts exist. While some deal with rudimentary items such as state boundaries, others help states carry out their policy objectives and administrative functions. Although several bistate compacts exist, others have as many as fifty signatories.[3] For example, all fifty states signed the Drivers License Compact to facilitate nationwide recognition of licenses issued in the respective states.

☐ Local Governments Under the Constitution

Local governments have no express power under the U.S. Constitution. A description of the relationship between states and local governments comes from Judge John F. Dillon, who in 1868 articulated a premise known as **Dillon's Rule.** Dillon's Rule states that all local governments—whether towns, villages, cities, or counties, or some other form—do not have any inherent sovereignty and instead must be authorized by state governments, which can create or abolish them (see Figure 3).

1	**U.S. government**
50	**State governments**
89,476	**Local governments**
3,033	County
19,492	Municipal (city)
16,519	Townships
13,051	School districts
37,387	Special districts
89,527	**TOTAL**

FIGURE 3 HOW MANY GOVERNMENTS EXIST IN THE UNITED STATES?

More than 89,000 governments exist in the United States. Most of these governments are found at the local level, and are divided between municipal governments, towns, and special districts, such as school districts. The most common form of government is the special district.

SOURCE: U.S. Census Bureau, www.census.gov/govs/cog/GovOrgTab033ss.html

Federalism and the Marshall Court

2 Determine the impact of the Marshall Court on federalism.

The nature of federalism, including its allocation of power between the national government and the states, has changed dramatically over the past 200 years. Much of this change has resulted from rulings of the U.S. Supreme Court, which has played a major role in defining the nature of the federal system. Few Supreme Courts have had a greater impact on the federal–state relationship than the one headed by Chief Justice John Marshall (1801–1835). In a series of decisions, he and his associates carved out an important role for the Court in defining the balance of power between the national government and the states. Three rulings in the early 1800s, *McCulloch* v. *Maryland* (1819), *Gibbons* v. *Ogden* (1824), and *Barron* v. *Baltimore* (1833), were particularly important.

☐ Defining National Power: *McCulloch* v. *Maryland* (1819)

McCulloch v. *Maryland* **(1819)** was the first major Supreme Court decision to define the relationship between the national and state governments. In 1816, Congress chartered the Second Bank of the United States. (The charter of the First Bank had been allowed to expire.) In 1818, the Maryland state legislature levied a tax requiring all banks not chartered by Maryland (that is, the Second Bank of the United States) to: (1) buy stamped paper from the state on which their bank notes were to be issued; (2) pay the state $15,000 a year; or, (3) go out of business. James McCulloch, the head cashier of the Baltimore branch of the Bank of the United States, refused to pay the tax, and Maryland brought suit against him. After losing in a Maryland state court, McCulloch appealed the decision to the U.S. Supreme Court by order of the U.S. secretary of the treasury. In a unanimous opinion, the Court answered the two central questions presented to it: Did Congress have the authority to charter a bank? And, if it did, could a state tax it?

Chief Justice John Marshall's answer to the first question—whether Congress had the right to establish a bank or another type of corporation—continues to stand as the classic exposition of the doctrine of implied powers and as a statement of the authority of a strong national government. Although the word "bank" does not appear in the Constitution, the Constitution enumerates powers that give Congress the authority to levy and collect taxes, issue a currency, and borrow funds. From these enumerated powers, Marshall found, it was reasonable to imply that Congress had the power to charter a bank, which could be considered "necessary and proper" to the exercise of its aforementioned enumerated powers.

Marshall next addressed whether any state government could tax a federal bank. To Marshall, this was not a difficult question. The national government depended on the people, not the states, for its powers. In addition, Marshall noted, the Constitution specifically called for the national law to be supreme. "The power to tax involves the power to destroy," wrote the chief justice.[4] Thus, the state tax violated the supremacy clause because individual states cannot interfere with operations of the national government, whose laws are supreme.

Dillon's Rule

A premise articulated by Judge John F. Dillon in 1868 which states that local governments do not have any inherent sovereignty and instead must be authorized by state governments that can create or abolish them.

McCulloch v. Maryland (1819)

The Supreme Court upheld the power of the national government and denied the right of a state to tax the federal bank, using the Constitution's supremacy clause. The Court's broad interpretation of the necessary and proper clause paved the way for later rulings upholding expansive federal powers.

Explore Your World

The United States has a federal system of government in which national and subnational political units known as states share power. A number of other countries, including Canada, Switzerland, India, and Nigeria, also have federal systems of government. However, most of the world's nations, including Great Britain, France, China, Japan, and Iran, have unitary systems, with authority concentrated in the central government. Although federal systems are relatively few in number, they tend to be large and politically important. This world map illustrates countries with federal systems of government in green. Countries with other systems of government are shown in gray.

Some subnational units in Brazil are based on cultural boundaries that precede Portuguese colonization. Other subnational units have been created for economic or administrative purposes.

Russia, the world's largest country by landmass, has a federal system comprised of 83 subnational units. The government was formed in 1993 after the dissolution of the Soviet Union.

Since India's independence from Great Britain in 1947, its federal system has united citizens speaking thousands of languages and from a variety of diverse religions.

Malaysia has what is known as an asymmetric federation. Some subnational units have more power than others.

CRITICAL THINKING QUESTIONS

1. Study the map to identify what economic, cultural, and political characteristics the countries with federal systems have in common. Why might these characteristics have led to the adoption of federal systems?

2. Examine countries such as India, Nigeria, and Germany. What challenges might these countries face in maintaining a federal system in a region where most other countries choose a different form of government?

3. What other countries might be likely candidates for adopting federal systems in the future? Why do you think these countries are particularly good candidates?

★ ★

The Living Constitution

> *Full Faith and Credit shall be given in each State to the public Acts, Records, and judicial Proceedings of every other State.* — ARTICLE IV, SECTION 1

The full faith and credit clause of Article IV of the Constitution rests on principles borrowed from international law that require one country to recognize contracts made in another country, absent a compelling public policy reason to the contrary. In the United States, this principle applies to the relationship between states.

The full faith and credit clause requires a state to recognize public acts and court proceedings of another state. In 1997, the Supreme Court ruled that the full faith and credit clause mandates that state courts always honor the judgments of other state courts, even if it entails going against state public policy or existing state laws. Failure to do so would allow a single state to "rule the world," said Supreme Court Justice Ruth Bader Ginsburg during oral argument.[a]

For the most part, interpretation of the full faith and credit clause has not been controversial. That is changing, however, as advocates of same-sex marriage have suggested that marriages of same-sex couples performed and legally sanctioned in one state must be recognized in another state, as is the case with heterosexual marriages.

In the mid-1990s, the possible legalization of marriage between same-sex couples threw numerous state legislatures and the U.S. Congress into a virtual frenzy.

Twenty-five states passed laws in 1996 and 1997 to bar legal recognition of same-sex marriages. The U.S. Congress also got involved by passing what is called the Defense of Marriage Act (DOMA), which President Bill Clinton signed into law in 1996. This federal law aimed to undercut possible state recognition of same-sex marriages by permitting states to disregard such marriages even if they are legal in other states. The constitutionality of this law, however, is questionable. The U.S. Constitution does not formally give Congress legislative authority to create exceptions to the full faith and credit clause. As a result, some observers believe that such an exception would require a constitutional amendment. The Obama administration, moreover, has stated that it does not support DOMA and believes it is unconstitutional.

CRITICAL THINKING QUESTIONS

1. How could a same-sex couple married in one state be granted a divorce in a state that does not recognize same-sex marriage?
2. Should states or the federal government be allowed to create public policy exceptions to the full faith and credit clause?

[a]Oral argument in *Baker* v. *General Motors Corporation*, 522 U.S. 222 (1998), noted in Linda Greenhouse, "Court Weighs Whether One State Must Obey Another's Courts," *New York Times* (October 16, 1997): A25.

The Court's decision in *McCulloch* has far-reaching consequences even today. Lawmakers use the necessary and proper clause to justify federal action in many areas, including social welfare problems. Furthermore, had Marshall allowed the state of Maryland to tax the federal bank, states possibly could have attempted to tax all federal agencies located within their boundaries, a costly proposition that could have driven the federal government into insurmountable debt.[5]

Gibbons v. Ogden (1824)
The Supreme Court upheld broad congressional power to regulate interstate commerce. The Court's broad interpretation of the Constitution's commerce clause paved the way for later rulings upholding expansive federal powers.

☐ Affirming National Power: *Gibbons* v. *Ogden* (1824)

Shortly after *McCulloch*, the Marshall Court had another opportunity to rule in favor of a broad interpretation of the scope of national power. *Gibbons* v. *Ogden* (1824) involved a dispute that arose after the New York state legislature granted to Robert Fulton the exclusive right to operate steamboats on the Hudson River.[6] Simultaneously, Congress licensed a ship to sail on the same waters. By the time the case reached the Supreme Court, it was complicated both factually and procedurally. Suffice it to say that both New York and New Jersey wanted to control shipping on the lower Hudson River. But, *Gibbons* actually addressed one simple, very important question: What was the scope of Congress's authority under the commerce clause? The states argued that "commerce," as mentioned in Article I, should be interpreted narrowly to include only direct dealings in products. In *Gibbons*, however, the Supreme Court ruled that Congress's power to regulate interstate commerce included the power to regulate commercial activity as well, and that the commerce power had no limits except those specifically found in the Constitution.

Thus, New York had no constitutional authority to grant a monopoly to a single steamboat operator, an action that interfered with interstate commerce.[7]

☐ Limiting the Bill of Rights: *Barron* v. *Baltimore* (1833)

In 1833, in one of Chief Justice Marshall's last major cases on the federal–state relationship, *Barron* v. *Baltimore* **(1833),** the Court addressed the issue of whether the due process clause of the Fifth Amendment applied to actions of the states.[8] John Barron, a Baltimore businessman, ran a successful docking business off the city's wharf. As the city entered a period of extensive construction, dirt was deposited onto Barron's wharf. In addition, sand and silt drifted to his section of the wharf, making it unusable as a harbor for ships. Barron sued the city and state for damages, arguing that the city took his lands "without just compensation," as guaranteed by the Fifth Amendment of the U.S. Constitution. The Marshall Court ruled that Barron had no federal claim because enumerated rights contained in the Bill of Rights bound only the national government.[9]

Dual Federalism: States' Rights, the Civil War, and Reconstruction

3 Describe the emergence and decline of dual federalism.

In the early to mid-1800s, a national crisis began over the division of power between the states and the federal government. One major battleground in this struggle was the issue of slavery, which the pro-states' rights southern states fought to maintain. In contrast, many northern states, where commercial and manufacturing interests were more powerful, favored greater national power. Chief Justice Roger B. Taney (1835–1863), who succeeded John Marshall, saw the Court as an arbiter of those competing state and nationalist views. In a series of cases involving the scope of Congress's power under the commerce clause, the Taney Court further developed the nationalist doctrines first enunciated by Marshall but also emphasized the authority of states to make laws "necessary to their well being and prosperity."[10]

Over time, Chief Justice Taney and the Court also began to articulate further the notions of concurrent power and **dual federalism.** Dual federalism posits that having separate and equally powerful state and national governments is the best constitutional arrangement. Adherents of this theory typically believe that the national government should not exceed its constitutionally enumerated powers, and as stated in the Tenth Amendment, all other powers are, and should be, reserved to the states or to the people.

☐ The States Assert Their Powers: Nullification

While the courts worked to carve out the appropriate roles for each level of government in the federal system, the political debate over states' rights swirled in large part over what is called **nullification,** the right of a state to declare a federal law void. As early as 1798, Congress approved the very unpopular Alien and Sedition Acts, which were passed by the Federalist Congress to prevent criticism of the national government. Thomas Jefferson, James Madison, and others who opposed the acts suggested that states had the right to nullify any federal law that, in the opinion of the states, violated the Constitution. The U.S. Supreme Court, however, never decided the issue, because the Alien and Sedition Acts expired before the Court could hear a challenge to them.

The question of nullification arose again in 1828, when the national government enacted a tariff act, most commonly referred to as the "Tariff of Abominations," that raised duties on raw materials, iron, hemp, and flax and reduced protections against imported woolen goods. John C. Calhoun, who served as vice president from 1825 to 1832 under President Andrew Jackson, broke with Jackson over the tariff bill because

---

Barron v. Baltimore (1833)
The Supreme Court ruled that the due process clause of the Fifth Amendment did not apply to the actions of states. This decision limited the Bill of Rights to the actions of Congress alone.

dual federalism
The belief that having separate and equally powerful levels of government is the best arrangement, often referred to as layer-cake federalism.

nullification
The right of a state to declare void a federal law.

it badly affected his home state of South Carolina. Not only did South Carolinians have to pay more for raw materials because of the tariff bill, but it was also becoming increasingly difficult for them to sell their dwindling crops abroad for a profit. Calhoun thus resurrected arguments made by some of the Framers and formulated the theory of nullification to justify South Carolina's refusal to abide by the federal tariff law.

Calhoun theorized that the federal government functioned merely as the agent of the states (the people and the individual state governments) and that the Constitution was simply a compact providing instructions on how the agent was to act. Thus, according to Calhoun, the U.S. Supreme Court could not pass judgment on the constitutional validity of acts of Congress. Calhoun posited that if the people of any individual state did not like an act of Congress, they could hold a convention to nullify that act. If a state contested an act, the law would have no force until three-fourths of all the states ratified an amendment expressly giving Congress that power. Then, if the nullifying state still did not wish to be bound by the new provision, it could secede, or withdraw, from the union.

☐ States' Rights and the *Dred Scott* Decision

Debate over nullification only forestalled debate on the inevitable slavery issue. By the 1850s, the country could wait no longer. In cases such as ***Dred Scott v. Sandford*** **(1857)**, the Court tried to manage the slavery issue by resolving questions of ownership, the status of fugitive slaves, and slavery in the new territories.[11] The Court generally settled these cases in favor of slavery and states' rights within the framework of dual federalism.

Dred Scott, for example, was born into slavery about 1795. In 1833, his original owners sold him to a family in Missouri. Later he tried to buy his freedom. His ability to take this action was questioned, so abolitionists gave money to support a test case seeking Scott's freedom. They believed his prior residence with a family living in free states and the Wisconsin Territory, which prohibited slavery, made Scott a free man, even though he now lived in a slave state, Missouri. In 1857, after many delays, the U.S. Supreme Court ruled 7–2 that Scott was not a citizen of the United States. "Slaves," said the Court, "were never thought of or spoken of except as property." The Court also found that Congress lacked the authority to ban slavery in the territories. In so doing, this decision narrowed the scope of national power, while it enhanced that of the states. Eventually, however, no form of federalism could accommodate the existence of slavery, and the nation marched toward inevitable war with itself.

☐ Reconstruction and the Transformation of Dual Federalism

The Civil War forever changed the nature of federalism. The concepts of nullification and dual federalism, as well as their emphasis on the role of the states, were destroyed along with the southern states' attempt at a confederacy. In the aftermath of the Civil War and the addition of the Thirteenth, Fourteenth, and Fifteenth Amendments to the Constitution, a profound change occurred in the reunited nation's concept of federalism.

The Supreme Court, too, often stepped in to limit state powers in favor of a stronger national government. The Court also recognized the need for national involvement in projects such as railroad construction, canal building, and the development of new technology, such as the telegraph.[12] And, beginning in the 1880s, the Court allowed Congress to regulate many aspects of economic relationships, such as outlawing monopolies, a type of regulation formerly considered to exist exclusively in the realm of the states. By the 1890s, passage of laws such as the Interstate Commerce Act and the Sherman Anti-Trust Act allowed Congress to establish itself as the supreme player in a growing national economy.

Some boundaries to this growing national role did exist, however. In 1895, for example, the United States filed suit against four sugar refiners, alleging that the sale of those four companies would give their buyer control of 98 percent of the U.S. sugar-refining business. The Supreme Court ruled that congressional efforts to control monopolies (through passage of the Sherman Anti-Trust Act) did not grant Congress the authority to prevent the sale of these sugar-refining businesses, because manufacturing was not

Dred Scott v. Sandford **(1857)**
The Supreme Court concluded that the U.S. Congress lacked the constitutional authority to bar slavery in the territories. This decision narrowed the scope of national power, while it enhanced that of the states.

commerce. Therefore, the Court found the companies and their actions to lie beyond the scope of Congress's regulatory authority.[13]

☐ Amending the National–State Relationship

Sixteenth Amendment
Amendment to the U.S. Constitution that authorized Congress to enact a national income tax.

Seventeenth Amendment
Amendment to the U.S. Constitution that made senators directly elected by the people, removing their selection from state legislatures.

cooperative federalism
The intertwined relationship between the national, state, and local governments that began with the New Deal, often referred to as marble-cake federalism.

In response to the Court's ruling on the income tax, Congress and the state legislatures were moved to ratify the **Sixteenth Amendment.** The Sixteenth Amendment gave Congress the power to levy and collect taxes on incomes without apportioning them among the states. The revenues taken in by the federal government through taxation of personal income "removed a major constraint on the federal government by giving it access to almost unlimited revenues."[14] If money is power, the income tax and the revenues it generated greatly enhanced the power of the federal government and its ability to enter policy areas in which it formerly had few funds to spend.

The **Seventeenth Amendment,** ratified in 1913, similarly enhanced the power of the national government at the expense of the states. This amendment terminated the state legislatures' election of senators and placed their election in the hands of the people. With senators no longer directly accountable to the state legislatures, states lost their principal protectors in Congress.

While the ratification of the Sixteenth and Seventeenth Amendments set the stage for expanded national government, the catalyst for dual federalism's demise was a series of economic events that ended in the cataclysm of the Great Depression:

- Throughout the 1920s, bank failures were common.
- In 1921, the nation experienced a severe slump in agricultural prices.
- In 1926, the construction industry went into decline.
- In the summer of 1929, inventories of consumer goods and automobiles were at an all-time high.
- On October 29, 1929, stock prices, which had risen steadily since 1926, crashed, taking with them the entire national economy.

Despite the severity of these indicators, Presidents Calvin Coolidge and Herbert Hoover took little action, believing that the national depression comprised an amalgamation of state economic crises better dealt with by state and local governments. It would take the election of President Franklin D. Roosevelt in 1932 to both respond to this crisis and forever change the relationship between state and national governments.

Cooperative Federalism: The Growth of National Government

4   Explain how cooperative federalism led to the growth of the national government at the expense of the states.

 ost political scientists likened the federal system before the 1930s to a layer cake: in most policy areas, each level or layer of government—national, state, and local—had clearly defined powers and responsibilities. By contrast, the metaphor of marble-cake federalism refers to what political scientists call **cooperative federalism,** a term that describes the intertwined relations among the national, state, and local governments that began during this period. States began to take a secondary, albeit important, cooperative role in the scheme of governance, as did many cities. One political scientist described the new balance of power as:

> Wherever you slice through it you reveal an inseparable mixture of differently colored ingredients.... Vertical and diagonal lines almost obliterate the horizontal ones, and in some places there are unexpected whirls and an imperceptible merging of colors, so that it is difficult to tell where one ends and the other begins.[15]

How Has the Federal-State Relationship Evolved?

The balance of power between the national and state governments has evolved over time. In the early years of the new republic, the nation maintained a system of dual federalism, often referred to as layer cake federalism. This relationship transformed into a marble cake form of federalism known as cooperative federalism during the 1930s with the passage of President Franklin D. Roosevelt's New Deal. This image illustrates the changing national–state relationship, building on the cake metaphor.

PROGRESSIVE FEDERALISM

The modern relationship between the states and federal government is both cooperative and coercive, depending on the issue area.

THE GREAT SOCIETY

One of the hallmarks of President Lyndon B. Johnson's Great Society program was offering federal financial aid to states in the form of grants-in-aid.

GROWING NATIONAL INTERVENTION IN THE ECONOMY

The needs of a growing and more technologically advanced nation required the intervention of the national government in economic affairs such as regulating business and constructing roads, railroads, and ports.

DUAL FEDERALISM

The division of national and state powers envisioned by the Framers; each government had separate spheres of authority dictated by the Constitution.

NEW FEDERALISM AND THE DEVOLUTION REVOLUTION

Republican President Ronald Reagan and Republicans in Congress demanded that the national government return some administrative authority to state governments.

THE NEW DEAL AND COOPERATIVE FEDERALISM

The Great Depression and the New Deal signaled the beginning of a new era in federalism where the state and national governments worked together to address a broad array of policy issues, including job creation, health and welfare.

CIVIL WAR AND RECONSTRUCTION

The Civil War and the defeat of the states' rights South began to alter the division of power between state and national governments.

○ 2010s

○ 1980s

○ 1960s

○ 1930s

○ 1880s

○ 1860s

○ 1800s

CRITICAL THINKING QUESTIONS

1. What kinds of events appear to be catalysts for changes in the federal system?

2. Consider the progression from layer to layer. Between which layers did the most change occur? Why was this change more definitive than that between the other layers?

3. How have changes to the federal system affected the lives of citizens? How are these changes seen in the everyday functions of government?

☐ A Need for National Action Arises: The New Deal

Rampant unemployment (historians estimate it was as high as 40 to 50 percent) was the hallmark of the Great Depression. In 1933, to combat severe problems facing the nation, newly elected President Franklin D. Roosevelt (FDR) proposed a variety of innovative programs, collectively called the **New Deal,** and ushered in a new era in American politics. FDR used the full power of the presidency, as well as his highly effective communication skills, to sell the American public and Congress on a new level of government intervention intended to stabilize the economy and reduce personal suffering. Most politicians during the New Deal period (1933–1939) agreed that to find national solutions to the Depression, which was affecting citizens of every state in the union, the national government would have to exercise tremendous authority.

In the first few weeks of the legislative session after FDR's inauguration, Congress passed a series of acts creating new federal agencies and programs proposed by the president. These new agencies, often known by their initials, created what many termed an alphabetocracy. Among the more significant programs were the Federal Housing Administration (FHA), which provided federal financing for new home construction; the Civilian Conservation Corps (CCC), a work relief program for farmers and homeowners; and the Agricultural Adjustment Administration (AAA) and National Recovery Administration (NRA), which imposed restrictions on production in agriculture and many industries while also providing subsidies to farmers.

New Deal programs forced all levels of government to work cooperatively with one another. Local governments, especially those of cities, were embraced as equal partners in an intergovernmental system for the first time and became players in the national political arena because many members of Congress wanted to bypass state legislatures, where urban interests usually were underrepresented. FDR also relied on big-city Democratic political machines to turn out voters to support his programs.

Those who feared these unprecedented changes in the federal system quickly challenged the constitutionality of the programs in court. And, at least initially, the U.S. Supreme Court often agreed with them. Through the mid-1930s, the Court continued to rule that certain aspects of New Deal programs went beyond the authority of Congress to regulate commerce. A series of decisions ruling various aspects of New Deal programs unconstitutional reflected the Court's *laissez-faire,* or hands-off, attitude toward the economy, which the justices viewed as a state problem.

FDR and Congress were livid. FDR's frustration with the Court prompted him to suggest what ultimately was nicknamed his "Court-packing plan." Knowing that he could do little to change the minds of those already on the Court, FDR suggested enlarging its size from nine to thirteen justices. This plan would have given him the opportunity to pack the Court with a majority of justices predisposed toward the constitutional validity of the New Deal.

Even though Roosevelt was popular, the Court-packing plan was not.[16] Congress and the public expressed outrage over even the suggestion of tampering with an institution of government. Even the Court appeared to respond to this threat. In 1937, it reversed its series of anti–New Deal decisions, concluding that Congress (and therefore the national government) had broad authority to legislate in any area as long as what was regulated affected commerce in any way. The Court also upheld the constitutionality of most of the massive New Deal relief programs, including the National Labor Relations Act of 1935, which authorized collective bargaining between unions and employees;[17] the Fair Labor Standards Act of 1938, which set a national minimum wage; and the Agricultural Adjustment Act of 1938, which provided crop subsidies to farmers.[18] Congress then used these newly recognized powers to legislate in a wide range of areas, including maximum hour laws and regulation of child labor.

Federal Grants to State and Local Governments

| **5** | Describe how the federal budget is used to further influence state and local governments' policies. |

categorical grant
Grant that appropriates federal funds to states for a specific purpose.

New Federalism
Federal–state relationship proposed by Reagan administration during the 1980s; hallmark is returning administrative powers to the state governments.

block grant
A large grant given to a state by the federal government with only general spending guidelines.

President Franklin D. Roosevelt's New Deal programs increased the flow of national dollars to the states for a variety of public works programs, including building and road construction. In the boom times of World War II, when the nation needed most able-bodied Americans to work, even more new federal programs were introduced. These programs often redefined national–state relationships and made the national government a major player in domestic policy. Until the 1960s, however, the national government constructed most federal grant programs in cooperation with the states, with emphasis on assisting the states in fulfilling their traditional responsibilities to protect the health, welfare, and safety of their citizens.

Today, the national government provides grants from its general revenues to states, local governments, nonprofit organizations, and even individuals. These grants are given for a number of purposes including: (1) providing state and local governments with additional funds; (2) setting national standards for national problems, such as clean air and water; and (3) attempting to financially equalize rich and poor states and localities. Federal grants are of several types. These include categorical grants, block grants, and programmatic requests.

☐ Categorical Grants

Categorical grants are grants for which Congress appropriates funds for specific purposes. Categorical grants allocate federal dollars by a precise formula, often based on population. They are subject to detailed conditions imposed by the national government. Often they are made available on a matching basis; that is, states must contribute money to match federal funds, although the national government may pay as much as 90 percent of the total. Categorical grants may be used by the national government to alter states' policy priorities or to coerce states to adopt particular policy objectives. With large sums of money at stake, states will often neglect their own wants and needs to follow the leadership of the national government.

These grants became more prominent mechanisms of coercion in 1964, when President Lyndon B. Johnson launched his Great Society program, which included what LBJ called a "War on Poverty." The Great Society program was a broad attempt to combat poverty and discrimination through urban renewal, education reform, and unemployment relief. In a frenzy of activity in Washington not seen since the New Deal, the national government channeled federal funds to states, to local governments, and even to citizen action groups. Funding these nonprofit organizations allowed liberal members of Congress to bypass not only conservative state legislatures but also conservative mayors and councils in the South and in cities such as Chicago, who were perceived as disinclined to help their poor, often African American, constituencies.

☐ Block Grants

In 1980, former California Republican Governor Ronald Reagan became president, pledging to advance what he called **New Federalism** and a return of power to the states. The hallmark of this action was the consolidation of many categorical grants into fewer, less restrictive **block grants**—large amounts of money given to states with only general spending guidelines. Many of these went to education and health care.[19]

Perhaps not surprisingly, these reforms were popular with governors, who urged the consolidation of even more programs into block grants. Calls to revamp the welfare system, in particular, were popular with citizens and governments alike. These reforms were ultimately realized during the mid-1990s, when a Republican-controlled Congress

Which States Win and Lose the Federal Aid Game?

The national government collects taxes from everyone, but it doesn't always spend money in the state where it gets it. Instead, the federal government transfers wealth from state to state. Recipient states receive more money than they pay in federal taxes, while donor states pay more in federal taxes than they receive. In 2007, there were 19 donor states and 31 recipient states. The political explanation for which states were donors and recipients is surprising.

Who pays? DELAWARE, MINNESOTA, NEW JERSEY, and CONNECTICUT
all paid at least $6,000 more in federal taxes per person than they received in federal aid.
15 other states were net donors.

Net Donor: Over $5,000 Per Person	Connecticut $6,241	New Jersey $6,644	Minnesota $7,431	Delaware $12,285
Net Donor: Between $1 and $5,000 per person	Ohio $49	North Carolina $1,108	Massachusetts $2,133	Rhode Island $2,732
	Georgia $434	California $1,466	Colorado $2,176	Illinois $3,640
	Washington $773	Nevada $1,616	Nebraska $2,850	New York $4,502
	Wisconsin $1,000	Arkansas $1,723	Texas $2,243	

Who receives? ALASKA took in twice the federal money in 2007 that it paid in
taxes. 31 states are recipient states. Of the top six recipient states, four are southern.

Net Recipient: Over $5,000 Per Person	Alaska -$7,448	New Mexico -$7,143	Mississippi -$6,765	Virginia -$6,239	West Virginia -$5,820	Alabama -$5,130
Net Recipient: Between $1 and $5,000 per person	Hawaii -$4983	South Carolina -$3,756	Arizona -$1,976	Utah -$792	Pennsylvania -$385	
	North Dakota -$4,856	Kentucky -$3,012	Idaho -$1,281	Indiana -$723	Oklahoma -$376	
	South Dakota -$4,414	Maryland -$3,010	Wyoming -$1,205	Tennessee -$603	New Hampshire -$349	
	Maine -$4,221	Vermont -$2,854	Missouri -$1,190	Florida -$581	Michigan -$171	
	Montana -$4,149	Louisiana -$2,180	Iowa -$1,075	Oregon -$474	Kansas -$154	

SOURCE: Data from United States Internal Revenue Service; *Statistical Abstract of the United States 2012;* and *U.S. Census of Population and Housing, 2010.*

Who are the Recipient States

Recipient states by party

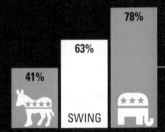

41% SWING 63% 78%

- 18 out of 23 Republican-voting states (78%) are recipient states compared to 8 out of the 19 Democratic-voting states (42%).

Recipient states by poverty level

53% Low 63% Average 69% High

- 9 of 13 states with high poverty levels are recipient states (69%), while only 9 of 17 states with low poverty levels are recipient states (53%).

Investigate Further

Concept How do we determine donor and recipient states? Per person, we subtract the federal aid dollars sent to a state from the federal tax dollars paid in a state. If the result is positive, a state is a donor state, otherwise it's a recipient state.

Connection What relationship exists between politics and whether a state is a recipient or donor? Recipient states are most often Republican in national politics, while donor states tend to be more Democratic in national politics.

Cause Is there a policy explanation for which states are recipient states? The federal government fights poverty by moving money around the country. Recipient states usually have higher poverty levels and lower average incomes. Therefore, they tend to pay less federal tax than they receive per person.

Take a Closer Look

Federal grants have become an increasingly important part of state budgets. While these grant programs may help states to develop new initiatives or implement federal programs, they may also create intergovernmental dependency that can have disastrous consequences. Unlike the national government, most state governments are required to balance their budgets. So, when federal revenues decline, they must often be accompanied by cuts in state government programs and services. To better understand the nature and consequences of this dependency, examine the pie graph and photo below.

As this pie graph from the Census Bureau indicates, two-thirds of state revenues came from taxes, service charges, and other sources, with the balance between the three varying from state to state.

States, on average, received 35.5% of their revenues from the federal government.

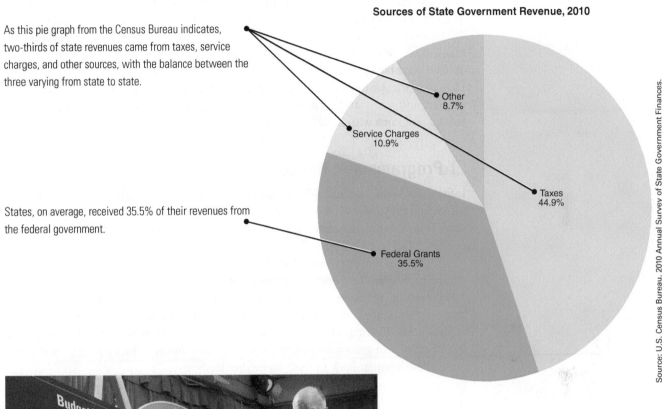

Sources of State Government Revenue, 2010

Other
8.7%

Service Charges
10.9%

Taxes
44.9%

Federal Grants
35.5%

Source: U.S. Census Bureau. 2010 Annual Survey of State Government Finances.

Depending on the federal government for funds can have significant implications for states. When fewer federal dollars flow, states are forced to cut programs. Here, California Governor Jerry Brown (D) discusses a number of ways to address his state's projected $16 billion budget shortfall in 2012.

CRITICAL THINKING QUESTIONS

1. Are state governments too dependent on federal dollars? Should they be required to find other ways to raise revenues? What mechanisms seem most equitable?

2. Should federal governments be required to fully fund any mandates they pass along to state governments? What are the pros and cons of such an arrangement?

3. How do you think cuts in federal dollars affect the demands that state governments place on local governments such as municipalities and special districts?

programmatic request
Federal funds designated for special projects within a state or congressional district.

under Speaker of the House Newt Gingrich (R–GA) and President Bill Clinton replaced the existing federal welfare program with a program known as Temporary Assistance for Needy Families (TANF). TANF returned much of the administrative power for welfare programs to the states and became a hallmark of what became known as the "devolution revolution."

☐ Unfunded Mandates

Another component of Congress' efforts to devolve greater authority back to the state governments during the 1990s was the passage of the Unfunded Mandates Reform Act of 1995. This act prevented Congress from passing costly federal programs without debate on how to fund them and addressed a primary concern of state governments, many of which held the view that federal programs were encompassing a growing part of their state budgets and were in violation of their sovereign policy-making authority. However, the Unfunded Mandates Reform Act has proved notoriously difficult to enforce, and many states charge the national government with continuing to create federal programs with insufficient funding.

☐ Programmatic Requests

Informally known as earmarks, **programmatic requests** are federal funds designated for special projects within a state or congressional district that direct specific exemptions from taxes or mandated fees. Federal funds have been provided for special projects since the first Congress.

The use of these grants exploded in the past two decades. The transportation budget, in particular, has benefited from earmarks; from 1996 to 2005, it increased by 1,150 percent. Programmatic requests are not competitively awarded, and have thus become very controversial owing to the use of paid political lobbyists who try to secure federal funds for their clients, be they states, cities, universities, or nonprofit groups. Members of Congress also attempt to secure these funds to bring programs and economic development back to their home districts.

Judicial Federalism

> **6** Explore the role of the judiciary as arbiter of federal–state conflicts.

The U.S. Supreme Court has always played an important role as the umpire of the federal system. When governmental powers, especially those of the state and national governments, come into conflict, it is the Court's job to determine which government is supreme. As detailed throughout this chapter, the Court has played the role of umpire at many transformational times in American history, including the founding, the Civil War, and during the Great Depression. The modern Supreme Court is no exception.

☐ The Rehnquist Court

From the 1930s until the 1980s, the Court's decisions largely expanded federal power at the expense of states. Beginning in the late 1980s, however, the Court's willingness to allow Congress to regulate in a variety of areas waned. This revolution was led by a group of new justices appointed by President Ronald Reagan. These judges, including Justices Sandra Day O'Connor, Antonin Scalia, and Anthony Kennedy, were committed to the notion of states' rights and to rolling back federal intervention in many areas. The leadership of a conservative chief justice, William H. Rehnquist, only served to intensify the changing perspective.

According to one observer, the federalism decisions made by the Rehnquist Court in the 1980s and 1990s were "a reexamination of the country's most basic constitutional arrangements."[20] The Court's decisions largely agreed with the Republican states' rights view evident in the policies of the Reagan administration and the Contract with America Congresses. For example, in *U.S. v. Lopez* (1995), which involved the conviction of a student charged with carrying a concealed handgun onto school property, a five-person majority of the Court ruled that Congress lacked constitutional authority under the commerce clause to regulate guns within 1,000 feet of a school.[21] The majority concluded that, however well-intentioned, gun control laws, even those involving schools, were not substantially related to interstate commerce. Thus, they were a state, not a federal, matter.

☐ The Roberts Court

In 2005, following the death of Chief Justice Rehnquist, President George W. Bush appointed Chief Justice John Roberts to head the Supreme Court. In its early years, the conservative Roberts Court appeared tentative to address high-profile federalism cases. However, during its 2011 term, the Court thrust itself into the federalism debate, deciding a series of visible cases related to the balance of national and state power. These cases considered issues such as immigration (discussed in the opening vignette), redistricting, and health care.[22] Much to the surprise of many Court-watchers, in both the immigration and health care cases, the Roberts Court sided with the power of the national government. Whether these decisions are a temporary departure from the norm or a harbinger of a new era in federalism remains to be seen. Like the Court's federalism decisions of previous eras, they may also simply be the result of a strategic Court seeking to maintain its institutional prestige by following the will of the people.

Toward Reform: Attempts to Balance National and State Power

> **7** Assess the challenges in balancing national and state powers and the consequences for policy making.

As we have seen throughout this chapter, attempting to find equilibrium between the powers and responsibilities of national and state governments is one of the greatest challenges of a federal system. The roles and relative strengths of the national and state governments in the United States have changed over time and continue to evolve today. Here, we explore the current status of this relationship, and examine its consequences for policy making.

☐ The Price of Federalism

In 1995, political scientist Paul E. Peterson published his seminal exploration of the balance between state and national powers, *The Price of Federalism*.[23] In this book, Peterson considered how governments should best divide policy-making responsibility into two broad issue areas: redistributive and developmental policies. Redistributive policies are those whereby the government collects money (usually through taxation) from one group of citizens to finance a service, such as health care or welfare, for another group of citizens. In contrast, developmental policies are those designed to strengthen a government's economic standing, such as building roads and other infrastructure. The national government's greater financial resources and ability to ensure a uniform standard, Peterson argued, made it better suited to handle redistributive programs. In contrast, developmental programs would be best left to state governments, which are closer to the people and better able to assess and address regional needs.

The problem with this arrangement—and the price of American federalism—is that, historically, the division of power has not followed this pattern. The national government and members of Congress in particular have had reelection incentives to create and fund programs that have a direct impact on constituents. As a result, administration of redistributive policies often fell to the states, perhaps with federal financial assistance.

In more recent years, however, the federal government, while not totally abandoning developmental projects, has begun to take greater responsibility for redistributive policies. One such example is the passage of the No Child Left Behind Act of 2001 (NCLB), the first comprehensive federal education legislation.

States are not entirely satisfied with these steps toward policy efficiency. Under the Tenth Amendment, state and local governments traditionally have controlled education policy. Many states and localities view NCLB as an unprecedented **preemption** of state and local powers.

◻ Progressive Federalism

During his first term, President Barack Obama appeared receptive to a pragmatic movement known as **progressive federalism.** Advocates of progressive federalism view the relationship between the states and the national government as both coercive and cooperative.[24] The form taken by the relationship depends chiefly on the political environment at each level of government. The best and first option is when the federal government is able to reach consensus and establish a national standard. However, failing the national government's ability to enact a particular proposal, national policy makers may embrace states' efforts to address that policy issue, particularly when those in power agree with the outcome of the state policy-making process.

Perhaps the most visible attempt by the Obama administration to create a national mandate was the passage of the 2010 Patient Protection and Affordable Care Act, which established a variety of mechanisms to ensure that nearly all Americans had access to health insurance. Part of this health care reform legislation also included significant changes in the Medicaid program administered by the state governments. Almost immediately after the ink was dry on the president's signature on the act, a group of state governments challenged the constitutionality of the act. They charged that it exceeded the federal government's

preemption
A concept that allows the national government to override state or local actions in certain policy areas.

progressive federalism
A pragmatic approach to federalism that views relations between national and state governments as both coercive and cooperative.

David Sipress / The New Yorker Collection / www.cartoonbank.com

"Stop! Wait! Government's no longer the problem—it's the solution."

HOW DO VIEWS ON THE ROLE OF GOVERNMENT CHANGE?

Depending on the party in power and the political climate, the national government may be viewed as either a necessary evil or simply evil. Progressive federalism acknowledges both of these viewpoints, taking a pragmatic approach to balancing the authority of state and national governments.

power to regulate interstate commerce. The Supreme Court, however, upheld the constitutionality of the law, citing the federal government's power to tax as a justification for Congress' authority to enact the health care reform legislation.

In other areas, the Obama administration permitted state governments to take the lead. In 2009, for example, Obama allowed the state of California to impose stricter limits on greenhouse gas emissions from cars and trucks than those established by the Environmental Protection Agency (EPA). This resolved a long-standing conflict between the states and the federal government and opened the door for a number of other states to follow California's lead.

Not everyone views progressive federalism positively. Critics, including the U.S. Chamber of Commerce, have called progressive federalism "free-for-all federalism." They charge that the emission standards, in particular, will lead to a costly "patchwork of laws impacting a troubled [automotive] industry."[25] Complying with a variety of state standards, they note, is more costly than meeting one national standard. It is also more expensive to monitor and lobby the legislatures of fifty states than it is to address only the EPA.

On MyPoliSciLab

Review the Chapter

 Listen to **Chapter** on **MyPoliSciLab**

Roots of the Federal System

1 Trace the roots of the federal system and the Constitution's allocation of powers between the national and state governments.

The national government has both enumerated and implied powers under the Constitution. National and state governments share an additional group of concurrent powers. Other powers are reserved to the states or the people or expressly denied to both governments. The powers of the national government are ultimately declared supreme. Local governments are not expressly mentioned in the constitution but are formed when state governments delegate their sovereign authority.

Federalism and the Marshall Court

2 Determine the impact of the Marshall Court on federalism.

The Supreme Court under the leadership of John Marshall played a key role in defining the relationship and powers of the national government through its broad interpretations of the supremacy and commerce clauses.

Dual Federalism: States' Rights, the Civil War, and Reconstruction

3 Describe the emergence and decline of dual federalism.

Dual federalism was characterized by a system of separate but equally powerful state and national governments. This system was exemplified by states' authority to regulate issues such as slavery, evident in the doctrine of nullification and the Supreme Court's decision in *Dred Scott* v. *Sanford* (1857). The Civil War changed forever the nature of federalism. A further departure from dual federalism became evident with the ratification of the Sixteenth and Seventeenth Amendments in 1913.

Cooperative Federalism: The Growth of National Government

4 Explain how cooperative federalism led to the growth of the national government at the expense of the states.

The notion of equally powerful but separate national and state governments met its demise in the wake of the Great Depression. Franklin D. Roosevelt's New Deal ushered in an era of cooperative federalism, in which the powers of the national and state and local governments became more integrated, working together to solve shared problems.

Federal Grants to State and Local Governments

5 Describe how the federal budget is used to further influence state and local governments' policies.

The federal government provides money to states in a number of ways, including categorical grants, block grants, and programmatic requests. Problems may result when the federal government creates programs without providing sufficient funds. These are called unfunded mandates.

Judicial Federalism

6 Explore the role of the judiciary as an arbiter of federal–state conflicts.

The Supreme Court has always been an important arbiter of the relationship between national and state governments. While many of the decisions of the Rehnquist Court favored state governments, more recent decisions by the Roberts Court have favored national power in areas such as immigration and health care.

Toward Reform: Attempts to Balance National and State Power

7 Assess the challenges in balancing national and state powers and the consequences for policy making.

The roles and relative strengths of the national and state governments have changed over time. Some political scientists argue that the national government is best suited for redistributive policy and the states for developmental policy. Progressive approaches to federalism combine coercion and cooperation to achieve desired policy objectives.

Learn the Terms

✓ **Study** and **Review** the **Flashcards**

Barron v. *Baltimore* (1833)
bill of attainder
block grant
categorical grant
concurrent powers
cooperative federalism
Dillon's Rule
Dred Scott v. *Sandford* (1857)
dual federalism
enumerated powers

ex post facto law
extradition clause
federal system
full faith and credit clause
Gibbons v. *Ogden* (1824)
implied powers
interstate compacts
McCulloch v. *Maryland* (1819)
New Deal
New Federalism

nullification
preemption
privileges and immunities clause
programmatic requests
progressive federalism
reserved powers
Seventeenth Amendment
Sixteenth Amendment
Tenth Amendment
unitary system

Test Yourself

✓ **Study** and **Review** the **Practice Tests**

1. Under the Constitution, both the national and state governments

  a. are totally autonomous.
  b. do not share any powers.
  c. are accountable to the people.
  d. can regulate interstate commerce.
  e. are able to establish local governments.

2. The Tenth Amendment provides for

  a. states' reserved powers.
  b. states' implied powers.
  c. concurrent state and federal powers.
  d. enumerated federal powers.
  e. taking private property for public purposes.

3. In *Gibbons* v. *Ogden*, the U.S. Supreme Court

  I. articulated an expansive view of congressional powers.
  II. gave Robert Fulton the exclusive right to operate steamships on the Hudson River.
  III. concluded that commerce should be given a broad definition.

  IV. declared that the states had sole authority to regulate commerce.

  a. I only
  b. II and III
  c. I and II
  d. III and IV
  e. I and III

4. The Supreme Court held in *Barron* v. *Baltimore* that

  a. Congress had broad powers to regulate interstate commerce.
  b. the Bill of Rights did not apply to state governments.
  c. Congress lacked the ability to ban slavery.
  d. the city of Baltimore could not nullify laws passed by Congress.
  e. states could not tax the federal bank.

5. Nullification

a. was used to justify South Carolina's refusal to abide by federal tariff laws.

b. is a political maneuver in which Congress purposefully invalidates state laws by passing national laws.

c. is a principle that allows states to invalidate laws from other states.

d. played no part in the development of the Civil War.

e. was deemed unconstitutional after the Supreme Court invalidated the Alien and Sedition Acts.

6. The Great Depression led to

a. a variety of innovative programs to combat terrorism.

b. greater adherence to the philosophy of dual federalism.

c. a growth in national government activity.

d. a provision allowing the election of President Franklin D. Roosevelt for four terms.

e. the increased use of unfunded mandates.

7. New Federalism favors _____ over _____ grants.

a. block/categorical

b. categorical/block

c. funded mandates/categorical

d. block/unfunded mandates

e. block/funded mandates

8. In general, the Rehnquist Court's federalism decisions empowered

a. both state and national governments.

b. the state governments at the expense of the national government.

c. the national government at the expense of the states.

d. neither the state nor the national government.

e. local governments at the expense of the state and national governments.

9. The No Child Left Behind Act is an example of

a. a block grant.

b. returning power to the states.

c. a funded mandate.

d. preemption.

e. a categorical grant.

10. According to the text, which of the following best exemplifies the cooperative aspects of progressive federalism?

a. Bailing out the failing automobile industry

b. Health care reform

c. Allowing states to set emissions standards

d. Creating of the U.S. Department of Education

e. Reforming Social Security and Medicare

Explore Further

Bowman, Ann O'Meara, and Richard C. Kearney. *State and Local Government*, 8th ed. Belmont, CA: Wadsworth, 2010.

Chemerinsky, Erwin. *Enhancing Government: Federalism for the 21st Century*. Stanford, CA: Stanford Law Books, 2008.

Ebel, Robert D., and John E. Petersen. *The Oxford Handbook of State and Local Government*. New York: Oxford University Press, 2012.

Gerston, Larry N. *American Federalism: A Concise Introduction*. Armonk, NY: M. E. Sharpe, 2007.

Gray, Virginia, Russell L. Hanson, and Thad Kousser, eds. *Politics in the American States: A Comparative Analysis*, 10th ed. Washington, DC: CQ Press, 2012.

Grodzins, Morton. *The American System: A View of Government in the United States*. Chicago: Rand McNally, 1966.

LaCroix, Alison. *The Ideological Origins of American Federalism*. Cambridge, MA: Harvard University Press, 2010.

Mayer, M. H. *Homeland Security and Federalism: Protecting America from Outside the Beltway*. New York: Praeger, 2009.

Nugent, John D. *Safeguarding Federalism: How States Protect Their Interests in National Policymaking*. Norman: University of Oklahoma Press, 2009.

O'Toole, Laurence L., ed. *American Intergovernmental Relations: Foundations, Perspectives, and Issues*, 4th ed. Washington, DC: CQ Press, 2007.

Peterson, Paul E. *The Price of Federalism*. Washington, DC: Brookings Institution, 1995.

Rivlin, Alice, Timothy J. Conlan, and Paul Posner. *Intergovernmental Management for the 21st Century*. Washington, DC: Brookings Institution, 2007.

Smith, Kevin B., ed. *State and Local Government, 2013–2014 ed.* Washington, DC: CQ Press, 2012.

Smith, Kevin B., Alan Greenblatt, and Michele Mariani Vaughn. *Governing States and Localities*, 3rd ed. Washington, DC: CQ Press, 2010.

Stephens, G. Ross, and Nelson Wikstrom. *American Intergovernmental Relations: A Fragmented Federal Polity*. New York: Oxford University Press, 2006.

To learn more about federalism, go to the American Council on Intergovernmental Relations at **govinfo.library.unt.edu/ amcouncil/federalism.html.**

To learn more about state and local governments, go to State and Local Government on the Net at **www.statelocalgov.net/.**

To learn more about Supreme Court cases on federalism, go to the Oyez Project at **www.oyez.org.**

Credits

Credits are listed in order of appearance.

Lewis W Hine/Getty Images; Paula Bronstein/Getty Images; Charles Dharapak/AP Images; Rich Pedroncelli/AP Images ; David Sipress/The New Yorker Collection/www.cartoonbank.com

Answer Key

1. c; 2. a; 3. e; 4. b; 5. a; 6. c; 7. a; 8. b; 9. d; 10. c

Notes

1. Randal C. Archibold, "Arizona Enacts Stringent Law on Immigration," *New York Times* (April 23, 2010): A1.

2. *Arizona* v. *United States*, 567 U.S.____(2012).

3. John Mountjoy, "Interstate Cooperation: Interstate Compacts Make a Comeback," Council of State Governments, www.csg.org.

4. *McCulloch* v. *Maryland*, 17 U.S. 316 (1819).

5. For more on *McCulloch*, see Richard E. Ellis, *Aggressive Nationalism:* McCulloch *v.* Maryland *and the Foundation of Federal Authority in the Young Republic* (New York: Oxford University Press, 2008).

6. *Gibbons* v. *Ogden*, 22 U.S. 1 (1824).

7. For more on *Gibbons*, see Thomas H. Cox, Gibbons v. Ogden: *Law and Society in the Early Republic* (Athens, OH: Ohio University Press, 2010).

8. *Barron* v. *Baltimore*, 32 U.S. 243 (1833).

9. For more on *Barron*, see Brendan J. Doherty, "Interpreting the Bill of Rights and the Nature of Federalism: *Barron* v. *City of Baltimore*." *Journal of Supreme Court History* 32 (2007): 211–28.

10. *Abelman* v. *Booth*, 62 U.S. 506 (1859).

11. *Dred Scott* v. *Sandford*, 60 U.S. 393 (1857).

12. *Pensacola Telegraph* v. *Western Union*, 96 U.S. 1 (1877).

13. *U.S.* v. *E. C. Knight*, 156 U.S. 1 (1895).

14. John O. McGinnis, "The State of Federalism," Testimony before the Senate Government Affairs Committee, May 5, 1999.

15. Morton Grodzins, "Centralization and Decentralization in the American Federal System," in Robert A. Goldwin, ed., *A Nation of States* (Chicago: Rand McNally, 1963), 3–4.

16. Jeff Shesol, *Supreme Power: Franklin Roosevelt vs. the Supreme Court* (New York: W.W. Norton, 2010).

17. *NLRB* v. *Jones and Laughlin Steel Co.*, 301 U.S. 1 (1937).

18. *Wickard* v. *Filburn*, 317 U.S. 111 (1942).

19. Richard P. Nathan, Fred C. Doolittle, and Associates, *Reagan and the States* (Princeton, NJ: Princeton University Press, 1987), 4.

20. Linda Greenhouse, "The Rehnquist Court and Its Imperiled States' Rights Legacy," *New York Times* (June 12, 2005): A3.

21. *U.S.* v. *Lopez*, 514 U.S. 549 (1995).

22. *Arizona* v. *United States*, 567 U.S. ____ (2012) and *National Federation of Independent Business* v. *Sebelius*, 567 U.S. ____(2012).

23. Paul E. Peterson, *The Price of Federalism* (Washington, DC: Brookings Institution, 1995).

24. Peter Harkness, "What Brand of Federalism Is Next?" *Governing* (January 2012): http://www.governing.com/columns/potomac-chronicle/gov-col-what-brand-of-federalism-is-next.html.

25. William J. Kovacs, quoted in John Schwartz, "Obama Seems to Be Open to a Broader Role for States," *New York Times* (January 30, 2009): A16.

Civil Liberties

From Chapter 4 of *Essentials of American Government: Roots and Reform,* 2012 Election Edition. Karen O'Connor. Copyright © 2014 by Pearson Education, Inc. Published by Pearson Education, Inc. All rights reserved.

Civil Liberties

T he Bill of Rights, written in 1789, set forth to define the natural rights of the citizens of the United States. It was also intended to limit the new national government's ability to overstep its authority. The Fourth Amendment, for example, guards against unreasonable search and seizure. Specifically, the amendment states that it protects "the right of people to be secure in their persons, houses, papers, and effects." The Fourth Amendment also provides guidelines regarding obtaining a warrant in order to conduct a search.

Through this amendment, the government ensured that the people of the United States were guaranteed both their privacy and autonomy. However, interpreting the Fourth Amendment—as well as many other amendments—has posed significant challenges for the modern judiciary. Determining what constitutes an "unreasonable" search or when a law enforcement officer has "probable cause," especially, prove difficult in practice. Constantly evolving technology and social and political norms can also pose unique challenges for the criminal justice system.

Two cases decided during the Supreme Court's 2012 term illustrate the ongoing challenges of the Fourth Amendment. In the first case, the Court was asked to rule on whether or not law enforcement officers could plant GPS tracking devices on a suspected criminal's vehicle. The Court ultimately decided that, although the purpose of the search, monitoring a suspected criminal's activity, was the same as an extended investigation, implanting a tracking device on the suspect's vehicle compromised the suspect's expectation of privacy. Though the Court did not explicitly state that a warrant was necessary, observers noted that the ruling was construed in such a way that using a GPS device to track a suspect's activity without a warrant would be unlikely to stand up to legal challenge.[1]

In a second case, the Court considered whether invasive strip searches could be performed on all individuals entering a prison. In this case, the justices acknowledged the diversity of problems facing the criminal justice system today, including concealed weapons, gang tattoos, and smuggled drugs or other illegal substances. In so doing, they noted that if any suspected criminal

1	2	3	4	5	6	7
Trace the constitutional roots of civil liberties.	Describe the First Amendment guarantee of freedom of religion.	Outline the First Amendment guarantees of and limitations on freedom of speech, press, assembly, and petition.	Summarize changes in the interpretation of the Second Amendment right to keep and bear arms.	Analyze the rights of criminal defendants found in the Bill of Rights.	Explain the origin and significance of the right to privacy.	Evaluate how reforms to combat terrorism have affected civil liberties

JUDICIAL INTERPRETATION HAS REDEFINED THE FOURTH AMENDMENT The Supreme Court plays an important role in interpreting the U.S. Constitution and applying its principles to a changing America. Vehicles are one Fourth Amendment issue that has continuously troubled the Court. Above, police officers search a vehicle during the Prohibition Era. Below, a Department of Homeland Security agent uses technological devices to search a van at the U.S.-Mexico border.

MyPoliSciLab Videos

 Watch on MyPoliS

The Big Picture Find out how the events of September 11, 2001 transformed civil liberties in the United States. Author Alixandra B. Yanus reviews the acts that were passed by the government after that day, and demonstrates why it can be troubling to accept civil liberties for all people.

The Basics What are civil liberties and where do they come from? In this video, you will learn about our First Amendment guarantees and about protections the Bill of Rights provides those accused of crimes. In the process, you'll discover how our liberties have changed over time to reflect our changing values and needs.

In Context Uncover the importance of civil liberties in a changing American society. University of Massachusetts at Boston political scientist Maurice T. Cunningham identifies the origins of our civil liberties and evaluates the clash between national security and civil liberties in a post 9/11 age.

Thinking Like a Political Scientist What are some of the challenges facing political scientists in regards to civil liberties? In this video, University of Massachusetts at Boston political scientist Maurice T. Cunningham raises some of the thought provoking questions regarding civil liberties that have arisen during the last decade.

In the Real World The American legal system and the American people have both struggled over whether the death penalty should be imposed in this country. In this segment, we'll hear what citizens have to say about the death penalty.

So What? Like having the freedom to read whatever book or magazine you want without censorship? In this video, author Alixandra B. Yanus lays out the civil liberties Americans enjoy (and take for granted) and explains how these liberties can sometimes run into conflict with each other.

was entering the general prison population, law enforcement officers had an interest in ensuring the safety of the prison and of society. Thus, performing a general strip search, even without a warrant, was permissible.[2]

In each of these cases, the Supreme Court was asked to consider issues related to the Fourth Amendment that the Framers could never have imagined. The brilliance of the civil liberties codified by the First Congress is that the Bill of Rights remains a relatively stable statement of our natural rights as Americans, even as technology has evolved. With judicial interpretation, the sentiments expressed more than 200 years ago still apply to the modern world.

• • •

Civil liberties are the personal guarantees and freedoms that government cannot abridge, by law, constitution, or judicial interpretation. As guarantees of "freedom to" action, they place limitations on the power of the government to restrain or dictate an individual's actions. **Civil rights,** in contrast, provide freedom from arbitrary or discriminatory treatment by government or individuals.

Questions of civil liberties often present complex problems. We must decide how to determine the boundaries of speech and assembly—or, how much control over our personal liberties we give to police or other law enforcement officials. Moreover, during times of war, it is important to consider the liberties accorded to those who oppose war or are suspected of anti-government activities.

Resolution of civil liberties questions often falls to the judiciary, which must balance the competing interests of the government and the people. Thus, in many of the cases discussed in this chapter, a conflict arises between an individual or group of individuals seeking to exercise what they believe to be a liberty and the government, be it local, state, or national, seeking to control the exercise of that liberty in an attempt to keep order and preserve the rights (and safety) of others. In other cases, two liberties clash, such as a physician's and her patients' right to easy access to a medical clinic such as Planned Parenthood versus a pro-life advocate's liberty to picket that clinic. In this chapter, we explore the various dimensions of civil liberties guarantees contained in the U.S. Constitution and the Bill of Rights.

Roots of Civil Liberties: The Bill of Rights

1   Trace the constitutional roots of civil liberties.

Recognition of the increased power of the new national government led Anti-Federalists to stress the need for a bill of rights. Anti-Federalists and many others were confident they could control the actions of their own state legislators, but they did not trust the national government to protect civil liberties.

The notion of including a bill of rights in the Constitution was not popular at the Constitutional Convention. When George Mason of Virginia suggested adding such a bill to the preface of the proposed Constitution, representatives unanimously defeated his resolution.[3] In subsequent ratification debates, Federalists argued that a bill of rights was unnecessary, putting forward three main arguments in opposition.

1. A bill of rights was unnecessary in a constitutional republic founded on the idea of popular sovereignty and inalienable, natural rights. Moreover, most state constitutions contained bills of rights, so federal guarantees were unnecessary.

2. A bill of rights would be dangerous. According to Alexander Hamilton in *Federalist No. 84*, since the national government was one of enumerated powers (that is, it had only the powers listed in the Constitution), "Why declare that things shall not be done which there is no power to do?"

civil liberties
The personal guarantees and freedoms that the government cannot abridge by law, constitution, or judicial interpretation.

civil rights
The government-protected rights of individuals against arbitrary or discriminatory treatment by governments or individuals.

Bill of Rights
The first ten amendments to the U.S. Constitution, which largely guarantee specific rights and liberties.

Ninth Amendment
Part of the Bill of Rights that makes it clear that enumerating rights in the Constitution or Bill of Rights does not mean that others do not exist.

Tenth Amendment
The final part of the Bill of Rights that defines the basic principle of American federalism in stating that the powers not delegated to the national government are reserved to the states or to the people.

due process clause
Clause contained in the Fifth and Fourteenth Amendments; over the years, it has been construed to guarantee a variety of rights to individuals.

substantive due process
Judicial interpretation of the Fifth and Fourteenth Amendments' due process clauses that protects citizens from arbitrary or unjust state or federal laws.

3. A national bill of rights would be impractical to enforce. Its validity would largely depend on public opinion and the spirit of the people and government.

Some Framers, however, came to support the idea. After the Philadelphia convention, James Madison conducted a lively correspondence with Thomas Jefferson about the need for a national bill of rights. Jefferson supported such guarantees far more quickly than did Madison. But, the reluctant Madison soon found himself in a close race against James Monroe for a seat in the House of Representatives in the First Congress. The district was largely Anti-Federalist. In an act of political expediency, Madison issued a new series of public letters similar to *The Federalist Papers,* in which he vowed to support a bill of rights. Once elected to the House, Madison made good on his promise and became the prime author of the Bill of Rights. Still, he considered Congress to have far more important matters to handle and viewed his work on the Bill of Rights as "a nauseous project."[4]

With fear of political instability running high, Congress worked quickly to approve Madison's draft. The proposed Bill of Rights was sent to the states for ratification in 1789, the same year the first Congress convened. By 1791, the states had approved most of its provisions.

The **Bill of Rights,** the first ten amendments to the Constitution, contains numerous specific guarantees against encroachment by the new government, including those of free speech, press, and religion. The Ninth and Tenth Amendments, favored by the Federalists, note that the Bill of Rights is not exclusive. The **Ninth Amendment** makes clear that this special listing of rights does not mean that others do not exist. The **Tenth Amendment** reiterates that powers not delegated to the national government are reserved to the states or to the people.

The Incorporation Doctrine: The Bill of Rights Made Applicable to the States

The Framers intended the Bill of Rights to limit the national government's power to infringe on the rights and liberties of the citizenry. In *Barron* v. *Baltimore* (1833), the Supreme Court ruled that the Bill of Rights limited only the actions of the U.S. government and not those of the states.[5] In 1868, however, the Fourteenth Amendment was added to the U.S. Constitution. Its language suggested that some or even all protections guaranteed in the Bill of Rights might be interpreted to prevent state infringement of those rights. Section 1 of the Fourteenth Amendment reads: "No State shall . . . . deprive any person of life, liberty, or property, without due process of law." Questions about the scope of "liberty" as well as the meaning of "due process of law" continue even today to engage legal scholars and jurists.

Until nearly the turn of the twentieth century, the Supreme Court steadfastly rejected numerous arguments for interpreting the **due process clause** in the Fourteenth Amendment in such a way as to make various provisions in the Bill of Rights applicable to the states. In 1897, however, the Court began to increase its jurisdiction over the states by holding them to a **substantive due process** standard whereby they had the legal burden to prove that their laws constituted a valid exercise of power to regulate the health, welfare, or public morals of citizens.[6] Interference with state power, however, was rare, and states passed sedition laws (laws that made it illegal to speak or write any political criticism that threatened to diminish respect for the government, its laws, or public officials), anticipating that the U.S. Supreme Court would uphold their constitutionality. When Benjamin Gitlow, a member of the Socialist Party, printed 16,000 copies of a manifesto in which he urged workers to overthrow the U.S. government, he was convicted of violating a New York state law that prohibited such advocacy. Although his conviction was upheld, in *Gitlow* v. *New York* (1925), the U.S. Supreme Court noted that states were not completely free to limit forms of political expression. The Court argued that certain "fundamental personal rights and liberties" were protected from impairment by the Fourteenth Amendment's due process clause.[7]

Gitlow, with its finding that states could not abridge free speech protections, was the first decision to clearly articulate the **incorporation doctrine.** In *Near* v. *Minnesota* (1931), the U.S. Supreme Court further developed this doctrine by holding that a state law violated the First Amendment's freedom of the press.[8]

☐ Selective Incorporation and Fundamental Freedoms

The Supreme Court has not made all specific guarantees in the Bill of Rights applicable to the states through the due process clause of the Fourteenth Amendment, as shown in Table 1. Instead, the Court has used the process of **selective incorporation** to limit the rights of states by protecting against abridgement of **fundamental freedoms.** These freedoms—defined by the Court as essential to order, liberty, and justice—are subject to the Court's most rigorous standard of review.

The Court set out the rationale for selective incorporation in *Palko* v. *Connecticut* (1937).[9] Frank Palko was charged with first-degree murder for killing two Connecticut police officers, found guilty of a lesser charge of second-degree murder, and sentenced to life imprisonment. Connecticut appealed. Palko was retried, found guilty of first-degree murder, and sentenced to death. Palko then appealed his second conviction, arguing that it violated the Fifth Amendment's prohibition against double jeopardy because the due process clause of the Fourteenth Amendment had made the Fifth Amendment applicable to the states.

The Supreme Court disagreed. In an opinion written by Justice Benjamin Cardozo, the Court ruled that the due process clause bound states only to those rights that were

incorporation doctrine
An interpretation of the Constitution holding that the due process clause of the Fourteenth Amendment requires state and local governments to guarantee the rights stated in the Bill of Rights.

selective incorporation
A judicial doctrine whereby most, but not all, protections found in the Bill of Rights are made applicable to the states via the Fourteenth Amendment.

fundamental freedoms
Those rights defined by the Court as essential to order, liberty, and justice and therefore entitled to the highest standard of review.

TABLE 1 HOW HAS SELECTIVE INCORPORATION MADE THE BILL OF RIGHTS APPLICABLE TO THE STATES?

Amendment	Right	Date	Case Incorporated
I	Speech	1925	*Gitlow* v. *New York*
	Press	1931	*Near* v. *Minnesota*
	Assembly	1937	*DeJonge* v. *Oregon*
	Religion	1940	*Cantwell* v. *Connecticut*
II	Bear arms	2010	*McDonald* v. *City of Chicago*
III	No quartering of soldiers		Not incorporated
IV	No unreasonable searches or seizures	1949	*Wolf* v. *Colorado*
	Exclusionary rule	1961	*Mapp* v. *Ohio*
V	Just compensation	1897	*Chicago, B&Q R.R. Co.* v. *Chicago*
	Self-incrimination	1964	*Malloy* v. *Hogan*
	Double jeopardy	1969	*Benton* v. *Maryland*
	Grand jury indictment		Not incorporated
VI	Public trial	1948	*In re Oliver*
	Right to counsel	1963	*Gideon* v. *Wainwright*
	Confrontation of witnesses	1965	*Pointer* v. *Texas*
	Impartial trial	1966	*Parker* v. *Gladden*
	Speedy trial	1967	*Klopfer* v. *North Carolina*
	Compulsory trial	1967	*Washington* v. *Texas*
	Criminal trial	1968	*Duncan* v. *Louisiana*
VII	Civil jury trial		Not incorporated
VIII	No cruel and unusual punishment	1962	*Robinson* v. *California*
	No excessive bail	1971	*Schilb* v. *Kuebel*

"of the very essence of a scheme of ordered liberty." The Fifth Amendment's double jeopardy clause was not, in the Court's view, among these rights. The Court overruled its decision in 1969.[10]

Today, selective incorporation requires states to respect freedoms of press, speech, and assembly, among other liberties. The Court has not incorporated other guarantees, such as those contained in the Third and Seventh Amendments (housing of soldiers and jury trials in civil cases), because it has yet to consider them sufficiently fundamental to national notions of liberty and justice.

First Amendment Guarantees: Freedom of Religion

2 Describe the First Amendment guarantee of freedom of religion.

The **First Amendment** to the Constitution begins, "Congress shall make no law respecting an establishment of religion, or prohibiting the free exercise thereof." This statement sets the boundaries of governmental action. The **establishment clause** directs the national government not to sanction an official religion. The **free exercise clause** ("or prohibiting the free exercise thereof") guarantees citizens that the national government will not interfere with their practice of religion. These guarantees, however, are not absolute.

☐ The Establishment Clause

Through the years, the Court has been divided over the interpretation of the establishment clause. Does this clause erect a total wall between church and state, as favored by Thomas Jefferson, or does it allow some governmental accommodation of religion?

First Amendment
Part of the Bill of Rights that imposes a number of restrictions on the federal government with respect to civil liberties, including freedom of religion, speech, press, assembly, and petition.

establishment clause
The first clause of the First Amendment; it directs the national government not to sanction an official religion.

free exercise clause
The second clause of the First Amendment; it prohibits the U.S. government from interfering with a citizen's right to practice his or her religion.

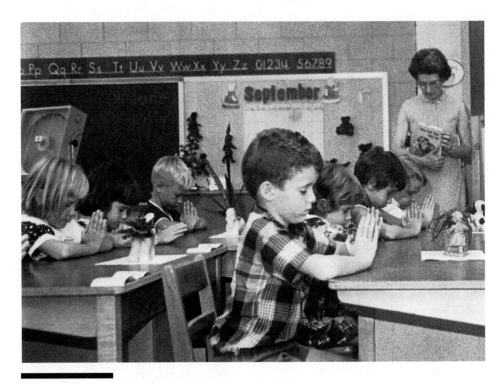

SHOULD CHILDREN BE REQUIRED TO PRAY IN PUBLIC SCHOOLS?
School prayer is just one of the thorny questions the Supreme Court has addressed under the establishment clause. Though the Court has usually decided against prayer in schools, even when it is student-led, many educational institutions maintain this practice.

While the Supreme Court has upheld the constitutionality of many kinds of church/state entanglements, such as public funding to provide sign language interpreters for deaf students in religious schools,[11] the Court has held fast to the rule of strict separation between church and state when issues of mandatory prayer in school are involved. In *Engel* v. *Vitale* (1962), for example, the Court ruled that the recitation in public school classrooms of a brief nondenominational prayer drafted by the local school board was unconstitutional.[12] One year later, in *Abington School District* v. *Schempp* (1963), the Court ruled that state-mandated Bible reading or recitation of the Lord's Prayer in public schools was also unconstitutional.[13]

The Court has gone back and forth in its effort to find a workable way to deal with church/state questions. In 1971, in *Lemon* v. *Kurtzman,* the Court tried to carve out a three-part test for laws dealing with religious establishment issues. According to the **Lemon test,** a practice or policy was constitutional if it: (1) had a legitimate secular purpose; (2) neither advanced nor inhibited religion; and, (3) did not foster an excessive government entanglement with religion.[14] But, the Supreme Court often has sidestepped the *Lemon* test altogether and has appeared more willing to lower the wall between church and state as long as school prayer is not involved. In 1981, for example, the Court ruled unconstitutional a Missouri law prohibiting the use of state university buildings and grounds for "purposes of religious worship." The law had been used to ban religious groups from using school facilities.[15]

In 1995, the Court signaled that it was willing to lower the wall even further. In a case involving the University of Virginia, a 5–4 majority held that the university violated the free speech rights of a fundamentalist Christian group when it refused to fund the group's student magazine. Justice David Souter highlighted the importance of this decision in his dissent: "The Court today, for the first time, approves direct funding of core religious activities by an arm of the state."[16] The Court under Chief Justice John Roberts, however, has demonstrated that boundaries to these accommodations exist. In 2010, in *Christian Legal Society* v. *Martinez*, the Court ruled that the University of California Hastings College of Law could deny recognition and therefore funding to the Christian Legal Society because the group limited its membership to those who shared a common faith orientation.

For more than a quarter-century, the Supreme Court basically allowed "books only" as an aid to religious schools, noting that the books go to children, not to schools. But, in 2000, the Court voted 6–3 to uphold the constitutionality of a federal aid provision that allowed the government to lend books and computers to religious schools.[17] And, in 2002, by a bitterly divided 5–4 vote, the Supreme Court concluded that governments can give parents money to send their children to private or religious schools.[18] Basically, the Court now appears willing to support programs as long as they provide aid to religious and nonreligious schools alike, and the money goes to persons who exercise free choice over how it is used.

Prayer in school also continues to be an issue. In 1992, the Court persisted in its unwillingness to allow organized prayer in public schools by finding unconstitutional the saying of prayer at a middle school graduation.[19] And, in 2000, the Court ruled that student-led, student-initiated prayer at high school football games violated the establishment clause.

Establishment issues, however, do not always focus on education. In 2005, for example, the Supreme Court, in a 5–4 decision, narrowly upheld the *Lemon* test by ruling that a privately donated courthouse display, which included the Ten Commandments and 300 other historical documents illustrating the evolution of American law, violated the First Amendment's establishment clause.[20]

But, in 2010, the Court appeared to reverse course. In a 5–4 decision, the Court ruled that a white cross erected on a World War I memorial on federal lands in the Mojave Desert was constitutional. According to Justice Anthony Kennedy, who wrote the majority opinion, the cross "is not merely a reaffirmation of Christian beliefs" but a symbol "often used to honor and respect" heroism. This opinion leaves state and local governments to ponder what kind of religious displays in public settings will be constitutional.[21]

Lemon test

Three-part test created by the Supreme Court for examining the constitutionality of religious establishment issues.

☐ The Free Exercise Clause

The free exercise clause of the First Amendment proclaims that "Congress shall make no law . . . prohibiting the free exercise [of religion]." Although the free exercise clause of the First Amendment guarantees individuals the right to be free from governmental interference in the exercise of their religion, this guarantee, like other First Amendment freedoms, is not absolute.

The free exercise clause may also pose difficult questions for the courts to resolve. In the area of free exercise, the Court often has had to confront questions of "What is a god?" and "What is a religious faith?"—questions that theologians have grappled with for centuries. In 1965, for example, in a case involving three men who were denied conscientious objector deferments during the Vietnam War because they did not subscribe to "traditional" organized religions, the Court ruled unanimously that belief in a supreme being was not essential for recognition as a conscientious objector.[22] Thus, the men were entitled to the deferments because their views paralleled those who objected to war and who belonged to traditional religions. In contrast, despite the Court's having ruled that Catholic, Protestant, Jewish, and Buddhist prison inmates must be allowed to hold religious services,[23] as early as 1987, the Court ruled that Islamic prisoners could be denied the same right for security reasons.[24]

Furthermore, when secular law conflicts with religious law, the right to exercise one's religious beliefs is often denied—especially if a minority or an unpopular or "suspicious" group holds the religious beliefs in question. Thus, the U.S. Supreme Court has interpreted the Constitution to mean that governmental interests can outweigh free exercise rights. The Court has upheld as constitutional state statutes barring the use of certain illegal drugs (such as peyote), snake handling, and polygamy—all practices once part of some religious observances—when states have shown compelling reasons to do so.[25]

First Amendment Guarantees: Freedoms of Speech, Press, Assembly, and Petition

> **3** Outline the First Amendment guarantees of and limitations on freedom of speech, press, assembly, and petition.

Explore on
MyPoliSciLab
Simulation: You Are a
Police Officer

T he Supreme Court has, to varying degrees, scrutinized the remaining guarantees protected by the First Amendment. During times of war, for example, the Court generally has allowed Congress and the chief executive extraordinary leeway in limiting First Amendment freedoms. Below, we provide historical background and current judicial interpretations of the freedoms of speech, press, assembly, and petition.

☐ Freedoms of Speech and the Press

A democracy depends on a free exchange of ideas, and the First Amendment shows that the Framers were well aware of this fact. Historically, one of the most volatile issues of constitutional interpretation has centered on the First Amendment's mandate that "Congress shall make no law . . . abridging the freedom of speech or of the press." As with the establishment and free exercise clauses of the First Amendment, the Court has not interpreted speech and press clauses as absolute bans on government regulation. This leeway in interpretation has led to thousands of cases seeking both broader and narrower judicial interpretations of the scope of the amendment.

Explore Your World

Free speech and free press are central values in most industrialized democracies such as the United States. In these countries, citizens and the media act as powerful watchdogs over the government's actions. However, in other countries such as Russia in the 1920s and North Korea in 2012, the government controls and monitors the media. This means that the government's message—as illustrated in the posters below—may be the only viewpoint citizens can learn, understand, and espouse.

This Russian poster was created during the 1920s. It illustrates the rise of the Russian economy and advocates for the Russian government's Five Year Plan. Note the images of prominent Russian Communist Party leaders, including Joseph Stalin, on the engine.

This propaganda poster from North Korea in 2012 depicts the image of a fist coming down on two people. The words on the poster, roughly translated, state, "Let's strike them with a single blow." This photo was taken at a rally against the South Korean president. Note how many people in the crowd have responded by raising a single fist.

CRITICAL THINKING QUESTIONS

1. How do these posters represent their country of origin? How do they represent other countries? What message does this send about global politics?

2. How do these posters use emotional appeals to induce support from citizens? Is this an appropriate tactic?

3. Can you think of any examples in which the U.S. government (or other western governments) employed tactics such as those seen in these posters? How were they similar, and how were they different?

Over the years, the Court has employed a hierarchical approach in determining what the government can and cannot regulate, with some liberties getting greater protection than others. Generally, the Court has granted thoughts the greatest protection and actions or deeds the least. Words have fallen somewhere in the middle, depending on their content and purpose.

prior restraint
Constitutional doctrine that prevents the government from prohibiting speech or publication before the fact; generally held to be in violation of the First Amendment.

THE ALIEN AND SEDITION ACTS When the states ratified the First Amendment in 1791, it was considered to protect against **prior restraint** of speech or expression, or to guard against the prohibition of speech or publication before the fact. Faced with increasing criticism of the Federalist government by Democratic-Republicans in 1798, the Federalist Congress, with President John Adams's blessing, enacted the Alien and Sedition Acts. These acts banned any criticism of the Federalist government by the growing numbers of Democratic-Republicans, making the publication of "any false, scandalous writing against the government of the United States" a criminal offense. Although the law clearly flew in the face of the First Amendment's ban on prior restraint, the Adams administration successfully prosecuted and partisan Federalist judges imposed fines and jail terms on at least ten Democratic-Republican newspaper editors. The acts became a major issue in the 1800 presidential election campaign, which led to the election of Thomas Jefferson, a vocal opponent of the acts. He quickly pardoned all who had been convicted under their provisions, and the Democratic-Republican Congress allowed the acts to expire before the Federalist-controlled U.S. Supreme Court had an opportunity to rule on the constitutionality of these First Amendment infringements.

SLAVERY, THE CIVIL WAR, AND RIGHTS CURTAILMENTS After the public outcry over the Alien and Sedition Acts, the national government largely refrained from regulating speech. But, in its place, the states, which were not yet bound by the Bill of Rights through selective incorporation, began to prosecute those who published articles critical of governmental policies. In the 1830s, at the urging of abolitionists (those who sought an end to slavery), the publication or dissemination of any positive information about slavery became a punishable offense in the North. In the opposite vein, in the South, supporters of slavery enacted laws to prohibit publication of any anti-slavery sentiments. Southern postmasters, for example, refused to deliver northern abolitionist newspapers, a step that amounted to censorship of the U.S. mail.

During the Civil War, President Abraham Lincoln took several steps that actually were unconstitutional. He made it unlawful to print any criticisms of the national government or of the Civil War, effectively suspending the free press protections of the First Amendment. Lincoln went so far as to order the arrest of several newspaper editors critical of his conduct of the war and ignored a Supreme Court decision saying that these practices were unconstitutional.

After the Civil War, states also began to prosecute individuals for seditious speech if they uttered or printed statements critical of the government. Between 1890 and 1900, for example, more than one hundred state prosecutions for sedition took place.[26] Moreover, by the dawn of the twentieth century, public opinion in the United States had grown increasingly hostile toward the commentary of Socialists and Communists who attempted to appeal to growing immigrant populations. Groups espousing socialism and communism became the targets of state laws curtailing speech and the written word (see the earlier discussion of *Gitlow* v. *New York*).

WORLD WAR I AND ANTI-GOVERNMENTAL SPEECH The next major efforts to restrict freedom of speech and the press did not occur until Congress, at the urging of President Woodrow Wilson during World War I, passed the Espionage Act in 1917. The government convicted nearly 2,000 Americans of violating its various provisions, especially prohibitions on urging resistance to the draft or distributing anti-war leaflets. In *Schenck* v. *U.S.* (1919), the Supreme Court upheld this act, ruling that Congress had a right to restrict speech "of such a nature as to create a clear and present danger that will bring about the substantive evils that Congress has a right to prevent."[27] Under this **clear and present danger test** the circumstances surrounding an incident are important. Anti-war leaflets, for example, may be permissible during peacetime, but during World War I they were considered too dangerous.

Still, for decades, the Supreme Court wrestled with what constituted a danger. Finally, in *Brandenburg* v. *Ohio* (1969), the Court fashioned a new test for deciding whether the government could regulate certain kinds of speech: the **direct incitement test.** Now, the government could punish the advocacy of illegal action only if "such advocacy is directed to inciting or producing imminent lawless action and is likely to incite or produce such action."[28] The requirement of "imminent lawless action" makes it more difficult for the government to punish speech and publication and is consistent with the Framers' notion of the special role played by these elements in a democratic society.

☐ Protected Speech and Press

The expression of ideas through speech and the press is a cornerstone of a free society. In line with this thinking, the U.S. Supreme Court has accorded constitutional protection to a number of aspects of speech and the press, even though the content of such expression may be objectionable to some citizens or the government. Here, we discuss the implications of this protection with respect to prior restraint, symbolic speech, and hate speech.

LIMITING PRIOR RESTRAINT As we have seen with the Alien and Sedition Acts, although Congress attempted to limit speech before the fact as early as 1798, the U.S. Supreme Court did not take a firm position on this issue until the 1970s. In *New York Times Co.* v. *U.S.* (1971), also called the Pentagon Papers case, the Supreme Court ruled that the U.S. government could not block the publication of secret Department of Defense documents illegally furnished to the *Times* by anti-war activists.[29] In 1976, the U.S. Supreme Court went even further, noting in *Nebraska Press Association* v. *Stuart* that any attempt by the government to prevent expression carried "'a heavy presumption' against its constitutionality."[30]

SYMBOLIC SPEECH In addition to the general protection accorded to pure speech, the Supreme Court has extended the reach of the First Amendment to **symbolic speech,** a means of expression that includes symbols or signs. In the words of Justice John Marshall Harlan, these kinds of speech are part of the "free trade in ideas."[31]

The Supreme Court first acknowledged that symbolic speech was entitled to First Amendment protection in *Stromberg* v. *California* (1931).[32] In that case, the Court overturned a communist youth camp director's conviction under a state statute prohibiting the display of a red flag, a symbol of opposition to the U.S. government. In a similar vein, the right of high school students to wear black armbands to protest the Vietnam War was upheld in *Tinker* v. *Des Moines Independent Community School District* (1969).[33]

In recent years, however, the Court has appeared less willing to support the standards established in *Tinker*. In a case commonly referred to as the "Bong Hits 4 Jesus" case, the Court ruled that a student's free speech rights were not violated when a school suspended him for displaying what the Court characterized as a "sophomoric" banner at an Olympic torch relay parade.[34]

HATE SPEECH In the 1990s, a particularly thorny First Amendment issue emerged as cities and universities attempted to prohibit what they viewed as hate speech. In *R.A.V.* v. *City of St. Paul* (1992), a St. Paul, Minnesota, ordinance that made it a crime to engage in speech or action likely to arouse "anger," "alarm," or "resentment" on the basis of race, color, creed, religion, or gender was at issue. The Court ruled 5–4 that a

clear and present danger test
Test articulated by the Supreme Court in *Schenck* v. *U.S.* (1919) to draw the line between protected and unprotected speech; the Court looks to see "whether the words used" could "create a clear and present danger that they will bring about substantive evils" that Congress seeks "to prevent."

direct incitement test
Test articulated by the Supreme Court in *Brandenburg* v. *Ohio* (1969) holding that the First Amendment protects advocacy of illegal action unless imminent lawless action is intended and likely to occur.

symbolic speech
Symbols, signs, and other methods of expression generally considered to be protected by the First Amendment.

libel

False written statement that defames a person's character.

slander

Untrue spoken statements that defame the character of a person.

New York Times Co. **v.** *Sullivan* **(1964)**

Case in which the Supreme Court concluded that "actual malice" must be proven to support a finding of libel against a public figure.

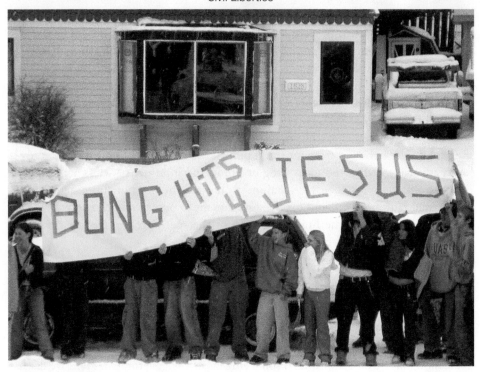

HOW BROAD IS THE RIGHT TO SYMBOLIC SPEECH?

In a 2007 case, the Supreme Court ruled that a school district was within its rights to suspend a student for displaying this banner, because it was intended to promote illegal drug use, even though it occurred off school property.

white teenager who burned a cross on a black family's front lawn, thereby committing a hate crime under the ordinance, could not face charges under that law because the First Amendment prevents governments from "silencing speech on the basis of its content."[35] In 2003, the Court narrowed this definition, ruling that state governments could constitutionally restrict cross burning when it occurred with the intent of racial intimidation.[36]

☐ Unprotected Speech and Press

Although the Supreme Court has allowed few governmental bans on most types of speech, some forms of expression lack protection. In 1942, the Supreme Court set forth the rationale by which it would distinguish between protected and unprotected speech. According to the Court, libel, fighting words, and obscenity are not protected by the First Amendment because "such expressions are no essential part of any exposition of ideals, and are of such slight social value as a step to truth that any benefit that may be derived from them is clearly outweighed by the social interest in order and morality."[37]

LIBEL AND SLANDER **Libel** is a false written statement that defames the character of a person. If the statement is spoken, it is **slander.** In many nations—such as Great Britain, for example—suing someone for libel is relatively easy. In the United States, however, the standards of proof reach much higher. A person who believes that he or she has been a victim of libel must show that the statements made were untrue. Truth is an absolute defense against the charge of libel, no matter how painful or embarrassing the revelations.

Individuals that the U.S. Supreme Court considers "public persons or public officials" often find it more difficult to sue for libel or slander. *New York Times Co.* **v.** *Sullivan* **(1964)** was the first major libel case considered by the Supreme Court.[38] An Alabama state court found the *Times* guilty of libel for printing a full-page advertisement accusing

Alabama officials of physically abusing African Americans during various civil rights protests. (Civil rights activists, including former First Lady Eleanor Roosevelt, paid for the ad.) The Supreme Court overturned the conviction and established that a finding of libel against a public official could stand only if "actual malice," or a knowing disregard for the truth, was shown. Proof that the statements were false or negligent was not sufficient to demonstrate actual malice.

fighting words

Words that "by their very utterance inflict injury or tend to incite an immediate breach of peace." Fighting words are not subject to the restrictions of the First Amendment.

FIGHTING WORDS In 1942, the Court stated that **fighting words,** or words that "by their very utterance inflict injury or tend to incite an immediate breach of peace," are not subject to the restrictions of the First Amendment.[39] Federal and state governments can therefore regulate fighting words, which include "profanity, obscenity, and threats."

OBSCENITY The current standard by which the Court judges obscenity was laid out by Chief Justice Warren E. Burger, who wrote the opinion in *Miller* v. *California* (1973). To make it easier for states to regulate obscene materials, the justices concluded that lower courts must ask, "whether the work depicts or describes, in a patently offensive way, sexual conduct specifically defined by state law." The courts also would determine "whether the work, taken as a whole, lacks serious literary, artistic, political, or scientific value." The Court also noted that local standards might affect its assessment of obscenity, under the rationale that what the citizens of New York City find acceptable might not be the case in Maine or Mississippi.[40]

Time and contexts clearly have altered the Court's and, indeed, much of America's perceptions of what works are obscene. But, the Supreme Court has allowed communities great leeway in drafting statutes to deal with obscenity and, even more importantly, other forms of questionable expression. In 1991, for example, the Court voted 5–4 to allow Indiana to ban totally nude erotic dancing, concluding that the statute furthered a substantial governmental interest in creating order in society and regulating morals, and therefore did not violate the First Amendment.[41]

While lawmakers have been fairly effective in restricting the sale and distribution of obscene materials, Congress has found it difficult to monitor the Internet. Since 1996, Congress has passed several laws designed to prohibit the transmission of obscene or "harmful" materials over the Internet to anyone under age eighteen. For many years, the Supreme Court repeatedly found these laws unconstitutional.[42] But, in 2008, a seven-justice majority decided that the PROTECT Act, which outlawed the sale or transmission of child pornography, was not overly broad and did not abridge the freedom of speech guaranteed by the First Amendment.[43]

☐ Freedoms of Assembly and Petition

"Peaceful assembly for lawful discussion cannot be made a crime," Chief Justice Charles Evans Hughes wrote in the 1937 case of *DeJonge* v. *Oregon*, which incorporated the First Amendment's freedom of assembly clause.[44] Despite this clear assertion, and an even more ringing declaration in the First Amendment, the fundamental freedoms of assembly and petition have been among the most controversial, especially in times of war. As with other First Amendment freedoms, the Supreme Court often has become the arbiter between the freedom of the people to express dissent and government's authority to limit controversy in the name of national security.

Because the freedom to assemble hinges on peaceful conduct, the freedoms of assembly and petition relate directly to those of speech and the press. If the words spoken or actions taken at any event cross the line of constitutionality, the First Amendment may no longer protect events such as parades or protests. Absent that protection, leaders and attendees may be subject to governmental regulation and even arrest, incarceration, or civil fines.

writs of *habeas corpus*

Petition requesting that a judge order authorities to prove that a prisoner is being held lawfully and that allows the prisoner to be freed if the government's case does not persuade the judge. *Habeas corpus* rights imply that prisoners have a right to know what charges are being made against them.

ex post facto law

Law that makes an act punishable as a crime even if the action was legal at the time it was committed.

bill of attainder

A law declaring an act illegal without a judicial trial.

The Second Amendment:
The Right to Keep and Bear Arms

> **4**   Summarize changes in the interpretation of the Second Amendment right to keep and bear arms.

During colonial times, the colonists' distrust of standing armies was evident. Most colonies required all white men to keep and bear arms and deputized these men to defend their settlements against Indians and European powers. The colonists viewed these local militias as the best way to keep order and protect liberty.

The Framers added the Second Amendment to the Constitution to ensure that Congress could not pass laws to disarm state militias. This amendment appeased Anti-Federalists, who feared that the new Constitution would abolish the right to "keep and bear arms." It also preserved an unstated right—the right to revolt against governmental tyranny.

Through the early 1920s, few state statutes were passed to regulate firearms (and generally these laws dealt with the possession of firearms by slaves). The Supreme Court's decision in *Barron* v. *Baltimore* (1833), which refused to incorporate the Bill of Rights to the state governments, prevented federal review of those state laws.[45] Moreover, in *Dred Scott* v. *Sandford* (1857), Chief Justice Roger B. Taney listed the right to own and carry arms as a basic right of citizenship.[46]

In 1934, Congress passed the National Firearms Act in response to the explosion of organized crime in the 1920s and 1930s, which stemmed from Prohibition. The act imposed taxes on automatic weapons and sawed-off shotguns. In *U.S.* v. *Miller* (1939), a unanimous Court upheld the constitutionality of the act, stating that the Second Amendment was intended to protect a citizen's right to own ordinary militia weapons, which did not include sawed-off shotguns.[47] For nearly seventy years following *Miller*, the Court did not directly address the Second Amendment. Then, in *D.C.* v. *Heller* (2008), when the Court offered some clarification, ruling that the Second Amendment protected an individual's right to own a firearm for personal use in Washington, D.C.[48]

In light of the Court's ruling, the D.C. City Council adopted new gun control laws requiring gun registration and prohibiting assault weapons and large-capacity magazines. A U.S. District Court ruled that these laws were valid and within the scope of the *Heller* decision.[49] And, in 2010, the Supreme Court broadened the ownership rights in *Heller* to include citizens of all states. It also incorporated the Second Amendment.[50]

The Rights of Criminal Defendants

> **5**   Analyze the rights of criminal defendants found in the Bill of Rights.

Article I of the Constitution guarantees a number of rights for persons accused of crimes. Among those are **writs of *habeas corpus,*** or court orders in which a judge requires authorities to prove they are holding a prisoner lawfully and that allow the prisoner to be freed if the government's case does not persuade the judge. In addition, *habeas corpus* rights imply that prisoners have a right to know what charges are being made against them.

Article I of the Constitution also prohibits *ex post facto* **laws,** those that make an act punishable as a crime even if the act was legal at the time it was committed. And, Article I prohibits **bills of attainder,** laws declaring an act illegal without a judicial trial.

How Do States Restrict the Right to Bear Arms?

The scope and application of the Second Amendment is a contentious and sensitive issue in American politics. Can, for example, citizens carry concealed weapons for self-protection? Does this right extend to possession of a rapid-fire submachine gun? As the image below illustrates, interstate variations in the number and severity of regulations on gun ownership are significant.

AK - 0

WA - 15
MT - 2
ND - 2
MN - 14
ME - 7
OR - 15
ID - 2
SD - 4
WI - 3
VT - 6
NH - 6
NY - 62
MA - 65
RI - 44
CT - 58
WY - 4
MI - 25
NB - 5
IA - 7
PA - 26
NJ - 72
NV - 5
UT - 0
CO - 15
IL - 35
IN - 4
OH - 7
DE - 13
MD - 45
KS - 4
MO - 4
WV - 4
VA - 12
CA - 81
KY - 2
NC - 16
AZ - 0
NM - 4
OK - 2
AR - 4
TN - 8
SC - 8
MS - 4
AL - 14
GA - 8
TX - 4
LA - 2
FL - 3
HI - 50

2011 State Rankings for Gun Law Strength

0-10 | 11-24 | 25-49 | 50-74 | 75-100

State Laws Governing Firearms

76%	53%	33%	22%	20%	14%
Right to carry concealed weapons	Right to carry prohibited	License to purchase handguns	Handgun waiting periods	Gun bans	Long gun waiting periods

CRITICAL THINKING QUESTIONS

1. How do gun control laws vary across the nation? What geographic patterns do you observe? Why do you observe these patterns?

2. Which gun control laws are most and least common? How do you explain these variations?

3. Should the national government have broader latitude to control ownership, sale, use, and manufacture of guns and firearms? Is it permissible under the constitution? Should this be a state responsibility?

SOURCES: Legal Community Against Violence's Web site and reports were the primary sources used for determining points awarded for each state. Visit www.LCAV.org. National Rifle Association Institute for Legislative Action, "Compendium of State Laws Governing Firearms."

Fourth Amendment
Part of the Bill of Rights that reads: "The right of the people to be secure in their persons, houses, papers, and effects, against unreasonable searches and seizures, shall not be violated, and no Warrants shall issue, but upon probable cause, supported by Oath or affirmation, and particularly describing the place to be searched, and the persons or things to be seized."

The Fourth, Fifth, Sixth, and Eighth Amendments supplement these rights with a variety of procedural guarantees, often called due process rights. In this section, we examine how the courts have interpreted and applied these guarantees in an attempt to balance personal liberty and national safety and security.

☐ The Fourth Amendment and Searches and Seizures

The **Fourth Amendment** to the Constitution protects people from unreasonable searches by the federal government. Moreover, it sets forth in some detail what may not be searched unless a warrant is issued, underscoring the Framers' concern with preventing government abuses.

The purpose of this amendment was to deny the national government the authority to make general searches. Over the years, in a number of decisions, the Supreme Court has interpreted the Fourth Amendment to allow the police to search: (1) the person arrested; (2) things in plain view of the accused person; and, (3) places or things that the arrested person could touch or reach or that are otherwise in the arrestee's immediate control.

Warrantless searches often occur if police suspect that someone is committing or is about to commit a crime. In these situations, police may stop and frisk the individual under suspicion. In 1989, the Court ruled that "reasonable suspicion" presented sufficient justification for stopping a suspect—a much lower standard than probable cause.[51]

Searches can also be made without a warrant if police obtain consent. In the case of homes, this consent must come from all occupants present at the time of the search. The police cannot conduct a warrantless search of a home if one of the occupants objects.[52] In contrast, under the open fields doctrine first articulated by the Supreme Court in 1924, if you own a field, and even if you post "No Trespassing" signs, the police can search your field without a warrant to see if you are engaging in illegal activity, such as growing marijuana, because you cannot reasonably expect privacy in an open field.[53]

In situations involving no arrests, police must obtain search warrants from a "neutral and detached magistrate" prior to conducting more extensive searches of houses, cars, offices, or any other place where an individual would reasonably have some expectation of privacy.[54] Thus, firefighters can enter your home to fight a fire without a warrant. But, if they decide to investigate the cause of the fire, they must obtain a warrant before they reenter.[55]

Cars have proven problematic for police and the courts because of their mobile nature. As noted by Chief Justice William H. Taft as early as 1925, "the vehicle can quickly be moved out of the locality or jurisdiction in which the warrant must be sought."[56] Historically, then, the Court has been lenient about the scope of automobile searches. In 2002, for example, an unusually unanimous Court ruled that the totality of the circumstances had to be considered in evaluating whether a border patrol officer acted lawfully in stopping a suspicious minivan. This ruling gave law enforcement officers more leeway to pull over suspicious motorists.[57] And, courts do not require search warrants in possible drunk driving situations. Thus, police in some states can require a Breathalyzer test to determine whether you have been driving with a blood alcohol level in excess of legal limits.[58]

More recently, the Roberts Court has attempted to limit law enforcement's power in some situations. In 2009, for example, the Court ruled that a warrantless vehicle search conducted after the driver voluntarily left his car and entered into police control was not legal. For a warrantless vehicle search to be legal, it needed to be both narrowly construed and the defendant needed to be able to access his vehicle.[59] And, in 2012, the Supreme Court limited law enforcement's ability to use GPS tracking devices on criminal suspects' vehicles.[60]

Testing for drugs, too, is an especially thorny search and seizure issue. While many private employers and professional athletic organizations routinely require drug tests upon application or as a condition of employment, governmental requirements present constitutional questions about the scope of permissible searches and seizures. In 1989, the Supreme Court ruled that mandatory drug and alcohol testing of employees involved in accidents was constitutional.[61] In 1995, the Court declared random drug testing of public high school athletes constitutional.[62] And, in 2002, the Court upheld the constitutionality of a Tecumseh, Oklahoma, policy that required mandatory drug testing of high school students participating in any extracurricular activities. Thus, prospective band, choir, debate, or drama club members were subject to the same kind of random drug testing undergone by athletes.[63]

☐ The Fifth Amendment: Self-Incrimination and Double Jeopardy

The **Fifth Amendment** provides a variety of guarantees protecting those charged with a crime. It requires, for example, that individuals accused in the most serious cases be allowed to present their case before a grand jury, a group of citizens charged with determining whether enough evidence exists for a case to go to trial. The Fifth Amendment also states that "No person shall be . . . compelled in any criminal case to be a witness against himself." "Taking the Fifth" is shorthand for exercising one's constitutional right not to self-incriminate. The Supreme Court has interpreted this guarantee to be "as broad as the mischief against which it seeks to guard," finding that criminal defendants do not have to take the stand at trial to answer questions, nor can a judge make mention of their failure to do so as evidence of guilt.[64] Moreover, lawyers cannot imply that a defendant who refuses to take the stand must be guilty or have something to hide.

This right not to incriminate oneself also means that prosecutors cannot use as evidence in a trial any of a defendant's statements or confessions that he or she did not make voluntarily. As is the case in many areas of law, however, judicial interpretation of the term "voluntary" has changed over time.

In earlier times, it was not unusual for police to beat defendants to obtain their confessions. In 1936, however, the Supreme Court ruled that convictions for murder based solely on confessions given after physical beatings were unconstitutional.[65] Police then began to resort to other measures for forcing confessions. Defendants, for example, faced questioning for hours on end with no sleep or food, or threats of physical violence until they were mentally beaten into giving confessions.

Miranda v. *Arizona* **(1966)** was the Supreme Court's response to coercive efforts used in obtaining confessions that were not truly voluntary. On March 3, 1963, an eighteen-year-old girl was kidnapped and raped on the outskirts of Phoenix, Arizona. Ten days later, police arrested Ernesto Miranda, a poor, mentally disturbed man with a ninth-grade education. In a police-station lineup, the victim identified Miranda as her attacker. Police then took Miranda to a separate room and questioned him for two hours. At first he denied guilt. Eventually, however, he confessed to the crime and wrote and signed a brief statement describing the crime and admitting his guilt. At no time did police tell him that he did not have to answer any questions or that he could be represented by an attorney.

After Miranda's conviction, his case was appealed on the grounds that his Fifth Amendment right not to incriminate himself had been violated because the police had coerced his confession. Writing for the Court, Chief Justice Earl Warren, himself a former district attorney and a former California state attorney general, noted that because police have a tremendous advantage in any interrogation situation, the law must grant criminal suspects greater protection. A confession obtained in the manner of Miranda's was not truly voluntary; thus, it was inadmissible at trial.

To provide guidelines for police to implement *Miranda*, the Court mandated that: "Prior to any questioning, the person must be warned that he has a right to remain silent, that any statements he does make may be used as evidence against him, and that he has a right to the presence of an attorney, either retained or appointed."[66] In response to this mandate from the Court, police routinely began to read suspects what are now called their *Miranda* **rights,** a practice you undoubtedly have seen repeated over and over in movies and TV police dramas.

Fifth Amendment

Part of the Bill of Rights that imposes a number of restrictions on the federal government with respect to the rights of persons suspected of committing a crime. It provides for indictment by a grand jury and protection against self-incrimination, and prevents the national government from denying a person life, liberty, or property without the due process of law. It also prevents the national government from taking property without just compensation.

Miranda **v.** *Arizona* **(1966)**

A landmark Supreme Court ruling holding that the Fifth Amendment requires individuals arrested for a crime to be advised of their right to remain silent and to have counsel present.

Miranda **rights**

Statements required of police that inform a suspect of his or her constitutional rights protected by the Fifth Amendment, including the right to an attorney provided by the court if the suspect cannot afford one.

double jeopardy clause
Part of the Fifth Amendment that protects individuals from being tried twice for the same offense in the same jurisdiction.

exclusionary rule
Judicially created rule that prohibits police from using illegally seized evidence at trial.

Sixth Amendment
Part of the Bill of Rights that sets out the basic requirements of procedural due process for federal courts to follow in criminal trials. These include speedy and public trials, impartial juries, trials in the state where the crime was committed, notice of the charges, the right to confront and obtain favorable witnesses, and the right to counsel.

Although the Burger Court did not enforce the reading of *Miranda* rights as vehemently as had the Warren Court, Chief Justice Warren E. Burger, Warren's successor, acknowledged that they had become an integral part of established police procedures.[67] The more conservative Rehnquist and Roberts Courts, however, have been more willing to weaken *Miranda* rights, allowing coerced confessions and employing much more flexible standards for the admission of evidence.[68]

The Fifth Amendment also mandates: "nor shall any person be subject for the same offense to be twice put in jeopardy of life or limb." Called the **double jeopardy clause,** it protects individuals from being tried twice for the same crime in the same jurisdiction. Thus, if a jury acquits a defendant of a murder charge, the defendant cannot be retried in that jurisdiction for the offense even if new information is unearthed that could further point to guilt. But, if a defendant was tried in a state court, he or she could still face charges in a federal court or vice versa.

The Fourth and Fifth Amendments and the Exclusionary Rule

In *Weeks* v. *U.S.* (1914), the U.S. Supreme Court adopted the **exclusionary rule,** which bars the use of illegally seized evidence at trial. Thus, although the Fourth and Fifth Amendments do not prohibit the use of evidence obtained in violation of their provisions, the exclusionary rule is a judicially created remedy to deter constitutional violations. In *Weeks,* for example, the Court reasoned that allowing police and prosecutors to use the "fruits of a poisonous tree" (a tainted search) would only encourage that activity.[69]

In balancing the need to deter police misconduct against the possibility that guilty individuals could go free, the Warren Court decided that deterring police misconduct was more important. In *Mapp* v. *Ohio* (1961), the Warren Court ruled "all evidence obtained by searches and seizures in violation of the Constitution, is inadmissible in a state court."[70] This historic and controversial case put law enforcement officers on notice that if they violated any constitutional rights in the search for evidence, their efforts would be for naught because federal or state trials could not accept tainted evidence.

In 1976, the Court noted that the exclusionary rule "deflects the truth-finding process and often frees the guilty."[71] Since then, the Court has carved out a variety of limited "good faith exceptions" to the exclusionary rule, allowing the use of tainted evidence in a variety of situations, especially when police have a search warrant and, in good faith, conduct the search on the assumption that the warrant is valid, even though it is subsequently found invalid. Since the purpose of the exclusionary rule is to deter police misconduct, and in this situation no police misconduct exists, the courts have permitted introduction of the seized evidence at trial. Another exception to the exclusionary rule is "inevitable discovery." Courts may allow illegally seized evidence if such evidence would likely have been discovered in the course of continuing investigation.

The Sixth Amendment and the Right to Counsel

The **Sixth Amendment** guarantees to an accused person "the Assistance of Counsel in his defense." In the past, this guarantee meant only that an individual could hire an attorney to represent him or her in court. Since most criminal defendants are too poor to hire private lawyers, this provision gave little assistance to many who found themselves on trial. Recognizing this, Congress required federal courts to provide an attorney for defendants who could not afford one. Capital cases (in which the death penalty is a possibility) were the first to require this provision;[72] eventually, in all federal criminal cases, the poor received legal counsel.[73] The Court also began to expand the right to counsel to other state offenses but did so in a piecemeal fashion that gave the states little direction. Given the high cost of legal counsel, this ambiguity often made it cost-effective for the states not to provide counsel at all.

Take a Closer Look

The due process rights contained in the Fourth, Fifth, Sixth, and Eighth Amendments to the U.S. Constitution provide a variety of protections for those accused of a crime. Perhaps nowhere are these privileges on display more than in the American courtroom, as shown in the photo below.

The Sixth Amendment provides a right to a trial by jury. This is the jury box.

The Sixth Amendment provides for a right to counsel for the accused. The defense sits to the judge's right, and the prosecution to the left.

The Sixth Amendment provides for a right to a speedy, public, and impartial trial in a court of law. According to the Fifth Amendment, however, no one may be tried twice for the same crime.

The Fifth Amendment prevents defendants from self-incrimination, but they may voluntarily take the stand. The Sixth Amendment provides for the right to confront witnesses.

The judge plays a crucial role in the sentencing process. The Eighth Amendment protects against excessive fines and bail, as well as cruel and unusual punishment.

CRITICAL THINKING QUESTIONS

1. Do the accused have any rights beyond those highlighted in this photo? Are those rights reflected or protected anywhere in the courtroom?

2. What observations can you make about the geography of the courtroom? How does the utilization of space reflect the goals of the American judicial system?

3. Does the American judicial system provide too many protections for those accused of a crime? Should suspected criminals be guilty until proven innocent?

Eighth Amendment
Part of the Bill of Rights that states: "Excessive bail shall not be required, nor excessive fines imposed, nor cruel and unusual punishments inflicted."

These ambiguities came to an end with the Court's decision in *Gideon* v. *Wainwright* (1963).[74] Writing for the Court, Justice Hugo Black explained, "lawyers in criminal courts are necessities, not luxuries." Therefore, the Court concluded, the state must provide an attorney to indigent defendants in felony cases. In emphasis of the Court's point, the jury acquitted Gideon when he was retried with a lawyer to argue his case.

The Burger and Rehnquist Courts gradually expanded the *Gideon* rule. The justices first applied this standard to cases that were not felonies[75] and, later, to many cases in which probation and future penalties were possibilities. In 2008, the Court also ruled that the right to counsel began at the accused's first appearance before a judge.[76]

The issue of legal representation also extends to questions of competence. Various courts have held that lawyers who fell asleep during trial, failed to put forth a defense, or were drunk during the proceedings were "adequate." In 2005, however, the Supreme Court ruled that the Sixth Amendment's guarantees required lawyers to take reasonable steps to prepare for their clients' trial and sentencing, including examination of their prior criminal history.[77]

☐ The Sixth Amendment and Jury Trials

The Sixth Amendment (and, to a lesser extent, Article III of the Constitution) provides that a person accused of a crime shall enjoy the right to a speedy and public trial by an impartial jury—that is, a trial in which a group of the accused's peers act as a fact-finding, deliberative body to determine guilt or innocence. It also gives defendants the right to confront witnesses against them. The Supreme Court has held that jury trials must be available if a prison sentence of six or more months is possible.

Impartiality is a requirement of jury trials that has undergone significant change, with the method of jury selection being the most frequently challenged part of the process. Historically, lawyers had used peremptory challenges (those for which no cause needs to be given) to exclude minorities from juries, especially when the defendant was a member of a minority group. In 1954, for example, the U.S. Supreme Court ruled that Hispanics were entitled to a jury trial that included other Hispanics.[78] And, in 1986, the Court ruled that the use of peremptory challenges specifically to exclude African American jurors violated the equal protection clause of the Fourteenth Amendment.[79]

In 1994, the Supreme Court answered the major remaining question about jury selection: can lawyers exclude women from juries through their use of peremptory challenges? This question arose frequently because in rape trials and sex discrimination cases, one side or another often considers it advantageous to select jurors on the basis of their sex. The Supreme Court ruled that the equal protection clause prohibits discrimination in jury selection on the basis of gender. Thus, lawyers cannot strike all potential male jurors because of the belief that males might be more sympathetic to the arguments of a man charged in a paternity suit, a rape trial, or a domestic violence suit, for example.[80]

The right to confront witnesses at trial also is protected by the Sixth Amendment. In 1990, however, the Supreme Court ruled that this right was not absolute, and the testimony of a six-year-old alleged child abuse victim via one-way closed-circuit TV was permissible. The clause's central purpose, said the Court, was to ensure the reliability of testimony by subjecting it to rigorous examination in an adversarial proceeding.[81] In this case, the child was questioned out of the presence of the defendant, who was in communication with his defense and prosecuting attorneys. The defendant, along with the judge and jury, watched the testimony.

☐ The Eighth Amendment and Cruel and Unusual Punishment

Among its protections, the **Eighth Amendment** prohibits "cruel and unusual punishments," a concept rooted in the English common-law tradition. Today the United States is the only western nation to put people to death for committing crimes. Not

HOW DO STATES VARY IN THEIR APPLICATION OF THE DEATH PENALTY?

This cartoon offers a social commentary on the frequent administration of the death penalty in Texas, which leads the nation in the number of executions. The state of Texas has accounted for a third of the nation's executions since 1976, a fact that is particularly remarkable after considering that the death penalty is illegal in sixteen states and rarely used in many others.

surprisingly, tremendous state-by-state differences exist in the imposition of the death penalty. Texas leads the nation in the number of executions each year.

In the 1960s, the NAACP (National Association for the Advancement of Colored People) Legal Defense and Educational Fund (LDF), believing that African Americans received the death penalty more frequently than members of other groups, orchestrated a carefully designed legal attack on its constitutionality.[82] Public opinion polls revealed that in 1971, on the eve of the LDF's first major death sentence case to reach the Supreme Court, public support for the death penalty had fallen below 50 percent. With the timing just right, in *Furman v. Georgia* (1972), the Supreme Court effectively put an end to capital punishment, at least in the short run.[83] The Court ruled that because the death penalty often was imposed in an arbitrary manner, it constituted cruel and unusual punishment in violation of the Eighth and Fourteenth Amendments. Following *Furman,* several state legislatures enacted new laws designed to meet the Court's objections to the arbitrary nature of the sentence. In 1976, in *Gregg v. Georgia,* the Supreme Court in a 7–2 decision ruled that Georgia's rewritten death penalty statute was constitutional.[84]

Although as recently as 2008 the Supreme Court has upheld the constitutionality of the death penalty by lethal injection,[85] it has made some exceptions. The Court, for example, has exempted two key classes of people from the death penalty: those who are what the law calls mentally retarded and those under the age of eighteen.[86]

PROTECTING THE WRONGFULLY CONVICTED At the state level, a move to at least stay executions gained momentum in March 2000, when Governor George Ryan (R–IL) ordered a moratorium on all executions. Ryan, a death penalty proponent, became disturbed by new evidence collected as a class project by Northwestern University students. The students unearthed information that led to the release of thirteen men on the state's death row. The specter of allowing death sentences to continue in the face of evidence indicating so many wrongful convictions prompted Ryan's much

Should the Government Apply the Death Penalty?

The United States is the only advanced democracy that practices capital punishment. Proponents arg death penalty is a deterrent to violent crimes, but since 1992, public support for it has declined. A m. ericans still believe the death penalty should exist, but there are racial differences among supporters

Death Penalty Supporters by Race

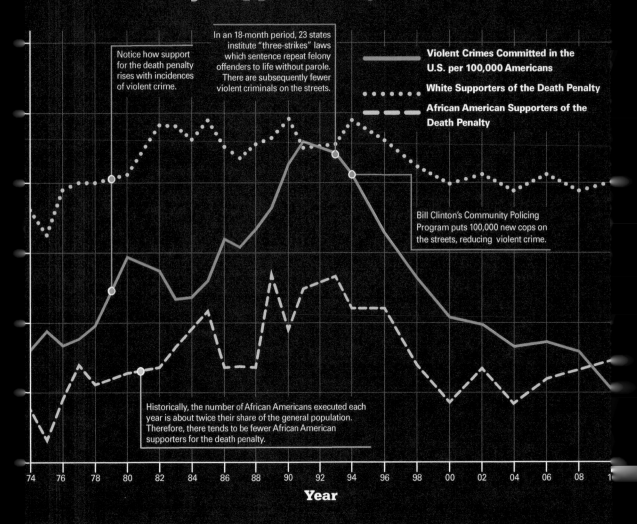

Notice how support for the death penalty rises with incidences of violent crime.

In an 18-month period, 23 states institute "three-strikes" laws which sentence repeat felony offenders to life without parole. There are subsequently fewer violent criminals on the streets.

Violent Crimes Committed in the U.S. per 100,000 Americans

White Supporters of the Death Penalty

African American Supporters of the Death Penalty

Bill Clinton's Community Policing Program puts 100,000 new cops on the streets, reducing violent crime.

Historically, the number of African Americans executed each year is about twice their share of the general population. Therefore, there tends to be fewer African American supporters for the death penalty.

Year

JRCE: Data from General Social Survey, 1972-2010; Bureau of Justice Statistics, U.S. Department of Justice.

Investigate Further

Concept How widespread is erican support for using the death alty? A majority of Americans endorse ital punishment, but support is stronger ong whites than African Americans. The al disparities are due in part to the fact African Americans are more likely to be death row than non-Hispanic whites.

Connection Is support for the death penalty related to lower crime rates? When violent crime goes up nationally, so does support for the death penalty because supporters believe it will decrease the crime rate. However, this effect is contested by death penalty opponents and those who see other explanations for less crime.

Cause Are there any co explanations for the decline of besides the death penalty? The least two non-death penalty re for the decline of crime: increa spending to put more cops on and states using stiffer senten repeat felony offenders.

publicized action. Soon thereafter, the Democratic governor of Maryland followed suit after receiving evidence that blacks were much more likely to be sentenced to death than whites; however, the Republican governor who succeeded him lifted the stay.

Before leaving office in January 2003, Illinois Governor Ryan continued his anti–death-penalty crusade by commuting the sentences of 167 death-row inmates, giving them life in prison instead. This action constituted the single largest anti–death-penalty action since the Court's decision in *Gregg*, and it spurred national conversation on the death penalty, which, in recent polls, has seen its lowest levels of support since 1978.

In another effort to verify that those on death row are not there in error, several states offer free DNA testing to death-row inmates. The U.S. Supreme Court recognized the potential exculpatory power of DNA evidence in *House* v. *Bell* (2006). In this case, the Court ruled that a Tennessee death-row inmate who had exhausted other federal appeals was entitled to an exception to more stringent federal appeals rules because DNA and related evidence suggested his innocence.[87] The Supreme Court, further, has ruled that although inmates do not have an automatic right to DNA testing, it is within their civil rights to file a lawsuit seeking this relief.[88]

right to privacy
The right to be left alone; a judicially created principle encompassing a variety of individual actions protected by the penumbras cast by several constitutional amendments, including the First, Third, Fourth, Ninth, and Fourteenth Amendments.

The Right to Privacy

6 Explain the origin and significance of the right to privacy.

To this point, we have discussed rights and freedoms that have been derived from specific guarantees contained in the Bill of Rights. However, the U.S. Supreme Court also has given protection to rights not enumerated specifically in the Constitution. Although silent about the **right to privacy,** the Bill of Rights contains many indications that the Framers expected some areas of life to be off limits to governmental regulation. The liberty to practice one's religion guaranteed in the First Amendment implies the right to exercise private, personal beliefs. As early as

---

The Living Constitution

The enumeration in the Constitution, of certain rights, shall not be construed to deny or disparage others retained by the people. —NINTH AMENDMENT

This amendment simply reiterates the belief that rights not specifically enumerated in the Bill of Rights exist and are retained by the people. It was added to assuage the concerns of Federalists, such as James Madison, who feared that the enumeration of so many rights and liberties in the first eight amendments to the Constitution would result in the denial of rights that were not enumerated.

Until 1965, the Ninth Amendment was rarely mentioned by the Court. In that year, however, it was used for the first time by the Court as a positive affirmation of a particular liberty—marital privacy. Although privacy is not mentioned in the Constitution, it was—according to the Court—one of those fundamental freedoms that

the drafters of the Bill of Rights implied as retained. Since 1965, the Court has ruled in favor of a host of fundamental liberties guaranteed by the Ninth Amendment, often in combination with other specific guarantees, including the right to have an abortion.

CRITICAL THINKING QUESTIONS

1. How can the U.S. justice system dictate the definition of a fundamental right if the Constitution does not specifically enumerate that right?

2. Are there other implied rights that should be protected by the Ninth Amendment?

1928, Justice Louis Brandeis hailed privacy as "the right to be left alone—the most comprehensive of rights and the right most valued by civilized men."[89] Not until 1965, however, did the Court attempt to explain the origins of this right.

☐ Birth Control

Today, most Americans take access to birth control for granted. Grocery stores sell condoms, and some TV stations air ads for them. Easy access to birth control, however, was not always the case. *Griswold* v. *Connecticut* (1965) involved a challenge to the constitutionality of an 1879 Connecticut law prohibiting the dissemination of information about and/or the sale of contraceptives.[90] In *Griswold*, seven justices decided that various portions of the Bill of Rights, including the First, Third, Fourth, Ninth, and Fourteenth Amendments, cast what the Court called "penumbras" (unstated liberties on the fringes or in the shadow of more explicitly stated rights), thereby creating zones of privacy, including a married couple's right to plan a family. Thus, the Connecticut statute was ruled unconstitutional because it violated marital privacy, a right the Court concluded could be read into the U.S. Constitution through interpreting several amendments.

Later, the Court expanded the right to privacy to include the right of unmarried individuals to have access to contraceptives. "If the right of privacy means anything," wrote Justice William J. Brennan Jr., "it is the right of the individual, married or single, to be free from unwarranted governmental intrusion into matters so fundamentally affecting a person as the decision to bear or beget a child."[91] This right to privacy formed the basis for later decisions from the Court, including the right to secure an abortion.

☐ Abortion

In 1973, in one of the most controversial decisions ever handed down, seven members of the Court agreed that the decision to carry a pregnancy to term is a woman's fundamental right. The woman whose case became the catalyst for pro-choice and pro-life groups was Norma McCorvey, an itinerant circus worker. The mother of a toddler she was

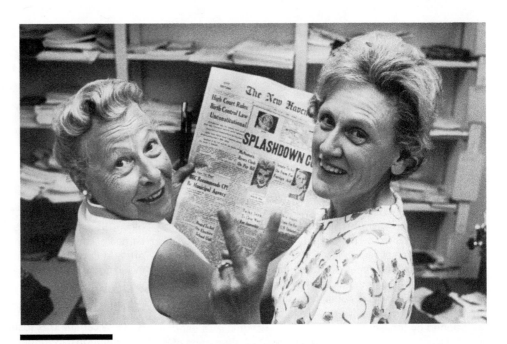

WHAT WAS THE OUTCOME OF *GRISWOLD* V. *CONNECTICUT* (1965)?

In this photo, Estelle Griswold (left), executive director of the Planned Parenthood League of Connecticut, and Cornelia Jahncke, its president, celebrate the Supreme Court's ruling in *Griswold* v. *Connecticut* (1965). *Griswold* invalidated a Connecticut law that made selling contraceptives or disseminating information about contraception to married couples illegal.

unable to care for, McCorvey could not leave another child in her mother's care. So, she decided to terminate her second pregnancy. She was unable to secure a legal abortion, and the conditions she found when seeking an illegal abortion frightened her. McCorvey turned to two young Texas lawyers who were aiming to challenge Texas's restrictive statute and were looking to bring a lawsuit with just such a plaintiff. McCorvey, who was unable to obtain a legal abortion, later gave birth and put the baby up for adoption. Nevertheless, she allowed her lawyers to proceed, with her as their plaintiff. Her lawyers used the pseudonym Jane Roe for McCorvey in their challenge of the Texas law as enforced by Henry Wade, the district attorney for Dallas County, Texas.

When the case finally came before the Supreme Court, Justice Harry A. Blackmun, a former lawyer at the Mayo Clinic, relied heavily on medical evidence to rule that the Texas law violated a woman's constitutionally guaranteed right to privacy, which, he argued, included her decision to terminate a pregnancy. Writing for the majority in *Roe* v. *Wade* (1973), Blackmun divided pregnancy into three stages. In the first trimester, a woman's right to privacy gave her an absolute right (in consultation with her physician), free from state interference, to terminate her pregnancy. In the second trimester, the state's interest in the health of the mother gave it the right to regulate abortions, but only to protect the woman's health. Only in the third trimester—when the fetus becomes potentially viable—did the Court find that the state's interest in potential life outweighed a woman's privacy interests. Even in the third trimester, however, the Court ruled that abortions to save the life or preserve the health of the mother were legal.[92]

From the 1970s through the present, the right to an abortion and its constitutional underpinnings in the right to privacy have been under attack by well-organized pro-life groups. The administrations of Ronald Reagan and George Bush strongly opposed abortions, and their Justice Departments regularly urged the Court to overrule *Roe*. They came close to victory in *Webster* v. *Reproductive Health Services* (1989).[93] In *Webster,* the Court upheld state-required fetal viability tests in the second trimester, even though these tests increased the cost of an abortion considerably. The Court also upheld Missouri's refusal to allow abortions to be performed in state-supported hospitals or by state-funded doctors or nurses. Perhaps most noteworthy, however, was that four justices seemed willing to overrule *Roe* v. *Wade* and that Justice Antonin Scalia publicly rebuked his colleague, Justice Sandra Day O'Connor, then the only woman on the Court, for failing to provide the critical fifth vote to overrule *Roe*.

After *Webster,* states began to enact more restrictive legislation. In *Planned Parenthood of Southeastern Pennsylvania v. Casey* (1992), Justices Sandra Day O'Connor, Anthony Kennedy, and David Souter, in a jointly authored opinion, wrote that Pennsylvania could limit abortions as long as its regulations did not pose "an undue burden" on pregnant women.[94] The narrowly supported standard, by which the Court upheld a twenty-four-hour waiting period and parental consent requirements, did not overrule *Roe*, but clearly limited its scope by abolishing its trimester approach and substituting the undue burden standard for the trimester approach used in *Roe*.

In the early 1990s, newly elected pro-choice President Bill Clinton appointed two supporters of abortion rights, Ruth Bader Ginsburg and Stephen Breyer, to the Supreme Court. Meanwhile, Republican-controlled Congresses made repeated attempts to restrict abortion rights. In March 1996 and again in 1998, Congress passed and sent to President Clinton a bill to ban—for the first time—a specific procedure used in late-term abortions. The president repeatedly vetoed the federal Partial Birth Abortion Ban Act. Many state legislatures, nonetheless, passed their own versions of the law. In 2000, the Supreme Court, however, ruled 5–4 in *Stenberg* v. *Carhart* that a Nebraska partial birth abortion statute was unconstitutionally vague because it failed to contain an exemption for a woman's health. The law, therefore, was unenforceable and called into question the partial birth abortion laws of twenty-nine other states.[95]

But, by October 2003, Republican control of the White House and both houses of Congress facilitated passage of the federal Partial Birth Abortion Ban Act. Pro-choice

Roe v. *Wade* (1973)

The Supreme Court found that a woman's right to an abortion was protected by the right to privacy that could be implied from specific guarantees found in the Bill of Rights applied to the states through the Fourteenth Amendment.

groups immediately filed lawsuits challenging the constitutionality of this law. The Supreme Court heard oral arguments on the challenge to the federal ban the day after the 2006 midterm elections. In a 5–4 decision, *Gonzales* v. *Carhart* (2007), the Roberts Court revealed the direction it was heading in abortion cases. Over the strong objections of Justice Ginsburg, Justice Kennedy's opinion for the majority upheld the federal act, although, like the law at issue in *Stenberg,* it contained no exceptions for the health of the mother. Observers viewed this ruling as a significant step toward reversing *Roe* v. *Wade* altogether.

The Court's decision in *Gonzales* has empowered states to enact abortion regulations with new gusto. In 2010, for example, Nebraska enacted legislation prohibiting most abortions after twenty weeks. Other states, such as Oklahoma, have laws or are considering legislation that requires doctors to show women an ultrasound image of the fetus before they are allowed to abort. And, in Utah, a new law categorizes self-induced abortions as homicide.[96]

The implementation of these and other restrictions on access to abortion are currently the subject of significant litigation. There are, for example, more than ten cases related to the twenty-week ban winding their way through the judicial system. The U.S. Supreme Court is expected to rule on—and likely uphold—these limits as failing to impose an "undue burden" on a pregnant woman.

☐ Homosexuality

Not until 2003 did the U.S. Supreme Court rule that an individual's constitutional right to privacy, which provided the basis for the *Griswold* (contraceptives) and *Roe* (abortion) decisions, prevents states from criminalizing private sexual behavior. This monumental decision invalidated the laws of fourteen states.

In *Lawrence* v. *Texas* (2003), six members of the Court overruled its decision in *Bowers* v. *Hardwick* (1986), which had upheld anti-sodomy laws. They found the Texas law unconstitutional; five justices found it violated fundamental privacy rights.[97] Justice O'Connor agreed that the law was unconstitutional, but concluded it was an equal protection violation. Although Justice Antonin Scalia issued a stinging dissent, charging, "the Court has largely signed on to the so-called homosexual agenda," the majority of the Court was unswayed.

Toward Reform: Civil Liberties and Combating Terrorism

7 Evaluate how reforms to combat terrorism have affected civil liberties.

After September 11, 2001, the George W. Bush administration, Congress, and the courts all operated in what Secretary of State Condoleezza Rice dubbed "an alternate reality," in which Bill of Rights guarantees were suspended in a time of war, just as they had been in the Civil War and in World Wars I and II.[98] The USA PATRIOT Act, the Military Commissions Act, and a series of secret Department of Justice memos all altered the state of civil liberties in the United States. Here, we detail the provisions of these actions, as well as subsequent actions by the Barack Obama administration, and explain how they have affected the civil liberties discussed in this chapter.

☐ The First Amendment

Both the 2001 USA PATRIOT Act and the 2006 Military Commissions Act contain a variety of major and minor interferences with the civil liberties that Americans, as well as those visiting our shores, have come to expect. The USA PATRIOT Act, for example, violates the First Amendment's free speech guarantees by barring those who have been subject to search orders from telling anyone about those orders, even in situations in which no need for secrecy can be proven. It also authorizes the Federal Bureau of Investigation (FBI) to investigate citizens who choose to exercise their freedom of speech, without demonstrating that any parts of their speech might be labeled illegal.

In addition, respect for religious practices fell by the wayside in the wake of the war on terrorism. For example, many Muslim detainees captured in Iraq and Afghanistan were fed pork, a violation of basic Islamic dietary laws. Some were stripped naked in front of members of the opposite sex, another religious violation.

☐ The Fourth Amendment

The USA PATRIOT Act enhances the ability of the government to curtail specific search and seizure restrictions in four areas. First, it allows the government to examine an individual's private records held by third parties. This empowers the FBI to force anyone, including physicians, libraries, bookshops, colleges and universities, and Internet service providers, to turn over all records on a particular individual. Second, it expands the government's right to search private property without notice to the owner. Third, according to the ACLU, the act "expands a narrow exception to the Fourth Amendment that had been created for the collection of foreign intelligence information."[99] Finally, the act expands an exception for spying that collects "addressing information" about where and to whom communications are going, as opposed to what is contained in the documents.

Judicial oversight of these governmental powers is virtually nonexistent. Proper governmental authorities need only certify to a judge, without any evidence, that the requested search meets the statute's broad criteria. Moreover, the legislation deprives judges of the authority to reject such applications.

☐ Due Process Rights

Illegal incarceration and torture are federal crimes, and the Supreme Court ruled in 2004 that detainees have a right of *habeas corpus*.[100] However, the Bush administration argued that under the Military Commissions Act of 2006, alien victims of torture had significantly reduced rights of *habeas corpus*. The Military Commissions Act also eliminated the right to challenge "detention, transfer, treatment, trial, or conditions of confinement" of detainees. It allowed the government to declare permanent resident aliens to be enemy combatants and enabled the government to jail these people indefinitely without any opportunity to file a writ of *habeas corpus*. In 2008, in a surprising setback for the Bush administration, the Roberts Court ruled parts of the act unconstitutional, finding that any detainees could challenge their extended incarceration in federal court.[101]

Secret offshore prisons, known as black sites, have also held many suspected terrorists against their will. In September 2006, President Bush acknowledged the existence of these facilities, moving fourteen such detainees to the detention facility at Guantanamo Bay, Cuba. The conditions of this facility sparked intense debate, as opponents cited numerous accusations of torture as well as possible violations of human rights. Those in support of the continued use of Guantanamo declared the detainees unlawful combatants and not war criminals subject to the provisions of the Geneva Convention. After President Barack Obama took office in 2009, he vowed to close Guantanamo by January 2010 and move detainees to a facility in Illinois. By the end of 2012, however, Guantanamo Bay remained open.

Recent federal activity has also curtailed the Sixth Amendment right to trial by jury. Those people detained as enemy combatants often do not have access to the evidence against them and are subject to coercion or torture in the gathering of additional evidence. Trials of enemy combatants are closed, and people tried in these courts do not have a right to an attorney of their choosing. The Supreme Court limited the federal government's activity in these tribunals, but the Military Commissions Act returned these powers to the executive branch.[102] The Obama administration, to the surprise of many observers, also has done little to restore the rights revoked by these acts and has, in fact, further limited some detainees' ability to challenge their incarceration.

Finally, great controversy has surrounded the Eighth Amendment's prohibition on cruel and unusual punishment. Since shortly after the terrorist attacks of September 11, 2001, rumors abounded that many prisoners detained by the U.S. government faced inhumane treatment. In 2004, for example, photos of cruel treatment of prisoners held by the U.S. military in Abu Ghraib, Iraq surfaced. These photos led to calls for investigations at all levels of government. On the heels of this incident, the Justice Department declared torture "abhorrent" in a December 2004 legal memo. That position lasted but a short time. After Alberto Gonzales was sworn in as attorney general in February 2005, the Department of Justice issued a secret memo endorsing harsh interrogation techniques. According to one Justice Department memo, interrogation practices were not considered illegal unless they produced pain equivalent to that with organ failure or death. Among the techniques authorized by the government were combinations of "painful physical and psychological tactics, including head-slapping, simulated drowning, and frigid temperatures."[103] The most controversial of these techniques is waterboarding, which simulates drowning. Although the Obama administration has harshly attacked the use of such tactics and techniques, it announced that those who committed these acts during the Bush administration would not be prosecuted.[104]

On MyPoliSciLab

Review the Chapter

 Listen to **Chapter** on **MyPoliSciLab**

Roots of Civil Liberties: The Bill of Rights

 1   Trace the constitutional roots of civil liberties.

Most of the Framers originally opposed the Bill of Rights. Anti-Federalists, however, continued to stress the need for a bill of rights during the drive for ratification of the Constitution, and some states tried to make their ratification contingent on the addition of a bill of rights. Thus, during its first session, Congress sent the first ten amendments to the Constitution, the Bill of Rights, to the states for their ratification. Later, the addition of the Fourteenth Amendment allowed the Supreme Court to apply some of the amendments to the states through a process called selective incorporation.

First Amendment Guarantees: Freedom of Religion

2   Describe the First Amendment guarantee of freedom of religion.

The First Amendment guarantees freedom of religion. The establishment clause, which prohibits the national government from establishing a religion, does not, according to Supreme Court interpretation, create an absolute wall between church and state. While the national and state governments may generally not give direct aid to religious groups, the Court has held that many forms of aid, especially those that benefit children, are constitutionally permissible. In contrast, the Court has generally barred mandatory prayer in public schools. The Court has allowed some governmental regulation of religious practices under the free exercise clause.

First Amendment Guarantees: Freedoms of Speech, Press, Assembly, and Petition

3 | Outline the First Amendment guarantees of and limitations on freedom of speech, press, assembly, and petition.

Historically, one of the most volatile subjects of constitutional interpretation has been the First Amendment's mandate that "Congress shall make no law . . . abridging the freedom of speech or of the press." As with the establishment and free exercise clauses of the First Amendment, the Court has not interpreted the speech and press clauses as absolute bans against government regulation. The Supreme Court has ruled against prior restraint, thus protecting freedom of the press. The Court has also protected symbolic speech and hate speech as long as they do not become action. Areas of speech and publication unprotected by the First Amendment include libel, fighting words, and obscenity and pornography. The freedoms of peaceable assembly and petition are directly related to the freedoms of speech and the press. As with other First Amendment rights, the Supreme Court has become the arbiter between the people's right to dissent and the government's need to promote security.

The Second Amendment: The Right to Keep and Bear Arms

4 | Summarize changes in the interpretation of the Second Amendment right to keep and bear arms.

Initially, the right to bear arms was envisioned in terms of state militias. Over the years, states and Congress have enacted various gun ownership restrictions with little Supreme Court interpretation. However, the Court ruled in *D.C.* v. *Heller* (2008) and *McDonald* v. *City of Chicago* (2010) that the Second Amendment protects an individual's right to own a firearm.

The Rights of Criminal Defendants

5 | Analyze the rights of criminal defendants found in the Bill of Rights.

The Fourth, Fifth, Sixth, and Eighth Amendments provide a variety of procedural guarantees to individuals accused of crimes. The Fourth Amendment prohibits unreasonable searches and seizures, and the Court has generally refused to allow evidence seized in violation of this safeguard to be used at trial. The Fifth Amendment protects those who have been charged with crimes. It mandates the use of grand juries in cases of serious crimes. It also guarantees that "no person shall be compelled to be a witness against himself." The Supreme Court has interpreted this provision to require the government to inform the accused of his or her right to remain silent. The Court has also interpreted this provision to require exclusion of illegally obtained confessions at trial. Finally, the Fifth Amendment's double jeopardy clause protects individuals from being tried twice for the same crimes in the same jurisdiction. The Court's interpretation of the Sixth Amendment's guarantee of "assistance of counsel" stipulates that the government provide counsel to defendants unable to pay for it in cases subject to prison sentences. The Sixth Amendment also requires an impartial jury, although the meaning of impartial continues to evolve through judicial interpretation. The judicial view is that the Eighth Amendment's ban against "cruel and unusual punishments" does not bar imposition of the death penalty.

The Right to Privacy

6 | Explain the origin and significance of the right to privacy.

The right to privacy is a judicially created right carved from the penumbras (unstated liberties implied by more explicitly stated rights) of several amendments, including the First, Third, Fourth, Ninth, and Fourteenth Amendments. The Court has found statutes that limit access to birth control, prohibit abortion, and ban homosexual acts to be unconstitutional under this right.

Toward Reform: Civil Liberties and Combating Terrorism

7 | Evaluate how reforms to combat terrorism have affected civil liberties.

After the terrorist attacks of September 11, 2001, Congress and the executive branch enacted reforms that dramatically altered civil liberties in the United States. Critics charge that the changes have significantly compromised a host of constitutional guarantees, while supporters say that they are necessary to protect national security in a time of war.

Learn the Terms

 Study and **Review** the **Flashcards**

bill of attainder
Bill of Rights
civil liberties
civil rights
clear and present danger test
direct incitement test
double jeopardy clause
due process clause
Eighth Amendment
establishment clause
exclusionary rule
ex post facto law
Fifth Amendment

fighting words
First Amendment
Fourth Amendment
free exercise clause
fundamental freedoms
incorporation doctrine
Lemon test
libel
Miranda rights
Miranda v. *Arizona* (1966)
New York Times Co. v. *Sullivan*
   (1964)
Ninth Amendment

prior restraint
right to privacy
Roe v. *Wade* (1973)
selective incorporation
Sixth Amendment
slander
substantive due process
symbolic speech
Tenth Amendment
writ of *habeas corpus*

Test Yourself

 Study and **Review** the **Practice Tests**

1. Which amendment did the Court use to make some provisions of the Bill of Rights applicable to the states?

a. Fifth

b. Tenth

c. Eleventh

d. Fourteenth

e. Fifteenth

2. Which of the following was NOT used as an argument against adding a bill of rights to the Constitution?

a. A constitutional republic is founded upon the idea of popular sovereignty and inalienable rights.

b. Federal guarantees were unnecessary because most state constitutions contained their own bills of rights.

c. The government should not enumerate what it could not do.

d. A national bill of rights would be nearly impossible to enforce.

e. The Constitution already contained protections for individual rights.

3. The U.S. Supreme Court has interpreted the establishment clause to mean that

a. reciting prayer in classrooms is constitutional, as long as the prayer is nondenominational.

b. state university grounds cannot be used for worship.

c. a privately owned display of the Ten Commandments in a courthouse is unconstitutional.

d. faculty-led prayer at high school football games is constitutional.

e. governments may provide aid to religious schools as long as the aid goes to children and not to religious goals.

4. Which form of speech is protected under the First Amendment?

a. Libel

b. Symbolic speech

c. Slander

d. Fighting words

e. Obscenity

5. Which is NOT considered a protected form of speech?

a. Carrying a "Bong Hits 4 Jesus" banner during a school-sanctioned parade

b. Wearing black armbands to protest a war

c. Publishing secret documents in a newspaper

d. Displaying a symbol of opposition to the U.S. government

e. Burning the American flag

6. The U.S. Supreme Court first ruled that the Second Amendment protects an individual's right to own a firearm in certain jurisdictions

a. in the early 1800s, when laws were passed to limit possession of firearms by slaves.

b. when Justice Roger B. Taney considered the right to own and carry arms a basic right of citizenship.

c. in *D.C.* v. *Heller* in 2008.

d. when a law that made sawed-off shotguns illegal was overturned in the 1930s.

e. in *Barron* v. *Baltimore* in 1833.

7. Traditionally, the Supreme Court has ruled that the Fourth Amendment requires a warrant for police to search

a. the person arrested.

b. things in plain view of the accused.

c. employees of the federal or state government.

d. places or things in the arrestee's immediate control.

e. the home of the accused.

8. When suspects are arrested and read their *Miranda* rights, the authorities are informing them of their _____ Amendment rights.

a. Second

b. Third

c. Fourth

d. Fifth

e. Seventh

9. The U.S. Supreme Court ruled that the controversial 2003 federal Partial Birth Abortion Ban Act was

a. a law that could be passed only by the states.

b. unconstitutional because it contained no health exceptions for the mother.

c. constitutional despite its lack of a health exception for the mother.

d. unconstitutional because it violated the three-trimester approach created by *Roe* v. *Wade* (1973).

e. constitutional based on the precedent established in *Planned Parenthood of Southeastern Pennsylvania* v. *Casey* (1992).

10. The major act passed in the aftermath of September 11, 2001, to combat terrorism in the United States was the

a. Military Commissions Act.

b. JUSTICE Act.

c. Detention and Retention Act.

d. Habeas Corpus Act.

e. USA PATRIOT Act.

Explore Further

Abrams, Floyd. *Speaking Freely: Trials of the First Amendment*. New York: Viking, 2006.

Ackerman, Bruce. *Before the Next Attack: Preserving Civil Liberties in an Age of Terrorism*. New Haven, CT: Yale University Press, 2007.

Baird, Robert M., and Stuart E. Rosenbaum. *Death Penalty: Debating the Moral, Legal, and Political Issues*. Amherst, NY: Prometheus Books, 2010.

Cole, David, and James X. Dempsey. *Terrorism and the Constitution: Sacrificing Civil Liberties in the Name of National Security*, 3rd ed. Washington, DC: First Amendment Foundation, 2006.

Darmer, M. Katherine B., Robert M. Baird, and Stuart E. Rosenbaum, eds. *Civil Liberties vs. National Security in a Post 9/11 World*. Amherst, NY: Prometheus, 2004.

Gates, Henry Louis, Jr., ed. *Speaking of Race, Speaking of Sex: Hate Speech, Civil Rights, and Civil Liberties*. New York: New York University Press, 1995.

Ivers, Gregg, and Kevin T. McGuire, eds. *Creating Constitutional Change*. Charlottesville: University Press of Virginia, 2004.

Lane, Frederick S. *American Privacy: The 400-Year History of Our Most Contested Right*. Boston: Beacon Press, 2009.

Lendler, Marc. *Gitlow v. New York: Every Idea an Incitement*. Lawrence, Kansas: University Press of Kansas, 2012.

Lewis, Anthony. *Gideon's Trumpet*, reissue ed. New York: Vintage Books, 1989.

———. *Make No Law: The Sullivan Case and the First Amendment*, reprint ed. New York: Random House, 1992.

O'Connor, Karen. *No Neutral Ground: Abortion Politics in an Age of Absolutes*. Boulder, CO: Westview, 1996.

Romero, Anthony D., and Dina Temple-Raston. *In Defense of Our America: The Fight for Civil Liberties in the Age of Terror*. New York: William Morrow, 2007.

Sando, Philippe. *Torture Teams: Rumsfeld's Memo and the Betrayal of American Values*. New York: Palgrave Macmillan, 2008.

Wheeler, Leigh Anne. *How Sex Became a Civil Liberty*. New York: Oxford University Press, 2012.

To learn more about differing views on civil liberties, go to the home pages for the following groups:
American Civil Liberties Union at **www.aclu.org**
People for the American Way at **www.pfaw.org**
American Center for Law and Justice at **www.aclj.org**
The Federalist Society at **www.fed-soc.org**

To learn more about the Supreme Court cases discussed in this chapter, go to Oyez: U.S. Supreme Court Media at **www.oyez.org**, and search on the case name. Or, go to the Legal Information Institute of Cornell University's Law School at **www.law.cornell.edu/supct/cases/topic.htm**, where you can search cases by topic.

To learn more about civil liberties protections for homosexuals, go to Human Rights Campaign at **www.hrc.org**, and Lambda Legal at **www.lambdalegal.org**.

Credits

Answer Key

1. d; 2. e; 3. e; 4. b; 5. a; 6. c; 7. e; 8. d; 9. c; 10. e

Notes

1. *U.S.* v. *Jones,* 564 U.S. ____ (2012); Robert Barnes, "Supreme Court: Warrants Needed in GPS Tracking," *Washington Post* (January 23, 2012).

2. *Florence* v. *Board of Chosen Freeholders of the County of Burlington,* 566 U.S. ____ (2012).

3. The absence of a bill of rights led Mason to refuse to sign the proposed Constitution, noting that he "would sooner chop off his right hand than put it to the Constitution as it now stands." Quoted in Eric Black, *Our Constitution: The Myth That Binds Us* (Boulder, CO: Westview, 1988), 75.

4. Quoted in Jack N. Rakove, "Madison Won Passage of the Bill of Rights but Remained a Skeptic," *Public Affairs Report* (March 1991): 6.

5. *Barron* v. *Baltimore,* 32 U.S. 243 (1833).

6. *Allgeyer* v. *Louisiana,* 165 U.S. 578 (1897).

7. *Gitlow* v. *New York,* 268 U.S. 652 (1925).

8. *Near* v. *Minnesota,* 283 U.S. 697 (1931). For more about *Near,* see Fred W. Friendly, *Minnesota Rag: The Dramatic Story of the Landmark Case That Gave New Meaning to Freedom of the Press* (New York: Random House, 1981).

9. *Palko* v. *Connecticut,* 302 U.S. 319 (1937).

10. *Benton* v. *Maryland,* 395 U.S. 784 (1969).

11. *Zobrest* v. *Catalina Foothills School District,* 506 U.S. 813 (1992).

12. *Engel* v. *Vitale,* 370 U.S. 421 (1962).

13. *Abington School District* v. *Schempp,* 374 U.S. 203 (1963).

14. *Lemon* v. *Kurtzman,* 403 U.S. 602 (1971).

15. *Widmar* v. *Vincent,* 454 U.S. 263 (1981).

16. *Rosenberger* v. *University of Virginia,* 515 U.S. 819 (1995).

17. *Mitchell* v. *Helms,* 530 U.S. 793 (2000).

18. *Zelman* v. *Simmons-Harris,* 536 U.S. 639 (2002).

19. *Lee* v. *Weisman,* 505 U.S. 577 (1992).

20. *McCreary County* v. *ACLU of Kentucky,* 545 U.S. 844 (2005).

21. *Salazar* v. *Buono,* 559 U.S. ____ (2010).

22. *U.S.* v. *Seeger,* 380 U.S. 163 (1965).

23. *Cruz* v. *Beto,* 405 U.S. 319 (1972).

24. *O'Lone* v. *Shabazz,* 482 U.S. 342 (1987).

25. *Employment Division, Dept. of Human Resources of Oregon* v. *Smith,* 494 U.S. 872 (1990).

26. David M. O'Brien, *Constitutional Law and Politics,* vol. 2: *Civil Rights and Civil Liberties* (New York: Norton, 1991), 345.

27. *Schenck* v. *U.S.,* 249 U.S. 47 (1919).

28. *Brandenburg* v. *Ohio,* 395 U.S. 444 (1969).

29. *New York Times Co.* v. *U.S.,* 403 U.S. 713 (1971).

30. *Nebraska Press Association* v. *Stuart,* 427 U.S. 539 (1976).

31. *Abrams* v. *U.S.,* 250 U.S. 616 (1919).

32. *Stromberg* v. *California,* 283 U.S. 359 (1931).

33. *Tinker* v. *Des Moines Independent Community School District,* 393 U.S. 503 (1969).

34. *Morse* v. *Frederick,* 551 U.S. 393 (2007).

35. *R.A.V.* v. *City of St. Paul,* 505 U.S. 377 (1992).

36. *Virginia* v. *Black,* 538 U.S. 343 (2003).

37. *Chaplinsky* v. *New Hampshire,* 315 U.S. 568 (1942).

38. *New York Times Co.* v. *Sullivan,* 376 U.S. 254 (1964).

39. *Chaplinsky* v. *New Hampshire,* 315 U.S. 568 (1942).

40. *Miller* v. *California,* 413 U.S. 15 (1973).

41. *Barnes* v. *Glen Theater,* 501 U.S. 560 (1991).

42. *Reno* v. *American Civil Liberties Union,* 521 U.S. 844 (1997); David G. Savage, "Ban on 'Virtual' Child Porn Is Upset by Court," *Los Angeles Times* (April 17, 2002): A1; and *Ashcroft* v. *American Civil Liberties Union,* 542 U.S. 656 (2004).

43. *U.S.* v. *Williams,* 553 U.S. 285 (2008).

44. *DeJonge* v. *Oregon,* 229 U.S. 353 (1937).

45. *Barron* v. *Baltimore,* 32 U.S. 243 (1833).

46. *Dred Scott* v. *Sandford,* 60 U.S. 393 (1857).

47. *U.S.* v. *Miller,* 307 U.S. 174 (1939).

48. *D.C.* v. *Heller,* 554 U.S. 290 (2008).

49. *Heller* v. *District of Columbia,* civil action 08-1289 (2010).

50. *McDonald* v. *City of Chicago,* 561 U.S. ____ (2010).

51. *U.S.* v. *Sokolov,* 490 U.S. 1 (1989).

52. *Georgia* v. *Randolph,* 547 U.S. 103 (2006).

53. *Hester* v. *U.S.*, 265 U.S. 57 (1924).
54. *Johnson* v. *U.S.*, 333 U.S. 10 (1948).
55. *Michigan* v. *Tyler*, 436 U.S. 499 (1978).
56. *Carroll* v. *U.S.*, 267 U.S. 132 (1925).
57. *U.S.* v. *Arvizu*, 534 U.S. 266 (2002).
58. *South Dakota* v. *Neville*, 459 U.S. 553 (1983).
59. *Arizona* v. *Gant*, 556 U.S. 332 (2009).
60. *United States* v. *Jones*, 564 U.S. _____ (2012).
61. *Skinner* v. *Railway Labor Executives' Association*, 489 U.S. 602 (1989).
62. *Vernonia School District* v. *Acton*, 515 U.S. 646 (1995).
63. *Board of Education of Independent School District No. 92 of Pottawatomie County* v. *Earls*, 536 U.S. 822 (2002).
64. *Counselman* v. *Hitchcock*, 142 U.S. 547 (1892).
65. *Brown* v. *Mississippi*, 297 U.S. 278 (1936).
66. *Miranda* v. *Arizona*, 384 U.S. 436 (1966).
67. *Rhode Island* v. *Innis*, 446 U.S. 291 (1980).
68. *Arizona* v. *Fulminante*, 499 U.S. 279 (1991).
69. *Weeks* v. *U.S.*, 232 U.S. 383 (1914).
70. *Mapp* v. *Ohio*, 367 U.S. 643 (1961).
71. *Stone* v. *Powell*, 428 U.S. 465 (1976).
72. *Powell* v. *Alabama*, 287 U.S. 45 (1932).
73. *Johnson* v. *Zerbst*, 304 U.S. 458 (1938).
74. *Gideon* v. *Wainwright*, 372 U.S. 335 (1963).
75. *Argersinger* v. *Hamlin*, 407 U.S. 25 (1972).
76. *Rothgery* v. *Gillespie County*, 554 U.S. 191 (2008).
77. *Rompilla* v. *Beard*, 545 U.S. 374 (2005).
78. *Hernandez* v. *Texas*, 347 U.S. 475 (1954).
79. *Batson* v. *Kentucky*, 476 U.S. 79 (1986).
80. *J.E.B.* v. *Alabama*, 511 U.S. 127 (1994).
81. *Maryland* v. *Craig*, 497 U.S. 836 (1990).
82. See Michael Meltsner, *Cruel and Unusual: The Supreme Court and Capital Punishment* (New York: Random House, 1973).
83. *Furman* v. *Georgia*, 408 U.S. 238 (1972).
84. *Gregg* v. *Georgia*, 428 U.S. 153 (1976).
85. *Baze* v. *Rees*, 553 U.S. 35 (2008).
86. *Atkins* v. *Virginia*, 536 U.S. 304 (2002); and *Roper* v. *Simmons*, 543 U.S. 551 (2005).
87. *House* v. *Bell*, 547 U.S. 518 (2006).
88. *Skinner* v. *Switzer*, 562 U.S. _____ (2011).
89. *Olmstead* v. *U.S.*, 277 U.S. 438 (1928).
90. *Griswold* v. *Connecticut*, 381 U.S. 481 (1965).
91. *Eisenstadt* v. *Baird*, 410 U.S. 113 (1972).
92. *Roe* v. *Wade*, 410 U.S. 113 (1973).
93. *Webster* v. *Reproductive Health Services*, 492 U.S. 490 (1989).
94. *Planned Parenthood of Southeastern Pennsylvania* v. *Casey*, 505 U.S. 833 (1992).
95. *Stenberg* v. *Carhart*, 530 U.S. 914 (2000).
96. Alison Young, "States Seek New Ways to Restrict New Abortions," *USA Today* (April 26, 2010): 1A.
97. *Bowers* v. *Hardwick*, 478 U.S. 186 (1986); and *Lawrence* v. *Texas*, 539 U.S. 558 (2003).
98. Jennifer Levin, "Alternative Reality About Public, War," *Associated Press* (May 29, 2007).
99. "Surveillance Under the USA Patriot Act," American Civil Liberties Union, April 3, 2003.
100. *Rasul* v. *Bush*, 542 U.S. 466 (2004).
101. *Boumediene* v. *Bush*, 553 U.S. 723 (2008).
102. *Hamdan* v. *Rumsfeld*, 548 U.S. 557 (2006).
103. Shane Scott, David Johnston, and James Risen, "Secret U.S. Endorsement of Severe Interrogations," *New York Times* (October 7, 2007): A1.
104. Jennifer Loven and Devlin Barrett, "CIA Officials Won't Be Prosecuted for Waterboarding, Obama Admin Says," *Huffington Post* (April 16, 2009), www.huffingtonpost.com.

Civil Rights

Civil Rights

W almart stores are the nation's largest employer, with more than 2 million employees. Of those employees, two-thirds are women. Management at Walmart stores, however, is 86 percent male.

Beginning in 2000, Betty Dukes, a Walmart worker from California, attempted to address this gap in hiring—as well as the resultant gap in men's and women's wages—by filing a case alleging that Walmart engaged in systematic sex discrimination. Dukes claimed that, despite six years of work for the company, she was repeatedly denied opportunities to attend management training seminars. As a result, she was unable to advance from her hourly work to a salaried, better-paying position within the company.

Eventually Dukes joined forces with other female Walmart employees who felt discriminated against on the basis of their sex. Among these was Christine Kwapnoski, a Walmart worker from New Hampshire who, when she asked why she had not been promoted in fifteen years, was told, "Blow the cobwebs off your makeup" and "doll up." Eventually, cases like those filed by Dukes and Kwapnoski reached class action status. Ultimately, the litigants claimed to represent more than 1.6 million women who had worked at Walmart since 1998.

It took more than ten years for the women's case to reach the Supreme Court. In 2011, however, the Court heard and decided the case of *Walmart* v. *Dukes*. Ultimately, in a 5-4 decision, the Court reached no conclusion on the merits of the women's sex discrimination or pay equity claims. Instead, the Court ruled that a group of 1.6 million women was simply too large and too diverse for the suit to move forward as a class action lawsuit. The individual plaintiffs were encouraged to begin litigation again, working on their own to show discrimination by Walmart stores.

Plaintiffs such as Dukes and Kwapnoski have continued to fight in individual suits. But, they are not alone. Experts estimate that more that 12,000 sex discrimination lawsuits against Walmart are still ongoing. In the meantime, critics charge, so is the discrimination and corporate culture that makes a 1.6 million-person class action lawsuit fathomable.

But, pay equity isn't only an issue at Walmart. Across the country, women only make about 75 to 80 cents for every dollar that similarly situated men earn. Despite the passage of well-intentioned legislation such as the Equal Pay Act of 1963, Title VII of the Civil Rights Act of 1964, and the Lilly Ledbetter Fair Pay Act of 2009, many women lack the courage or the ability to speak up

1	**2**	**3**	**4**	**5**	**6**
Trace the efforts from 1800 to 1890 of African Americans and women to win the vote.	Outline developments in African Americans' and women's push for equality from 1890 to 1954.	Analyze the civil rights movement and the effects of the Civil Rights Act of 1964.	Assess statutory and constitutional remedies for discrimination pursued and achieved by the women's rights movement.	Describe how other groups have mobilized in pursuit of their own civil rights.	Evaluate the ongoing debate concerning civil rights and affirmative action.

WOMEN IN THE WORKPLACE The tasks performed by women in the workplace have changed over time. Above, women work in the knitting mills of Lowell, Massachusetts, during the mid-1800s. Below, a female employee stocks shelves at a modern Walmart store.

MyPoliSciLab Videos

 Watch on **MyPoliS**

 The Big Picture How did groups in America realize that they were being discriminated against? And what have they chosen to do about it? Author Karen O'Connor explains why the ongoing struggle for civil rights continues to be a major topic of discussion in American politics.

The Basics Discover whether we have always had civil rights and whether all American citizens have them. Watch as ordinary people answer questions about where our civil rights come from and how we won them. Consider what equal treatment and protection under the law means today.

Have all Americans always had civil rights?

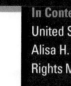 **In Context** Discover how civil rights issues have permeated our society since the United States was founded. In the video, University of Oklahoma political scientist Alisa H. Fryar talks about how civil rights has expanded in scope since the Civil Rights Movement of the twentieth century.

Thinking Like a Political Scientist Where are we headed in terms of civil rights research in the United States? University of Oklahoma political scientist Alisa H. Fryar discusses how current research on voting rights, municipal election methods, and education address civil rights issues.

 In the Real World The Defense of Marriage Act declares that the federal government does not recognize same-sex marriage. Is that constitutional? Hear real people argue both sides as they discuss their beliefs about same-sex marriage, and find out how public opinion has changed dramatically over the years.

So What? Why do women pay more for dry cleaning than men? Author Karen O'Connor dispels the myth that discrimination no longer exists in the United States by looking at the ways men and women are treated, and argues that there is still more to be done to reach equality.

against sex discrimination. When the livelihoods of families and children depend on a paycheck from a working woman, something—even when it is less than what a male counterpart might make—often seems better than nothing. Thus, the issue of pay equity, like other civil rights issues discussed in this chapter, can often be a difficult one for policy makers to tackle.[1]

• • •

Since the Framers wrote the Constitution, concepts of **civil rights**—the government-protected rights of individuals against arbitrary or discriminatory treatment by governments or individuals based on categories such as race, sex, national origin, age, religion, or sexual orientation—have changed dramatically. The Fourteenth Amendment, one of three Civil War Amendments ratified from 1865 to 1870, introduced the notion of equality into the Constitution by specifying that a state could not deny "any person within its jurisdiction equal protection of the laws." Throughout history, the Fourteenth Amendment's equal protection guarantees have been the lynchpin of efforts to expand upon the original intent of the amendment. Today, this amendment protects a variety of groups from discrimination.

Since passage of the Civil War Amendments, the expansion of civil rights to more and more groups has followed a fairly consistent pattern. In this chapter, we will explore how notions of equality and civil rights have changed in the United States.

civil rights
The government-protected rights of individuals against arbitrary or discriminatory treatment by governments or individuals.

Roots of Suffrage: 1800–1890

1 Trace the efforts from 1800 to 1890 of African Americans and women to win the vote.

The period from 1800 to 1890 was one of tremendous change and upheaval in America. Despite the Civil War and the freeing of slaves, the promise of equality guaranteed to African Americans by the Civil War Amendments failed to become a reality. Woman's rights activists also began to make claims for equality, often using the arguments enunciated for the abolition of slavery, but they, too, fell far short of their goals.

□ Slavery and Congress

As the nation grew westward in the early 1800s, conflicts between northern and southern states intensified over the free versus slave status of new states admitted to the union. The first major crisis occurred in 1820, when Missouri applied for admission to the union as a slave state—that is, one in which slavery would be legal. Missouri's admission would have weighted the Senate in favor of slavery and therefore was opposed by northern senators. To resolve this conflict, Congress passed the Missouri Compromise of 1820. The Compromise prohibited slavery north of the geographical boundary at 36 degrees latitude. This act allowed the union to admit Missouri as a slave state. To maintain the balance of slave and free states, Maine was carved out of a portion of Massachusetts.

□ The First Civil Rights Movements: Abolition and Women's Rights

The Missouri Compromise solidified the South in its determination to keep slavery legal, but it also fueled the fervor of those opposing it. William Lloyd Garrison, a white New Englander, galvanized the abolitionist movement in the early 1830s. A newspaper editor, Garrison (along with Arthur Tappan) founded the American Anti-Slavery Society in 1833; by 1838, it had more than 250,000 members. Given the U.S. population today, the National Association for the Advancement of Colored People (NAACP) would need 3.8 million members to have the same kind of overall proportional membership. (In 2013, NAACP membership was approximately 300,000.)

Thirteenth Amendment
One of the three Civil War Amendments; specifically bans slavery in the United States.

Black Codes
Laws denying most legal rights to newly freed slaves; passed by southern states following the Civil War.

Slavery was not the only practice that people began to question in the decades following the Missouri Compromise. In 1840, for example, Elizabeth Cady Stanton and Lucretia Mott, who were to found the first woman's rights movement, attended the 1840 meeting of the World Anti-Slavery Society in London with their husbands. In spite of their long journey, they were not permitted to participate in the convention because they were women. As they sat in a mandated area apart from the male delegates, they compared their status to that of the slaves they sought to free. They concluded that women were not much better off than slaves, and they resolved to address this issue.

The Seneca Falls Convention in 1848 attracted people from other states as well as New York. Attendees passed resolutions demanding the abolition of legal, economic, and social discrimination against women. All of the resolutions reflected the attendees' dissatisfaction with contemporary moral codes; divorce and criminal laws; and the limited opportunities for women in education, the church, medicine, law, and politics. Ironically, only the call for "woman suffrage"—a call to give women the right to vote—failed to win unanimous approval. Most who attended the Seneca Falls Convention continued to press for woman's rights along with the abolition of slavery. Similar conventions took place later across the Northeast and Midwest. At an 1851 meeting in Akron, Ohio, for example, former slave Sojourner Truth delivered her famous "Ain't I a Woman?" speech, calling on women to recognize the plight of their black sisters.

☐ The 1850s: The Calm Before the Storm

By 1850, much had changed in America: the Gold Rush had spurred westward migration, cities grew as people were lured from their farms, railroads and the telegraph increased mobility and communication, and immigrants flooded into the United States. The woman's movement gained momentum, and slavery continued to tear the nation apart. Harriet Beecher Stowe's *Uncle Tom's Cabin*, a novel that depicted the evils of slavery, further inflamed the country. *Uncle Tom's Cabin* sold more than 300,000 copies in 1852. Equivalent sales today would top 4 million copies.

The tremendous national reaction to *Uncle Tom's Cabin*, which later prompted President Abraham Lincoln to call Stowe "the little woman who started the big war," had not yet faded when a new controversy over the Missouri Compromise became the lightning rod for the first major civil rights case addressed by the U.S. Supreme Court. In *Dred Scott* v. *Sandford* (1857)the Court ruled that the Missouri Compromise, which prohibited slavery north of a set geographical boundary, was unconstitutional. Furthermore, the Court added that slaves were not U.S. citizens and, as a consequence, could not bring suits in federal court.

☐ The Civil War and Its Aftermath: Civil Rights Laws and Constitutional Amendments

The Civil War had many causes, but slavery was clearly a key issue. During the war (1861–1865), abolitionists continued to press for an end to slavery. They were partially rewarded when President Abraham Lincoln issued the Emancipation Proclamation, which provided that all slaves in states still in active rebellion against the United States would be freed automatically on January 1, 1863. Designed as a measure to gain favor for the war in the North, the Emancipation Proclamation did not free all slaves—it freed only those who lived in the Confederacy. Complete abolition of slavery did not occur until congressional passage and ultimate ratification of the Thirteenth Amendment in 1865.

The **Thirteenth Amendment** was the first of the three Civil War Amendments. It banned all forms of "slavery [and] involuntary servitude." Although the federal government required the southern states to ratify the Thirteenth Amendment as a condition of readmission to the Union after the war, most former Confederate states passed laws designed to restrict opportunities for newly freed slaves. These **Black Codes** denied most legal rights to newly freed slaves by prohibiting African Americans from voting, sitting on juries, or even appearing in public places. Although Black Codes differed from state to state, all empowered local law enforcement officials to arrest

The Living Constitution

Neither slavery nor involuntary servitude, except as a punishment for crime whereof the party shall have been duly convicted, shall exist within the United States, or any place subject to their jurisdiction. —THIRTEENTH AMENDMENT, SECTION 1

This amendment, the first of three Civil War Amendments, abolished slavery throughout the United States and its territories. It also prohibited involuntary servitude.

Based on his wartime authority, in 1863, President Abraham Lincoln issued the Emancipation Proclamation abolishing slavery in the states that were in rebellion against the United States. Abolishing slavery in the Union, however, proved more challenging. Congress could not end this practice by statute. Thus, the proposed Thirteenth Amendment was forwarded to the states on February 1, 1865. With its adoption, said one of its sponsors, it relieved Congress "of sectional strifes."

Initially, some doubted if any groups other than newly freed African slaves were protected by the provisions of the amendment. Soon, however, the Supreme Court went on to clarify this question by noting: "If Mexican peonage or the Chinese coolie labor system shall develop slavery of the Mexican or Chinese race within our territory, this amendment may safely be trusted to make it void."[a]

In the early 1900s, the Supreme Court was called on several times to interpret section 1 of the amendment,

especially in regard to involuntary servitude. Thus, provisions of an Alabama law that called for criminal sanctions and jail time for defaulting sharecroppers were considered unconstitutional, and Congress enacted a law banning this kind of involuntary servitude.

More recently, the Thirteenth Amendment has been invoked to seek a stop to the estimated 100,000 to 300,000 American children and teens forced into sex trafficking each year. Like some slaves, many of the children are forced to have sex multiple times at the will and for the financial benefit of their "owners." Still, most federal and state programs target helping adults and not the young.

CRITICAL THINKING QUESTIONS

1. Is forcing prison inmates to work as part of a "chain gang" a form of involuntary servitude? Why or why not?

2. Why have the federal and state governments largely failed to stop or minimize the sex trafficking of minors?

[a] *The Slaughterhouse Cases*, 83 U.S. 36 (1873).

unemployed blacks, fine them for vagrancy, and hire them out to employers to satisfy their fines. Some state codes even required African Americans to work on plantations or as domestics. The Black Codes laid the groundwork for Jim Crow laws, which later would institute segregation in all walks of life in the South.

An outraged Congress enacted the Civil Rights Act of 1866 to invalidate some state Black Codes. President Andrew Johnson vetoed the legislation, but—for the first time in history—Congress overrode a presidential veto. The Civil Rights Act formally made African Americans citizens of the United States and gave Congress and the federal courts the power to intervene when states attempted to restrict the citizenship rights of male African Americans in matters such as voting. Congress reasoned that African Americans were unlikely to succeed if they had to file discrimination complaints in state courts, where most judges were elected. Passage of a federal law allowed African Americans to challenge discriminatory state practices in federal courts, where the president appointed judges for life.

Because controversy remained over the constitutionality of the act (since the Constitution gives states the right to determine qualifications of voters), Congress proposed the **Fourteenth Amendment** simultaneously with the Civil Rights Act to guarantee, among other things, citizenship to all freed slaves. Other key provisions of the Fourteenth Amendment barred states from abridging "the privileges or immunities of citizenship" or depriving "any person of life, liberty, or property, without due process of law." Finally, the Fourteenth Amendment includes the **equal protection clause,** which prohibits states from denying "any person within its jurisdiction the equal protection of the laws."

Fourteenth Amendment
One of the three Civil War Amendments; guarantees equal protection and due process of the law to all U.S. citizens.

equal protection clause
Section of the Fourteenth Amendment that guarantees all citizens receive "equal protection of the laws."

Fifteenth Amendment
One of the three Civil War Amendments; specifically enfranchised newly freed male slaves.

Jim Crow laws
Laws enacted by southern states that required segregation in public schools, theaters, hotels, and other public accommodations.

Civil Rights Cases (1883)
Name attached to five cases brought under the Civil Rights Act of 1875. In 1883, the Supreme Court decided that discrimination in a variety of public accommodations, including theaters, hotels, and railroads, could not be prohibited by the act because such discrimination was private, not state, discrimination.

poll tax
A tax levied in many southern states and localities that had to be paid before an eligible voter could cast a ballot.

Unlike the Thirteenth Amendment, which had near-unanimous support in the North, the Fourteenth Amendment faced opposition from many women because it failed to guarantee them suffrage. Congress also passed the **Fifteenth Amendment** in early 1869. It guaranteed the "right of citizens" to vote regardless of their "race, color or previous condition of servitude." Sex was not mentioned.

☐ Civil Rights, Congress, and the Supreme Court

Continued southern resistance to African American equality led Congress to pass the Civil Rights Act of 1875, designed to grant equal access to public accommodations such as theaters, restaurants, and transportation. The act also prohibited the exclusion of African Americans from jury service. But, after federal occupation of the South (Reconstruction) ended in 1877, southern states quickly moved to limit African Americans' access to the ballot. Other forms of discrimination also came about by judicial decisions upholding **Jim Crow laws,** which required segregation in public schools and facilities, including railroads, restaurants, and theaters.

All these laws, at first glance, appeared to conflict with the Civil Rights Act of 1875. In 1883, however, a series of cases decided by the Supreme Court severely damaged the vitality of the 1875 act. The *Civil Rights Cases* (1883) were five separate cases involving convictions of private individuals found to have violated the Civil Rights Act by refusing to extend accommodations to African Americans in theaters, a hotel, and a railroad.[2] In deciding these cases, the Supreme Court ruled that Congress could prohibit only state or governmental action, but not private acts of discrimination. The Court thus concluded that Congress had no authority to outlaw private discrimination in public accommodations. The Court's opinion in the *Civil Rights Cases* provided a moral reinforcement for the Jim Crow system. Southern states viewed the Court's ruling as an invitation to gut the reach and intent of the Thirteenth, Fourteenth, and Fifteenth Amendments.

In devising ways to make certain that African Americans did not vote, southern states had to sidestep the intent of the Fifteenth Amendment. This amendment did not guarantee suffrage; it simply said that states could not deny anyone the right to vote on the basis of race or color. To exclude African Americans in a way that seemed racially neutral, southern states used three devices before the 1890s: (1) **poll taxes** (small taxes on the right to vote that often came due when poor African American

WHAT DID JIM CROW LAWS DO?
Throughout the South, examples of Jim Crow laws abounded. As noted in the text, there were Jim Crow schools, restaurants, hotels, and businesses. Some buildings even had separate "white" and "colored" facilities, such as the public drinking fountains shown here. Notice the obvious difference in quality.

sharecroppers had the least amount of money on hand); (2) some form of property-owning qualifications; and, (3) "literacy" or "understanding" tests, which allowed local voter registration officials to administer difficult reading-comprehension tests to potential voters whom they did not know.

These voting restrictions had an immediate impact. By the late 1890s, black voting fell by 62 percent from the Reconstruction period, while white voting fell by only 26 percent. To make certain these laws did not further reduce the numbers of poor or uneducated white voters, many southern states added a **grandfather clause** to their voting qualification provisions, granting voting privileges to those citizens who failed to pass a wealth or literacy test only if their grandfathers had voted before Reconstruction. Grandfather clauses effectively denied the descendents of slaves the right to vote.

The Push for Equality, 1890–1954

| 2 | Outline developments in African Americans' and women's push for equality from 1890 to 1954. |

The Progressive era (1890–1920) was characterized by a concerted effort to reform political, economic, and social affairs. Evils such as child labor, the concentration of economic power in the hands of a few industrialists, limited suffrage, political corruption, business monopolies, and prejudice against African Americans all were targets of progressive reform. Distress over the inferior legal status of African Americans increased with the U.S. Supreme Court's decision in *Plessy v. Ferguson* **(1896),** a case that some commentators point to as the Court's darkest hour.[3]

In *Plessy,* the Court upheld the constitutionality of a Louisiana law mandating racial segregation on all public trains. The justices based the decision on their belief that separate facilities for blacks and whites provided equal protection of the laws. After all, they reasoned, the Louisiana statute did not prevent Plessy from riding the train; it required only that the races travel separately. Justice John Marshall Harlan was the lone dissenter. He argued that "the Constitution is colorblind" and that it was senseless to hold constitutional a law "which, practically, puts the badge of servitude and degradation upon a large class of our fellow citizens."

Not surprisingly, the separate-but-equal doctrine enunciated in *Plessy v. Ferguson* soon came to mean only separate, as new legal avenues to discriminate against African Americans made their way into law throughout the South. By 1900, equality for African Americans was far from the promise first offered by the Civil War Amendments. Again and again, the Supreme Court nullified the intent of the amendments and sanctioned racial segregation; southern states avidly followed its lead.[4]

☐ The Founding of Key Groups

In 1909, a handful of individuals active in a variety of progressive causes, including woman suffrage and the fight for better working conditions for women and children, met to discuss the idea of a group devoted to addressing the problems of the "Negro." Major race riots had occurred in several American cities, and progressive reformers were concerned about these outbreaks of violence and the possibility of others. Oswald Garrison Villard, the influential publisher of the *New York Evening Post*—and the grandson of William Lloyd Garrison—called a conference to discuss the matter. This group soon evolved into the National Association for the Advancement of Colored People (NAACP).

The NAACP was not the only new group. The struggle for woman's rights was revitalized in 1890, when the National and American Woman Suffrage Associations merged. The new organization, the National American Woman Suffrage Association (NAWSA), was headed by Susan B. Anthony. Unlike NWSA, which had sought a wide

grandfather clause
Voter qualification provision in many southern states that allowed only those citizens whose grandfathers had voted before Reconstruction to vote unless they passed a wealth or literacy test.

Plessy v. *Ferguson* **(1896)**
Supreme Court case that challenged a Louisiana statute requiring that railroads provide separate accommodations for blacks and whites. The Court found that separate-but-equal accommodations did not violate the equal protection clause of the Fourteenth Amendment.

variety of expanded rights for women, this new association largely devoted itself to securing woman suffrage. The proliferation of woman's groups during the Progressive era greatly facilitated its task. In addition to the rapidly growing temperance movement—whose members pressed to ban the sale of alcohol, which many women blamed for a variety of social ills—woman's groups sprang up to seek goals such as maximum hour or minimum wage laws for women, improved sanitation, public morals, and education.

NAWSA based its claim to the right to vote largely on the fact that women, as mothers, should be enfranchised. The new woman's movement—called the **suffrage movement** because of its focus on voting rights—soon took on racist and nativist overtones. Suffragists argued that if undereducated African American men and immigrants could vote, why couldn't women?

By 1917, the new woman's movement had more than 2 million members. In 1920, a coalition of woman's groups, led by NAWSA and the newer, more radical National Woman's Party, was able to secure ratification of the **Nineteenth Amendment** to the Constitution through rallies, protest marches, and the support of President Woodrow Wilson. The Nineteenth Amendment guaranteed all women the right to vote—fifty years after the Fifteenth Amendment had enfranchised African American males.

After passage of the suffrage amendment in 1920, the fragile alliance of diverse woman's groups that had come together to fight for the vote quickly disintegrated. Women returned to their home groups, such as the NCL or the Woman's Christian Temperance Union, to pursue their individualized goals. In fact, after the tumult of the suffrage movement, organized activity on behalf of women's rights did not reemerge in national politics until the 1960s. In the meantime, the NAACP continued to fight racism and racial segregation. Its activities and those of others in the civil rights movement would later give impetus to a new women's movement.

☐ Litigating for Equality

During the 1930s, leaders of the NAACP began to sense that the time was right to launch a full-scale challenge to the constitutionality of *Plessy*'s separate-but-equal doctrine in the federal courts. Clearly, the separate-but-equal doctrine and the proliferation of Jim Crow laws barred any hope of full equality for African Americans. Traditional legislative channels were unlikely to work, given African Americans' limited or nonexistent political power. Thus, the federal courts and a litigation strategy were the NAACP's only hopes. The NAACP mapped out a long-range plan that would first target segregation in professional and graduate education.

TEST CASES The NAACP opted first to challenge the constitutionality of Jim Crow law schools. In 1935, all southern states maintained fully segregated elementary and secondary schools. Colleges and universities also were segregated, and most states did not provide for postgraduate education for African Americans. NAACP lawyers chose to target law schools because they were institutions that judges could well understand, and integration there would prove less threatening to most whites.

Lloyd Gaines, a graduate of Missouri's all-black Lincoln University, sought admission to the all-white University of Missouri Law School in 1936. The school immediately rejected him. In the separate-but-equal spirit, the state offered to build a law school at Lincoln (although no funds were allocated for the project) or, if he did not want to wait, to pay his tuition at an out-of-state law school. Gaines rejected the offer, sued, lost in the lower courts, and appealed to the U.S. Supreme Court.

The attorneys filed Gaines's case at a promising time. As our discussion of federalism illustrates, a constitutional revolution of sorts occurred in Supreme Court decision making in 1937. Prior to this, the Court was most receptive to, and interested in, the protection of economic liberties. In 1937, however, the Court began to regard the protection of individual freedoms and personal liberties as important issues. Thus, in 1938, Gaines's lawyers pleaded his appeal to a far more sympathetic Supreme Court. NAACP attorneys argued that the creation of a separate law school of a laughable lesser caliber than that of the University of Missouri would not and could not afford Gaines an equal

Are All Forms of Discrimination the Same?

In *Loving* v. *Virginia* (1967), the Supreme Court ruled unconstitutional all laws that restricted marriage based solely on race. Today, a similar debate revolves around marriage for same-sex couples. Public opposition to interracial marriage declined dramatically after the Court's decision — as shown in the 1972 and 1988 data. Has opinion about same-sex marriage changed in a similar way?

"Should Interracial Marriage Be Legal?"

1972	REGION	YES	NO
	Northeast	71%	26%
	Midwest	61%	35%
	South	43%	53%
	Rocky Mountains	54%	41%
	Pacific Coast	74%	24%

1988	REGION	YES	NO
	Northeast	85%	11%
	Midwest	76%	21%
	South	62%	35%
	Rocky Mountains	89%	11%
	Pacific Coast	87%	12%

In 2004, Massachusetts became the first state to legalize same-sex marriage. Now, 40% of Americans live in a state where same-sex unions or marriages are legal.

A majority in the South and a sizable minority in the Rocky Mountains supported outlawing interracial marriage.

Today, the Pacific Coast holds a majority of support for same-sex marriage.

By 1988, there was growing and widespread acceptance for interracial marriage, even in the South and Rocky Mountains.

In 1988, solid majorities disagreed with same-sex marriage across the U.S. As of 2012, the strongest prohibitions to same-sex union are found in the South.

"Should Same-Sex Marriage Be Legal?"

1988	REGION	YES	NO
	Northeast	12%	63%
	Midwest	12%	66%
	South	8%	78%
	Rocky Mountains	12%	63%
	Pacific Coast	16%	62%

2010	REGION	YES	NO
	Northeast	54%	30%
	Midwest	50%	41%
	South	38%	46%
	Rocky Mountains	45%	44%
	Pacific Coast	52%	33%

SOURCE: General Social Survey data from 1972, 1988, and 2010.

Investigate Further

Concept How do we measure discrimination of interracial and same-sex marriage? Pollsters ask if a person agrees or disagrees with policy proposals, such as laws that recognize same-sex or interracial marriage. By watching the responses over time, we are able to determine change in public opinion.

Connection How does geography help predict public opinion on interracial marriage and same-sex marriage? The American South and Rocky Mountains are historically more conservative regions, and more resistant to changing definitions of marriage. But, even in these regions, opinion on interracial and same-sex marriage has become more liberal over time.

Cause Does opinion about marriage influence policy or vice versa? After the Supreme Court settled the matter of interracial marriage in 1967, public opinion followed suit across the country. Support for same-sex marriage has also changed over time, but policies vary by state. Legalization is more common where public opinion is most favorable, and bans are most common where support lags.

Brown v. Board of Education (1954)

U.S. Supreme Court decision holding that school segregation is inherently unconstitutional because it violates the Fourteenth Amendment's guarantee of equal protection.

education. The justices agreed and ruled that Missouri had failed to meet the separate-but-equal requirements of *Plessy*. The Court ordered Missouri either to admit Gaines to the school or to set up a law school for him.[5]

Recognizing the importance of the Court's ruling, the NAACP, in 1939, created a separate, tax-exempt legal defense fund to devise a strategy that would build on the Missouri case and bring about equal educational opportunities for all African American children. The first head of the NAACP Legal Defense and Educational Fund, commonly referred to as the LDF, was Thurgood Marshall, who later became the first African American to serve on the U.S. Supreme Court. Sensing that the Court would be more amenable to the NAACP's broader goals if it were first forced to address a variety of less threatening claims to educational opportunity, Marshall and the LDF brought a series of carefully crafted test cases to the Court.

The first case involved H.M. Sweatt, a forty-six-year-old African American mail carrier who applied for admission to the all-white University of Texas Law School in 1946. Rejected on racial grounds, Sweatt sued. The judge gave the state six months to establish a law school or to admit Sweatt to the university. The state legislature then authorized $3 million for the creation of the Texas State University for Negroes. One hundred thousand dollars of that money was allotted for a new law school in Austin across the street from the state capitol building. It consisted of three small basement rooms, a library of 10,000 books, access to the state law library, and three part-time first-year instructors as the faculty. Sweatt declined the opportunity to attend the substandard university and instead chose to continue his legal challenge.

The Supreme Court handled this case together with another case involving graduate education.[6] The eleven southern states filed an *amicus curiae* (friend of the court) brief, in which they argued that *Plessy* should govern both cases. The LDF received assistance, however, from an unexpected source—the U.S. government. In a dramatic departure from the past, President Harry S Truman directed his Department of Justice to file an *amicus* brief urging the Court to overrule *Plessy*.

Although the Court did not overrule *Plessy*, the justices found that measures taken by the states in each case failed to live up to the strictures of the separate-but-equal doctrine. The Court unanimously ruled that the remedies to each situation were inadequate to afford a sound education.

In 1950, after the Court had handed down these decisions, the LDF concluded that the time had come to launch a full-scale attack on the separate-but-equal doctrine. The Court's decisions were encouraging, and the position of the U.S. government and the population in general (and especially outside the South) appeared more receptive to an outright overruling of *Plessy*.

BROWN V. BOARD OF EDUCATION

Brown v. *Board of Education* (1954) actually was five cases brought from different areas of the South and border states involving public elementary or high school systems that mandated separate schools for blacks and whites.[7] In *Brown*, LDF lawyers, again led by Thurgood Marshall, argued that the equal protection clause of the Fourteenth Amendment made *Plessy*'s separate-but-equal doctrine unconstitutional, and that if the Court was still reluctant to overrule *Plessy*, the only way to equalize the schools was to integrate them. A major component of the LDF's strategy was to prove that the intellectual, psychological, and financial damage done to African Americans as a result of segregation prevented any court from finding that the separate-but-equal policy was consistent with the intent of the Fourteenth Amendment's equal protection clause.

On May 17, 1954, Chief Justice Earl Warren delivered the fourth opinion of the day, *Brown* v. *Board of Education*. Writing for the Court, Warren stated:

> To separate [some school children] from others . . . solely because of their race generates a feeling of inferiority as to their status in the community that may affect their hearts and minds in a way very unlikely ever to be undone. We conclude, unanimously, that in the field of public education the doctrine of "separate but equal" has no place.

Brown was, without doubt, the most important civil rights case decided in the twentieth century.[8] It immediately evoked an uproar that shook the nation. Some segregationists gave the name Black Monday to the day the decision was handed down. The governor of South Carolina denounced the decision, saying, "Ending segregation would mark the beginning of the end of civilization in the South as we know it."[9]

The Civil Rights Movement

3 Analyze the civil rights movement and the effects of the Civil Rights Act of 1964.

 lthough it did not create immediate legal change, *Brown* served as a catalyst for a civil rights movement across the United States, and especially in the South. The decision emboldened activists and gave them faith that the government might one day change its segregationist policies in all areas of the law.[10]

☐ School Desegregation After *Brown*

One year after *Brown*, in a case referred to as *Brown* v. *Board of Education II* (1955), the Court ruled that racially segregated systems must be dismantled "with all deliberate speed."[11] Many politicians in the South entered into a near conspiracy to avoid the mandates of *Brown II*. In Arkansas, for example, Governor Orval Faubus, who was facing a reelection bid, announced that he would not "be a party to any attempt to force acceptance of change to which people are overwhelmingly opposed."[12] The day before school was to begin, he declared that National Guardsmen would surround Little Rock's Central High School to prevent African American students from entering. While the federal courts in Arkansas continued to order desegregation, the governor remained adamant. Finally, President Dwight D. Eisenhower sent federal troops to Little Rock to protect the rights of the nine African American students attending Central High.

In reaction to the governor's illegal conduct, the Court broke with tradition and issued a unanimous decision in *Cooper* v. *Aaron* (1958), which was filed by the Little Rock School Board and asked the federal district court for a delay of two and one-half years in implementing desegregation plans. Each justice signed the opinion individually, underscoring his own support for the notion that "no state legislator or executive or judicial officer can war against the Constitution without violating his undertaking to support it."[13] The state's actions thus were ruled unconstitutional and its "evasive schemes" illegal.

☐ A New Move for African American Rights

In 1955, soon after *Brown II,* the civil rights movement took another step forward—this time in Montgomery, Alabama. Rosa Parks, the local NAACP's Youth Council adviser, decided to challenge the constitutionality of the segregated bus system. First, Parks and other NAACP officials began to raise money for litigation and made speeches around town to garner public support. Then, on December 1, 1955, Rosa Parks made history when she refused to leave her seat in the front of the colored section of the bus to make room for a white male passenger without a seat. Police arrested her for violating an Alabama law banning integration of public facilities, including buses. After being freed on bond, Parks and the NAACP decided to enlist city clergy to help her cause. At the same time, they distributed 35,000 handbills calling for African Americans to boycott the Montgomery bus system on the day of Parks's trial. Black ministers used Sunday services to urge their members to support the boycott. On Monday morning, African Americans walked, carpooled, or used black-owned taxicabs. That night, local ministers decided the boycott should continue. A new, twenty-six-year-old minister, the Reverend Martin Luther King Jr., was selected to lead the newly formed Montgomery Improvement Association.

As the boycott dragged on, Montgomery officials and local business owners (who were suffering negative economic consequences) began to harass the city's African American citizens. The black residents held out, despite suffering personal hardship for their actions, ranging from harassment to job loss to bankruptcy. In 1956, a federal court ruled that the segregated bus system violated the equal protection clause of the Fourteenth Amendment. After a year-long boycott, African American Montgomery residents ended their protest when city officials ordered the public transit system to integrate. The first effort at nonviolent protest had been successful. Organized boycotts and other forms of nonviolent protest, including sit-ins at segregated restaurants and bus stations, were to follow.

☐ Formation of New Groups

The recognition and respect earned by the Reverend Martin Luther King Jr. within the African American community helped him launch the Southern Christian Leadership Conference (SCLC) in 1957, soon after the end of the Montgomery Bus Boycott. Unlike the NAACP, which had northern origins and had come to rely largely on litigation as a means of achieving expanded equality, the SCLC had a southern base and was rooted more closely in black religious culture. The SCLC's philosophy reflected King's growing belief in the importance of nonviolent protest and civil disobedience.

Eventually, the SCLC and the Student Non-violent Coordinating Committee (SNCC), largely made up of activist college students, dominated the new civil rights movement. Whereas the SCLC generally worked with church leaders in a community, SNCC was much more of a grassroots organization. Always perceived as more radical than the SCLC, SNCC tended to focus its organizing activities on the young, both black and white.

In addition to joining the sit-in bandwagon, SNCC also came to lead what were called freedom rides, designed to shine the spotlight on segregated public accommodations. Bands of college students and other civil rights activists traveled by bus throughout the South in an effort to force bus stations to desegregate.

While SNCC continued to sponsor sit-ins and freedom rides, in 1963 King launched a series of massive nonviolent demonstrations in Birmingham, Alabama, long considered a major stronghold of segregation. Thousands of blacks and whites marched to Birmingham in a show of solidarity. Peaceful marchers were met there by the Birmingham police commissioner, who ordered his officers to use dogs, clubs, and fire hoses on the marchers. Americans across the nation were horrified as they witnessed on television the brutality and abuse heaped on the protesters. As the marchers had hoped, the shocking scenes helped convince President John F. Kennedy to propose important civil rights legislation.

☐ The Civil Rights Act of 1964

Both the SCLC and SNCC sought full implementation of U.S. Supreme Court decisions dealing with race and an end to racial segregation and discrimination. The cumulative effect of collective actions including sit-ins, boycotts, marches, and freedom rides—as well as the tragic bombings, lynchings, and other deaths inflicted in retaliation—led Congress to pass the first major piece of civil rights legislation since the post–Civil War era, the Civil Rights Act of 1964, followed the next year by the Voting Rights Act of 1965. Several events led to consideration of the two pieces of legislation.

In 1963, President John F. Kennedy requested that Congress pass a law banning discrimination in public accommodations. Seizing the moment, the Reverend Martin Luther King Jr. called for a monumental march on Washington, D.C., to demonstrate widespread support for far-ranging anti-discrimination legislation. It was clear that

Take a Closer Look

Throughout history, literature has played a significant role in raising the public's awareness of important civil rights issues. Movements for greater rights for African Americans, women, Hispanics, and American Indians, among others, have all been aided by the power of prose. Although some of these texts were works of fiction, and others nonfiction, all helped to energize and mobilize a growing social movement.

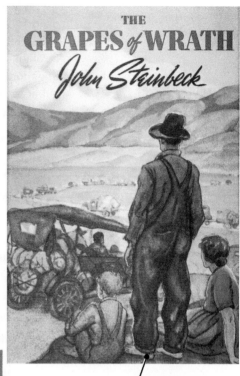

Uncle Tom's Cabin, written by Harriet Beecher Stowe in 1852, is one of the most widely circulated texts of all time. It depicted the realities of slavery, helped to inspire the abolition movement, and was a catalyst for the Civil War.

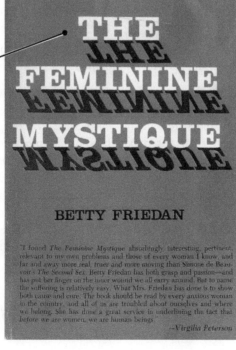

Betty Friedan's *The Feminine Mystique* was first published in 1963. It played an important role in helping housewives and other women realize that they were not alone in their feelings of discontent. As a result, it served as one of the inspirations for the 1960's women's movement.

The Grapes of Wrath, written by John Steinbeck in 1939, did not focus on a Hispanic family. However, its story of California tenant farmers struggling to survive resonated with many Hispanic rights activists and helped to motivate movements for farm workers' rights.

CRITICAL THINKING QUESTIONS

1. How do the visuals of these texts depict the plight and despair faced by minority groups?
2. What other texts have been significant in mobilizing social and political change for disadvantaged groups? How are they similar to and different from the books shown here?
3. Why do you think literature has been so effective in mobilizing citizens for social change? What does writing add that everyday life cannot? How will the Internet change this?

Civil Rights Act of 1964

Wide-ranging legislation passed by Congress to outlaw segregation in public facilities and discrimination in employment, education, and voting; created the Equal Employment Opportunity Commission.

national legislation outlawing discrimination was the only answer: southern legislators would never vote to repeal Jim Crow laws. The March on Washington for Jobs and Freedom was held in August 1963, only a few months after the Birmingham demonstrations. More than 250,000 people heard King deliver his famous "I Have a Dream" speech from the Lincoln Memorial. Before Congress had the opportunity to vote on any legislation, however, President Kennedy was assassinated on November 22, 1963, in Dallas, Texas.

When Vice President Lyndon B. Johnson, a southern-born, former Senate majority leader, succeeded Kennedy as president, he put civil rights reform at the top of his legislative priority list, and civil rights activists gained a critical ally. Thus, through the 1960s, the movement subtly changed its focus from peaceful protest and litigation to legislative lobbying. Its scope broadened from integration of school and public facilities and voting rights to preventing housing and job discrimination and alleviating poverty.

In spite of strong presidential support and the sway of public opinion, the Civil Rights Act of 1964 did not sail through Congress. Southern senators, led by South Carolina's Strom Thurmond, a Democrat who later switched to the Republican Party, conducted the longest filibuster in the history of the Senate. For eight weeks, Thurmond led the effort to hold up voting on the civil rights bill. Once passed, the **Civil Rights Act of 1964:**

- Outlawed arbitrary discrimination in voter registration and expedited voting rights lawsuits.

- Barred discrimination in public accommodations engaged in interstate commerce.

- Authorized the Department of Justice to initiate lawsuits to desegregate public facilities and schools.

- Provided for the withholding of federal funds from discriminatory state and local programs.

- Prohibited discrimination in employment on grounds of race, creed, color, religion, national origin, or sex.

- Created the Equal Employment Opportunity Commission (EEOC) to monitor and enforce the bans on employment discrimination.

As practices thought to be in violation of the law continued, other changes continued to sweep the United States. African Americans in the North, who believed that their brothers and sisters in the South were making progress against discrimination, found themselves frustrated. Northern blacks, too, were experiencing high unemployment, poverty, and discrimination, and had little political clout. Some, including African American Muslim leader Malcolm X, even argued that, to survive, African Americans must separate themselves from white culture in every way. These increased tensions resulted in violent race riots in many major cities from 1964 to 1968, when many African Americans in the North took to the streets, burning and looting to vent their rage. The assassination of the Reverend Martin Luther King Jr. in 1968 triggered a new epidemic of race riots.

The Women's Rights Movement

4 Assess statutory and constitutional remedies for discrimination pursued and achieved by the women's rights movement.

s in the abolition movement of the 1800s, women from all walks of life participated in the civil rights movement. Women were important members of new groups such as SNCC and the SCLC, as well as more traditional groups such as the NAACP, yet they often found themselves treated as second-class citizens. At one point during an SNCC national meeting, its male chair proclaimed:

"The only position for women in SNCC is prone."[14] Statements and attitudes such as these led some women to found early women's liberation groups that generally were quite radical but small in membership. Others established more traditional groups, such as the National Organization for Women (NOW).

☐ The Equal Rights Amendment

Not all women agreed with the concept of full equality for women. Nevertheless, from 1923 to 1972, a proposal for an equal rights amendment was made in every session of every Congress. Every president between Harry S Truman and Richard M. Nixon backed it, and by 1972 public opinion favored its ratification.

Finally, in 1972, in response to pressure from NOW, the National Women's Political Caucus, and a wide variety of other feminist groups, Congress voted in favor of the **Equal Rights Amendment** (ERA) by overwhelming majorities (84–8 in the Senate; 354–24 in the House). The amendment provided that:

> Equality of rights under the law shall not be denied or abridged by the United States or by any state on account of sex.
>
> The Congress shall have the power to enforce, by appropriate legislation, the provisions of this article.

Within a year, twenty-two states ratified the amendment, most by overwhelming margins, but the tide soon turned. By 1978, one year before the expiration deadline for ratification, thirty-five states had voted for the amendment—three short of the three-fourths necessary for ratification. Efforts in key states such as Illinois and Florida failed as opposition to the ERA intensified. Faced with the prospect of defeat, ERA supporters heavily lobbied Congress to extend the deadline for ratification. Congress extended the ratification period by three years, but to no avail. No additional states ratified the amendment, and three more rescinded their votes.

What began as a simple correction to the Constitution turned into a highly controversial proposed change. Even though large percentages of the public favored the ERA, opponents needed to stall ratification in only thirteen states, while supporters had to convince legislators in thirty-eight. Ironically, the success of women's rights activists in the courts was hurting the effort. When women first sought the ERA in the late 1960s, the Supreme Court had yet to rule that women were protected from any kind of discrimination by the Fourteenth Amendment's equal protection clause, thus highlighting the need for an amendment. But, as the Court widened its interpretation of the Constitution to protect women from some sorts of discrimination, many felt the need for a new amendment was less urgent. The proposed amendment died without ratification on June 30, 1982. Since 1982, the amendment has been reintroduced in every session of Congress.

☐ The Equal Protection Clause and Constitutional Standards of Review

The Fourteenth Amendment protects all U.S. citizens from state action that violates equal protection of the laws. Most laws, though, are subject to what is called the rational basis or minimum rationality test. This lowest level of scrutiny means that governments must show a rational foundation for any distinctions they make. As early as 1937, however, the Supreme Court recognized that certain freedoms were so fundamental that a very heavy burden would fall on any government seeking to restrict those rights. WhenWhen fundamental freedoms such as those guaranteed by the First Amendment or **suspect classifications** such as race are involved, the Court uses a heightened standard of review called **strict scrutiny** to determine the constitutional validity of the challenged practices, as detailed in Table 1.

Equal Rights Amendment
Proposed amendment to the Constitution that states "Equality of rights under the law shall not be denied or abridged by the United States or any state on account of sex."

suspect classification
Category or class, such as race, that triggers the highest standard of scrutiny from the Supreme Court.

strict scrutiny
A heightened standard of review used by the Supreme Court to determine the constitutional validity of a challenged practice.

TABLE 1 WHAT ARE THE STANDARDS OF REVIEW FASHIONED BY THE COURT UNDER THE EQUAL PROTECTION CLAUSE?

Type of Classification: *What kind of statutory classification is at issue?*	Standard of Review: *What standard of review will be used?*	Test: *What does the Court ask?*	Example: *How does the Court apply the test?*
Fundamental freedoms (including religion, speech, assembly, press), suspect classifications (including race, alienage, and national origin)	Strict scrutiny or heightened standard	Is the classification necessary to the accomplishment of a permissible state goal? Is it the least restrictive way to reach that goal?	*Brown* v. *Board of Education* (1954): Racial segregation not necessary to accomplish the state's goal of educating its students.
Gender	Intermediate standard	Does the classification serve an important governmental objective, and is it substantially related to those ends?	*Craig* v. *Boren* (1976): Keeping drunk drivers off the roads may be an important governmental objective, but allowing eighteen-to twenty-one-year-old women to drink alcoholic beverages while prohibiting men of the same age from drinking is not substantially related to that goal.
Others (including age, wealth, mental capacity, and sexual orientation)	Minimum rationality standard	Is there any rational foundation for the discrimination?	*Romer* v. *Evans* (1996): Colorado state constitutional amendment denying equal rights to homosexuals is unconstitutional.

In legal terms, this means that if a statute or governmental practice makes a classification based on race, the statute is presumed to be unconstitutional unless the state can provide "compelling affirmative justifications"—that is, unless the state can prove that the law in question is necessary to accomplish a permissible goal and that it is the least restrictive means of accomplishing that goal.

During the 1960s and into the 1970s, the Court routinely struck down as unconstitutional practices and statutes that discriminated on the basis of race. The Court ruled that "whites-only" public parks and recreational facilities, tax-exempt status for private schools that discriminated, and statutes prohibiting interracial marriage were unconstitutional. In contrast, the Court refused to consider whether the equal protection clause might apply to discrimination against women. Finally, in a case argued in 1971 by Ruth Bader Ginsburg (later an associate justice of the Supreme Court) as director of the Women's Rights Project of the ACLU, the Supreme Court ruled that an Idaho law granting a male parent automatic preference over a female parent as the administrator of their deceased child's estate violated the equal protection clause of the Fourteenth Amendment. *Reed* v. *Reed* (1971), the Idaho case, turned the tide in terms of constitutional litigation. Although the Court did not rule that sex was a suspect classification, it concluded that the equal protection clause of the Fourteenth Amendment prohibited unreasonable classifications based on sex.[15]

Since 1976, the Court has applied the intermediate standard of constitutional review to most claims involving gender that it has heard. Thus, the Court has found the following practices in violation of the Fourteenth Amendment:

- Single-sex public nursing schools.[16]
- Laws that consider males adults at twenty-one years but females adults at eighteen years.[17]
- Laws that allow women, but not men, to receive alimony.[18]
- State prosecutors' use of peremptory challenges to reject male or female potential jurors to create more sympathetic juries.[19]
- Virginia's maintenance of an all-male military college, the Virginia Military Institute.[20]

In contrast, the Court has upheld the following governmental practices and laws:

- Draft registration provisions for males only.[21]
- State statutory rape laws that apply only to female victims.[22]
- Different requirements for a child's acquisition of citizenship based on whether the citizen parent is a mother or a father.[23]

The level of review used by the Court is crucial. Clearly, a statute excluding African Americans from draft registration would be unconstitutional. But, because gender is not subject to the same higher standard of review used in racial discrimination cases, the Court ruled the exclusion of women from requirements of the Military Selective Service Act permissible because it considered the government policy to serve "important governmental objectives."[24]

This history perhaps clarifies why women's rights activists continue to argue that until the passage of the Equal Rights Amendment, women will never enjoy the same rights as men. An amendment would raise the level of scrutiny applied by the Court to gender-based claims, although indications are clear that the Supreme Court of late favors requiring states to meet a tougher test than *Craig* and show "exceedingly persuasive justifications" for their actions.[25]

☐ Statutory Remedies for Sex Discrimination

In part because of the limits of the intermediate standard of review and the fact that the equal protection clause applies only to governmental discrimination, women's rights activists began to look for statutory solutions to discrimination. The **Equal Pay Act of 1963,** the first such piece of legislation, requires employers to pay women and men equal pay for equal work. Women have won important victories under the act, but a large wage gap between women and men continues to exist, even beginning with the first paycheck issued to men and women with equal jobs, education, and experience. Women's earnings in 2012 equaled about 75 to 80 percent of men's earnings, depending on location and occupation.

In 2007, the U.S. Supreme Court tested the boundaries of the Equal Pay Act. The justices heard the case of Lilly Ledbetter, the lone female supervisor at a Goodyear tire factory in Alabama. Ledbetter charged that sex discrimination throughout her career had led her to earn substantially less than her male counterparts. In a 5–4 decision, the Court ruled that Ledbetter and other women could not seek redress of grievances under the provisions of the Equal Pay Act for discrimination that had occurred over a period of years. Justice Ruth Bader Ginsburg, the only woman on the Court at the time, took the uncommon action of reading her dissent from the bench. Speaking for herself and Justices David Souter, John Paul Stevens, and Stephen Breyer, she angrily noted, "In our view, the court does not

Equal Pay Act of 1963
Legislation that requires employers to pay men and women equal pay for equal work.

Clay Bennett. Christian Science Monitor

GENDER GAP IN WAGES

'Three-fourths of a penny for your thoughts...'

WHAT ARE THE PRACTICAL CONSEQUENCES OF PAY EQUITY?

This cartoon pokes fun at a serious issue in gender equality: pay equity. In 2012, women earned between 75 and 80 cents for every $1.00 earned by their similarly situated male counterparts.

Title IX

Provision of the Education Amendments of 1972 that bars educational institutions that receive federal funds from discriminating against female students.

comprehend, or is indifferent to, the insidious way in which women can be victims of pay discrimination."[26] In 2009, the first official act of President Barack Obama was to sign the Lilly Ledbetter Fair Pay Act, which overruled the Court's decision bearing her name.

Another important piece of legislation is Title VII of the Civil Rights Act of 1964, which prohibits gender discrimination by private (and, after 1972, public) employers. Much litigation has focused on this act, too. Key victories under Title VII include:

- Consideration of sexual harassment as sex discrimination.[27]
- Inclusion of law firms, which many argued were private partnerships, in the coverage of the act.[28]
- A broad definition of what can be considered sexual harassment, including same-sex harassment.[29]
- Allowance of voluntary programs to redress historical discrimination against women.[30]

Finally, **Title IX** of the Education Amendments of 1972 bars educational institutions that receive federal funds from discriminating against female students. Title IX, which parallels Title VII, greatly expanded the opportunities for women in elementary, secondary, and postsecondary institutions. Most of today's college students do not go through school being excluded from home economics or technology education classes because of their sex. Nor, probably do many attend schools that have no team sports for females. Yet, this was commonly the case in the United States prior to passage of Title IX.[31] Nevertheless, sport facilities, access to premium playing times, and quality equipment remain unequal in many high schools and colleges. Major rulings by the U.S. Supreme Court that uphold the provisions of Title IX include:

- Holding school boards or districts responsible for both student-on-student harassment and harassment of students by teachers.[32]
- Allowing retaliatory lawsuits by coaches on behalf of their sports teams denied equal treatment by school boards.[33]

Other Groups Mobilize for Rights

5 Describe how other groups have mobilized in pursuit of their own civil rights.

frican Americans and women are not the only groups that have suffered unequal treatment under the law. Denial of civil rights has led other disadvantaged groups to mobilize. Their efforts parallel in many ways the efforts made by African Americans and women.

☐ Hispanic Americans

Hispanics are the largest minority group in the United States. But, Hispanic population growth in the United States is not a new phenomenon. In 1910, the Mexican Revolution forced Mexicans seeking safety and employment into the United States. And, in 1916, New Mexico entered the union officially as a bilingual state—the only one in the United States.

Early Hispanic immigrants, many of whom were from families who had owned land when parts of the Southwest were still under Mexico's control, formed the League of United Latin American Citizens (LULAC) in 1929. LULAC continues to be the largest Hispanic organization in the United States, with local councils in every state and Puerto Rico.

As large numbers of immigrants from Mexico and Puerto Rico entered the United States, they quickly became a source of cheap labor, with Mexicans initially tending to settle in the Southwest, where they most frequently found employment as migratory farm workers, and Puerto Ricans mainly moving to New York City. Both groups gravitated to

Explore Your World

Good fences make good neighbors, or so the adage goes. Throughout history, many countries have adopted this perspective. Beginning in the seventh century B.C., for example, China fortified its borders by constructing the Great Wall. And, following World War II, Germans built the Berlin Wall to divide the city of Berlin into East (communist) and West (democratic). Today, many politicians call for the construction of a "fence" or a "wall" between the United States and Mexico to stem illegal immigration and drug trafficking. Building a fence, however, poses a dilemma; although it may increase domestic security, it may also strain relations with allies around the world.

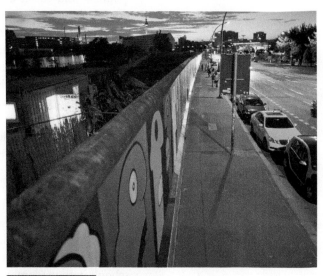

This photo of the Berlin Wall, taken after the reunification of Germany, illustrates the lasting effects of the division of the German capital. Note the contrast between the vibrancy of the West and the desertion of the East.

Construction on the Great Wall of China began as early as 700 B.C. It extends for more than 13,000 miles along the border of China and Mongolia.

This photo illustrates a small section of the fence between the United States and Mexico in the American Southwest. The fence remains an ongoing debate; more than 300 miles of fence have been constructed in California, Arizona, and New Mexico. Work continues in these states, as well as Texas.

CRITICAL THINKING QUESTIONS

1. What similarities do you see between the walls or fences depicted here? What important differences do you observe?
2. Does each of these walls have the same implications for domestic and foreign policy? Why or why not?
3. Is a border fence constitutional? What combination of physical boundaries and legal constraints should the United States use to protect its borders from illegal immigrants? What about the civil rights of immigrants?

their own neighborhoods, where life revolved around the Roman Catholic Church and the customs of their homeland, and both groups largely lived in poverty. Still, in 1954, the same year as *Brown*, Hispanics won a major victory when, in *Hernandez* v. *Texas*, the Supreme Court struck down discrimination based on race and ethnicity.[34] In *Hernandez*, the Court ruled unanimously that Mexican Americans had the right to a jury that included other Mexican Americans.

A push for greater Hispanic rights began in the mid-1960s, just as a wave of Cuban immigrants started to establish homes in Florida, dramatically altering the political and social climate of Miami and neighboring towns and cities in South Florida. This new movement, marked by the establishment of the National Council of La Raza in 1968, incorporated many tactics drawn from the African American civil rights movement, including sit-ins, boycotts, marches, and other activities designed to heighten publicity for their cause. In one earlier example, in 1965, Cesar Chavez and Dolores Huerta organized migrant workers into the United Farm Workers Union, which would become the largest such union in the nation, and led them in a strike against produce growers in California. Organizers eventually coupled this strike with a national boycott of various farm products.

Hispanics also have relied heavily on litigation to secure legal change. Key groups are the Mexican American Legal Defense and Educational Fund (MALDEF) and the Puerto Rican Legal Defense and Education Fund (renamed LatinoJustice PRLDEF). MALDEF began its life in 1968 after members of LULAC met with NAACP LDF leaders and, with their assistance, secured a $2.2-million start-up grant from the Ford Foundation. The founders of MALDEF originally created it to bring test cases before the Supreme Court with the intent to force school districts to allocate more funds to schools with predominantly low-income minority populations, to implement bilingual education programs, to require employers to hire Hispanics, and to challenge election rules and apportionment plans that undercount or dilute Hispanic voting power.

MALDEF has been successful in expanding voting rights and electoral opportunities to Hispanic Americans under the Voting Rights Act of 1965 (renewed in 2006 for ten years) and the U.S. Constitution's equal protection clause. In 1973, for example, it won a major victory when the Supreme Court ruled that multimember electoral districts (in which more than one person represents a single district) in Texas discriminated against African Americans and Hispanics.[35] In multimember systems, legislatures generally add members to larger districts instead of drawing smaller districts in which a minority candidate could garner a majority of the votes necessary to win.

The organization's success in educational equity cases came more slowly. In 1973, for example, in *San Antonio Independent School District* v. *Rodriguez*, the Supreme Court refused to find that a Texas law under which the state appropriated a set dollar amount to each school district per pupil, while allowing wealthier districts to enrich educational programs from other funds, violated the equal protection clause of the Fourteenth Amendment.[36] In 1989, however, MALDEF won a case in which a state district judge elected by the voters of only a single county declared the state's entire method of financing public schools to be unconstitutional under the state constitution.[37] And, in 2004, it entered into a settlement with the state of California in a case brought four years earlier to address, in MALDEF's words, "the shocking inequities facing public school children across the state."[38]

MALDEF continues to litigate in a wide range of areas of concern to Hispanics. High on its agenda today are affirmative action, the admission of Hispanic students to state colleges and universities, health care for undocumented immigrants, and challenging redistricting practices that make it more difficult to elect Hispanic legislators. To ensure that Hispanics are adequately represented, it also litigates to challenge many state redistricting plans. MALDEF and other Hispanic rights groups, for example, have played a major role in challenging redistricting plans in the state of Texas. As a result of these legal challenges, the U.S. Supreme Court has repeatedly found unconstitutional redistricting plans that divide geographically compact Hispanic populations into many congressional districts, thus diluting Hispanic representation.[39]

MALDEF also stands at the fore of legislative lobbying for expanded rights. Since 2002, it has worked to oppose restrictions concerning driver's license requirements for undocumented immigrants, to gain greater rights for Hispanic workers, and to ensure that redistricting plans do not silence Hispanic voters. MALDEF also focuses on the rights of Hispanic immigrants and workers.

☐ American Indians

American Indians are the first true Americans, and their status under U.S. law is unique. The U.S. Constitution considers Indian tribes distinct governments, a situation that has affected the treatment of these Americans by Congress and the Supreme Court.

For years, Congress and the courts manipulated the law to promote westward expansion of the United States. The Northwest Ordinance of 1787, passed by the Continental Congress, specified that "good faith should always be observed toward the Indians; their lands and property shall never be taken from them without their consent, and their property rights, and liberty, they shall never be invaded or disturbed, unless in just and lawful wars authorized by Congress." The federal government did not follow this pledge. During the eighteenth and nineteenth centuries, it isolated American Indians on reservations as it confiscated their lands and denied them basic political rights. The U.S. government administered Indian reservations, and American Indians often lived in squalid conditions.

With passage of the Dawes Act in 1887, however, the government switched policies, promoting assimilation over separation. This act gave each American Indian family land within the reservation; the rest was sold to whites, thus reducing Indian lands from about 140 million acres to about 47 million. Moreover, to encourage American Indians to assimilate, the act mandated sending their children to boarding schools off the reservation. It also banned native languages and rituals. American Indians did not become U.S. citizens, nor were they given the right to vote, until 1924.

At least in part because tribes were small and scattered (and the number of members declining), American Indians formed no protest movement in reaction to these drastic policy changes. Not until the 1960s did American Indians began to mobilize. During this time, American Indian activists, many trained by the American Indian Law Center at the University of New Mexico, began to file hundreds of test cases in the federal courts involving tribal fishing rights, tribal land claims, and taxation of tribal profits. The Native American Rights Fund (NARF), founded in 1970, became the NAACP LDF of the American Indian rights movement.

American Indians have won some very important victories concerning hunting, fishing, and land rights. Tribes all over the country have sued to reclaim lands they maintain the United States stole from them, often more than 200 years ago. These land rights allow American Indians to host gambling casinos across the country, frequently on tribal lands abutting cities and states where gambling is illegal. This phenomenon has resulted in billions of dollars of revenue for Indian tribes. These improvements in American Indians' economic affairs have helped to increase their political clout. Tribes are donating to political campaigns of candidates predisposed to policies favorable to tribes. The Agua Caliente Band of Cahuilla Indians, for example, donated $7.5 million to political campaigns in just one year alone. These large expenditures, American Indians claim, are legal, because as sovereign nations they are immune from federal and state campaign finance disclosure laws. The political involvement of American Indian tribes will most likely continue to grow as their casinos—and the profits of those ventures—proliferate.

Like the civil rights and women's rights movements, the movement for American Indian rights has had a radical as well as a more traditional branch. In 1973, for example, national attention centered on the plight of Indians when members of the radical American Indian Movement took over Wounded Knee, South Dakota, the site of the U.S. Army's massacre of 150 Indians in 1890. Just two years before the protest, the treatment of Indians had been highlighted in Dee Brown's best-selling *Bury My Heart at Wounded Knee,* which in many ways served to mobilize public opinion against the oppression of American Indians in the same way *Uncle Tom's Cabin* had against slavery.[40]

☐ Asian and Pacific Island Americans

One of the most significant difficulties for Asian and Pacific Island Americans has been finding a Pan-Asian identity. Originally, Asian and Pacific Island Americans were far more likely to identify with their individual Japanese, Chinese, Korean, or Filipino heritage.[41] Not until 1977 did the U.S. government decide to use "Asian and Pacific Island" for all of these origins. Some subgroups have even challenged this identity; in the 1990s, native Hawaiians unsuccessfully requested to be categorized with American Indians, with whom they felt greater affinity.

Discrimination against Asian and Pacific Island immigrants developed over time in the United States. In 1868, Congress passed a law allowing free migration from China, because workers were needed to complete building an intercontinental railroad. But in 1882, Congress passed the Chinese Exclusion Act, which was the first act to restrict the immigration of any identifiable nationality. This legislation implicitly invited more discriminatory laws against the Chinese, which closely paralleled the Jim Crow laws affecting African Americans.

Several Supreme Court cases also slowed the progress of Asian and Pacific Island Americans. This began to change in 1886, when the Court decided the landmark case of *Yick Wo* v. *Hopkins,* using the rational basis test highlighted in Table 1. A number of events precipitated this decision. Discriminatory provisions in the California Constitution prevented Chinese people from practicing many professions. However, the Chinese in California were allowed to open laundries. And, many immigrants did. In response to this growing trend, the city of San Francisco passed a ban on laundries operating in wooden buildings, two-thirds of which were owned by persons of Chinese ancestry. The Court in *Yick Wo* found that the law violated the Fourteenth Amendment in its application since one ethnic group was being targeted.[42]

In 1922, the Court took a step backward, ruling that Asian and Pacific Island Americans were not white and therefore not entitled to full citizenship rights.[43] Conditions became even worse, especially for those of Japanese descent, after the Japanese attack on

HOW WERE JAPANESE AMERICANS TREATED DURING WORLD WAR II?

The internment of Japanese Americans during World War II was a low point in American history. In *Korematsu* v. *U.S.* (1944), the U.S. Supreme Court upheld the constitutionality of this action.

Pearl Harbor in 1941. In response to the attack, President Franklin D. Roosevelt issued Executive Order 9066, which led to the internment of over 130,000 Japanese Americans, Italian Americans, and German Americans, some of whom were Jewish refugees. More than two-thirds of those confined to internment camps were U.S. citizens. The Supreme Court upheld the constitutionality of these camps in *Korematsu* v. *U.S.* (1944).

During the 1960s and 1970s, Asian and Pacific Island Americans, like many other groups discussed in this chapter, began to organize for equal rights. Filipino farm workers, for example, joined with Mexicans to form the United Farm Workers Union. In 1973, the Movement for a Free Philippines emerged to oppose the government of Ferdinand Marcos, the president of the Philippines. Soon, it joined forces with the Friends of Filipino People, also founded in 1973. These groups worked with the Free Legal Assistance Group (FLAG) to openly oppose the Vietnam War and, with the aid of the Roman Catholic Church, established relief organizations for Filipinos in the United States and around the world.

In the 1970s and 1980s, Japanese Americans also mobilized, lobbying the courts and Congress for reparations for their treatment during World War II. In 1988, Congress passed the Civil Liberties Act, which apologized to the interned and their descendents and offered reparations to them and their families.

Today, myriad Asian and Pacific Island Americans are the fastest-growing minority group. They target diverse political venues. In California, in particular, they have enjoyed success in seeing more men and women elected at the local and state levels.

☐ Gays and Lesbians

Until very recently, gays and lesbians have experienced many challenges in achieving anything approximating equal rights.[44] However, gays and lesbians have, on average, far higher household incomes and educational levels than other minority groups, and they are beginning to convert these advantages into political clout at the ballot box. They have also recently benefited from changes in public opinion. Like African Americans and women, gays and lesbians have worked through the courts to achieve incremental legal change. In the late 1970s, gay and lesbian activists dedicated to ending legal restrictions on the civil rights of homosexuals founded Lambda Legal, the National Center for Lesbian Rights, and Gay and Lesbian Advocates and Defenders (GLAD).[45] These groups have won important legal victories concerning HIV/AIDS discrimination, insurance policy survivor benefits, and even some employment issues. However, progress in other areas has relied on changing voters' and policy makers' hearts and minds.[46]

In 1993, for example, President Bill Clinton tried to ban discrimination against homosexuals in the armed services. Eventually, Clinton compromised with congressional and military leaders on what was called the "Don't Ask, Don't Tell" (DADT) policy. The military would no longer ask gays and lesbians if they were homosexual, but it barred them from revealing their sexual orientation under threat of discharge. Despite the compromise, the armed services discharged thousands on the basis of their sexual orientation. Government officials called the policy into question as the wars in Iraq and Afghanistan increased America's need for active-duty military personnel.

In 2010, a federal district court judge ruled the "Don't Ask" policy unconstitutional. She also issued an injunction directing the Department of Defense to refrain from enforcing the policy. As a result of these rulings and increasing public pressure, in late 2010, Congress passed and President Barack Obama signed into law a formal repeal of DADT. In September 2011, the policy officially ended, paving the way for many military members to openly acknowledge their homosexuality.

Changes in public opinion have also opened the door for greater legal and constitutional protection for gay and lesbian rights.[47] In 1996, for example, the U.S. Supreme Court ruled that an amendment to the Colorado Constitution that denied homosexuals the right to seek protection from discrimination was unconstitutional under the equal protection clause of the Fourteenth Amendment.

Less than ten years later, these sentiments were reflected in the Court's decision in *Lawrence* v. *Texas* (2003). In this case, the Court reversed an earlier ruling, finding a Texas statute banning sodomy to be unconstitutional. Writing for the majority, Justice Anthony

How Do Governments Regulate Same-Sex Marriage?

Under the federal system of government created by the Framers, marriage has historically been a state responsibility. Thus, in the past ten years, states have been very active in passing legislation on this issue. State legislatures and voters have chosen to adopt a wide array of laws, with some states fully supporting same-sex marriages, others refusing all unions, and many choosing legislation between the two extremes.

ALLOWING SAME-SEX PARTNERSHIPS

9 STATES
Allow Civil Unions

9 STATES
Allow Same-Sex Marriages

10 STATES
Allow Domestic Partnerships

PROHIBITIONS ON SAME-SEX PARTNERSHIPS

8 STATES
Statutory Ban on Same-Sex Marriages

10 STATES
Constitutional Ban on Same-Sex Marriages

20 STATES
Constitutional Ban on All Same-Sex Unions

CRITICAL THINKING QUESTIONS

1. How do the numbers of states allowing and prohibiting same-sex unions vary? What may be the cause of these differences?

2. What are the differences between the tiers of each cake? Why might states adopt laws that vary so widely?

3. Should the United States move toward full marriage equality for homosexual couples? Why or why not?

Kennedy stated, "[homosexuals'] right to liberty under the due process clause gives them the full right to engage in their conduct without intervention of the government."[48]

Following the Court's ruling in *Lawrence,* many Americans were quick to call for additional rights for homosexuals. A good number of corporations responded to this amplified call. For example, Walmart announced it would ban job discrimination based on sexual orientation. In addition, editorial pages across the country praised the Court's ruling, arguing that the national view toward homosexuality had changed.[49] In November 2003, the Massachusetts Supreme Court further agreed when it ruled that denying homosexuals the right to civil marriage was unconstitutional under the commonwealth's constitution. The U.S. Supreme Court later refused to hear an appeal of this case, paving the way for legality of same-sex marriage.

While voters, legislators, and courts in more liberal states took action to legalize these unions, the Religious Right mobilized against them. In 2004, many conservative groups and Republican politicians made same-sex marriage a key issue. Initiatives or referenda prohibiting same-sex marriage were placed on eleven state ballots, and voters overwhelmingly passed all of them. The 2006 mid-term elections also saw same-sex marriage bans on several state ballots, but the issue seemed to lack the emotional punch of the 2004 effort in the context of plummeting presidential approval and the war in Iraq.

In 2008, California and Connecticut joined Massachusetts in legalizing same-sex marriages. Same-sex couples traveled to California, especially, to legally marry. But, in November 2008, California voters passed a ballot proposition amending the state constitution to make same-sex marriages illegal again. This provision, however, did not pass legal muster in the courts; litigation is ongoing.

Ongoing litigation also focuses on the constitutionality of the 1996 Defense of Marriage Act (DOMA), a federal law defining marriage as between one man and one woman. Several district courts around the nation have declared the law to be an unconstitutional violation of the Fourteenth Amendment's equal protection clause. It is likely to take a Supreme Court decision to settle the issue.[50]

☐ Americans with Disabilities

In the aftermath of World War II, many veterans returned to a nation unequipped to handle their disabilities. The Korean and Vietnam Wars made the problems of disabled veterans all the more clear. These veterans saw the successes of African Americans, women, and other minorities, and they, too, began to lobby for greater protection against discrimination.[51] In 1990, in coalition with other disabled people, veterans finally convinced Congress to pass the Americans with Disabilities Act (ADA). The statute defines a disabled person as someone with a physical or mental impairment that limits one or more "life activities," or who has a record of such impairment. It thus extends the protections of the Civil Rights Act of 1964 to all citizens with physical or mental disabilities. It guarantees access to public facilities, employment, and communication services. Furthermore, it requires employers to acquire or modify work equipment, adjust work schedules, and make existing facilities accessible to those with disabilities.

In 1999, the U.S. Supreme Court issued a series of four decisions redefining and limiting the scope of the ADA. The cumulative impact of these decisions dramatically limited the number of people who can claim coverage under the act. Moreover, these cases "could profoundly affect individuals with a range of impairments—from diabetes and hypertension to severe nearsightedness and hearing loss—who are able to function in society with the help of medicines or aids but whose impairments may still make employers consider them ineligible for certain jobs."[52] Thus, pilots who need glasses to correct their vision cannot claim discrimination when employers fail to hire them, even though their vision is correctable.[53] In the 2004 case of *Tennessee* v. *Lane,* however, the Court ruled 5–4 that disabled persons could sue states that failed to make reasonable accommodations to ensure that courthouses are handicapped accessible.[54]

The largest national nonprofit organization lobbying for expanded civil rights for the disabled is the American Association of People with Disabilities (AAPD). Acting affirmative action

Policies designed to give special attention or compensatory treatment to members of a previously disadvantaged group.

Explore on
MyPoliSciLab
Simulation: You Are a
Mayor

on behalf of over 56 million Americans who suffer from some form of disability, it works in coalition with other disability organizations to make certain that the ADA is implemented fully. The activists who founded AAPD lobbied for the ADA and recognized that "beyond national unity for ADA and our civil rights, people with disabilities did not have a venue or vehicle for working together for common goals."[55]

Toward Reform: Civil Rights and Affirmative Action

6   Evaluate the ongoing debate concerning civil rights and affirmative action.

Many civil rights debates center on the question of equality of opportunity versus equality of results. Most civil rights and women's rights organizations argue that taking race and gender into account in fashioning remedies for discrimination is the only way to overcome the lingering and pervasive burdens of racism and sexism, respectively. They argue that the Constitution is not, and should not be, blind to color or sex.

Other groups believe that if the use of labels to discriminate against a group was once wrong, the use of those same labels to help a group should likewise be wrong. They argue that laws should be neutral, or color-blind. According to this view, quotas and other forms of **affirmative action,** policies designed to give special attention or compensatory treatment to members of a previously disadvantaged group, are unconstitutional.

The debate over affirmative action and equality of opportunity became particularly intense during the presidential administration of Ronald Reagan. In *Regents of the University of California* v. *Bakke* (1978), a sharply divided Court concluded that Bakke's rejection had been illegal because the use of strict quotas was inappropriate.[56] The medical school, however, was free to "take race into account," said the Court.

Bakke was followed by a 1979 case in which the Court ruled that a factory and a union could voluntarily adopt a quota system in selecting black workers over more senior white workers for a training program.[57] These kinds of programs outraged blue-collar Americans, who traditionally had voted for the Democratic Party. In 1980, they abandoned the party in droves to support Ronald Reagan, an ardent foe of affirmative action.

For a time, despite the addition of Reagan-appointed Justice Sandra Day O'Connor to the Court, the justices continued to uphold affirmative action plans, especially when clear-cut evidence of prior discrimination was present. In 1987, for example, the Court ruled for the first time that a public employer could use a voluntary plan to promote women even if no judicial finding of prior discrimination existed.[58]

In all these affirmative action cases, the Reagan administration strongly urged the Court to invalidate the plans in question, but to no avail. Changes on the Court, however, including the 1986 elevation of William H. Rehnquist, a strong opponent of affirmative action, to chief justice, signaled an end to advances in civil rights law. In a three-month period in 1989, the Supreme Court handed down five civil rights decisions limiting affirmative action programs and making it harder to prove employment discrimination.

In February 1990, congressional and civil rights leaders unveiled legislation designed to overrule the Court's decisions, which, according to the bill's sponsor, "were an abrupt and unfortunate departure from its historic vigilance in protecting the rights of minorities."[59] The bill passed both houses of Congress but was vetoed by President Reagan's successor, George Bush, and Congress failed to override the veto. In late 1991, however, Congress and the White House reached a compromise on a weaker version of the civil rights bill, which passed by overwhelming majorities in both houses of Congress. The Civil Rights Act of 1991 overruled all five Supreme Court rulings.

By 2002, the U.S. Supreme Court once again found the affirmative action issue ripe for review. In *Grutter* v. *Bollinger* (2003), the Court voted to uphold the constitutionality of the University of Michigan's Law School admissions policy, which gave preference to minority applicants.[60] However, in *Gratz* v. *Bollinger* (2003), the Court struck down Michigan's undergraduate point system, which gave minority applicants twenty automatic points simply because they were minorities.[61]

Together, these cases set the stage for a new era in affirmative action in the United States. Although the use of strict quotas and automatic points is not constitutional, the Court clearly believes that some preferential treatment has its place, at least until greater racial and ethnic parity is achieved. However, as Justice Sandra Day O'Connor noted in *Grutter*, "a program must remain flexible enough to ensure that each applicant is evaluated as an individual and not in a way that makes an applicant's race or ethnicity the defining feature of his or her application."

In 2012, however, the Court called even this standard into question by accepting a case involving a white applicant denied admission at the University of Texas at Austin. A ruling is expected during the Court's 2012–13 term.[62]

On MyPoliSciLab

Review the Chapter

 Listen to Chapter on MyPoliSciLab

Roots of Suffrage: 1800–1890

 1 Trace the efforts from 1800 to 1890 of African Americans and women to win the vote.

When the Framers tried to compromise on the issue of slavery, they only postponed dealing with a volatile question that eventually would rip the nation apart. Ultimately, the Civil War brought an end to slavery. Among its results were the triumph of the abolitionist position and the adoption of the Thirteenth, Fourteenth, and Fifteenth Amendments. During this period, women also sought expanded rights, especially the right to vote, to no avail.

The Push for Equality, 1890–1954

2 Outline developments in African Americans' and women's push for equality from 1890 to 1954.

Although the Civil War Amendments became part of the Constitution, the Supreme Court limited their application. As legislatures throughout the South passed Jim Crow laws, the NAACP was founded in the early 1900s to press for equal rights for African Americans. Woman's groups also were active during this period, successfully lobbying for passage of the Nineteenth Amendment, which ensured them the right to vote.

The Civil Rights Movement

 3 Analyze the civil rights movement and the effects of the Civil Rights Act of 1964.

In 1954, the U.S. Supreme Court ruled in *Brown* v. *Board of Education* that racially segregated state school systems were unconstitutional. This victory empowered African Americans as they sought an end to other forms of pervasive discrimination. Bus boycotts, sit-ins, freedom rides, pressure for voting rights enforcement, and massive nonviolent demonstrations became common tactics. These efforts culminated in passage of the Civil Rights Act of 1964, which gave African Americans another weapon in their legal arsenal.

The Women's Rights Movement

 4 Assess statutory and constitutional remedies for discrimination pursued and achieved by the women's rights movement.

After passage of the Equal Pay Act of 1963 and the Civil Rights Act of 1964, a new women's rights movement arose. Several women's rights groups were created. Some sought a constitutional amendment (the Equal Rights Amendment) as a remedy for discrimination; it would elevate the standard of review for sex-based claims. In general, strict scrutiny, the most stringent standard, is applied to race-based claims and cases involving fundamental freedoms. The Court developed an intermediate standard of review to assess the constitutionality of sex discrimination claims. All other claims are subject to the rational basis test.

Other Groups Mobilize for Rights

5 Describe how other groups have mobilized in pursuit of their own civil rights.

Building on the successes of African Americans and women, other groups, including Hispanics, American Indians, Asian and Pacific Island Americans, gays and lesbians, and those with disabilities, organized to litigate for expanded civil rights and to lobby for anti-discrimination laws.

Toward Reform: Civil Rights and Affirmative Action

6 Evaluate the ongoing debate concerning civil rights and affirmative action.

All of the groups discussed in this chapter have yet to reach full equality. Affirmative action, a policy designed to remedy education and employment discrimination, continues to generate controversy.

Learn the Terms

 Study and **Review** the **Flashcards**

affirmative action
Black Codes
Brown v. *Board of Education* (1954)
civil rights
Civil Rights Act of 1964
Civil Rights Cases (1883)
Equal Pay Act of 1963
equal protection clause

Equal Rights Amendment
Fifteenth Amendment
Fourteenth Amendment
grandfather clause
Jim Crow laws
Nineteenth Amendment
Plessy v. *Ferguson* (1896)
poll tax

strict scrutiny
suffrage movement
suspect classification
Thirteenth Amendment
Title IX

Test Yourself

 Study and **Review** the **Practice Tests**

1. The Fourteenth Amendment, which provided legal protection for the rights of citizens, did NOT include

a. African Americans.
b. those with a "previous condition of servitude."
c. women.
d. those over twenty-one years old.
e. immigrants.

2. Why did Elizabeth Cady Stanton and Lucretia Mott found the first woman's rights movement in the nineteenth century?

a. They escaped from slavery and joined forces with William Lloyd Garrison.
b. After attending an abolitionist meeting, they concluded that women were not much better off than slaves.
c. They were jailed for attempting to hold a woman's rights convention in Seneca Falls in 1848.
d. William Lloyd Garrison and Frederick Douglass encouraged them to leave the abolition movement to pursue their own causes.
e. Their husbands and sons made comments implying women were undeserving of suffrage rights.

3. Which law(s), passed after the Civil War Amendments, reverted many African Americans back to conditions similar to those characterizing their previous lifestyles?

a. Equal protection clause
b. Civil Rights Act of 1875
c. Fifteenth Amendment

d. Civil Rights Act of 1866
e. Black Codes

4. Woman's rights advocates won the right to vote with the ratification of the

a. Eighteenth Amendment.
b. Nineteenth Amendment.
c. Twentieth Amendment.
d. Seventeenth Amendment.
e. Sixteenth Amendment.

5. *Brown* v. *Board of Education* (1954) ruled that segregation in schools is unconstitutional because:

a. there were not enough law schools for African Americans.
b. all schools should be integrated.
c. it violates the Fourteenth Amendment's guarantee of equal protection.
d. postgraduate programs were not offered to African Americans.
e. African Americans had fought in World War II and should therefore be afforded adequate schooling.

6. The Civil Rights Act of 1964 did all of the following EXCEPT:

a. create a commission to monitor workplace discrimination.

b. prohibit discrimination in employment based on race, creed, color, religion, national origin, or sex.

c. allow discrimination in voter registration.

d. allow the withholding of federal funds from discriminatory programs.

e. establish Department of Justice monitoring of southern elections.

7. Which standard of review does the U.S. Supreme Court apply to practices involving alleged gender discrimination?

a. Strict scrutiny

b. Heightened standard

c. Intermediate standard

d. Minimum rationality

e. Suspect class scrutiny

8. Which of these issues has NOT been a subject of litigation and lobbying on behalf of Hispanic rights groups?

a. Education

b. Immigration

c. Workers' rights

d. Driver's licensing

e. Protection of native lands

9. Which group did President Franklin D. Roosevelt's executive order NOT force into internment camps after the attack on Pearl Harbor?

a. German Americans

b. Irish Americans

c. Italian Americans

d. Jewish refugees

e. Japanese Americans

10. Which of the following statements is true about affirmative action programs in the United States?

a. Affirmative action programs are widespread with virtually no limitations.

b. Affirmative action programs have been deemed unconstitutional.

c. Affirmative action programs can be used, but they must pass the strict scrutiny test.

d. Numerical quotas are the only means by which affirmative action can be applied.

e. Racial and ethnic parity has made affirmative action programs obsolete.

Explore Further

Anderson, Terry H. *The Pursuit of Fairness: A History of Affirmative Action.* New York: Oxford University Press, 2005.

Delgado, Richard. *Justice at War: Civil Liberties and Civil Rights During Times of Crisis.* New York: New York University Press, 2005.

Freeman, Jo. *The Politics of Women's Liberation.* New York: Backinprint.com, 2000.

Klarman, Michael. *From the Closet to the Altar: Courts, Backlash, and the Struggle for Same-Sex Marriage.* New York, Oxford University Press, 2012.

Longmore, Paul, and Lauri Umansky. *The New Disability History: American Perspectives.* New York: New York University Press, 2001.

Lovell, George I. *This Is Not Civil Rights: Discovering Rights Talk in 1939 America.* Chicago: University of Chicago Press, 2012.

Mansbridge, Jane J. *Why We Lost the ERA.* Chicago: University of Chicago Press, 1986.

McClain, Paula D., and Joseph Stewart Jr. *"Can We All Get Along?": Racial and Ethnic Minorities in American Politics,* 5th ed. Boulder, CO: Westview, 2009.

McGlen, Nancy E., Karen O'Connor, Laura Van Assendelft, and Wendy Gunther-Canada. *Women, Politics, and American Society,* 5th ed. New York: Longman, 2010.

Reed, Adolph, Jr., ed. *Without Justice for All: The New Liberalism and Our Retreat from Racial Equity.* Boulder, CO: Westview, 2001.

Rodriguez, Marc. *Rethinking the Chicano Movement.* New York: Routledge, 2013.

Wilkins, David E., and Heidi Kiiwetinepinesiik Stark. *American Indian Politics and the American Political System,* 3rd ed. New York: Rowman and Littlefield, 2010.

Williams, Juan. *Eyes on the Prize: America's Civil Rights Years, 1954–1965.* New York: Penguin, 1987.

Wilson, William Julius. *The Bridge over the Racial Divide: Rising Inequality and Coalition Politics,* 2nd ed. Berkeley: University of California Press, 2001.

Zia, Hellen. *Asian American Dreams: The Emergence of an American People.* New York: Farrar, Straus and Giroux, 2000.

To learn more about civil rights issues in the United States, go to the Leadership Conference on Civil and Human Rights at **www.civilrights.org,** where a coalition of 150 civil rights organizations provides coverage of a host of civil rights issues as well as links to breaking news related to civil rights.

To learn more about the ACLU Women's Rights Project, go to its Web site at **www.aclu.org/womensrights/index.html.**

To learn more about ongoing efforts to achieve greater rights for gay and lesbian Americans, see **http://lambdalegal.org.**

To learn more about disability advocacy groups, go to the Web site for the American Association of People with Disabilities at **www.aapd.com.**

Credits

Credits are listed in order of appearance.

Answer Key

1. c; 2. e; 3. b; 4. b; 5. c; 6. c; 7. c; 8. e; 9. b; 10. c

Notes

1. This vignette draws on Abigail Lofberg, "Pay Equity: Calling Out Walmart's Two Wealthiest Women," *Huffington Post* (June 4, 2012): http://www.huffingtonpost.com; Roberta Guise, "Women's Pay Equity Still a Sore Point," *San Francisco Gate* (April 10, 2011): http://www.sfgate.com; *Walmart* v. *Dukes,* 564 U.S. ____ (2011).

2. *Civil Rights Cases,* 109 U.S. 3 (1883).

3. *Plessy* v. *Ferguson,* 163 U.S. 537 (1896).

4. *Williams* v. *Mississippi,* 170 U.S. 213 (1898); and *Cummins* v. *Richmond County Board of Education,* 175 U.S. 528 (1899).

5. *Missouri* ex rel. *Gaines* v. *Canada,* 305 U.S. 337 (1938).

6. *Sweatt* v. *Painter,* 339 U.S. 629 (1950); and *McLaurin* v. *Oklahoma,* 339 U.S. 637 (1950).

7. *Brown* v. *Board of Education,* 347 U.S. 483 (1954).

8. But see Gerald Rosenberg, *The Hollow Hope: Can Courts Bring About Social Change?* (Chicago: University of Chicago Press, 1991).

9. Juan Williams, *Eyes on the Prize: America's Civil Rights Years, 1954–1965* (New York: Penguin, 1987), 10.

10. Michael McCann, "Reform Litigation on Trial," *Law and Social Inquiry* 17(1992): 715–43.

11. *Brown* v. *Board of Education II,* 349 U.S. 294 (1955).

12. Quoted in Williams, *Eyes on the Prize,* 37.

13. *Cooper* v. *Aaron,* 358 U.S. 1 (1958).

14. Jo Freeman, *The Politics of Women's Liberation* (New York: Longman, 1975), 57.

15. *Reed* v. *Reed,* 404 U.S. 71 (1971).

16. *Mississippi University for Women* v. *Hogan,* 458 U.S. 718 (1982).

17. *Craig* v. *Boren,* 429 U.S. 190 (1976).

18. *Orr* v. *Orr,* 440 U.S. 268 (1979).

19. *J.E.B.* v. *Alabama* ex rel. *TB,* 440 U.S. 268 (1979).

20. *U.S.* v. *Virginia,* 518 U.S. 515 (1996).

21. *Rostker* v. *Goldberg,* 453 U.S. 57 (1981).

22. *Michael M.* v. *Superior Court of Sonoma County,* 450 U.S. 464 (1981).

23. *Nguyen* v. *INS,* 533 U.S. 53 (2001).

24. *Rostker* v. *Goldberg,* 453 U.S. 57 (1981).

25. *U.S.* v. *Virginia,* 518 U.S. 515 (1996).

26. *Ledbetter* v. *Goodyear Tire and Rubber Co.,* 550 U.S. 618 (2007).

27. *Meritor Savings Bank* v. *Vinson,* 477 U.S. 57 (1986).

28. *Oncale* v. *Sundowner Offshore Services, Inc.,* 523 U.S. 75 (1998).

29. *Hishon* v. *King & Spalding,* 467 U.S. 69 (1984).

30. *Johnson* v. *Transportation Agency,* 480 U.S. 616 (1987).

31. Joyce Gelb and Marian Lief Palley, *Women and Public Policies* (Charlottesville: University of Virginia Press, 1996).

32. *Davis* v. *Monroe County Board of Education,* 526 U.S. 629 (1999).

33. *Jackson* v. *Birmingham Board of Education,* 544 U.S. 167 (2005).

34. *Hernandez* v. *Texas,* 347 U.S. 475 (1954).

35. *White* v. *Register,* 412 U.S. 755 (1973).

36. *San Antonio Independent School District* v. *Rodriguez,* 411 U.S. 1 (1973).

37. *Edgewood Independent School District* v. *Kirby,* 777 S.W.2d 391 (Texas 1989).

38. "MALDEF Pleased with Settlement of California Public Schools Inequity Case, *Williams* v. *California,*" (August 13, 2004): www.maldef.org.

39. *LULAC* v. *Perry,* 548 U.S. 399 (2006); and "Redistricting in Texas," *New York Times* (January 20, 2012): www.nytimes.com.

40. Dee Brown, *Bury My Heart at Wounded Knee* (New York: Holt, Rinehart and Winston, 1971).

41. Roger Daniels, *Asian America: Chinese and Japanese in the United States Since 1850* (Seattle: University of Washington Press, 1988).

42. *Yick Wo* v. *Hopkins,* 118 U.S. 356 (1886).

43. *Ozawa* v. *U.S.,* 260 U.S. 178 (1922).

44. Diane Helene Miller, *Freedom to Differ: The Shaping of the Gay and Lesbian Struggle for Civil Rights* (New York: New York University Press, 1998).

45. Sarah Brewer et al., "Sex and the Supreme Court: Gays, Lesbians, and Justice," in Craig A. Rimmerman, Kenneth D. Wald, and Clyde Wilcox, eds., *The Politics of Gay Rights* (Chicago: University of Chicago Press, 2000): 377–408.

46. Evan Gerstmann, *The Constitutional Underclass: Gays, Lesbians, and the Failure of Class-Based Equal Protection* (Chicago: University of Chicago Press, 1999).

47. *Romer* v. *Evans*, 517 U.S. 620 (1996).

48. *Lawrence* v. *Texas*, 539 U.S. 558 (2003).

49. Joan Biskupic, "Court's Opinion on Gay Rights Reflects Trends," *USA Today* (July 18, 2003): 2A.

50. *Perry* v. *Brown*, 671 F.3d 1052 (9th Circuit, 2012).

51. David Pfeiffer, "Overview of the Disability Movement: History, Legislative Record and Political Implications," *Policy Studies Journal* (Winter 1993): 724–42; and "Understanding Disability Policy," *Policy Studies Journal* (Spring 1996): 157–74.

52. Joan Biskupic, "Supreme Court Limits Meaning of Disability," *Washington Post* (June 23, 1999): A1.

53. *Sutton* v. *United Air Lines, Inc.,* 527 U.S. 471 (1999).

54. *Tennessee* v. *Lane,* 541 U.S. 509 (2004).

55. American Association of People with Disabilities, www.aapd.com.

56. *Regents of the University of California* v. *Bakke,* 438 U.S. 265 (1978).

57. *United Steelworkers of America* v. *Weber,* 443 U.S. 193 (1979).

58. *Johnson* v. *Santa Clara County,* 480 U.S. 616 (1987).

59. Ruth Marcus, "Hill Coalition Aims to Counter Court in Job Bias," *Washington Post* (February 8, 1990): A10.

60. *Grutter* v. *Bollinger,* 539 U.S. 306 (2003).

61. *Gratz* v. *Bollinger,* 539 U.S. 244 (2003).

62. *Fisher* v. *Texas,* _____ U.S. _____ (2013).

Congress

Congress

T he U.S. Constitution creates Congress as the legislative branch of government. Its primary goals are to make the laws of the nation, as well as to represent citizens' interests in national politics. However, in recent Congresses, neither of these objectives has been particularly apparent.

As a result, the modern Congress has a serious image problem. Its approval ratings reached a new low in August of 2012, when only 10 percent of Americans said they approved of the institution. The 112th House of Representatives and Senate have passed a staggeringly low number of pieces of legislation—and many of the laws that have passed have been ceremonial or simple renewals of existing programs. As a result, the legislative branch—once the most powerful political institution in the world—has been branded as a "do-nothing" institution, fraught with political conflict and weakened by partisan gridlock.

The lack of legislation passed by Congress, critics note, does not owe to a lack of important issues facing the nation. When Congress adjourned for the election in September 2012, the issues facing the institution were staggering. Farmers in the Midwest faced serious droughts and a need for governmental relief. The national debt was swelling by the minute. Unemployment was hovering near 10 percent. Questions remained about the persistence of President George W. Bush's tax cuts for the middle class. And, no budget had been passed for the upcoming fiscal year, skirting the issues of funding for programs as varied and significant as Medicare, Medicaid, and national defense. Moreover, the American people—and the presidential candidates—appeared to demand action on a range of other issues, including education, student grants and loans, access to abortion and contraceptives, gay marriage, and the implementation of health care reform.

What caused such dramatic inactivity in the 112th Congress? To some degree, that depends on whom you ask. Democratic Party officials, including House Democratic Leader Nancy Pelosi (D-CA), very vocally blamed the Republican majority in the House for failing to schedule debates and votes on significant pieces of legislation. They noted the accomplishments of recent Democratic-controlled Congresses as evidence for the fact that the problem was particularistic to the politics of the Republican Party and Speaker of the House John Boehner's (R-OH) unwillingness to compromise.

Republicans, on the other hand, blamed the Democrats in the Senate. They accused Majority Leader Harry Reid (D-NV) for the lack of legislative output, noting that even when the House passes

1	2	3	4	5	6
Trace the roots of the legislative branch outlined by the U.S. Constitution.	Characterize the demographic attributes of members of Congress, and identify factors that affect their chances for reelection.	Assess the role of the committee system, political parties, and congressional leadership in organizing Congress.	Identify three of the most significant powers of Congress.	Analyze the factors that influence how members of Congress make decisions.	Evaluate the strategic interactions between Congress, the president, the courts, and the people.

CONGRESS FUNCTIONS AS THE NATION'S LAWMAKING BODY The basic structure, rules, and procedures of Congress have changed very little since the 1940s, shown above. However, the interpersonal dynamics, policy issues, and role of the media have led to dramatically different outcomes in the modern Congress, shown below.

MyPoliSciLab Videos

The Big Picture Is Congress actually representative of the American people? Author Alixandra B. Yanus compares what Congress is supposed to do with what it actually does, and offers some suggestions as to why Americans have become increasingly disillusioned with their representatives.

The Basics Why do we have two houses of Congress? This video reveals the answer to this question and explores the differences between the two houses in their organization and procedures. You will also learn how a bill becomes a law, how Congress is organized, and how members of Congress represent you.

In Context Discover the role that the Framers expected Congress to serve in the U.S. government. Columbia University political scientist Greg Wawro discusses how Congress has become more expansive in its powers. Listen as Greg Wawro also delves into the process of creating coalitions in Congress to achieve policy results.

Think Like a Political Scientist Why has the United States become more polarized in the last decade? Columbia University political scientist Greg Wawro examines this central question and explains why polarization may be correlated to the income gap between the wealthy and the poor. He also explores recent research on the Senate as a super-majoritarian institution.

In the Real World Congress today is the most divided it has been since the end of World War II. It is also the least effective. Is compromise the answer? Real people consider the benefits and the dangers of compromise, and they discuss issues—like abortion—where compromise seems impossible.

So What? Want to change the way your government operates? In this video, author Alixandra B. Yanus reveals why Congress may actually listen to what you have to say. Find out how you can get involved in your state government and how Congress can help you accomplish your goals.

or considers legislation, Reid and the Democrats are often unwilling to discuss the issue in the Senate. This resistance, they noted, is particularly evident when it comes to issues of the budget and financial reform—some of the most important issues facing the country today.

Ironically, it may be exactly this type of hyperpartisanship and finger-pointing that has produced such a low approval rating among the American people. To these citizens, many of whom are not especially interested in politics, an unwillingness to compromise for the good of the nation often looks a lot like a failure of representation. Increasingly, therefore, citizens ask why members of Congress are so focused on dividing into Democrats and Republicans—rather than uniting as Americans.

• • •

The Framers' original conception of Congress's authority was much narrower than it is today. Those in attendance at the Constitutional Convention wished to create a legislative body that would be able to make laws as well as raise and spend revenues. Over time, Congress has attempted to maintain these roles, but changes in demands made on the national government have allowed the executive and judicial branches to gain powers at the expense of the legislative branch. Moreover, the power and the importance of individual members have grown.

Today, members of Congress must combine and balance the roles of lawmaker, budgeter, and policy maker with acting as a representative of their district, their state, their party, and sometimes their race, ethnicity, or gender. Not surprisingly, this balancing act often results in role conflict.

In this chapter, we analyze the powers of Congress and the competing roles members play as they represent the interests of their constituents, make laws, and oversee actions of the other two branches of government. We also show that as these functions have changed throughout U.S. history, so has Congress itself.

bicameral legislature
A two-house legislature.

Roots of the Legislative Branch of Government

1   Trace the roots of the legislative branch outlined by the U.S. Constitution.

A rticle I of the Constitution describes the structure of the legislative branch of government. The Great Compromise at the Constitutional Convention resulted in the creation of a lower house, the House of Representatives, and an upper house, the Senate. Any two-house legislature, such as the one created by the Framers, is called a **bicameral legislature.** The population of any given state determines the number of representatives that state sends to the House of Representatives. In contrast, two senators represent each state in the Senate, regardless of the state's population.

The U.S. Constitution sets forth the formal, or legal, requirements for membership in the House and Senate. As agreed to at the Constitutional Convention, House members must be at least twenty-five years of age; senators, thirty. Members of the House must be citizens of the United States for at least seven years; those elected to the Senate, at least nine years. Both representatives and senators must be legal residents of the states from which they are elected.

The eligible electorate in each congressional district votes to elect members of the House of Representatives to two-year terms. The Framers expected that House members would be more responsible to the people, both because they were elected directly by them and because they were up for reelection every two years. The U.S. Constitution requires that a census, which entails the counting of all Americans, be conducted every ten years. Until the first census could be taken, the Constitution fixed the number of representatives in the House of Representatives at sixty-five. In 1790, one member

The Living Constitution

> *The Congress shall have power ... to establish a uniform Rule of Naturalization.*
>
> —ARTICLE I, SECTION 8, CLAUSE 4

This clause places authority to draft laws concerning naturalization in the hands of Congress. The power of Congress over naturalization is exclusive—meaning that no state can bestow U.S. citizenship on anyone. Citizenship is a privilege, and Congress may make laws limiting or expanding the criteria.

The word "citizen" was not defined constitutionally until ratification in 1868 of the Fourteenth Amendment, which sets forth two kinds of citizenship: by birth and through naturalization. Throughout American history, Congress has imposed a variety of limits on naturalization, originally restricting it to "free, white persons." "Orientals" were excluded from eligibility in 1882. At one time, those affiliated with the Communist Party and those who lacked "good moral character" (a phrase that was construed to bar homosexuals, drunkards, gamblers, and adulterers) were deemed unfit for citizenship. These restrictions no longer carry the force of law, but they do underscore the power of Congress in this matter.

Congress continues to retain the right to naturalize large classes of individuals, as it did in 2000, when it granted automatic citizenship rights to all minor children adopted abroad as long as at least one adoptive parent was an American citizen. Naturalized citizens, however, do not necessarily possess the full rights of citizenship enjoyed by other Americans, such as the right to run for president. Congress at any time, subject only to Supreme Court review, can limit the rights and liberties of naturalized citizens, especially in times of national crisis. In the wake of the September 11, 2001, terrorist attacks, when it was revealed that one-third of the forty-eight al-Qaeda–linked operatives who took part in some sort of terrorist activities against the United States were lawful permanent residents or naturalized citizens, Congress called for greater screening by the U.S. Bureau of Citizenship and Immigration Services for potential terrorists.

CRITICAL THINKING QUESTIONS

1. Is Congress the appropriate institution to have the power over immigration and naturalization? Why or why not?

2. Is racial profiling by the U.S. Bureau of Citizenship and Immigration Services and other government entities an appropriate action in the name of national security? Why or why not?

---

apportionment
The process of allotting congressional seats to each state according to its proportion of the population, following the decennial census.

bill
A proposed law.

---

represented about 30,000 people. But, as the population of the new nation grew and states were added to the union, the House became larger and larger. In 1910, it expanded to 435 members, and in 1929, its size was fixed at that number by statute. When Alaska and Hawaii became states in the 1950s, however, the number of seats increased to 437. The number reverted to 435 in 1963. In 2012, the average number of people in a district was 713,000.

Each state is granted its share of these 435 representatives on the basis of its population. After each U.S. Census, a constitutionally mandated process called **apportionment** adjusts the number of seats allotted to each state. After seats are apportioned, state legislatures must redraw congressional districts to reflect population shifts, thereby ensuring that each member in Congress represents approximately the same number of residents. This process of redrawing congressional districts to reflect increases or decreases in the number of seats allotted to a state, as well as population shifts within a state, is called redistricting. It is discussed in greater detail later in this chapter.

Senators are elected to six-year terms, and originally state legislatures chose them because the Framers intended senators to represent their states' interests in the Senate. State legislators lost this influence over the Senate with the ratification of the Seventeenth Amendment in 1913, which provides for the direct election of senators by voters. Then, as now, one-third of all senators are up for reelection every two years.

The Constitution specifically gives Congress its most important powers: the authorities to make laws and raise and spend revenues. No **bill**, or proposed law, can

HOW LONG ARE MEMBERS' TERMS?

Members of the Senate serve six-year terms, while members of the House of Representatives serve for two years. There are no term limits, so members may run for reelection for a unlimited number of terms. The advantages of incumbency make turnover in Congress very low; new members such as Tammy Duckworth (D-IL), a disabled Iraq War veteran, constitute only a small percentage of representatives.

become law without the consent of both houses. Examples of other powers shared by both houses include the power to declare war, raise an army and navy, coin money, regulate commerce, establish the federal courts and their jurisdiction, set forth rules of immigration and naturalization, and "make all Laws which shall be necessary and proper for carrying into Execution the foregoing Powers." As interpreted by the U.S. Supreme Court, the necessary and proper clause, found at the end of Article I, section 8, when coupled with one or more of the specific powers enumerated in Article I, section 8, has allowed Congress to increase the scope of its authority, often at the expense of the states.

Reflecting the different constituencies and size of each house of Congress (as well as the Framers' intentions), Article I gives special, exclusive powers to each house in addition to their shared role in law-making. For example, as noted in Table 1, the Constitution specifies that all revenue bills must originate in the House of Representatives.

Over the years, however, this mandate has become less clear, and it is not unusual to see budget bills being considered simultaneously in both houses. Ultimately, each house must approve all bills. The House also has the power of **impeachment,** or to charge the president, vice president, or other "civil officers," including federal judges, with "Treason, Bribery, or other high Crimes and Misdemeanors." But, only the Senate has authority to conduct impeachment trials, with a two-thirds yea vote being necessary to remove a federal official, such as the president or a judge, from office.

While the House and Senate share in the impeachment process, the Senate has the sole authority to approve major presidential appointments, including federal judges, ambassadors, and Cabinet- and sub–Cabinet-level positions. The Senate, too, must approve all presidential treaties by a two-thirds vote.

impeachment
The power delegated to the House of Representatives in the Constitution to charge the president, vice president, or other "civil officers," including federal judges, with "Treason, Bribery, or other high Crimes and Misdemeanors." This is the first step in the constitutional process of removing government officials from office.

TABLE 1 WHAT ARE THE KEY DIFFERENCES BETWEEN THE HOUSE OF REPRESENTATIVES AND THE SENATE?

Constitutional Differences	
House	**Senate**
435 voting members (apportioned by population)	100 voting members (two from each state)
Two-year terms	Six-year terms (one-third up for reelection every two years)
Initiates all revenue bills	Offers "advice and consent" on many major presidential appointments
Initiates impeachment procedures and passes articles of impeachment	Tries impeached officials
	Approves treaties

Differences in Operation	
House	**Senate**
More centralized, more formal; stronger leadership	Less centralized, less formal; weaker leadership
Committee on Rules fairly powerful in controlling time and rules of debate (in conjunction with the Speaker of the House)	No rules committee; limits on debate come through unanimous consent or cloture of filibuster
More impersonal	More personal
Power distributed less evenly	Power distributed more evenly
Members are highly specialized	Members are generalists
Emphasizes tax and revenue policy	Emphasizes foreign policy

Changes in the Institution	
House	**Senate**
Power centralized in the Speaker's inner circle of advisers	Senate workload increasing and institution becoming more formal; threat of filibusters more frequent than in the past
Procedures becoming more efficient	Becoming more difficult to pass legislation
Turnover is relatively high, although those seeking reelection almost always win	Turnover is moderate

The Members of Congress

2 Characterize the demographic attributes of members of Congress, and identify factors that affect their chances for reelection.

Members must attempt to appease several constituencies—party leaders, colleagues, and lobbyists in Washington, D.C., and voters at home.[1] In attempting to do so, members spend full days at home as well as in D.C. (see Table 2). According to one study of House members, average representatives made about forty trips back home to their districts each year.[2] One journalist has aptly described a member's days as a

> kaleidoscopic jumble: breakfast with reporters, morning staff meetings, simultaneous committee hearings to juggle, back-to-back sessions with lobbyists and constituents, phone calls, briefings, constant buzzers interrupting office work to make quorum calls and votes on the run, afternoon speeches, evening meetings, receptions, fund-raisers, all crammed into four days so they can race home for a weekend gauntlet of campaigning. It's a rat race.[3]

☐ Congressional Demographics

Congress is better educated, richer, more male, and whiter than the general population. Over two-thirds of the members of the House and Senate also hold advanced degrees.[4]

TABLE 2 WHAT IS A TYPICAL DAY LIKE FOR A MEMBER OF CONGRESS?

5:00 a.m.	Arrive at office.
7:00 a.m.	Give a tour of the U.S. Capitol to constituents.
8:00 a.m.	Eat breakfast with the House Shipbuilding Caucus.
9:00 a.m.	Meet with Speaker of the House and other members of Congress.
10:00 a.m.	Attend House Armed Services Committee hearing.
11:00 a.m.	Prepare for afternoon press conference, return phone calls, and sign constituent mail.
12:00 p.m.	Meet with constituents who want the member to join a caucus that may benefit the district.
1:00 p.m.	Read one of nine newspapers to keep track of current events.
2:00 p.m.	Attend Homeland Security Subcommittee hearing.
3:00 p.m.	Attend floor vote.
3:30 p.m.	Meet with group of high school students on front steps of Capitol.
4:15 p.m.	Return to office to sign more constituent mail and to meet with representatives from the American Heart Association.
5:00 p.m.	Attend Sustainable Energy and Environment Caucus meeting.
7:00 p.m.	Eat dinner with fellow members.
9:00 p.m.	Return to office to sign more constituent mail and read more newspapers.
11:00 p.m.	Leave office to go home.

SOURCE: Adapted from Bob Clark, "A Day in the Life ..." *Evening Tribune* (October 7, 2009), www.eveningtribune .com (accessed October 20, 2010).

Many members of both houses have significant inherited wealth, but given their educational attainment, which is far higher than the average American's, it is not surprising to find so many wealthy members of Congress. Almost half of all members of Congress are millionaires. The Senate, in fact, is often called the Millionaires Club. In 2011, the average net worth of a House member was $4.7 million, while the average net worth of a senator was $13.9 million.

The average age of House members is fifty-seven; Representative Aaron Schock (R–IL) was first elected to the House in 2008 at age twenty-eight and is still the youngest member of Congress. The average age of senators in the 112th Congress is sixty-three. Michael Lee (R–UT) is the youngest senator; he was first elected in 2010 at the age of thirty-nine.

The 2012 elections saw a record number of women, African Americans, and other minorities elected to Congress. By the 113th Congress, the total number of women members rose to seventy-seven in the House and twenty in the Senate. The number of African Americans in the House remained steady at forty-four. No African Americans currently serve in the Senate. Thirty-one Hispanics served in Congress. Also serving in the 112th Congress are eleven members of Asian or Pacific Island American heritage, and one American Indian, Tom Cole (R–OK). A record number—five—openly homosexual members and one bisexual member served in the House; one homosexual woman, Tammy Baldwin (D-WI) served in the Senate.

☐ Running for and Staying In Office

Despite the long hours and hard work required of senators and representatives, thousands of people aspire to these jobs every year. Yet, only 535 men and women (plus seven nonvoting members from American Samoa, the District of Columbia, Guam, the U.S. Virgin Islands, and Puerto Rico) actually serve in the U.S. Congress. Membership in one of the two major political parties is almost always a prerequisite for election, because election laws in various states often discriminate against independents (those without party affiliation) and minor-party candidates. The ability to raise money often is key to any member's victory, and many members spend nearly all of their free time on the phone, dialing for dollars, or attending fundraisers. Incumbency and redistricting also affect members' chances at reelection.

The People's House?

The Framers intended the House of Representatives to be the people's house. At least in theory, it is the more democratic of the two houses of Congress, and its members are intended to be closer to and more representative of the American population. Critics, however, charge that it is difficult for all citizens' interests to be heard in an institution whose members overrepresent some groups, while underrepresenting others, as shown in the infographic below.

PARTY

- Republican 242
- Democrat 192

GENDER

- Women 74
- Men 341

RACE

- White 349
- African American 44
- Hispanic 29
- Asian 12
- American Indian 1

RELIGION

- Protestant 248
- Catholic 132
- Jewish 27
- Mormon 10
- Orthodox 5
- Buddhist 3
- Muslim 2
- Hindu 2
- Other 6

SOURCE: Data from Jennifer E. Manning, "Membership of the 112th Congress: A Profile," *Congressional Research Service,* accessed online August 1, 2012.

CRITICAL THINKING QUESTIONS

1. Which demographic groups are most over and unde1rrepresented in Congress, compared to the population?

2. Can members provide substantive policy representation for citizens even if they are descriptively different? Why or why not?

3. Should actions be taken to make the House look more like the American people? Why or why not? What positives and negatives might result from these actions?

TABLE 3 WHAT ARE THE ADVANTAGES OF INCUMBENCY?

Name recognition. Members' names have been on the ballot before, and voters may associate their names with programs or social services they have brought to the district.

Credit claiming. Members may claim to be responsible for federal money brought to the district.

Casework. Members and their staffs help constituents solve problems with the government, including navigating red tape and tracking down federal aid.

Franking privilege. Members may send mail or newsletters for free by using their signature in place of a stamp.

Access to media. Members and their staffs may have relationships with reporters and may find it easy to spin stories or give quotes.

Ease in fund-raising. Incumbents' high reelection rates make them a safe bet for individuals or groups wanting to give donations in exchange for access.

Experience in running a campaign. Members have already put together a campaign staff, made speeches, and come to understand constituent concerns.

Redistricting. In the House, a member's district may be drawn to enhance electability.

incumbency
Already holding an office.

redistricting
The process of redrawing congressional districts to reflect increases or decreases in seats allotted to the states, as well as population shifts within a state.

gerrymandering
The drawing of congressional districts to produce a particular electoral outcome without regard to the shape of the district.

INCUMBENCY **Incumbency** helps members stay in office once they are elected.[5] It is often very difficult for outsiders to win because they don't have the advantages enjoyed by incumbents, including name recognition, access to free media, an inside track on fund-raising, and a district drawn to favor the incumbent (see Table 3).

It is not surprising, then, that, on average, 96 percent of incumbents who seek reelection win their primary and general election races.[6] In 2012, about 20 incumbent House members lost their reelection bids. The majority of those who lost were Republicans, and many of those members had been first elected in 2010.[7] In the Senate, however, only two members, Scott Brown (R-MA) and Richard Lugar (R-IN) ran for reelection and lost.

REDISTRICTING The process of redrawing congressional districts to reflect increases or decreases in seats allotted to the states, as well as population shifts within a state, is called **redistricting.** Redistricting is a largely political process. In most states, partisan state legislatures draw district lines. As a result, the majority party in the state legislature uses the redistricting process as an opportunity to ensure formation of voting districts that protect their majority. Hoping to avoid this sort of political conflict, some states, including Iowa and Arizona, appoint nonpartisan commissions or use some other independent means of drawing district lines. Although the processes vary in detail, most states require legislative approval of redistricting plans.

The redistricting process often involves **gerrymandering**—the drawing of congressional districts to produce a particular electoral outcome without regard to the shape of the district. Because of enormous population growth, the partisan implications of redistricting, and the requirement under the Voting Rights Act of 1965 for minorities to have an equal chance to elect candidates of their choice, legislators end up drawing oddly shaped districts to elect more members of their party.[8] Redistricting plans routinely meet with court challenges across the country (see Figure 1).

For a long time, the U.S. Supreme Court considered redistricting based on partisan considerations to be a political question not within the scope of constitutional law, but, rather, one worked out through the regular political process.[9] But, in recent years the Supreme Court has involved itself in some such cases and has ruled that:

- Congressional as well as state legislative districts must be apportioned on the basis of population.[10]

- District lines must be contiguous; one must be able to draw the boundaries of the district with a single unbroken line.[11]

- Purposeful gerrymandering of a congressional district to dilute minority strength is illegal under the Voting Rights Act of 1965.[12]

- Redrawing districts to enhance minority representation is constitutional if race is not the "predominate" factor.[13]

- States may redistrict more frequently than every ten years.[14]

163

The Original "Gerrymander" Cartoon, 1812

Congress

Texas 35th District, 2012

FIGURE 1 WHAT IS GERRYMANDERING?

Two drawings—one a mocking cartoon, the other all too real—show the bizarre geographical contortions that result from gerrymandering. The term was coined by combining the last name of the Massachusetts governor first credited with politicizing the redistricting process, Elbridge Gerry, and the word "salamander," which looked like the oddly shaped district that Gerry created.

SOURCES: David Van Biema, "Snakes or Ladders?" *Time* (July 12, 1993) © 1993, Time Inc. Reprinted by permission.

majority party

The political party in each house of Congress with the most members.

minority party

The political party in each house of Congress with the second most members.

party caucus (or conference)

A formal gathering of all party members.

How Congress Is Organized

3 Assess the role of the committee system, political parties, and congressional leadership in organizing Congress.

As demonstrated in Figure 2, the organization of both houses of Congress is closely tied to political parties and their strength in each house. The basic division in Congress is between majority and minority parties. The **majority party** in each house is the party with the most members. The **minority party** in each house is the party with the second most members.

At the beginning of each new Congress—the 113th Congress, for example, will sit in two sessions, one in 2013 and one in 2014—the members of each party formally gather in their **party caucus (or conference)** (see Figure 3 for the partisan composition of Congress). Historically, these caucuses have enjoyed varied powers, but today the party caucuses—now called caucus by House and Senate Democrats and conference by House and Senate Republicans—have several roles, including nominating or electing party officers, reviewing committee assignments, discussing party policy, imposing party discipline, setting party themes, and coordinating media, including talk radio. Conference and caucus chairs are recognized party leaders who work with other leaders in the House or Senate.[15]

Each caucus or conference has specialized committees that fulfill certain tasks. House Republicans, for example, have a Committee on Committees that makes committee assignments. The Democrats' Steering Committee performs this function. Each party also has congressional campaign committees to assist members in their reelection bids.

☐ Leadership in the House of Representatives

Even in the first Congress in 1789, the House of Representatives was almost three times larger than the Senate. It is not surprising, then, that from the beginning the House has shown tighter organization, more elaborate structure, and governance by stricter rules. Traditionally, loyalty to party leadership and voting along party lines have been more common in the House than in the Senate. House leaders also play a key role in moving the business of the House along. Historically, the Speaker of the House, the majority and minority leaders, and the Republican and Democratic House whips have made up the party leadership that runs the institution.

THE SPEAKER OF THE HOUSE The **Speaker of the House**, the chamber's most powerful position, is the only officer of the House of Representatives specifically mentioned in the Constitution. The entire House of Representatives elects the Speaker at the beginning of each new Congress. Traditionally, the Speaker is a member of the majority party. Although typically not the member with the longest service, the Speaker generally has served in the House for a long time and in other House leadership positions as an apprentice.

The Speaker presides over the House of Representatives, oversees House business, and is the official spokesperson for the House, as well as being second in the line of presidential succession (after the vice president). The Speaker is also expected to smooth the passage of party-backed legislation through the House. To aid in this process, the Speaker generally has great political influence within the chamber and in policy negotiations with the president.

LEADERSHIP TEAMS After the Speaker, the next most powerful people in the House are the majority and minority leaders, who are elected in their individual party

Speaker of the House
The only officer of the House of Representatives specifically mentioned in the Constitution; the chamber's most powerful position; traditionally a member of the majority party.

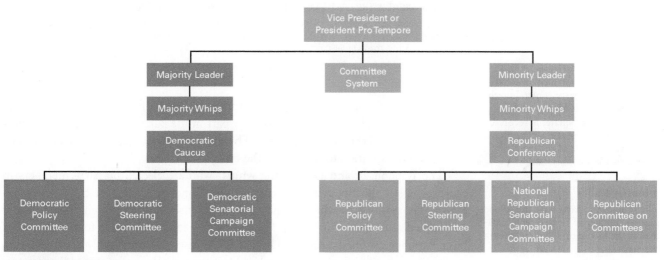

FIGURE 2 HOW ARE THE HOUSE OF REPRESENTATIVES AND THE SENATE ORGANIZED?

Parties play a very important role in organizing both the House and Senate. The majority and minority leaders are chosen by the party caucus or conference, as are other key leaders in the party hierarchy. This structure helps to organize operations and conflict in each of the institutions.

SOURCE: Adapted from Roger H. Davidson and Walter J. Oleszek, *Congress and Its Members,* 10th ed. (Washington, DC: CQ Press, 2006). Updated by the authors.

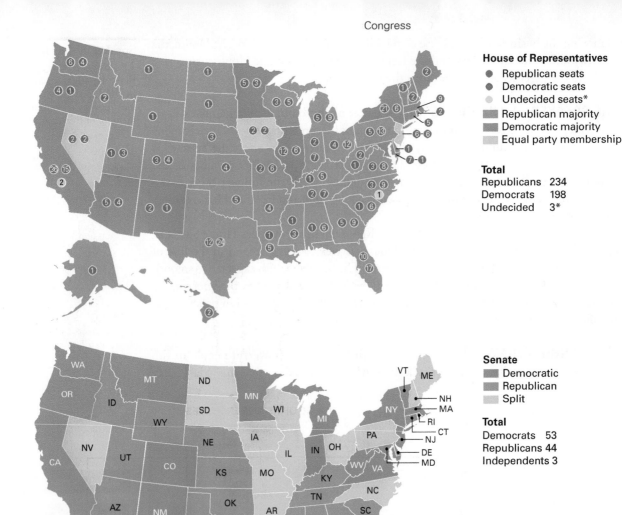

House of Representatives

- ● Republican seats
- ● Democratic seats
- ○ Undecided seats*
- ■ Republican majority
- ■ Democratic majority
- ■ Equal party membership

Total

Republicans	234
Democrats	198
Undecided	3*

Senate

- ■ Democratic
- ■ Republican
- ■ Split

Total

Democrats	53
Republicans	44
Independents	3

*As of mid-November 2012.

FIGURE 3 WHAT IS THE PARTISAN COMPOSITION OF THE 113TH CONGRESS?

The partisan composition of the 113th Congress is quite similar to that of the 112th Congress, with Republicans holding the majority in the House of Representatives and Democrats holding the majority in the Senate. Democrats made small gains in each of the houses, but it was not enough to switch overall control.

SOURCE: CNN Races and Results, http://www.cnn.com/election/2012/results/race/house and http://www.cnn.com/election/2012/results/race/senate.

majority leader

The head of the party controlling the most seats in the House of Representatives or the Senate; is second in authority to the Speaker of the House and in the Senate is regarded as its most powerful member.

minority leader

The head of the party with the second highest number of elected representatives in the House of Representatives or the Senate.

whip

Party leader who keeps close contact with all members of his or her party, takes vote counts on key legislation, prepares summaries of bills, and acts as a communications link within a party.

caucuses or conferences. The **majority leader** is the head of the party controlling the most seats in the House; his or her counterpart in the party with the second highest number of seats is the **minority leader.** The majority leader helps the Speaker schedule proposed legislation for debate on the House floor.

The Republican and Democratic **whips,** who are elected by party members in caucuses, assist the Speaker and majority and minority leaders in their leadership efforts. The position of whip originated in the British House of Commons, where it was named after the "whipper in," the rider who keeps the hounds together in a fox hunt. Party whips—first designated in the U.S. House of Representatives in 1899—do, as their name suggests, try to whip fellow Democrats or Republicans into line on partisan issues. They try to maintain close contact with all members on important votes, prepare summaries of content and implications of bills, take vote counts during debates and votes, and in general persuade members to toe the party line. Whips and their deputy whips also serve as communications links, distributing word of the party line from leaders to rank-and-file members and alerting leaders to concerns in the ranks.

Explore Your World

The structure of the U.S. Capitol reflects not only the bicameral legislature created by the Framers in Article I but also American culture. For example, the designer of the Capitol "Americanized" some of the columns on the building by sculpting ears of corn instead of traditional European acanthus leaves. Examine each of the photos below and consider how they reflect the characteristics of the state they represent.

Myanmar's (Burma) legislative building is one of the newest in the world, opening in 2010 after decades of controversy in that country gave way to parliamentary elections. The building's architecture echos the style of many Burmese temples in the region, but this lavish complex has spurred controversy, as the perfectly manicured lawns and brand new buildings contrast sharply with the poverty of many of the country's residents.

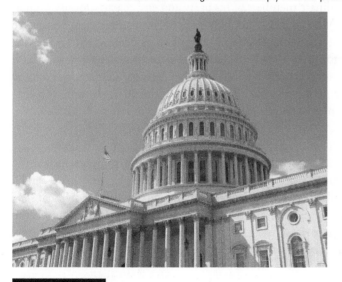

The most prominent feature of the U.S. Capitol is its dome, which is located in the center of the building. The wings on either side of the dome are home to the House of Representatives and the Senate.

The Hellenic Parliament meets in the Parliament House in Athens, Greece. The building sits elevated on a hill, above Constitution Square. Although the legislature is unicameral today, it was bicameral during some parts of the country's history.

CRITICAL THINKING QUESTIONS

1. What similarities and differences did you notice in the physical structures of the legislative buildings?

2. Why do you think each legislature looks the way it does? How has the country's governmental system influenced each building's appearance? How have cultural influences affected each building's appearance?

3. Assume two new countries have just been established: one has a unicameral legislature, and the other has a bicameral legislature. If you were to design a legislative building for each of these countries, how would each look and why?

president pro tempore
The official chair of the Senate; usually the most senior member of the majority party.

☐ Leadership in the Senate

Organization and formal rules never have played the same role in the Senate as in the House. Through the 1960s, the Senate was a gentlemen's club whose folkways—unwritten rules of behavior—governed its operation. In the 1960s and 1970s, senators became increasingly active on a variety of issues on and off the Senate floor, and extended debates often occurred on the floor without the rigid rules of courtesy that had once prevailed. These changes have made the majority leader's role as coalition-builder extraordinarily challenging.[16]

PRESIDING OFFICER The Constitution specifies that the presiding officer of the Senate is the vice president of the United States. Because he is not a member of the Senate, he votes only in the case of a tie.

The official chair of the Senate is the **president pro tempore,** or pro tem, whom the majority party selects and who presides over the Senate in the absence of the vice president. The position of pro tem today is primarily an honorific office generally awarded to the most senior senator of the majority party. Once elected, the pro tem stays in that office until the majority party in the Senate changes. Since presiding over the Senate can be a rather perfunctory duty, neither the vice president nor the president pro tempore actually performs the task very often. Instead, this particular duty rotates among junior members of the majority party of the chamber, allowing more senior members to attend meetings of greater importance.

MAJORITY LEADER The true leader of the Senate is the majority leader, elected to the position by the majority party. Because the Senate is a smaller and more collegial body, the majority leader is not nearly as powerful as the Speaker of the House. Senate Majority Leader Harry Reid (D–NV) discovered the many difficulties that may face a Senate leader trying to coordinate members of his party and ensure party loyalty, even in times of high partisanship. Most of Reid's troubles resulted from struggles to ensure the loyalty of moderate Democratic members on important votes dealing with economic recovery and health care reform. As a result of these challenges, but also because of high unemployment and foreclosure rates in his home state of Nevada, Reid appeared to be one of the most vulnerable members of the Senate during the 2010 election. He ultimately defeated Tea Party member Sharron Angle with help from many labor unions.

LEADERSHIP TEAMS The minority leader and the Republican and Democratic whips round out the leadership positions in the Senate and perform functions similar to those of their House counterparts. But, leading and whipping in the Senate can be quite a challenge. Senate rules always have given tremendous power to individual senators; in most cases senators can offer any kind of amendments to legislation on the floor, and an individual senator can bring all work on the floor to a halt indefinitely through a filibuster unless three-fifths of the senators vote to cut him or her off.[17]

☐ The Committee System

The saying "Congress in session is Congress on exhibition, whilst Congress in its committee rooms is Congress at work" may not be as true today as it was when Woodrow Wilson wrote it in 1885.[18] Still, "the work that takes place in the committee and subcommittee rooms of Capitol Hill is critical to the productivity and effectiveness of Congress."[19] Standing committees are the first and last places to which most bills go. Usually, committee members play key roles in floor debate about the merits of bills that have been introduced. When the House and Senate pass different versions of a bill, a conference committee with members of both houses meets to iron out the differences. Committee organization and specialization are especially important in the House of Representatives because of its size. The establishment of subcommittees allows for even greater specialization.

TYPES OF COMMITTEES Congressional committees are of four types: (1) standing; (2) joint; (3) conference; and, (4) select (or special).[20]

1. **Standing committees** are those to which bills are referred for consideration; they are so called because they continue from one Congress to the next.

2. **Joint committees** are standing committees that include members from both houses of Congress and are set up to conduct investigations or special studies. They focus public attention on major matters, such as the economy, taxation, or scandals.

3. **Conference committees** are special joint committees created to reconcile differences in bills passed by the House and Senate. A conference committee comprises members from the House and Senate committees that originally considered the bill.

4. **Select (or special) committees** are temporary committees appointed for specific purposes, such as investigating the September 11, 2001, terrorist attacks.

In the 112th Congress, the House had twenty standing committees, as shown in Table 4, each with an average of thirty-one members. Together, these standing committees had roughly ninety subcommittees that collectively acted as the eyes, ears, and hands

standing committee
Committee to which proposed bills are referred; continues from one Congress to the next.

joint committee
Standing committee that includes members from both houses of Congress set up to conduct investigations or special studies.

conference committee
Special joint committee created to reconcile differences in bills passed by the House and Senate.

select (or special) committee
Temporary committee appointed for a specific purpose.

TABLE 4 WHAT WERE THE COMMITTEES OF THE 112TH CONGRESS?

Standing Committees	
House	**Senate**
Agriculture	Agriculture, Nutrition, and Forestry
Appropriations	Appropriations
Armed Services	Armed Services
Budget	Banking, Housing, and Urban Affairs
Education and the Workforce	Budget
Energy and Commerce	Commerce, Science, and Transportation
Ethics	Energy and Natural Resources
Financial Services	Environment and Public Works
Foreign Affairs	Finance
Homeland Security	Foreign Relations
House Administration	Health, Education, Labor, and Pensions
Judiciary	Homeland Security and Governmental Affairs
Commercial and Administrative Law	Judiciary
The Constitution, Civil Rights, and Civil Liberties	*Administrative Oversight and the Courts*
Courts and Competition Policy	*Antitrust, Competition Policy, and Consumer Rights*
Crime, Terrorism, and Homeland Security	*The Constitution*
Immigration, Citizenship, Refugees, Border Security, and International Law	*Crime and Drugs*
Task Force on Antitrust	*Human Rights and the Law*
Natural Resources	*Immigration, Refugees, and Border Security*
Oversight and Government Reform	*Terrorism, Technology, and Homeland Security*
Rules	Rules and Administration
Science, Space, and Technology	Small Business and Entrepreneurship
Small Business	Veterans Affairs
Transportation and Infrastructure	
Veterans' Affairs	
Ways and Means	

Select, Special, and Other Committees		
House	**Senate**	**Joint Committees**
Intelligence	Select Ethics	Economic
	Select Intelligence	Taxation
	Special Aging	Library
	Indian Affairs	Printing

NOTE: The subcommittees of the House and Senate Judiciary Committees during the 112th Congress are listed in italics.

seniority
Time of continuous service on a committee.

of the House. They considered issues roughly parallel to those of the departments represented in the president's Cabinet. For example, there were committees on agriculture, education, the judiciary, veterans' affairs, transportation, and commerce.

Although most committees in one house parallel those in the other, the House Committee on Rules, for which no counterpart in the Senate exists, plays a major role in the House's law-making process. As an indication of this committee's importance, the Speaker directly appoints its chair and majority party members. This committee reviews most bills after they come from a committee and before they go to the full chamber for consideration. Performing a traffic cop function, the Committee on Rules gives each bill what is called a rule, which contains the date the bill will come up for debate and the time that will be allotted for discussion, and often specifies what kinds of amendments can be offered. Bills considered under a closed rule cannot be amended.

Standing committees have considerable power. They can kill bills, amend them radically, or hurry them through the process. In the words of former President Woodrow Wilson, once a bill is referred to a committee, it "crosses a parliamentary bridge of sighs to dim dungeons of silence whence it never will return."[21]

In the 112th Congress, the Senate had sixteen standing committees ranging in size from fifteen to twenty-nine members. It also had roughly seventy subcommittees, which allowed all majority party senators to chair at least one.

In contrast to members of the House, who hold few committee assignments (an average of 1.8 standing and three subcommittees), senators each serve on an average of three to four committees and seven subcommittees. Whereas the committee system allows House members to become policy or issue specialists, Senate members often are generalists.

Senate committees have the same power over framing legislation that House committees do, but the Senate, as an institution more open to individual input than the House, gives less deference to the work done in committees. In the Senate, legislation is more likely to be rewritten on the floor, where all senators can generally participate and add amendments.

COMMITTEE CHAIRS Committee chairs enjoy tremendous power and prestige, with authorization to select all subcommittee chairs, call meetings, and recommend majority members to sit on conference committees. Committee chairs may even opt to kill a bill by refusing to schedule hearings on it. They also have a large committee staff at their disposal and are often recipients of favors from lobbyists, who recognize the chair's unique position of power. Interpersonal skills, influence, and expertise are a chair's best resources.

Historically, committee chairs were the majority party members with the longest continuous service on the committee. Committee chairs in the House, unlike the Senate, are no longer selected by **seniority,** or time of continuous service on the committee. Instead, to ensure that candidates demonstrate party loyalty, party leaders interview potential chairs. Six years of service on a particular committee is the limit on all committee chairs.

COMMITTEE MEMBERSHIP Many newly elected members of Congress set their sights on certain committee assignments. Others are more flexible. Many legislators who desire particular committee assignments inform their party's selection committee of their preferences. They often request assignments based on their own interests or expertise or on a particular committee's ability to help their prospects for reelection. One political scientist has noted that members view committee assignments the way investors view stocks—they seek to acquire those that will add to the value of their portfolios.[22]

Some committees, such as Energy and Commerce, facilitate reelection by giving House members influence over decisions that affect large campaign contributors. Other committees, such as Education and the Workforce or Judiciary, attract members eager to work on the policy responsibilities assigned to the committee even if the appointment does them little good at the ballot box. Another motivator for certain committee assignments is the desire to have power and influence within the chamber. The Appropriations and Budget Committees provide that kind of reward for some members, given the monetary impact of the committees. Congress can approve programs, but unless money for them is appropriated in the budget, they are largely symbolic.

In both the House and the Senate, committee membership generally reflects party distribution within that chamber. For example, at the outset of the 113th Congress, Republicans held a majority of House seats and thus claimed about a 55 percent share of the seats on several committees. On committees more critical to the operation of the House or to the setting of national policy, the majority often takes a disproportionate share of the slots. Since the Committee on Rules regulates access to the floor for legislation approved by other standing committees, control by the majority party is essential for it to manage the flow of legislation. For this reason, no matter how narrow its margin in the chamber, the majority party makes up more than two-thirds of the Committee on Rules' membership.

Powers of Congress

4   Identify three of the most significant powers of Congress.

T he Framers wished to ensure that the national government had sufficient power to govern the states. Thus, Article I, section 7, of the Constitution details the procedures by which Congress can make laws and raise revenues. Article I, section 8, also details Congress's power to tax, spend, regulate commerce, coin money, and make "all Laws which shall be necessary and proper for carrying into Execution" those powers.

Today, Congress not only makes laws dealing with substantive policy but also spends significant time negotiating and trying to pass the nation's budget. In addition, in accordance with the system of checks and balances, it has a key oversight role. Through the War Powers Resolution, congressional review, approval of nominations, and impeachment, Congress can check the power of the executive and judicial branches.

☐ The Law-making Function

Congress's law-making power allows it to affect the day-to-day lives of all Americans and set policy for the future. Although proposals for legislation—be they about terrorism, Medicare, or tax policy—can come from the president, executive agencies, committee staffs, interest groups, or even private individuals, only members of the House or Senate can formally submit a bill for congressional consideration (although lobbyists initially draft many of them). Once a member of Congress introduces a bill, it usually reaches a dead end. Of the approximately 10,500 bills introduced during the 112th session, Congress voted fewer than 150 into law.

A bill must survive several stages before it becomes a law. One or more standing committees and both chambers must approve it, and if House and Senate versions differ, each house must accept a conference report resolving those differences. Multiple stopping points provide many opportunities for legislation to die or members to revise the content of legislation and may lead representatives to alter their views on a particular piece of legislation several times over. Thus, it is much easier to defeat a bill than to pass one (see Figure 4). The ongoing debates on the budget process are particularly illustrative of this problem.

COMMITTEE REFERRAL The House and Senate have parallel processes, and often the same bill is introduced in each chamber at the same time. One member of Congress must introduce a bill, but several other members (called co-sponsors) often sponsor a bill, in an attempt to show support for its aims. Once introduced, the bill is sent to the clerk of the chamber, who gives it a number (for example, HR 1 or S 1—indicating House or Senate bill number one, respectively). The bill is then printed, distributed, and sent to the appropriate committee or committees for consideration.

Take a Closer Look

Much of the work of Congress is accomplished in committee hearings and private meetings and negotiations. The activity that occurs on the floor of the U.S Senate and House of Representatives is, as a result, more informal than many citizens might expect. While one member is speaking in support of or opposition to a piece of legislation, other members—if they are even in the chamber—may be casting votes, talking with colleagues, or even milling around. Still, the floor proceedings of the U.S. Congress play an important role in the legislative process.

Each senator has a desk in the chamber, with Republicans on the left hand side of the presiding officer and Democrats on the right. Senators, however, rarely sit at these desks.

Clerks record senators' comments, tally votes, and maintain the operations of the institution. Behind the clerks sits a presiding officer. Officially, this member should be the vice president or the president pro tempore, but in practice, it is usually a junior member.

The member of the Senate speaking stands at a podium at the front and center of the chamber.

CRITICAL THINKING QUESTIONS

1. Why are formal legislative sessions important to the governmental process, even if little actual work is accomplished during this time?

2. Should members be required to spend more time in the chamber listening to their colleagues' speeches and participating in the legislative process? What would be the positives and negatives of this requirement?

3. Should some of the work traditionally accomplished on the floor of the House and Senate, such as voting and giving speeches, move online in the interest of efficiency? Why or why not?

The committee usually refers the bill to one of its subcommittees, whose staff researches the proposed legislation, and then the chair decides whether or not to hold hearings. The subcommittee hearings provide an opportunity for those on both sides of the issue to voice their opinions. Since the 1970s, most hearings have been open to the public. After the hearings, the subcommittee revises the bill and then votes to approve or defeat it. If the subcommittee votes in favor of the bill, it is returned to the full committee. There, it goes through **markup,** a session during which committee members can offer changes to a bill before it goes to the floor. The full committee may also reject the bill before it goes to the floor in either house.

FLOOR DEBATE The second stage of action takes place on the House or Senate floor. As previously discussed, in the House, before a bill may be debated on the floor,

markup
A session in which committee members offer changes to a bill before it goes to the floor.

FIGURE 4 HOW DOES A BILL BECOME A LAW?
A bill must go through a carefully prescribed process in both the House of Representatives and the Senate in order to be enacted into law. After a bill has passed both houses, differences must be reconciled and the proposed legislation must meet with the president's approval. As a result, though many bills are introduced, few actually become law.

hold

A procedure by which a senator asks to be informed before a particular bill or nomination is brought to the floor. This request signals leadership that a member may have objections to the bill (or nomination) and should be consulted before further action is taken.

filibuster

A formal way of halting Senate action on a bill by means of long speeches or unlimited debate.

cloture

Mechanism requiring the vote of sixty senators to cut off debate.

veto

The formal, constitutional authority of the president to reject bills passed by both houses of Congress, thus preventing them from becoming law without further congressional action.

pocket veto

If Congress adjourns during the ten days the president has to consider a bill passed by both houses of Congress, the bill is considered vetoed without the president's signature.

the Committee on Rules must approve it and give it a rule and a place on the calendar, or schedule. (House budget bills, however, do not go to the Committee on Rules.) In the House, the rule given to a bill determines limits on the floor debate and specifies what types of amendments, if any, may be attached to the bill. Once the Committee on Rules considers the bill, it is added to the calendar.

When the day arrives for floor debate, the House may choose to form a Committee of the Whole. This procedure allows the House to deliberate with only one hundred members present to expedite consideration of the bill. During this time, members may offer amendments, and the full House ultimately takes a vote. If the bill survives, it goes to the Senate for consideration if that body did not consider it simultaneously.

Unlike the House, whose size necessarily limits debate, the Senate may hold up bills by a hold or a filibuster. A **hold** is a procedure by which a senator asks to be informed before a particular bill (or nomination) is brought to the floor. This request signals the Senate leadership and the sponsors of the bill that a colleague may have objections to the bill (or nomination) and should be consulted before further action is taken.

Filibusters, a formal way of halting Senate action on a bill by means of long speeches or unlimited debate, grew out of the absence of rules to restrict speech in the Senate. The content of a filibuster has no limits as long as a senator keeps talking. A senator may read from a phone book, recite poetry, or read cookbooks to delay a vote. Often, a team of senators takes turns speaking to continue the filibuster in the hope of tabling or killing a bill. In 1964, for example, a group of northern liberal senators kept a filibuster alive for eighty-two days in an effort to prevent amendments that would weaken a civil rights bill. The use of filibusters has increased in recent years. Moreover, simply the threat of a filibuster can be quite potent; in the modern Senate, it often takes the assured votes of sixty senators for a bill to come to a final vote because of the threat of a filibuster.

Senators may end a filibuster in only one way. Sixty of them must sign a motion for **cloture.** After a cloture motion passes the Senate floor, members may spend no more than thirty additional hours debating the legislation at issue.

FINAL APPROVAL The third stage of action takes place when the two chambers of Congress approve different versions of the same bill. When this happens, they establish a conference committee to iron out the differences between the two versions. The conference committee, whose members are from the original House and Senate committees, hammers out a compromise, which is returned to each chamber for a final vote. Sometimes the conference committee fails to agree and the bill dies there. No changes or amendments to the compromise version are allowed. If the bill does not pass in both houses, it dies. If the bill passes, it is sent to the president, who has ten days to consider a bill. He has four options:

1. The president can sign the bill, at which point it becomes law.
2. The president can **veto** the bill, which is more likely to occur when the president is of a different party from the majority in Congress; Congress may override the president's veto with a two-thirds vote in each chamber, a very difficult task.
3. The president can wait the full ten days, at the end of which time the bill becomes law without his signature if Congress is still in session.
4. If Congress adjourns before the ten days are up, the president can choose not to sign the bill, which is called a **pocket veto.** To become law, the bill then has only one path: to be reintroduced in the next session of Congress and put through the process all over again.

☐ The Budgetary Function

Since the writing of the Constitution, Congress has enjoyed authority over the budgetary process. For much of American history, however, congressional budgets were piecemeal and made without an eye toward setting the course of public policy. By the 1920s, as a result of growing federal regulation and the bureaucracy, many policy makers sensed a need for greater centralization and order in the budgetary process. Thus, Congress passed and President Warren G. Harding signed into law the Budget and Accounting Act of 1921. This legislation required the president—for the first time—to submit a budget to Congress. The president's proposal would include the prior year's spending, projections, and proposals for the next year. Congress, in turn, could alter the allocation of appropriations but could not increase the total level of spending proposed by the president. To aid the executive branch in this role, the act also created the Bureau of the Budget. In 1970, the name of this agency was changed to the Office of Management and Budget.

This process continued relatively unfettered until the early 1970s, when tension between a Democratic-controlled Congress and a Republican president, Richard M. Nixon, exposed several shortcomings in the system. For example, although Congress authorized the expenditure of funds for many social problems, President Nixon refused to spend appropriated money on them. Angered and frustrated by Nixon's flagrant use of executive power, Congress solidified its role in the budgetary process by passing the Congressional Budget Act of 1974.

CONGRESSIONAL BUDGET ACT OF 1974 The **Congressional Budget Act of 1974** established the congressional budgetary process we use today. The act also created the Congressional Budget Office (CBO), a nonpartisan agency to help members make accurate estimations of revenues and expenditures and to lay out a plan for congressional action on the annual budget resolution, appropriations, reconciliation, and any other revenue bills. In general, these bills and resolutions establish levels of spending for the federal government and its agencies during the next fiscal year. (The federal government's fiscal year runs from October 1 of one year to September 30 of the next. Thus, the 2014 fiscal year runs from October 1, 2013, to September 30, 2014.) Although these levels rarely change dramatically from year to year, the programs and policies that receive increases and decreases in federal spending make a powerful statement about the goals of Congress and the president.

One special process detailed by the Congressional Budget Act of 1974 is **reconciliation.** The reconciliation procedure allows consideration of controversial issues affecting the budget by limiting debate to twenty hours, thereby ending the threat of a filibuster in the Senate. This process received a great deal of attention in 2010, when members of Congress used it to pass the health care reform bill.

The Congressional Budget Act of 1974 also includes a timetable intended to make sure that action on the budget occurs without unnecessary delay (see Table 5). Under this constraint, Congress must complete initial action on the budget resolution by April 15 of the preceding fiscal year. The budget resolution—or one or more continuing resolutions allowing the government to spend money at the same rates as the

Congressional Budget Act of 1974
Act that established the congressional budgetary process by laying out a plan for congressional action on the annual budget resolution, appropriations, reconciliation, and any other revenue bills.

reconciliation
A procedure that allows consideration of controversial issues affecting the budget by limiting debate to twenty hours, thereby ending threat of a filibuster.

TABLE 5 WHAT IS THE TIMELINE FOR THE CONGRESSIONAL BUDGETARY PROCESS?

Date	Action
First Monday in February	**President submits budget to Congress**—President's budget is prepared by the Office of Management and Budget; includes requested levels of spending for the next fiscal year.
February 15	**Budget outlooks**—Congressional Budget Office submits economic projections to the House and Senate Budget Committees.
April 15	**Budget resolution**—Congress must complete action on the initial version of a budget resolution.
May 15	**Appropriation begins**—House begins to consider appropriations bills.
June 10	**Appropriations Committee**—House Appropriations Committee should conclude consideration of appropriations issues.
June 15	**Reconciliation ends**—House must handle any reconciliation bills by this date.
June 30	**Appropriation ends**—Full House should conclude consideration of all appropriations bills.
October 1	**Fiscal year begins**—Government's fiscal year runs from October 1 to September 30.

1
2
3
4
5
6

pork
Legislation that allows representatives to bring money and jobs to their districts in the form of public works programs, military bases, or other programs.

programmatic requests
Federal funds designated for special projects within a state or congressional district.

War Powers Resolution
Passed by Congress in 1973; requires the authorization of Congress to deploy troops overseas and limits the time of their deployment.

congressional review
A process whereby Congress can nullify agency regulations by a joint resolution of legislative disapproval.

previous fiscal year—must receive approval by the start of the new fiscal year on October 1. When this does not occur, the federal government may shut down.

PORK AND PROGRAMMATIC REQUESTS Representatives often seek to win appropriations known as **pork,** legislation that allows representatives to bring money and jobs to their districts in the form of public works programs, military bases, or other programs. Many of these programs, once called earmarks but now called **programmatic requests,** are funds that an appropriations bill designates for specific projects within a state or congressional district. Legislators who bring jobs and new public works programs back to their districts are hard to defeat when up for reelection. But, ironically, these programs also attract much of the public criticism directed at the federal government in general and Congress in particular.

☐ The Oversight Function

Historically, Congress has performed its oversight function by holding committee hearings in which members question bureaucrats to determine if they are enforcing and interpreting the laws as intended by Congress. These hearings, now routinely televised, are among Congress's most visible and dramatic actions. Congress uses them not only to gather information but also to focus on particular executive branch actions. They often signal that Congress believes an agency needs to make changes in policy or performance before it next comes before the committee to justify its budget or actions. Congress also uses hearings to improve program administration.

Congress may also exercise its oversight powers in a number of other ways. It may, for example, use its powers under the War Powers Resolution or the Congressional Review Act of 1996 to examine actions taken by the president. The Senate also has the authority to offer advice and consent on executive and judicial branch nominees. Congress's ultimate oversight power, however, is the power to impeach other federal officials and remove them from office.

THE WAR POWERS RESOLUTION After years of playing second fiddle to a series of presidents from Theodore Roosevelt to Richard M. Nixon, a "snoozing Congress" was "aroused" and seized for itself the authority and expertise necessary to exercise its full foreign policy oversight powers over the chief executive.[23] In a delayed response to Lyndon B. Johnson's conduct of the Vietnam War, in 1973 Congress passed the **War Powers Resolution** over President Nixon's veto. The resolution permits the president to send troops into action only with the authorization of Congress or if the United States, its territories, or the armed forces are attacked. It also requires the president to notify Congress within forty-eight hours of committing troops to foreign soil. In addition, the president must withdraw troops within sixty days unless Congress votes to declare war. The president also must consult with Congress, if at all possible, prior to committing troops.

The War Powers Resolution, however, has had limited effectiveness in claiming an oversight role for Congress in international crisis situations. Presidents Gerald R. Ford, Jimmy Carter, and Ronald Reagan never consulted Congress in advance of committing troops, citing the need for secrecy and swift movement, although each president did notify Congress shortly after the deployment of troops abroad. They contended that the War Powers Resolution was probably unconstitutional because it limits presidential prerogatives as commander in chief.

CONGRESSIONAL REVIEW The Congressional Review Act of 1996 allows Congress to exercise its oversight powers by nullifying agency regulations. Under the home rule charter of the District of Columbia, the House and Senate may also nullify actions of the Washington, D.C., City Council. This process is called **congressional review.**[24] If using this oversight power, Congress has sixty days after the implementation of an administrative action to pass a joint resolution of legislative disapproval. The president must also have signed the resolution.

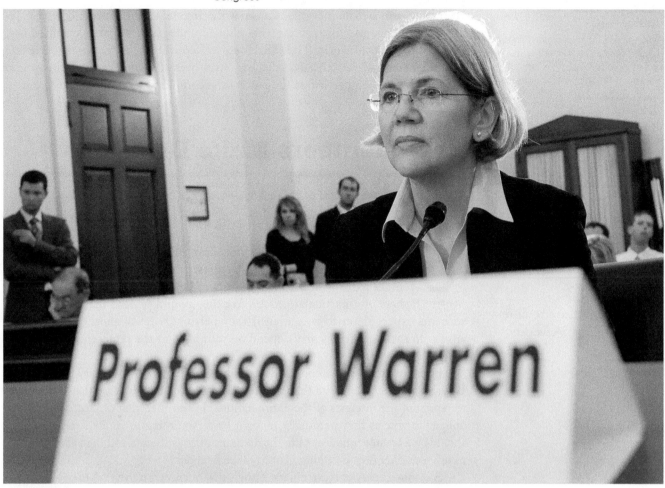

1
2
3
4
5
6

ON WHAT ISSUES DOES CONGRESS CONDUCT OVERSIGHT HEARINGS?

In 2008, Congress created the Troubled Assets Relief Program (TARP) to aid in restoring order and liquidity to the nation's financial system. It also created an Oversight Panel to assure that this program was working efficiently and effectively. Law Professor Elizabeth Warren, who in 2012 was elected to the Senate representing Massachusetts, chaired this committee. She is shown here testifying to the House Budget Committee.

CONFIRMATION OF PRESIDENTIAL APPOINTEES The Senate plays a special oversight function through its ability to confirm key members of the executive branch, as well as presidential appointments to the federal courts. Although the Senate generally confirms most presidential nominees, it does not always do so. A wise president considers senatorial reaction before nominating potentially controversial individuals to his administration or to the federal courts.

In the case of federal district court appointments, senators often have considerable say in the nomination of judges from their states through **senatorial courtesy,** a process by which presidents generally defer to the senators who represent the state where the vacancy occurs. Through the "blue slip" process, senators may submit a favorable or unfavorable review of a nominee; they may also choose not to comment. Despite this procedure, the judicial nominees of recent presidents have encountered particularly hostile Senates. "Appointments have always been the battleground for policy disputes," says one political scientist. But now, "what's new is the rawness of it—all of the veneer is off."[25]

IMPEACHMENT As discussed earlier, the impeachment process is Congress's ultimate oversight of the U.S. president and federal court judges. The U.S. Constitution is quite vague about the impeachment process, and much debate over it concerns what constitutes an impeachable offense. The Constitution specifies that Congress can impeach a president for treason, bribery, or other "high crimes and misdemeanors." Most commentators agree that the Framers intended this phrase to mean significant abuses of power.

senatorial courtesy

A process by which presidents generally allow senators from the state in which a judicial vacancy occurs to block a nomination by simply registering their objection.

House and Senate rules control how the impeachment process operates. Yet, because Congress uses the process so rarely, and under such disparate circumstances, few hard and fast rules exist. The U.S. House of Representatives has voted to impeach only seventeen federal officials. Of those, seven were convicted and removed from office, and three resigned before the process was completed.

How Members Make Decisions

5 Analyze the factors that influence how members of Congress make decisions.

Over the years, political theorists have offered various ideas about how any legislative body can best represent constituents' interests. Does it make a difference if the members of Congress come from or are members of a particular group? Are they bound to vote the way their constituents expect them to vote even if they personally favor another policy? Your answer to these questions may depend on your view of the representative function of legislators.

British political philosopher Edmund Burke (1729–1797), who also served in the British Parliament, believed that although he was elected from Bristol, it was his duty to represent the interests of the entire nation. He reasoned that elected officials were obliged to vote as they personally thought best. According to Burke, a representative should be a **trustee** who listens to the opinions of constituents and then can be trusted to use his or her own best judgment to make final decisions.

A second theory of representation holds that a representative should be a **delegate.** True delegates are representatives who vote the way their constituents would want them to, regardless of their own opinions. Delegates, therefore, must be ready and willing to vote against their conscience or personal policy preferences if they know how their constituents feel about a particular issue.

Not surprisingly, members of Congress and other legislative bodies generally do not fall neatly into either category. It is often unclear how constituents regard a particular issue, or conflicting opinions may arise within a single constituency. With these difficulties in mind, a third theory of representation holds that a **politico** alternately dons the hat of a trustee or delegate, depending on the issue. On matters of great concern to their constituents, representatives most likely will vote as delegates; on other matters, perhaps those less visible, representatives will act as trustees and use their own best judgment.[26]

In addition to weighing their representational role, members of Congress consider a number of other factors when deciding how to vote on a piece of legislation. Among these are political parties, constituents, interest groups and lobbyists, and staff and support agencies.

☐ Political Parties

The influence of political parties on members' votes cannot be overstated. In fact, congressional party unity, a measure of the solidarity of the members of a political party, has reached historically high levels in recent years. Members of both the Democratic and Republican Parties in the House and Senate vote together on approximately 90 percent of all legislation considered by those bodies.

The incentives for members to vote with their party also rarely have been higher—or more creative. In addition to lending members campaign support through party organizations or member-to-member political action committees (PACs), leadership in both houses may also offer committee assignments or chairs as rewards to members who toe the party line.

trustee

Role played by an elected representative who listens to constituents' opinions and then uses his or her best judgment to make a final decision.

delegate

Role played by an elected representative who votes the way his or her constituents would want, regardless of personal opinions.

politico

An elected representative who acts as a trustee or as a delegate, depending on the issue.

Explore on
MyPoliSciLab
Simulation: You Are a
Consumer Advocate

an Congress Get
nything Done?

government cannot operate without a budget, revenue, or appropriations. But over the past thirty years
members of Congress have grown so polarized that they cannot agree on a budget or much of anything
Polarization occurs when members of both parties move away from the moderate middle and share
asingly less common ground. Since 2001, Congress failed to pass a budget eight times, succeeding only
oving temporary budgets to keep government running. As the parties grow more polarized, Congress is
to pass a permanent budget and the national debt increases.

rty **Polarization**

As Congress grew even more polarized, it passed eight temporary budgets instead of confronting tough budget choices.

Despite growing party polarization, President Clinton managed to decrease the national debt throughout the 90s.

In 2011, Congress created a bipartisan "Supercommittee" to consider ways to cut annual deficits. Since then, the national debt has dropped again despite increased polarization in Congress.

In 1995, polarization increased and the Democrats lost control of Congress. The government shut down because the Republican Congress and Democratic president could not agree on a budget.

President Bush's 2001 tax cut was the last bill to influence the national debt. As people paid fewer taxes, national debt grew.

Year

zation is measured as the distance between the two parties' ideological scores as computed from data at Voteview.com.
CE: Data from Voteview and the U.S. Government Accountability Office.

vestigate **Further**

cept What is political polariza-
olarization occurs when members of
olitical parties consistently vote along
gical lines. Political scientists track
ation because it has nearly doubled
oast thirty years, and it tends to
e the government's ability to function.

Connection Is polarization related
to greater annual debt? On a yearly basis,
polarization is largely independent of the debt
incurred by the United States—notice, for
example, during the Clinton presidency how
polarization grew even as debt decreased.
However, as a long-term trend, national debt
and polarization in Congress increase
together.

Cause Does polarization impede
Congress's ability to create annual
budgets? Yes. The more polarized
Congress becomes, the more likely the
disagreements over permanent budget
solutions lead to temporary resolutions
barely stave off government shutdown.

logrolling
Vote trading; voting to support a colleague's bill in return for a promise of future support.

☐ Constituents

When they are voting, members of Congress always have in mind their constituents—the people who live and vote in a representative's home district or state. It is rare for a legislator to vote against the wishes of his or her constituents regularly, particularly on issues of social welfare, domestic policy, or other crucial issues.

Gauging how voters regard any particular issue often is not easy. Because it is virtually impossible to know how the folks back home feel on all matters, a representative's perception of his or her constituents' preferences is important. Even when voters have opinions, legislators may receive little guidance if they come from a narrowly divided district. Abortion is an issue about which many voters feel passionate, but a legislator whose district has roughly equal numbers of pro-choice and pro-life advocates can satisfy only a portion of his or her constituents.

☐ Colleagues and Caucuses

The range and complexity of issues confronting Congress means that no one can be up to speed on more than a few topics. When members must vote on bills concerning issues about which they know very little, they often turn for advice to colleagues who have served on the committee that handled the legislation. On issues that are of little interest to a legislator, **logrolling,** or vote trading, often occurs. Logrolling often takes place on specialized bills targeting money or projects to selected congressional districts. An unaffected member may exchange a yea vote now for the promise of a future yea vote on a similar piece of specialized legislation.

Members may also look to other representatives who share common interests. Special-interest caucuses created around issues, home states, regions, congressional class, or other commonalities facilitate this communication. Prior to 1995, these groups were more powerful. Several caucuses enjoyed formal status and were provided staff, office space, and budgets, which the Republican takeover ended. Today, however, all caucuses are informal in nature, although some, such as the Black and Hispanic Caucuses, are far more organized than others. The Congressional Caucus for Women's Issues, for example, has formal elections of its Republican and Democratic co-chairs and vice chairs, its members provide staff to work on issues of common concern to caucus members, and staffers meet regularly to facilitate support for legislation of interest to women.

☐ Interest Groups, Lobbyists, and Political Action Committees

A primary function of most lobbyists, whether they work for interest groups, trade associations, or large corporations, is to provide information to supportive or potentially supportive legislators, committees, and their staffs. It is likely, for example, that a representative knows the National Rifle Association's (NRA's) position on gun control legislation. What the legislator needs from the NRA is information and substantial research on the feasibility and impact of such legislation. How could the states implement such legislation? Is it constitutional? Will it really have an impact on violent crime or crime in schools? Organized interests can persuade undecided legislators or confirm the support of their friends by providing information that legislators use to justify the position they have embraced. They also can supply direct campaign contributions, volunteers, and publicity to members seeking reelection.

The high cost of campaigning has made members of Congress, especially those without huge personal fortunes, attentive to those who help pay the tab for such expenses. Political action committees (PACs) organized by interest groups are a major source of most members' campaign funding. When an issue arises that is of little consequence to a member's constituents, that member, not surprisingly, tends to support the positions of those interests who helped pay for the last campaign. After all, who wants to bite the hand that feeds him or her?

Interest groups also use grassroots appeals to pressure legislators by urging their members in a particular state or district to call, write, fax, e-mail, text, or tweet their senators or representatives. Lobbyists cannot vote, but constituents back home can and do.

☐ Staff and Support Agencies

Members of Congress rely heavily on their staffs for information on pending legislation.[27] House members have an average of fifteen staffers; senators, an average of thirty-five. Staff is divided between D.C. and district offices. When a bill is nonideological or one on which the member has no real position, staff members can be very influential. In many offices, they are the greatest influence on their boss's votes, and lobbyists are just as likely to contact key staffers as they are members.

Congressional committees and subcommittees also have their own dedicated staff to assist committee members. Additional help for members comes from support personnel at the Congressional Research Service (CRS) at the Library of Congress, the Government Accountability Office (GAO), and the Congressional Budget Office (CBO).

Toward Reform: Balancing Institutional Power

6	Evaluate the strategic interactions between Congress, the president, the courts, and the people.

The Framers envisioned that the Congress, the president, and the judiciary would have discrete powers, and that one branch would be able to hold the others in check. These checks and balances would also allow citizens to influence their government but temper the will of the people. Especially since the 1930s, the president often has held the upper hand in institutional power. In times of crisis or simply when it was unable to meet public demands for solutions, Congress has willingly handed over its authority to the chief executive. Even though the inherent powers of the chief executive give the president greater latitude, Congress does, of course, retain ultimate legislative authority to question executive actions and to halt administration activities by cutting off funds for programs a president wants. Similar checks and balances affect relations between Congress and the courts.

☐ Congress and the Executive

The balance of power between Congress and the president has fluctuated over time. The post–Civil War Congress tried to regain control of the vast executive powers that the recently slain President Abraham Lincoln had assumed. Angered at the refusal of Lincoln's successor, Andrew Johnson, to go along with its radical "reforms" of the South, Congress passed the Tenure of Office Act, which prevented the president, under threat of civil penalty, from removing any Cabinet-level appointees of the previous administration. Johnson accepted the challenge and fired Lincoln's secretary of war, who many believed guilty of heinous war crimes. The House voted to impeach Johnson, but the desertion of a handful of Republican senators prevented him from being removed from office. (The effort fell short by one vote.) Nonetheless, this attempt to remove the president greatly weakened his power, and the Congress again became the center of power and authority in the federal government.

Beginning in the early 1900s, however, a series of strong presidents acted at the expense of congressional power. Theodore Roosevelt, Franklin D. Roosevelt, and Lyndon B. Johnson viewed the presidency as carrying with it enormous powers. Especially since the presidency of Franklin D. Roosevelt, Congress has ceded to the president a major role in the legislative process.

☐ Congress and the Judiciary

As part of our system of checks and balances, the power of judicial review gives the Supreme Court the ability to review the constitutionality of acts of Congress. Historically, the Court has used this power very carefully. From 1787 to 1987, the Supreme Court struck down only 127 federal laws, for an average of less than one law per term. However, in recent years, the Court has struck down congressional legislation at a rate of nearly three laws per term. Thus, Congress must be increasingly mindful of the Court's reaction when it enacts new laws for the nation.[28]

Congress also interacts with the judiciary in a number of other ways. No matter how busy federal judges are, it is ultimately up to Congress to determine the number of judges on each court, as well as the boundaries of judicial districts and circuits. Congress also sets the jurisdiction of the federal courts. During recent Congresses, for example, several members, unhappy with Supreme Court actions on abortion and gay rights, pushed for a bill to prevent federal courts from hearing challenges related to these civil liberties issues. When Congress threatens the Court's jurisdiction, it is signaling its belief that federal judges have gone too far.

☐ Congress and the People

Congress, at least conceptually, is the people's branch of government. The people elect the members, who then are supposed to serve in the citizens' best interest. In recent years, however, citizens have increasingly questioned members' dedication to their representational role. In 2012, as shown in Figure 5, the congressional approval rate reached an all-time low of 10 percent; even individual members of Congress, who have generally had higher approval ratings than Congress as a whole, received a dismal 41 percent approval rating. These low approval numbers mirror the frustrations of the American people over the increasing partisanship and unproductivity of the institution.

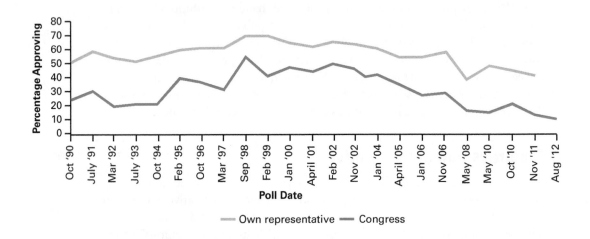

FIGURE 5 WHAT DO AMERICANS THINK ABOUT CONGRESS?

This graph shows the American public's views on Congress as an institution and individual members. Poll respondents were asked, "Do you approve or disapprove of the way Congress is handling its job?" and "Do you approve or disapprove of the way the representative from your district is handling his or her job?"

SOURCE: http://www.ropercenter.uconn.edu/data_access/tag/congressional_approval.html#.UDp_QERZt8ohttp; http://www.gallup.com/poll/156662/congress-approval-ties-time-low.aspx

Roots of the Legislative Branch of Government

1 Trace the roots of the legislative branch outlined by the U.S. Constitution.

The Constitution created a bicameral legislature with members of each body to be elected differently, and thus to represent different constituencies. Article I of the Constitution sets forth qualifications for office, states age minimums, and specifies how legislators are to be distributed among the states. The Constitution also requires that seats in the House of Representatives be apportioned by population. Thus, after every U.S. Census, state legislatures must redraw district lines to reflect population shifts. In addition, the Constitution also provides a vast array of enumerated and implied powers to Congress. Both houses of Congress share some, such as lawmaking and oversight, but not others, such as confirmation of presidential appointees.

The Members of Congress

2 Characterize the demographic attributes of members of Congress, and identify factors that affect their chances for reelection.

Members of Congress live in two worlds—in their home districts and in the District of Columbia. They must attempt to appease two constituencies: party leaders, colleagues, and lobbyists in Washington, D.C., on the one hand, and constituents in their home districts, on the other. In general, members of Congress are better educated, richer, more likely to be male, and more likely to be white than the general population, in terms of its makeup, and membership in one of the two major parties is almost always a prerequisite for election, as is the ability to raise money. When it comes to reelection, incumbency and redistricting also affect members' chances.

How Congress Is Organized

3 Assess the role of the committee system, political parties, and congressional leadership in organizing Congress.

Political parties play a major role in the way Congress is organized. The Speaker of the House is traditionally a member of the majority party, and the parties also control other leadership roles, such as majority and minority leaders and whips. In addition to the party leaders, Congress has a labyrinth of committees and subcommittees that cover the entire range of government policies, often with a confusing tangle of shared responsibilities. In these environments, many policies take shape and members make their primary contributions to solving public problems.

Powers of Congress

4 Identify three of the most significant powers of Congress.

The three most significant powers of Congress are its lawmaking, budgetary, and oversight functions. The road to enacting a bill into law is long and strewn with obstacles, and only a small share of the proposals introduced become law. The Congressional Budget Act of 1974 solidified Congress's role in the budgetary process. Congress conducts oversight in a number of ways, including through hearings. Congress also offers advice and consent on executive and judicial branch nominees and has the power to impeach federal officials and remove them from office.

How Members Make Decisions

5 Analyze the factors that influence how members of Congress make decisions.

Members' view of their representational role—as trustees, delegates, or politicos—influences how they make policy decisions. Legislators may also consider a number of other factors, including political party; constituents; colleagues and caucuses; staff and support agencies; and interest groups, lobbyists, and political action committees. When a bill is non-ideological or one on which a member has no real position, staff members may have the greatest influence on how a member of Congress votes.

Toward Reform: Balancing Institutional Power

6 Evaluate the strategic interactions between Congress, the president, the courts, and the people.

The balance of power between Congress and the executive branch has fluctuated tremendously over time. Congress was most powerful in the early years of U.S. history, but since the New Deal, the president has played an important role in proposing legislation and spending. An ongoing power struggle also characterizes legislative–judicial relations. Although the judiciary can declare acts of Congress unconstitutional, Congress also exercises control over the judiciary in a variety of ways. The people also hold an important check on all political institutions.

Learn the Terms

 Study and **Review** the **Flashcards**

apportionment
bicameral legislature
bill
cloture
conference committee
Congressional Budget Act of
    1974
congressional review
delegate
filibuster
gerrymandering
hold
impeachment

incumbency
joint committee
logrolling
majority leader
majority party
markup
minority leader
minority party
party caucus (or conference)
pocket veto
politico
pork
president pro tempore

programmatic requests
reconciliation
redistricting
select (or special) committee
senatorial courtesy
seniority
Speaker of the House
standing committee
trustee
veto
War Powers Resolution
whip

Test Yourself

 Study and **Review** the **Practice Tests**

1. Which power is NOT granted to Congress in Article I?

a. Regulating commerce with foreign nations and between the states

b. Declaring war

c. Raising and supporting an army and navy

d. Overruling Supreme Court decisions

e. Establishing rules for naturalization

2. All of these describe the House of Representatives EXCEPT:

a. initiates all revenue bills.

b. two-year terms served by members.

c. low turnover in membership.

d. decentralized power.

e. powerful Committee on Rules.

3. Much of the controversy surrounding redistricting comes from a process called:

a. gerrymandering.

b. reallocation.

c. census review.

d. incumbency.

e. demography.

4. The official who oversees House business and is second in line for presidential succession is

a. minority leader.

b. Speaker of the House.

c. vice president.

d. president pro tempore.

e. conference chair.

5. A party whip is

a. any new member of the majority party in the House.

b. a moderate member of any party.

c. a leader responsible for mobilizing party support.

d. a member designated to speak to the media on behalf of the party.

e. the longest serving member of each party.

6. The practice of halting Senate action on a bill through unlimited debate or long speeches is called a

a. hold.

b. filibuster.

c. veto.

d. cloture.

e. pocket veto.

7. Which of these is NOT a power of Congress that limits the president's power?

a. War Powers Resolution

b. Congressional review

c. Appointment

d. Senatorial courtesy

e. Oversight

8. Members of Congress rely heavily on all of these groups to educate them on specific political issues EXCEPT:

a. caucuses.

b. newspaper editors.

c. interest groups.

d. political parties.

e. lobbyists.

9. Political parties' influence on the votes of members of Congress is

a. decreasing rapidly.

b. decreasing slowly.

c. about the same as during the 1960s.

d. increasing.

e. almost nonexistent.

10. Which of the following statements is true regarding congressional approval?

a. Congressional approval is at historic highs.

b. Citizens generally think more highly of Congress than of their individual members.

c. Approval of Congress is higher than approval of all other political institutions.

d. Despite declining approval, members of Congress continue to be reelected at high rates.

e. Congressional approval has declined in every year since Watergate.

Explore Further

Adler, E. Scott, and John S. Lapinski, eds. *The Macropolitics of Congress.* Princeton, NJ: Princeton University Press, 2006.

Cox, Gary W., and Mathew D. McCubbins. *Setting the Agenda: Responsible Party Government in the U.S. House of Representatives.* New York: Cambridge University Press, 2005.

Davidson, Roger H., Walter J. Oleszek, and Frances E. Lee. *Congress and Its Members,* 13th ed. Washington, DC: CQ Press, 2011.

Dodd, Lawrence C. *Thinking About Congress: Essays on Congressional Change.* New York: Routledge, 2011.

Dodd, Lawrence C., and Bruce I. Oppenheimer, eds. *Congress Reconsidered,* 9th ed. Washington, DC: CQ Press, 2008.

Fenno, Richard F., Jr. *Home Style: House Members in Their Districts,* reprint ed. New York: Longman, 2009.

Mayhew, David R. *Congress: The Electoral Connection,* 2nd ed. New Haven, CT: Yale University Press, 2004.

Miler, Kristina C. *Constituency Representation in Congress: The View from Capitol Hill.* New York: Cambridge University Press, 2010.

Oleszek, Walter J. *Congressional Procedures and the Policy Process,* 8th ed. Washington, DC: CQ Press, 2010.

Price, David E. *The Congressional Experience: A View from the Hill,* 3rd ed. Boulder, CO: Westview Press, 2005.

Quirk, Paul J., and Sarah A. Binder, eds. *Institutions of American Democracy: The Legislative Branch.* New York: Oxford University Press, 2006.

Schickler, Eric, and Frances E. Lee, eds. *The Oxford Handbook of the American Congress.* New York: Oxford University Press, 2011.

Smith, Steven S. *Party Influence in Congress.* New York: Cambridge University Press, 2007.

Straus, Jacob R. *Party and Procedure in the United States Congress.* Lanham, MD: Rowman and Littlefield, 2012.

Theriault, Sean M. *Party Polarization in Congress.* New York: Cambridge University Press, 2008.

To learn more about the Senate, go to its official Web site at **www.senate.gov.**

To learn more about the House of Representatives, go to its official Web site at **www.house.gov.**

To learn more about the legislative branch, go to the Library of Congress's home page, named Thomas, in honor of President Thomas Jefferson, at **thomas.loc.gov.**

To learn more about members of Congress, go to the Congressional Biographical Directory at **bioguide.congress.gov.**

Credits

Credits are listed in order of appearance.

Answer Key

1. d; 2. d; 3. a; 4. b; 5. c; 6. b; 7. c; 8. b; 9. d; 10. d

Notes

1. Richard F. Fenno Jr., "U.S. House Members in Their Constituencies: An Exploration," *American Political Science Review* 71 (September 1977): 883–917.

2. Richard F. Fenno Jr., *Home Style: House Members in Their Districts* (New York: Longman, 2009), 32; and Judy Schneider and Michael L. Koempel, *Congressional Deskbook 2005–2007: 109th Congress* (Alexandria, VA: Capital Net, 2005).

3. Hedrick Smith, *The Power Game* (New York: Ballantine Books, 1989), 108.

4. Jennifer E. Manning, "Membership of the 111th Congress: A Profile," *Congressional Research Service Report for Congress* (July 19, 2010): http://opencrs.com.

5. Gary W. Cox and Jonathan N. Katz, "Why Did the Incumbency Advantage in U.S. House Elections Grow?" *American Journal of Political Science* 40 (May 1996): 478–97; Kenneth N. Bickers and Robert M. Stein, "The Electoral Dynamics of the Federal Pork Barrel," *American Journal of Political Science* 40 (November 1996): 1300–26; "2010 Overview: Incumbent Advantage," www.opensecrets.org; and Scott Ashworth and Ethan Bueno de Mesquita, "Electoral Selection, Strategic Challenger Entry, and the Incumbency Advantage," *Journal of Politics* 70 (October 2008): 1006–25.

6. Marjorie Randon Hershey, "Congressional Elections," in Gerald M. Pomper, et al., *The Election of 1992: Reports and Interpretations* (Chatham, NJ: Chatham House, 1993), 159.

7. Jennifer Steinhauer, "Republicans Retain House by Shoring Up Incumbents," *New York Times* (November 7, 2012): http://www.nytimes.com/2012/11/07/us/politics/republicans-stand-firm-in-controlling-the-house.html?pagewanted=all.

8. "How to Rig an Election," *Economist* (April 25, 2002): 51-54.

9. In *Davis* v. *Bandemer,* 478 U.S. 109 (1986), the Court found that gerrymandering was not a political question but was unable to determine a standard by which to judge constitutionality.

10. *Wesberry* v. *Sanders,* 376 U.S. 1 (1964).

11. *Reynolds* v. *Sims,* 377 U.S. 533 (1964).

12. *Thornburg* v. *Gingles,* 478 U.S. 30 (1986).

13. *Shaw* v. *Reno,* 509 U.S. 630 (1993).

14. *LULAC* v. *Perry,* 548 U.S. 399 (2006).

15. "What is the Democratic Caucus?": www.dcaucusweb.house.gov.

16. David R. Mayhew, "Supermajority Rule in the U.S. Senate," *PS: Political Science and Politics* 36 (January 2003): 31–36.

17. Barbara Sinclair, "The Struggle over Representation and Law-making in Congress: Leadership Reforms in the 1990s," in James A. Thurber and Roger H. Davidson, eds., *Remaking Congress: Change and Stability in the 1990s* (Washington, DC: CQ Press, 1995), 105.

18. Woodrow Wilson, *Congressional Government: A Study in American Politics* (Cambridge, MA: Riverside Press, 1885).

19. Roger H. Davidson, "Congressional Committees in the New Reform Era: From Combat to the Contract," in Thurber and Davidson, *Remaking Congress,* 28.

20. Christopher Deering and Steven S. Smith, *Committees in Congress,* 3rd ed. (Washington, DC: CQ Press, 1997).

21. Wilson, *Congressional Government.*

22. Kenneth A. Shepsle, *The Giant Jigsaw Puzzle: Democratic Committee Assignments in the Modern House* (Chicago: University of Chicago Press, 1978).

23. *Wall Street Journal* (April 13, 1973): 10.

24. "The Mysteries of the Congressional Review Act," *Harvard Law Review* 122 (June 2009): 2163–83.

25. Quoted in Stewart M. Powell, "Lee Fight Signals Tougher Battles Ahead on Nomination," *Commercial Appeal* (December 21, 1997): A15.

26. Warren E. Miller and Donald Stokes, "Constituency Influence in Congress," *American Political Science Review* 57 (March 1963): 45–57.

27. Barbara S. Romzek and Jennifer A. Utter, "Congressional Legislative Staff: Political Professionals or Clerks?" *American Journal of Political Science* 41 (October 1997): 1251–79; and Michael T. Heaney, "Brokering Health Policy: Coalitions, Parties, and Interest Group Influence," *Journal of Health Politics, Policy, and Law* 31 (October 2006): 887–944.

28. Russell A. Miller, "Lords of Democracy: The Judicialization of 'Pure Politics' in the United States and Germany," *Washington and Lee Law Review* 61 (2004): 587; Adam Liptak, "Court Under Roberts Is Most Conservative in Decades," *New York Times* (July 28, 2010): www.nytimes.com.

The Presidency

The Presidency

When Ronald Reagan died on June 5, 2004, many Americans, first in California and then in Washington, D.C., lined up for hours to pay their respects to the man who had been the fortieth president of the United States. Many people could see, for the first time in recent memory, the grandeur of a presidential state funeral. The first president to lie in state in the Rotunda of the Capitol since Lyndon B. Johnson died in January 1973, Reagan was one of only nine American presidents to receive that honor.

Presidential funerals underscore the esteem that most Americans accord the office of the president, regardless of its occupant. Just before the first president, George Washington, died, he made it known that he wanted his burial to be a quiet one, "without parade or funeral oration." He also requested a three-day delay of his burial—a common request at the time because of the fear of being buried alive. Despite these requests, Washington's funeral was a state occasion as hundreds of soldiers, with their rifles held backward, marched to Mount Vernon, Virginia, where he was interred. Across the nation, imitation funerals took place, and the military wore black armbands for six months.[1]

When President Abraham Lincoln was assassinated in 1865, his funeral became a nationwide event. He lay in state in the East Room of the White House, where more than 25,000 mourners came to pay their respects. Black cloth draped the room, and two dozen Union soldiers formed an honor guard. Following the funeral, a parade to the Capitol was held in Washington, D.C. Thousands of free blacks escorted Lincoln to the Rotunda, where he lay in state for another day. The body of the deceased president then embarked on a national train tour to his burial site in Springfield, Illinois, allowing Americans across the country an opportunity to grieve.

Today, one of the first things a president does upon taking office is to consider funeral plans. The military has a 138-page book devoted to the kind of ceremony and traditions so evident in the Reagan funeral: a horse-drawn caisson; a riderless horse with boots hung backward in the stirrups to indicate that the deceased will ride no more; a twenty-one-gun salute; and a flyover by military

1	**2**	**3**	**4**	**5**	**6**
Trace the development of the presidency and the provisions for choosing and replacing presidents.	Identify and describe the constitutional powers of the president.	Evaluate the development and expansion of presidential power.	Outline the structure of the presidential establishment and the functions of each of its components.	Explain the concept of presidential leadership and analyze the importance of public opinion.	Assess the president's role as policy maker.

PRESIDENTIAL FUNERALS ARE OCCASIONS FOR NATIONAL MOURNING. Above, the nation mourns President Abraham Lincoln, the first American president to be assassinated. Below, former presidents and vice presidents and their wives attend a funeral service for President Ronald Reagan in the National Cathedral in Washington, D.C., prior to his interment in California.

189

MyPoliSciLab Videos

 Watch on MyPoliS

The Big Picture How well do you know your president? In this video, author Alixandra B. Yanus describes how the relationship between the American people and the president has evolved, and what implications that change has had on the kinds of candidates who run for office.

The Basics What do presidents do? The simple answer is "an awful lot." In this video, you'll hear what ordinary people think about what presidents should do. In the process, you'll discover why there is often a gap between what we expect and what we get.

What makes a great president?

In Context Uncover the historical context that led the Framers to fear a strong executive. In this video University of Oklahoma political scientist Glen Krutz not only reveals the reason behind the Framers' apprehension, but also explores how this fear still restricts presidents today as they struggle to create new policies.

Thinking Like a Political Scientist Why do presidents try to persuade you to support their policies? In this video, University of Oklahoma political scientist Glen Krutz discloses why persuasion is vital to a president's success and how technology has created obstacles and opportunities for presidents.

In the Real World Should President Obama have used an executive order to change immigration policy? The president bypassed Congress to implement his own agenda. Find out why some people believe the president abused his powers and others think he was entirely justified.

So What? Find out what it takes to become president of the United States. In this video, author Alixandra B. Yanus explains the future of the presidency, and considers what ethnicities and demographics we can expect to hold the office in the coming years.

aircraft. Each president's family, however, has personalized their private, yet also public, opportunity to mourn. The Reagan family, for example, filed a 300-page plan for the funeral in 1989 and updated it regularly. President Gerald R. Ford filed a plan that was implemented after his death in 2006. Presidents Jimmy Carter and George Bush have also filed formal plans; Bill Clinton, George W. Bush, and Barack Obama have yet to do so.

The Reagan funeral also created a national time-out from the news of war, and even presidential campaigns halted in respect for the deceased president. One historian commented that the event gave Americans the opportunity to "rediscover . . . what holds us together instead of what pulls us apart."[2] This is often the role of presidents—in life or in death.

• • •

The authority granted to the president by the U.S. Constitution and through subsequent congressional legislation makes it a position with awesome power and responsibility. Not only did the Framers not envision such a powerful role for the president, but they also could not have foreseen the skepticism with which the modern media greet many presidential actions.

The modern media, used by successful presidents to help advance their agendas, have brought us closer to our presidents and made them seem more human, a mixed blessing for those trying to lead. Only two photographs exist of President Franklin D. Roosevelt in a wheelchair, his paralysis kept a closely guarded secret. Seven decades later, presidential candidate Mitt Romney was asked on national TV what he wore to bed.

Public opinion and confidence greatly affect a president's ability to get his programs adopted and his vision of the nation implemented. As one political scientist has noted, the president's power often rests on the power to persuade.[3] To persuade, he must have the capacity to forge links with members of Congress as well as gain the support of the American people and the respect of foreign leaders. The tension between public expectations about the presidency and the formal powers of the president permeate our discussion of how the office has evolved from its humble origins in Article II of the Constitution to its current stature.

Roots of the Office of President of the United States

1 Trace the development of the presidency and the provisions for choosing and replacing presidents.

nder the Articles of Confederation, no executive branch of government existed; the eighteen different men who served as the president of the Continental Congress of the United States of America were president in name only—they held no actual authority or power in the new nation. When the delegates to the Constitutional Convention met in Philadelphia to fashion a new government, the need for an executive branch to implement the laws made by Congress created little dissent. Although some delegates suggested that multiple executives would be preferable, the Framers eventually agreed that executive authority should be vested in one person. This agreement was relatively easy because the Framers felt certain that George Washington—whom they had trusted with their lives during the Revolutionary War—would become the first president of the new nation.

The manner of the president's election troubled the Framers for some time. Their solution to the dilemma was the creation of the Electoral College We leave the resolution of that issue aside and turn instead to details of the issues the Framers resolved quickly.

☐ Presidential Qualifications and Terms of Office

The Constitution requires the president (and the vice president, whose major function is to succeed the president in the event of his death or disability) to be a natural-born citizen of the United States, at least thirty-five years old, and a resident of the United States for fourteen years or longer.

WHO HAS SERVED AS PRESIDENT OF THE UNITED STATES?
Before Barack Obama, all of the people who served as president were white men. Here, four former presidents—George W. Bush, Bill Clinton Jimmy Carter, and George Bush—gather to celebrate the opening of the Clinton Presidential Library in 2004.

Twenty-Second Amendment
Adopted in 1951; prevents a president from serving more than two terms, or more than ten years if he came to office via the death, resignation, or impeachment of his predecessor.

impeachment
The power delegated to the House of Representatives in the Constitution to charge the president, vice president, or other "civil officers," including federal judges, with "Treason, Bribery, or other high Crimes and Misdemeanors." This is the first step in the constitutional process of removing government officials from office.

At one time the length of a president's term created controversy. Various delegates to the Constitutional Convention suggested four-, seven-, and eleven-year terms with no eligibility for reelection. The Framers ultimately reached agreement on a four-year term with eligibility for reelection. In the 1930s and 1940s, however, Franklin D. Roosevelt ran successfully in four elections as Americans fought first the Great Depression and then World War II. Despite Roosevelt's popularity, negative reaction to his long tenure in office led to passage (and ratification in 1951) of the **Twenty-Second Amendment.** It limits presidents to two four-year terms. A vice president who succeeds a president due to death, resignation, or impeachment is eligible for a maximum of ten years in office: two years of a president's remaining term and two elected terms, or more than two years of a president's term followed by one elected term.

During the Constitutional Convention, Benjamin Franklin staunchly supported inclusion of a provision allowing for **impeachment,** the first step in a formal process to remove a specified official from office. He noted that "historically, the lack of power to impeach had necessitated recourse to assassination."[4] Not surprisingly, then, Franklin urged the rest of the delegates to formulate a legal mechanism to remove the president and vice president. Impeachment is that mechanism.

Each house of Congress was given a role in the impeachment process to ensure that the chief executive could be removed only for "Treason, Bribery, or other high Crimes and Misdemeanors." The Framers empowered the House to impeach the president by a simple majority vote. The Senate then acts as a court of law and tries the president for the charged offenses, with the chief justice of the U.S. Supreme Court presiding. A two-thirds majority vote in the Senate on any count contained in the articles of impeachment is necessary to remove the president from office. The House of Representatives has impeached only two presidents, Andrew Johnson and Bill Clinton. The Senate removed neither man, however, from office.

In 1974, President Richard M. Nixon resigned from office rather than face the certainty of impeachment, trial, and removal from office for his role in covering up details about a break-in at the Democratic Party's national headquarters in the Watergate office complex. What came to be known simply as Watergate also produced

The Living Constitution

Whenever there is a vacancy in the office of the Vice President, the President shall nominate a Vice President who shall take office upon confirmation by a majority vote of both Houses of Congress.
—TWENTY-FIFTH AMENDMENT, SECTION 2

This clause of the Twenty-Fifth Amendment allows a president to fill a vacancy in the office of vice president with the consent of a simple majority of both Houses of Congress. The purpose of this amendment, which also deals with vacancies in the office of the president, was to remedy some structural flaws in Article II. When this amendment to the Constitution was proposed in 1965 (it was ratified in 1967), seven vice presidents had died in office and one had resigned. For over 20 percent of the nation's history, no vice president had been available to assume the office of the president in case of his death or infirmity. When John F. Kennedy was assassinated, Vice President Lyndon B. Johnson became president and the office of vice president was vacant. Since Johnson had suffered a heart attack as vice president, members of Congress were anxious to remedy the problems that might occur should no vice president be able to step in.

Richard M. Nixon followed Johnson as president, and during Nixon's presidency, the office of the vice president became empty twice. First, Vice President Spiro T. Agnew was forced to resign in the wake of charges of bribe taking, corruption, and income-tax evasion while an elected official in Maryland. His replacement was popular House Minority Leader Gerald R. Ford (R–MI), who had no trouble gaining a majority vote in both houses of Congress to confirm his nomination. When Nixon resigned rather than face certain impeachment, Ford became president and selected the former governor of New York, Nelson A. Rockefeller, to be his vice president. This chain of events set up for the first time in U.S. history a situation in which neither the president nor the vice president had been elected to those positions.

CRITICAL THINKING QUESTIONS

1. Why wasn't the Twenty-Fifth Amendment proposed until 1965? Why might a vice president be more necessary today than in the past?

2. Is it appropriate in a representative democracy to ever have a situation in which both the president and the vice president have not been popularly elected?

---

a major decision from the Supreme Court on the scope of what is termed **executive privilege.** In *U.S. v. Nixon* **(1974),** the Supreme Court ruled unanimously that no overriding executive privilege sanctioned the president's refusal to comply with a court order to produce information for use in the trial of the Watergate defendants.

☐ Rules of Succession

Through 2013, eight presidents have died in office from illness or assassination. William H. Harrison was the first president to die in office—he caught a cold at his inauguration in 1841 and died one month later. John Tyler thus became the first vice president to succeed to the presidency. In 1865, Abraham Lincoln became the first assassinated president.

Knowing that a system of orderly transfer of power was necessary, the Framers created the office of the vice president. To further clarify presidential succession, in 1947, Congress passed the Presidential Succession Act, which lists—in order—those in line to succeed the president (see Table 1).

The Succession Act has never been used because a vice president has always been available to take over when a president died in office. To ensure this will continue to be the case, the **Twenty-Fifth Amendment,** in fact, became part of the Constitution in 1967 as a response to the death of President John F. Kennedy. Should a vacancy occur in the office of the vice president, the Twenty-Fifth Amendment directs the president to appoint a new vice president, subject to the approval (by a simple majority) of both houses of Congress.

executive privilege
An implied presidential power that allows the president to refuse to disclose information regarding confidential conversations or national security to Congress or the judiciary.

U.S. v. Nixon (1974)
Supreme Court ruling on power of the president, holding that no absolute constitutional executive privilege allows a president to refuse to comply with a court order to produce information needed in a criminal trial.

Twenty-Fifth Amendment
Adopted in 1967 to establish procedures for filling vacancies in the office of president and vice president as well as providing for procedures to deal with the disability of a president.

Cabinet
The formal body of presidential advisers who head the fifteen executive departments. Presidents often add others to this body of formal advisers.

TABLE 1 WHAT IS THE PRESIDENTIAL LINE OF SUCCESSION?

1. Vice President	10. Secretary of Commerce
2. Speaker of the House	11. Secretary of Labor
3. President Pro Tempore of the Senate	12. Secretary of Health and Human Services
4. Secretary of State	13. Secretary of Housing and Urban Development
5. Secretary of the Treasury	14. Secretary of Transportation
6. Secretary of Defense	15. Secretary of Energy
7. Attorney General	16. Secretary of Education
8. Secretary of the Interior	17. Secretary of Veterans Affairs
9. Secretary of Agriculture	18. Secretary of Homeland Security

The Constitutional Powers of the President

2 Identify and describe the constitutional powers of the president.

 In contrast to Article I's laundry list of enumerated powers for the Congress, Article II details few specific presidential powers. Perhaps the most important section of Article II is its first sentence: "The executive Power shall be vested in a President of the United States of America." Nonetheless, the president's combined powers, discussed below, make him a major player in the policy process.

Explore on
MyPoliSciLab
Simulation: You Are a
First-Term President

☐ The Appointment Power

To help the president enforce laws passed by Congress, the Constitution authorizes him to appoint, with the advice and consent of the Senate, "Ambassadors, other public Ministers and Consuls, judges of the supreme Court, and all other Officers of the United States, whose Appointments are not herein otherwise provided for, and which shall be established by Law." Although this section of the Constitution deals only with appointments, behind that language lies a powerful policy-making tool. The president has the authority to make nearly 3,500 appointments to his administration (of which about 1,125 require Senate confirmation).[5] He also holds the power to remove many of his appointees at will. In addition, he technically appoints more than 75,000 military personnel. Many of these appointees are in positions to wield substantial authority over the course and direction of public policy. And, especially in the context of his ability to make appointments to the federal courts, his influence can last far past his term of office.

It is not surprising, then, that the president has, as one of his most important tasks, the selection of the right people. Presidents look for a blend of loyalty, competence, and integrity. Identifying these qualities in people constitutes a major challenge that every new president faces. Recent presidents have made an effort to create staffs that are more diverse, or, in President Bill Clinton's words, look "more like America."

In the past, when a president forwarded nominations to the Senate for its approval, the Senate traditionally gave his selections great respect—especially those for the **Cabinet,** an advisory group chosen by the president to help him make decisions and execute laws. In fact, until the Clinton administration, the Senate confirmed the vast majority (97 percent) of all presidential nominations.[6] This is no longer the case, as investigations into nominees' pasts and political wrangling in the Senate can delay the approval of nominees for months.

Delay or rejection of nominees can have a major impact on the course of an administration. Rejections leave a president without first choices, affect a president's relationship with the Senate, and influence how the public perceives the president. One method presidents have for persuading Congress to approve or disapprove nominees quickly is to make temporary appointments while Congress is in recess (thus, without congressional approval).

☐ The Power to Convene Congress

The Constitution requires the president to inform the Congress periodically of "the State of the Union" and authorizes the president to convene either one or both houses of Congress on "extraordinary Occasions." In *Federalist No. 77*, Hamilton justified the latter by noting that because the Senate and the chief executive enjoy concurrent powers to make treaties, "It might often be necessary to call it together with a view to this object, when it would be unnecessary and improper to convene the House of Representatives." The power to convene Congress had more importance when Congress did not sit in nearly year-round sessions.

☐ The Power to Make Treaties

The president's power to make treaties with foreign nations is checked by the Constitution's stipulation that at least two-thirds of the members of the Senate must approve all treaties. The chief executive can also "receive ambassadors," wording that has been interpreted to allow the president to recognize the existence of other nations.

The Senate also may require substantial amendment of a treaty prior to its approval. When President Jimmy Carter proposed the controversial Panama Canal Treaty in 1977 to turn the canal over to Panama, for example, the Senate demanded settlement of several conditions before approving the canal's return.

Presidents may also "unsign" treaties, a practice often met with dismay from other signatories. For example, the George W. Bush administration formally withdrew its support for the International Criminal Court (ICC), the first permanent court to prosecute war crimes, genocide, and other crimes against humanity.

Presidents also often use **executive agreements** to try sidestepping the constitutional "advice and consent" of the Senate requirement for ratification of treaties and the congressional approval requirement for trade agreements. Executive agreements allow the president to form secret and highly sensitive arrangements with foreign nations, without Senate approval. Presidents have used these agreements since the days of George Washington, and the courts have upheld their use. Although executive agreements are not binding on subsequent administrations, since 1900, many presidents have favored them over treaties.

☐ The Veto Power

In keeping with the system of checks and balances, then, the Framers gave the president veto power, but only as a "qualified negative." Although the president had the authority to **veto** any act of Congress (with the exception of joint resolutions that propose constitutional amendments), the Framers gave Congress the authority to override an executive veto by a two-thirds vote in each house. Congress, however, cannot usually muster enough votes to override a veto. Thus, of the approximately 2,500 presidential vetoes that have occurred in over 200 years, Congress has overridden only about a hundred.

☐ The Power to Preside over the Military as Commander in Chief

One of the most important executive powers is that over the military. Article II states that the president is "Commander in Chief of the Army and Navy of the United States." While the Constitution specifically grants Congress the authority to declare war, presidents since Abraham Lincoln have used the commander in chief clause in

executive agreements
Formal international agreements entered into by the president that do not require the advice and consent of the U.S. Senate.

veto
The formal, constitutional authority of the president to reject bills passed by both houses of Congress, thus preventing them from becoming law without further congressional action.

Take a Closer Look

The president of the United States is asked to wear many hats. A good number of these roles extend from the powers the Framers enumerated in Article II of the U.S. Constitution. Others have evolved out of necessity over time. As a result, the modern president fulfills at least six different professional roles: chief law enforcer, leader of the party, commander in chief, shaper of public policy, key player in the legislative process, and chief of state. Examine the examples, shown below, of recent presidents as they fulfilled these roles.

CHIEF LAW ENFORCER:
Troops sent by President Dwight D. Eisenhower enforce a federal court decision ordering the integration of public schools in Little Rock, Arkansas.

LEADER OF THE PARTY:
President Ronald Reagan mobilizes conservatives at the Republican National Convention, changing the nature of the party.

COMMANDER IN CHIEF:
President Barack Obama meets with members of the armed forces.

SHAPER OF PUBLIC POLICY:
President Richard M. Nixon cheers on the efforts of Apollo 11 astronauts as he celebrates U.S. space policy.

KEY PLAYER IN THE LEGISLATIVE PROCESS:
President Bill Clinton celebrates newly passed legislation at a bill-signing ceremony.

CHIEF OF STATE:
President John F. Kennedy and his wife Jacqueline pose for cameras with the president of France and his wife during the Kennedys' widely publicized 1961 trip to that nation.

CRITICAL THINKING QUESTIONS

1. Which of these presidential roles is most important? Why?

2. How are these roles derived from the enumerated powers of the presidency? How are they enhanced by the president's inherent powers?

3. How has the balance of power between these roles changed over time? Which roles have become more and less important, and why?

conjunction with the chief executive's duty to "take Care that the Laws be faithfully executed" to wage war (and to broaden various powers).

Modern presidents continually clash with Congress over the ability to declare war. The Vietnam War, in which 58,000 American soldiers were killed and 300,000 were wounded, was conducted (at a cost of $150 billion) without a congressional declaration of war.

During that highly controversial war, Presidents Johnson and Richard M. Nixon routinely assured members of Congress that victory was near. In 1971, however, publication of what were called *The Pentagon Papers* revealed what many people had suspected all along: the Johnson administration had systematically altered casualty figures and distorted key facts to place the progress of the war in a more positive light. Angered that this misinformation had led Congress to defer to the executive in the conduct of the Vietnam War, in 1973, Congress passed the **War Powers Resolution** to limit the president's authority to introduce American troops into hostile foreign lands without congressional approval. President Nixon vetoed the resolution, but both houses of Congress overrode it by a two-thirds majority.

Presidents since Nixon have continued to insist that the War Powers Resolution is an unconstitutional infringement on their executive power. Still, in 2001, President George W. Bush complied with the resolution when he sought, and both houses of Congress approved, a joint resolution authorizing the use of force against "those responsible for the recent [September 11] attacks launched against the United States." This resolution actually gave the president more open-ended authority to wage war than President Johnson had received from the Gulf of Tonkin Resolution in 1964. In October 2002, after President Bush declared Iraq to be a "grave threat to peace," the House (296–133) and Senate (77–23) also voted overwhelmingly to allow the president to use force in Iraq "as he determines to be necessary and appropriate," thereby conferring tremendous authority on Bush and future presidents to wage war.

☐ The Pardoning Power

Presidents can exercise a check on judicial power through their constitutional authority to grant reprieves or pardons. A **pardon** is an executive grant releasing an individual from the punishment or legal consequences of a crime before or after conviction, and restores all rights and privileges of citizenship. Presidents exercise complete pardoning power for federal offenses except in cases of impeachment, which cannot be pardoned. President Gerald R. Ford gave the most famous presidential pardon of all to former President Richard M. Nixon—who had not been formally charged with any crime— "for any offenses against the United States, which he, Richard Nixon, has committed or may have committed while in office." This unilateral, absolute pardon unleashed a torrent of public criticism against Ford and raised questions about whether Nixon had discussed the pardon with Ford before resigning. Many analysts attribute Ford's defeat in the 1976 election to that pardon.

The Development and Expansion of Presidential Power

3 Evaluate the development and expansion of presidential power.

very president brings to the position not only a vision of America but also expectations about how to use presidential authority. But, most presidents find accomplishing their goals much more difficult than they envisioned. As he was leaving office, for example, President Harry S Truman mused

---

War Powers Resolution
Passed by Congress in 1973; requires the authorization of Congress to deploy troops overseas and limits the time of their deployment.

pardon
An executive grant providing restoration of all rights and privileges of citizenship to a specific individual charged or convicted of a crime.

about what surprises awaited his successor, Dwight D. Eisenhower, a former general: "He'll sit here and he'll say, 'Do this! Do that!' And nothing will happen. Poor Ike—it won't be a bit like the army. He'll find it very frustrating."[7]

inherent powers
Powers that belong to the president because they can be inferred from the Constitution.

The formal powers enumerated in Article II of the Constitution and the Supreme Court's interpretation of those constitutional provisions limit a president's authority. The times in which the president serves, his confidantes and advisers, and his personality and leadership abilities all affect how he wields these powers. The 1950s postwar Era of Good Feelings and economic prosperity presided over by the grandfatherly Eisenhower, for instance, called for a very different leader from the one needed by the Civil War–torn nation governed by Abraham Lincoln.

During the Civil War, Lincoln believed he needed to act quickly for the very survival of the union. He frequently took action without first obtaining the approval of Congress. Among many of Lincoln's legally questionable acts were:

- He suspended the writ of *habeas corpus*, which allows those in prison to petition for release, citing the need to jail persons suspected of disloyal practices.
- He expanded the size of the U.S. Army above congressionally mandated ceilings.
- He ordered a blockade of southern ports without the approval of Congress.
- He closed the U.S. mail to treasonable correspondence.

Lincoln argued that his **inherent powers**, or powers that belong to the president because they can be inferred from the Constitution, allowed him to circumvent the Constitution in a time of war or national crisis. Since the Constitution conferred on the president the duty to make sure that the laws of the United States are faithfully executed, reasoned Lincoln, these acts were constitutional. He simply refused to allow the nation to crumble because of what he viewed as technical requirements of the Constitution. Because of his leadership during this crisis, Lincoln is generally ranked by historians as one of the best presidents (see Table 2).

☐ Creating the Modern Presidency

Since the 1930s, the general trend has been for presidential—as opposed to congressional—decision making to assume greater importance. The start of this trend can be traced to the four-term presidency of Franklin D. Roosevelt (FDR), who led the nation through several crises.

FDR took office in 1933 in the midst of the Great Depression, a major economic crisis in which a substantial portion of the U.S. workforce was unemployed. Noting the sorry state of the national economy in his inaugural address, FDR concluded: "This

TABLE 2 WHO WERE THE BEST U.S. PRESIDENTS?

According to Historians ...	According to American People ...
1. Lincoln	1. Reagan
2. Washington	2. Lincoln
3. F. Roosevelt	3. Clinton
4. T. Roosevelt	4. Kennedy
5. Truman	5. Washington
6. Kennedy	6. F. Roosevelt
7. Jefferson	7. Obama
8. Eisenhower	8. No opinion
9. Wilson	9. G. W. Bush (tie)
10. Reagan	9. Jefferson (tie)

SOURCES: C-SPAN 2009 Historians Survey of Presidential Leadership; Gallup Poll, February 2–5, 2011.

HOW DID ABRAHAM LINCOLN EXPAND PRESIDENTIAL POWERS?

During the Civil War, Lincoln assumed inherent powers that no president before him had claimed. He argued that these actions were necessary for the preservation of the union. After the war, the president's powers never returned to their previous levels. Here, Lincoln is shown meeting with military leaders following the battle of Antietam, one of the bloodiest battles of the Civil War.

nation asks for action and action now." To jump-start the American economy, FDR asked Congress for and was given "broad executive powers to wage a war against the emergency, as great as the power that would be given to me if we were in fact invaded by a foreign foe."[8]

Just as Abraham Lincoln had taken bold steps upon his inauguration, Roosevelt also acted quickly. He immediately fashioned a plan for national recovery called the New Deal, a package of bold and controversial programs designed to invigorate the failing American economy.

Roosevelt served an unprecedented twelve years in office; he was elected to four terms but died shortly after the beginning of the fourth. During his years in office, the nation went from the economic war of the Great Depression to the real international conflict of World War II. The institution of the presidency changed profoundly and permanently with the creation of new federal agencies to implement the New Deal.

Not only did FDR create a new bureaucracy to implement his pet programs, but he also personalized the presidency by establishing a new relationship between the president and the people. In his radio addresses, or fireside chats, as he called them, he spoke directly to the public in a relaxed and informal manner about serious issues.

To his successors, FDR left the modern presidency, including a burgeoning federal bureaucracy, an active and usually leading role in both domestic and foreign policy and legislation, and a nationalized executive office that used technology—first radio, then TV, and now the Internet—to bring the president closer to the public than ever before.

The Presidential Establishment

4 Outline the structure of the presidential establishment and the functions of each of its components.

As the responsibilities and scope of presidential authority grew over the years, so did the executive branch, including the number of people working directly for the president in the White House. The presidential establishment includes the vice president and his staff, the Cabinet, the first lady and her staff, the Executive Office of the President, and the White House staff. All help the president fulfill his duties as chief executive.

☐ The Vice President

Historically, presidents chose their vice presidents largely to balance—politically, geographically, or otherwise—the presidential ticket, with little thought given to the possibility that the vice president could become president. Franklin D. Roosevelt, for example, a liberal New Yorker, selected John Nance Garner, a conservative Texan, to be his running mate in 1932. After serving two terms, Garner—who openly disagreed with Roosevelt over many policies, including Roosevelt's decision to seek a third term—unsuccessfully sought the 1940 presidential nomination himself.

In 2008, then-Senator Barack Obama, accused of lacking foreign policy experience, chose Senator Joe Biden (D–DE) to balance the Democratic ticket. Obama and Biden ran for reelection in 2012. They were challenged by former Governor Mitt Romney and Representative Paul Ryan (R-WI). One of the main reasons Romney selected Ryan as his running mate was to energize social conservatives who had not been firmly behind Romney. Ryan, as chair of the House Budget Committee, also provided the Republican ticket with expertise in federal financial matters.

How much power a vice president has depends on how much the president is willing to give. Jimmy Carter was the first president to grant his vice president, Walter Mondale, more than ceremonial duties. In fact, Mondale was the first vice president to have an office in the White House. The last two vice presidents, Dick Cheney and Joe Biden, have attained significant powers and access to the president, elevating the office to new heights.

☐ The Cabinet

The Cabinet, which has no official basis in the Constitution but is implied by Article II, section 2, is an informal institution based on practice and precedent whose membership is determined by tradition and presidential discretion. By custom, this advisory group selected by the president includes the heads of major executive departments. Presidents today also include their vice presidents in Cabinet meetings, as well as any other agency heads or officials to whom they would like to accord Cabinet-level status. As a body, the Cabinet's major function is to help the president execute the laws and assist him in making decisions.

Over the years, the Cabinet has grown alongside the responsibilities of the national government. As interest groups, in particular, pressured Congress and the president to recognize their demands for services and governmental action, they often were rewarded by the creation of an executive department. Since a secretary heading an executive department automatically became a member of the president's Cabinet, powerful clientele groups, including farmers (Agriculture), business people (Commerce), workers (Labor), and teachers (Education), saw the creation of a department as a way to expand their access to the national government.

While the size of the president's Cabinet has increased over the years, the reliance of most presidents on their Cabinet secretaries has decreased. Some individual members of a president's Cabinet, however, may be very influential.

What Does the West Wing Say About the Presidency?

The White House, also known as the "President's Palace" or "Executive Mansion," is both a national symbol and a unique private residence. The West Wing of the White House also serves as office space for some of the president's closest advisors. It was added to the White House in 1902 and has been redesigned several times since then to serve the needs of the president. Most recently, for example, the White House swimming pool, added at the behest of President Franklin D. Roosevelt, was converted into the press room. Examine the diagram of the West Wing and consider how its layout reflects individuals' power and the president's policy priorities.

The national security advisor heads the administration's efforts on foreign policy and intelligence issues.

The location of the press secretary's office is symbolic of his role as an intermediary between the president and the press.

Since 1977, the vice president has had an office in the West Wing, which signifies his increasing role in policy making.

The chief of staff oversees the administration and acts as a gatekeeper to the president.

Although these offices are much smaller than in the Executive Office Building, the advisors who occupy them are much closer to the president.

Entrance

National Security Advisor

Vice President

Lobby

Press Secretary

Roosevelt Room

Cabinet Room

Rose Garden

Chief of Staff

Senior Advisers

Dining Room

Study

OVAL OFFICE

Press Briefing Room

To the Executive Residence

CRITICAL THINKING QUESTIONS

1. Whose offices are closest to the president? What statement does this make about these individuals' power and authority?

2. Whose offices are notably missing from the West Wing? Where are their offices located, and what statement does this make about these individuals' power and authority?

3. How might the allocation of West Wing office space vary from one administration to the next? Why might these variations occur?

Executive Office of the President (EOP)

A mini-bureaucracy created in 1939 to help the president oversee the executive branch bureaucracy.

☐ The First Lady

From the time of Martha Washington, first ladies (a term coined in 1849) have assisted presidents as informal advisers while making other, more public, and significant contributions to American society. Edith Bolling Galt Wilson was probably the most powerful first lady. When President Woodrow Wilson collapsed and was left partly paralyzed in 1919, she became his surrogate and decided whom and what the stricken president saw. Her detractors dubbed her "Acting First Man."

Eleanor Roosevelt also played a powerful and much criticized role in national affairs. Not only did she write a nationally syndicated daily newspaper column, but also she traveled and lectured widely, worked tirelessly on countless Democratic Party matters, and raised six children. After FDR's death, she shone in her own right as U.S. delegate to the United Nations, where she headed the commission that drafted the covenant on human rights. Later, she headed President John F. Kennedy's Commission on the Status of Women.

More recently, First Lady Michelle Obama, a lawyer who was an administrator at the University of Chicago Medical Center, has prioritized health and physical fitness. From planting an organic White House vegetable garden to visiting schools around the country, she has stressed the importance of healthy lunches and fresh food and encouraged children to make nutritious choices, viewing childhood obesity and childhood diabetes as a serious problem and policy priority.

☐ The Executive Office of the President (EOP)

In 1939, FDR established the **Executive Office of the President (EOP)** to oversee his New Deal programs. Its purpose was to provide the president with a general staff to help him direct the diverse activities of the executive branch. In fact, it is a mini-bureaucracy of several advisers and offices located in the ornate Eisenhower Executive Office Building next to the White House on Pennsylvania Avenue, as well as in the White House itself, where the president's closest advisers often are located.

The EOP has expanded to include several advisory and policy-making agencies and task forces. Over time, the units of the EOP have become the prime policy makers in their fields of expertise, as they play key roles in advancing the president's policy preferences. Among the EOP's most important members are the National Security Council, the Council of Economic Advisers, the Office of Management and Budget, the Office of the Vice President, and the Office of the U.S. Trade Representative.

The National Security Council (NSC) was established in 1947 to advise the president on American military affairs and foreign policy. The NSC comprises the president; the vice president; and the secretaries of state, defense, and treasury. The chair of the Joint Chiefs of Staff and the director of the Central Intelligence Agency also participate. Others, such as the White House chief of staff and the general counsel, may attend. The national security advisor runs the staff of the NSC, coordinates information and options, and advises the president.

Presidents can clearly indicate their policy preferences by the kinds of offices they include in the EOP. President Barack Obama's addition of an Economic Recovery Advisory Board to the EOP showed his concern about the economy and a desire to find ways to bring the country out of recession. President Obama has also appointed an unprecedented number of "czars," administrators given authority by the president over important policy priorities. The rise in the number of czars can be partially explained by the ever-growing number of organizations and groups now managed by the government, including those involving health, energy, and technology issues.

☐ The White House Staff

Although presidents organize the White House staff in different ways, they typically have a chief of staff whose job is to facilitate the smooth running of the staff and the executive branch of government. Successful chiefs of staff also have protected the president from mistakes and helped implement policies to obtain the maximum political advantage for the president. Other important White House aides include domestic, foreign, and economic policy strategists; the communications staff; the White House counsel; and a liaison between the president and Congress.

As presidents have tried to consolidate power in the White House, and as public demands on the president have grown, the size of the White House staff has increased—from fifty-one in 1943, to 247 in 1953, to a high of 583 in 1972. Since that time, staffs have been trimmed, generally running around 500. The Obama White House has approximately 490 staffers.

Presidential Leadership and the Importance of Public Opinion

5   Explain the concept of presidential leadership and analyze the importance of public opinion.

A president's success in having his programs adopted or implemented depends on many factors, including his leadership capabilities, his personality and powers of persuasion, his ability to mobilize public opinion in support of his actions, the public's perception of his performance, and Congress's perception of his public support.

☐ Presidential Leadership and Personality

Leadership is not easy to exercise, and it remains an elusive concept for scholars to identify and measure, but it is important to all presidents seeking support for their programs and policies. Moreover, ideas about the importance of effective leaders have

WHAT ROLE DO PRESIDENTIAL SPEECHES SERVE?
Presidents carefully choose favorable audiences that enable them to mobilize support for key initiatives. Here, President Barack Obama speaks to students and faculty at the University of North Carolina–Chapel Hill, encouraging them to lobby members of Congress against raising student loan interest rates.

deep roots in our political culture. Frequently, the difference between great and mediocre presidents centers on their ability to grasp the importance of leadership style. Truly great presidents, such as Lincoln and FDR, understood that the White House was a seat of power from which decisions could flow to shape the national destiny. They recognized that their day-to-day activities and how they went about them should be designed to bolster support for their policies and to secure congressional and popular backing that could translate their intuitive judgment into meaningful action. Mediocre presidents, on the other hand, have tended to regard the White House as "a stage for the presentation of performances to the public" or a fitting honor to cap a career.[9]

Political scientist Richard E. Neustadt calls the president's ability to influence members of Congress and the public "the power to persuade." Neustadt believes this power is crucial to presidential leadership because it enables presidents to get their policy goals enacted and win support for their policies in the electorate.[10] Persuasion may come from a variety of sources, including a president's natural charisma or ability to make people do things they would not ordinarily do.

At least one prominent psychologist has suggested that a president's personality may influence his success in the White House. Specifically, this scholar proposes that presidents with mood disorders may be best suited to lead when crises arise. Mania, for example, may lend itself to creative solutions in trying times. Similarly, political scientists and historians have long discussed Lincoln's melancholy and how it affected his ability to keep the nation together.[11]

☐ Going Public

Even before radio, TV, and the Internet, presidents tried to reach out to the public to gain support for their programs through what President Theodore Roosevelt called the bully pulpit. The development of commercial air travel, radio, newsreels, TV, computers, cell phones, and social media has made direct communication to larger numbers of voters easier. Presidents, first ladies, and other presidential advisers travel the world over to publicize their views and to build support on a personal level as well for administration programs.

Direct presidential appeals to the electorate, such as those often made by recent presidents, are referred to as "going public."[12] Going public means that a president bypasses the heads of members of Congress to gain support from the people, who can then place pressure on their elected officials in Washington.

☐ The President and Public Opinion

Presidents and other public figures often use approval ratings as tacit measures of their political capital: their ability to enact public policy simply because of their name and their office. People assume that presidents who have high approval ratings—as President George W. Bush did in the immediate aftermath of the September 11, 2001, terrorist attacks—are more powerful leaders with a mandate for action that comes largely by virtue of high levels of public support. These presidents are often able to use their clout to push controversial legislation, such as the USA PATRIOT Act, through Congress. A public appearance from a popular president can even deliver a hotly contested congressional seat or gubernatorial contest to the president's party.

In sharp contrast, low approval ratings often cripple presidents in the policy arena. Their low ratings can actually prevent favored policies from being enacted on Capitol Hill, even when their party controls the legislature, as many of their partisans locked in close elections shy away from being seen or affiliated with an unpopular president.

Presidential popularity, though, generally follows a cyclical pattern. These cycles have been recorded since 1938, when pollsters first began to track presidential popularity. Typically, presidents enjoy their highest level of public approval at the beginning of their terms and try to take advantage of this honeymoon period to get their programs passed by Congress as soon as possible (see Figure 1). Each action a president takes, however, is divisive—some people will approve, and others will disapprove.

What Influences a President's Public Approval?

olitical scientists watch a president's approval rating because it shows how much political capital is availab him, indicates how the public views the executive's performance, and helps us relate popular support to p ccess, such as dealing with foreign crises or managing the economy. Gallup approval ratings of two recent esidents are shown below; you can see how presidential approval is shaped by the economy and by events.

Bill Clinton was president during one of the largest economic expansions in American history and his popularity climbed with the tech-driven economic boom.

Public support for **George W. Bush** soared to record levels after the 9/11 terrorist attacks, but steadily dropped from that point onward. As economic growth slowed, and after a botched response to Hurricane Katrina in 2005, Bush's approval ratings never recovered.

Monica Lewinsky Scandal

War in Iraq

9/11

US-NATO Kosovo Intervention

WTC Garage Bombing

Oklahoma City Bombing

Saddam Hussein's Capture

Hurricane Katrina

Global Financial Crisis

Start of Clinton's 1st term
Start of Clinton's 2nd term
Start of Bush's 1st term
Start of Bush's 2nd term

80 — 40 — 0

93 94 95 96 97 98 99 00 01 02 03 04 05 06 07 08 0

Year

URCE: Data from the Gallup Presidential Job Approval Center.

nvestigate Further

oncept Do presidents gain or e popularity over the course of their m? For President Clinton, an initial s of popularity—due in part to onomic recession—was followed by rable gains in public support. George Bush's popularity peaked with the 1 attacks then systematically fell off.

Connection Is popularity tied to economic performance? Clearly Bill Clinton's popularity moved with the economy. As it grew, so too did Clinton's job approval. For President Bush, there may be correlation between economic approval and popularity, but it is masked for much of his term by the effects of war on public opinion.

Cause How do events shape the popularity of President Bush? The 9/ terrorist attacks led to a rally-round-the-f effect which defined George W. Bush's presidency. For a brief period, success ir the Iraq war boosted Bush's popularity until war fatigue and failure to manage other crises pulled his approval ratings to record low levels.

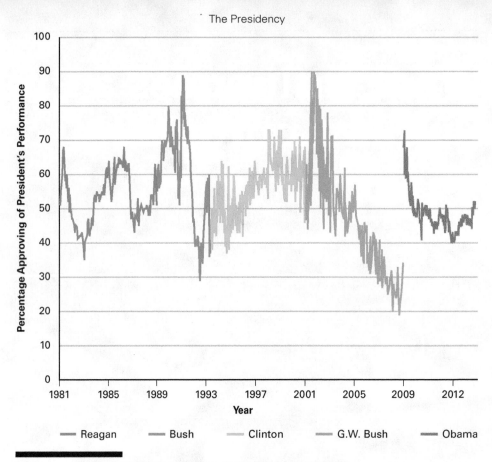

FIGURE 1 HOW DO PRESIDENTIAL APPROVAL RATINGS VARY OVER TIME?

Examine the line graph, which shows the percentage of the American public approving of the president's performance from 1981 through 2012. When is the president's approval the highest? The lowest? How does the president's approval rating change over his term? Based on partisanship?

SOURCE: http://www.gallup.com/poll/124922/presidential-approval-center.aspx

Toward Reform: The President as Policy Maker

6 Assess the president's role as policy maker.

W hen President Franklin D. Roosevelt sent his first legislative package to Congress, he broke the traditional model of law-making.[13] As envisioned by the Framers, the responsibility of making laws fell to Congress. Now FDR was claiming a leadership role for the president in the legislative process. Said the president of this new relationship: "It is the duty of the President to propose and it is the privilege of the Congress to dispose."[14] With those words and the actions that followed, FDR shifted the presidency into a law- and policy maker role. Now the president and the executive branch not only executed the laws but generally suggested them and proposed budgets to Congress to fund those proposals.

☐ The President's Role in Proposing and Facilitating Legislation

Modern presidents play a major role in setting the legislative agenda, especially in an era when the House and Senate are narrowly divided along partisan lines. Without working majorities, "merely placing a program before Congress is not enough," as President Lyndon B. Johnson once explained. "Without constant attention from the administration, most legislation moves through the congressional process at the speed of a glacier."[15]

Explore Your World

Executive mansions and palaces are often among the most ornate homes in the world. These homes exemplify the importance and prominence of the head of government. They may represent the state's culture or values. Their structure and functions may also vary, depending on whether the state has a presidential or a parliamentary system. Examine the structures shown below, with an eye toward these themes.

Christiansborg Palace in Copenhagen, Denmark, is the only building in the world that houses all three branches of a state's government. It is home to the prime minister, the Danish Supreme Court, and the Folketing, the Danish legislature.

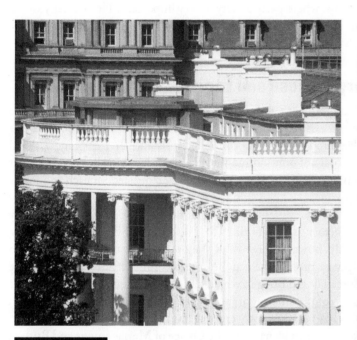

Though the White House, home of the American president, may appear modest on the outside, the residence area of the White House alone boasts 132 rooms, thirty-five bathrooms, and twenty-eight fireplaces.

Until 2002, the prime minister of Japan lived in the small brick residence shown in the back right hand side of this photo. However, the prime minister's residence has recently been upgraded to the larger glass building in the foreground.

CRITICAL THINKING QUESTIONS

1. How does each of these structures reflect the history and governmental system of the state it represents?

2. In states with parliamentary systems, how would you expect the residence of the head of government, the prime minister, to compare to the residence of the head of state, who is often a monarch? How does the combination of these roles affect the structure and functions of presidential residences?

3. Should presidents and prime ministers be provided an official residence at the citizens' expense? Why or why not?

Office of Management and Budget (OMB)

The office that prepares the president's annual budget proposal, reviews the budget and programs of the executive departments, supplies economic forecasts, and conducts detailed analyses of proposed bills and agency rules.

executive order

Rule or regulation issued by the president that has the effect of law. All executive orders must be published in the *Federal Register*.

signing statements

Occasional written comments attached to a bill signed by the president.

However, presidents have a hard time persuading Congress to pass their programs. Recent research by political scientists shows that presidents are much more likely to win on bills central to their announced agendas, such as President Barack Obama's victory on health care reform, than to secure passage of legislation proposed by others.[16]

Because presidents generally experience declining support for policies they advocate throughout their terms, it is important for a president to propose key plans early in his administration. Even President Lyndon B. Johnson, who was able to push nearly 60 percent of his programs through Congress, noted: "You've got to give it all you can, that first year ... before they start worrying about themselves.... You can't put anything through when half the Congress is thinking how to beat you."[17]

A president can also bolster support for his legislative package by calling on his political party. As the informal leader of his party, he should take that advantage to build coalitions in Congress, where party loyalty is very important. This strategy works best when the president has carried members of his party into office on his coattails as well as when his party has a majority in the legislature.

☐ The Budgetary Process and Legislative Implementation

Closely associated with a president's ability to have legislation passed is his capacity to secure funding for new and existing programs. A president sets national policy and priorities through his budget proposals and his continued insistence on their congressional passage. The budget proposal not only outlines the programs he wants but also indicates the importance of each program by the amount of funding requested for each and for its associated agency or department.

Because the Framers gave Congress the power of the purse, Congress had primary responsibility for the budgetary process until 1930. The economic disaster set off by the stock market crash of 1929, however, gave FDR the opportunity to involve himself in the congressional budgetary process, just as he inserted himself into the legislative process. In 1939, the Bureau of the Budget, which had been created in 1921 to help the president inform Congress of the amount of money needed to run the executive branch of government, was made part of the newly created Executive Office of the President. In 1970, President Nixon changed its name to the **Office of Management and Budget (OMB)** to clarify its function in the executive branch.

The OMB works exclusively for the president and employs hundreds of budget and policy experts. Major OMB responsibilities include preparing the president's annual budget proposal; assessing the costs of the president's proposals; and reviewing the progress, budget, and program proposals of the executive department agencies. It also supplies economic forecasts to the president and conducts detailed analyses of proposed bills and agency rules. OMB reports allow the president to attach price tags to his legislative proposals and defend his budget.

☐ Policy Making Through Executive Order

Proposing legislation and using the budget to advance policy priorities are not the only ways that presidents can affect the policy process, especially in times of highly divided government when the policies of the president and Congress may differ. Presidents may institute major policy changes by issuing an **executive order,** a rule or regulation set forth by the president that has the effect of law without congressional approval. Presidents Franklin D. Roosevelt and Harry S Truman used executive orders to seize mills, mines, and factories whose production was crucial to World War II and Korean War efforts. Roosevelt and Truman argued that these actions were necessary to preserve national security. The Supreme Court, however, eventually disagreed with the Truman administration in *Youngstown Sheet and Tube* v. *Sawyer* (1952). In that case, the Court unequivocally stated that Truman had overstepped the boundaries of his office as provided by the Constitution.[18]

Presidents may also issue **signing statements,** occasional written comments attached to a bill, when signing legislation. Often these written statements merely comment on the bill signed, but they sometimes include controversial claims by the president that some part of the legislation is unconstitutional and that he intends to disregard it or to implement it in other ways. Signing statements, thus, have become another way for the president to use his informal powers to make and influence public policy. For example, these statements invite litigation and may delay policy implementation. Because signing statements happen at the end of the legislative process, they also represent a largely unchecked way for the president to assert himself in the ongoing power struggle with Congress.

On MyPoliSciLab

Review the Chapter

 Listen to **Chapter** on **MyPoliSciLab**

Roots of the Office of President of the United States

1 Trace the development of the presidency and the provisions for choosing and replacing presidents.

To keep any one president from becoming too powerful, the Framers created an executive office with limited powers. They mandated that a president be at least thirty-five years old, a natural-born citizen, and a resident of the United States for fourteen years or more, and they opted not to limit the president's term of office. To further guard against tyranny, they made provisions for the removal of the president.

The Constitutional Powers of the President

2 Identify and describe the constitutional powers of the president.

The Framers gave the president a variety of specific constitutional powers in Article II, including the powers to appoint, to convene Congress, and to make treaties. The Constitution also gives the president the capacity to grant pardons and to veto acts of Congress. In addition, the president derives considerable power from being commander in chief of the military.

The Development and Expansion of Presidential Power

3 Evaluate the development and expansion of presidential power.

The development of presidential power has depended on the personal force of those who have held the office. George Washington, in particular, took several actions to establish the primacy of the president in national affairs and as chief executive of a strong national government. With only a few exceptions, subsequent presidents often let Congress dominate in national affairs. Franklin D. Roosevelt (FDR), however, took more power for the office of the president, and made more decisions in national and foreign affairs.

The Presidential Establishment

4 Outline the structure of the presidential establishment and the functions of each of its components.

As the responsibilities of the president have grown, so has the executive branch of government. FDR established the Executive Office of the President to help him govern. Perhaps the most important policy advisers are those closest to the president: the vice president, the White House staff, some members of the Executive Office of the President, and the first lady.

Presidential Leadership and the Importance of Public Opinion

5 Explain the concept of presidential leadership and analyze the importance of public opinion.

To gain support for his programs or proposed budget, the president uses a variety of skills, including personal leadership and direct appeals to the public. The president's leadership and personal style, which are affected by his character and his ability to persuade, determine how he goes about winning support. Since the 1970s, however, the American public has been increasingly skeptical of presidential actions, and few presidents have enjoyed the extended periods of popularity needed to help win support for programmatic change.

Toward Reform: The President as Policy Maker

6 Assess the president's role as policy maker.

Since FDR, the public has looked to the president to propose legislation to Congress. Through proposing legislation, advancing budgets, involvement in the regulatory process, and executive orders and agreements, presidents make policy.

Learn the Terms

 Study and **Review** the **Flashcards**

Cabinet
executive agreements
Executive Office of the President
  (EOP)
executive order
executive privilege

impeachment
inherent powers
Office of Management and Budget
  (OMB)
pardon
signing statements

Twenty-Fifth Amendment
Twenty-Second Amendment
U.S. v. Nixon (1974)
veto
War Powers Resolution

Test Yourself

 Study and **Review** the **Practice Tests**

1. Which of the following is a requirement to become president of the United States?

a. Be at least 35 years old

b. No prior criminal record

c. Have a valid U. S. passport

d. Be a resident of the United States for at least thirty years

e. Have previous government experience

2. Which of the following is a constitutional duty of the vice president?

a. In the event of an emergency, the vice president must stand in for the president.

b. The vice president is the director of foreign policy, often meeting with delegates from other nations and addressing international crises.

c. The vice president functions as the head of the Supreme Court, voting in the event of a tie.

d. The vice president is the president's official legislative liaison.

e. All of the above

3. Which of the following is NOT a role fulfilled by the modern president?

a. Chief of state

b. Commander in chief

c. Chief of party

d. Chief legislator

e. Chief of education

4. When creating treaties, the president must:

a. make binding treaties only with permission from the Supreme Court.

b. seek the approval of the Senate.

c. host delegates and ambassadors, but only with Senate approval.

d. rely only on the House of Representatives to negotiate all treaties related to international commerce.

e. operate only within the framework established by the United Nations.

5. The president's authority is defined by:

a. Supreme Court interpretation of international law.

b. the powers granted to the president by the Senate and the House of Representatives.

c. the implied and inherent powers extending from Article II of the Constitution.

d. the powers enumerated in the Bill of Rights.

e. the powers given to the president by Congress upon his appointment to office.

6. Which of the following is NOT selected by the president?

a. The Speaker of the House

b. The Cabinet

c. The vice president

d. The first lady

e. The national security advisor

7. Cabinet secretaries

a. may also serve simultaneously in Congress.

b. are elected by the American people.

c. have decreased in number and importance in the American political system.

d. may not identify with a particular political party.

e. have become less important presidential advisors over time.

8. How, according to political scientists, can American presidents best demonstrate their ability to lead?

a. By spending time abroad with foreign leaders

b. By increasing public attention to particular issues

c. By attending all sessions of Congress

d. By maintaining a wholesome family life

e. By visiting low-income constituencies across the country

9. What is the typical trend of a president's approval ratings throughout his tenure in office?

a. The rating usually remains consistent, regardless of the decisions made.

b. The rating is higher when entering office than the rating when leaving office.

c. The rating is lower when entering office than the rating when leaving office.

d. The rating is sporadic, based on the decisions made, and no pattern can be found.

e. Each president has had a unique rating pattern, and no systematic differences can be observed.

10. Which of the following is NOT a method that the president can use to make and influence public policy?

a. Signing statements to comment on bills

b. Suggesting changes to legislation

c. Using the budget to advance policy priorities

d. Issuing an executive order

e. Amending the Constitution

Explore Further

Barber, James David. *The Presidential Character: Predicting Presidential Performance in the White House,* 5th ed. New York: Longman, 2008.

Cronin, Thomas E., and Michael A. Genovese. *The Paradoxes of the American Presidency,* 3rd ed. New York: Oxford University Press, 2009.

Ghaemi, Nassir. *A First Rate Madness: Uncovering the Links Between Leadership and Mental Illness.* New York: Penguin, 2011.

Greenstein, Fred I. *The Presidential Difference: Leadership Style from FDR to Barack Obama,* 3rd ed. Princeton, NJ: Princeton University Press, 2009.

Han, Lori Cox. *New Directions in the American Presidency.* New York: Routledge, 2010.

Neustadt, Richard E. *Presidential Power and the Modern Presidents.* New York: Free Press, 1991.

Pfiffner, James P. *The Character Factor: How We Judge America's Presidents.* College Station: Texas A&M University Press, 2004.

———. *The Modern Presidency,* 6th ed. Belmont, CA: Wadsworth, 2010.

Pika, Joseph A., and John Anthony Maltese. *The Politics of the Presidency,* 8th ed. Washington, DC: CQ Press, 2012.

Rozell, Mark J. *Executive Privilege: Presidential Power, Secrecy, and Accountability.* Lawrence: University Press of Kansas, 2010.

Shesol, Jeff. *Supreme Power: Franklin Roosevelt vs. the Supreme Court.* New York: W.W. Norton, 2010.

Skowronek, Stephen. *The Politics Presidents Make: Leadership from John Adams to Bill Clinton.* Cambridge, MA: Harvard University Press, 1997.

Warshaw, Shirley Anne. *The Co-Presidency of Bush and Cheney.* Stanford, CA: Stanford University Press, 2009.

Wood, B. Dan. *The Politics of Economic Leadership: The Causes and Consequences of Presidential Rhetoric.* Princeton, NJ: Princeton University Press, 2007.

To learn more about the office of the president, go to the official White House Web site at **www.whitehouse.gov.** There you can track current presidential initiatives and legislative priorities, read press briefings, and learn more about presidential nominations and executive orders.

To learn more about past presidents, go to the National Archives Web site at **www.archives.gov/index.html.** There you can learn about the presidential libraries, view presidential documents, and hear audio of presidents speaking.

To learn more about the office of the vice president, go to **www.whitehouse.gov/vicepresident.**

To learn more about the initiatives favored by the first lady, go to **www.whitehouse.gov/firstlady.** The White House, also known as the "President's Palace" or "Executive Mansion," is both a national symbol and a unique private residence. The West Wing of the White House also serves as office space for some of the president's closest advisors. It was added to the White House in 1902 and has been redesigned several times since then to serve the needs of the president. Most recently, for example, the White House swimming pool, added at the behest of President Franklin D. Roosevelt, was converted into the press room. Examine the diagram of the West Wing and consider how its layout reflects individuals' power and the president's policy priorities.

Credits

Credits are listed in order of appearance.

Answer Key

1. a; 2. a; 3. e; 4. b; 5. c; 6. a; 7. e; 8. b; 9. b; 10. e

Notes

1. "Two Hundred Years of Presidential Funerals," *Washington Post* (June 10, 2004): C14.
2. Gail Russell Chaddock, "The Rise of Mourning in America," *Christian Science Monitor* (June 11, 2004): 1.
3. Richard E. Neustadt, *Presidential Power and the Modern Presidency* (New York: Free Press, 1991).
4. Winston Solberg, *The Federal Convention and the Formation of the Union of the American States* (Indianapolis, IN: Bobbs-Merrill, 1958), 235.
5. Craig Whitlock, "Gates Says Pentagon Faces Spending 'Crisis' over Congressional Inaction," *Washington Post* (January 28, 2011): Al.
6. Benjamin I. Page and Mark P. Petracca, *The American Presidency* (New York: McGraw-Hill, 1983), 262.
7. Quoted in Neustadt, *Presidential Power,* 9.
8. Quoted in Page and Petracca, *The American Presidency,* 57.
9. George Reedy, *The Twilight of the Presidency* (New York: New American Library, 1971), 38–39.
10. Neustadt, *Presidential Power,* 1–10.
11. Nassir Ghaemi, *A First Rate Madness: Uncovering the Links Between Leadership and Mental Illness* (New York: Penguin, 2011).
12. Samuel Kernell, *Going Public: New Strategies of Presidential Leadership,* 4th ed. (Washington, DC: CQ Press, 2006).
13. See Louis Fisher, *Constitutional Conflicts Between Congress and the President,* 7th ed. (Lawrence: University Press of Kansas, 2007).
14. Franklin D. Roosevelt, Press Conference, July 23, 1937.
15. Lyndon B. Johnson, *The Vantage Point* (New York: Holt, Rinehart and Winston, 1971), 448.
16. See Cary Covington, J. Mark Wrighton, and Rhonda Kinney, "A 'Presidency-Augmented' Model of Presidential Success on House Roll Call Votes," *American Journal of Political Science* 39 (November 1995): 1001–24; and Wayne P. Steger, "Presidential Policy Initiation and the Politics of Agenda Control," *Congress & the Presidency* 24 (Spring 1997): 102–14.
17. Quoted in Thomas E. Cronin, *The State of the Presidency,* 2nd ed. (Boston: Little, Brown, 1980), 169.
18. *Youngstown Sheet and Tube* v. *Sawyer,* 343 U.S. 579 (1952).

The Executive Branch and the Federal Bureaucracy

From Chapter 8 of *Essentials of American Government: Roots and Reform,* 2012 Election Edition. Karen O'Connor. Copyright © 2014 by Pearson Education, Inc. Published by Pearson Education, Inc. All rights reserved.

The Executive Branch and the Federal Bureaucracy

O n the afternoon of May 2, 2011, United States Navy SEAL Team Six performed the most significant counterterrorism assassination in the history of the United States. Two helicopters flew from Afghanistan to al-Qaeda founder Osama bin Laden's compound in Abbottabad, Pakistan. Despite difficulties with the first helicopter, the SEAL Team successfully landed and entered the compound. Several gunmen, including bin Laden's son, Khalid, confronted them immediately; the SEALs rebuffed the gunmen's attack. Reaching the third floor of the house, one member of the SEAL Team saw an armed man look outside a door. The SEAL fired on the male assailant, injuring him with the first shot; additional shots were fired, and the assailant was soon dead. When prompted, a child identified the man on the floor by name: Osama bin Laden.

The SEAL Team immediately relayed their victorious message to their commander in chief, President Barack Obama, and his Cabinet. In military language, they stated: "For God and country, I pass Geronimo, Geronimo, E.K.I.A." which meant, "Osama bin Laden, Enemy Killed In Action."

Although the SEAL Team carried out the on-the-ground attack that ultimately took bin Laden's life, their actions were supported by years of research and data collection by intelligence analysts in a variety of government agencies. Perhaps no bureaucrat was more dedicated to the cause than a Central Intelligence Agency employee known only as Miss One-Hundred Percent. In the

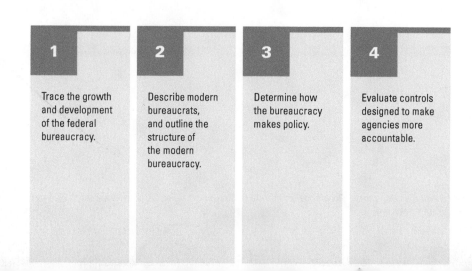

1	**2**	**3**	**4**
Trace the growth and development of the federal bureaucracy.	Describe modern bureaucrats, and outline the structure of the modern bureaucracy.	Determine how the bureaucracy makes policy.	Evaluate controls designed to make agencies more accountable.

BUREAUCRATS PLAY AN IMPORTANT ROLE AS ADVISERS TO THE PRESIDENT Above, President John F. Kennedy meets with his national security team in the wake of the Cuban Missile Crisis. Below, President Barack Obama and his national security team watch live coverage of the capture of Osama bin Laden.

MyPoliSciLab Videos

 The Big Picture From the IRS to the Department of Defense, bureaucracy exists to help Americans—so why does everyone hate it? Author Karen O'Connor defends public bureaucrats against the charges that they are lazy and inefficient, and provides some explanations for why they are so underappreciated.

The Basics What does the bureaucracy do? What is its role in our democracy? In this video, you will listen to what people think about bureaucrats and the job they do. You will also learn why the bureaucracy can have such a big impact on your life.

 In Context Why is the bureaucracy important in the policy-making process? In this video, University of North Texas political scientist Matthew Eshbaugh-Soha talks about not only the bureaucracy and its importance at the federal level, but also the role the federal bureaucracy plays in cooperation with state and local bureaucracies.

Thinking Like a Political Scientist Are bureaucracies democratic? And if so, how are they democratic? University of North Texas political scientist Matthew Eshbaugh-Soha tackles this question and also looks at political appointments and other important research topics associated with bureaucracies.

 In the Real World Is the federal bureaucracy too big and too powerful? Real people weigh in on this question and discuss whether they feel reducing the size of the bureaucracy is worth losing the protections that those agencies provide.

So What? Discover how bureaucracy affects you. Author Karen O'Connor examines a typical day in the life of a student, and highlights the ways that bureaucracy is present—from the water temperature of your shower to the brand of clothing that you wear.

days leading up to the attack, Miss One-Hundred Percent briefed the SEAL Team. During these meetings, she shared information about Bin Laden's compound, the location of the target within the compound, and the amount of time they would have to execute their orders. Once they returned to their base in Afghanistan, Miss One-Hundred Percent not only debriefed the SEALs, but she also identified bin Laden's body on behalf of the U.S. government, shedding tears for the success of her career's mission.

Without the cooperation of Miss One-Hundred Percent and others like her at the Central Intelligence Agency, Federal Bureau of Investigation, Department of Defense, and National Security Agency, just to name a few, the mission to capture and ultimately kill bin Laden would have been impossible. Employing this type of cooperation to solve large-scale national problems is the hallmark of the federal bureaucracy. The diverse programs and agencies that comprise the bureaucracy also enable government officials to work efficiently on many issues at once. In so doing, the executive branch can carry out orders handed down from officials in each of the three branches of government. For example, the mission to capture bin Laden, officially called Operation Neptune Spear, was confirmed and ordered by the president of the United States, acting as commander in chief of the armed forces. Funds appropriated by Congress were essential to its completion, and the U.S. Supreme Court may review its constitutionality.[1]

● ● ●

The **federal bureaucracy,** or the thousands of federal government agencies and institutions that implement and administer federal laws and programs, is frequently called the "fourth branch of government." Critics often charge that the bureaucracy is too large, too powerful, and too unaccountable to the people or even to elected officials. Many politicians, elected officials, and voters complain that the federal bureaucracy is too wasteful. However, few critics discuss the fact that state and local bureaucracies and bureaucrats, whose numbers are proportionately far larger, also implement laws and policies and are often far less accountable than those working for the federal government.

Many Americans—as evidenced by the success of the Tea Party movement—are uncomfortable with the prominent role of the federal government in their lives. Nevertheless, recent studies show that most users of federal agencies rate quite favorably the agencies and services they receive. Most of those polled drew sharp distinctions between particular agencies and the government as a whole. For example, only 20 percent of Americans in one poll expressed positive views toward federal agencies, whereas 61 percent of respondents voiced satisfaction with the agencies with which they have dealt.[2]

Harold D. Lasswell once defined political science as the "study of who gets what, when, and how."[3] Those questions of "what, when, and how" can perhaps best be answered by examining what the bureaucracy is, how it works, and how it is controlled—the topics in this chapter.

federal bureaucracy
The thousands of federal government agencies and institutions that implement and administer federal laws and programs.

Roots of the Federal Bureaucracy

1 Trace the growth and development of the federal bureaucracy.

I n 1789, three executive departments existed under the Articles of Confederation: Foreign Affairs, War, and Treasury, which President George Washington inherited as his Cabinet. A secretary headed each department, and the Department of State almost immediately became the new name for Foreign Affairs. To provide the president with legal advice, Congress also created the office of attorney general. From the beginning, individuals appointed as Cabinet secretaries (as well as the attorney general) were subject to approval by the U.S. Senate, but the president alone could remove them from office. Even the first Congress realized how important it was for a president to be surrounded by those in whom he had complete confidence and trust.

spoils system
The firing of public-office holders of a defeated political party to replace them with loyalists of the newly elected party.

patronage
Jobs, grants, or other special favors that are given as rewards to friends and political allies for their support.

Pendleton Act
Reform measure that established the principle of federal employment on the basis of open, competitive exams and created the Civil Service Commission.

merit system
A system of employment based on qualifications, test scores, and ability, rather than party loyalty.

civil service system
The merit system by which many federal bureaucrats are selected.

independent regulatory commission
An entity created by Congress outside a major executive department.

☐ The Civil War and the Growth of Government

The Civil War (1861–1865) permanently changed the nature of the federal bureaucracy. As the nation geared up for war, President Abraham Lincoln authorized the addition of thousands of new employees to existing departments. The Civil War also spawned the need for new government agencies in response to a series of poor harvests and distribution problems. President Lincoln (who understood that well-fed troops are necessary to conduct a war) created the Department of Agriculture in 1862, although it was not given full Cabinet-level status until more than twenty years later.

Congress also created the Pension Office in 1866 to pay benefits to the thousands of Union veterans who had fought in the war (more than 127,000 veterans initially were eligible for benefits). Justice, headed by the attorney general, became a Cabinet department in 1870, and Congress and the president added other departments through 1900.

☐ From the Spoils System to the Merit System

In 1831, describing President Andrew Jackson's populating the federal government with his political cronies, a New York senator commented, "To the victors belong the spoils." From his statement derives the term **spoils system** to describe the firing of public-office holders of the defeated political party and their replacement with loyalists of a new administration. The spoils system was a form of **patronage:** that is jobs, grants, or other special favors given as rewards to friends and political allies for their support. Political patronage often is defended as an essential element of the party system because it provides rewards and inducements for party workers. This system reached a high-water mark during Abraham Lincoln's presidency. By the time James A. Garfield, a former distinguished Civil War officer, was elected president in 1880, many reformers were calling for changes in the patronage system. On his election, thousands pressed Garfield for positions. Garfield resolved to reform the civil service, but his life was cut short by the bullets of an assassin who, ironically, was a frustrated job seeker.

Public reaction to Garfield's death and increasing criticism of the spoils system prompted Congress to pass the Civil Service Reform Act in 1883, more commonly known as the **Pendleton Act.** It established a **merit system** of federal employment on the basis of open, competitive exams and created a bipartisan three-member Civil Service Commission, which operated until 1978. Initially, the law covered only about 10 percent of positions in the federal **civil service system**, but later laws and executive orders extended coverage of the act to over 90 percent of all federal employees.

☐ Regulating Commerce

As the nation grew, so did the bureaucracy (see Figure 1). In the wake of the tremendous growth of big business (especially railroads), widespread price fixing, and other unfair business practices that occurred after the Civil War, Congress created the Interstate Commerce Commission (ICC) in 1887. In doing so, Congress was reacting to public outcries over exorbitant rates charged by railroad companies for hauling freight. It became the first **independent regulatory commission,** an entity outside a major executive department. Congress creates independent regulatory commissions such as the ICC, which generally focus on particular aspects of the economy. Commission members are appointed by the president and hold their jobs for fixed terms, but the president cannot remove them unless they fail to uphold their oaths of office. The creation of the ICC also marked a shift in the focus of the bureaucracy from service to regulation, giving the government—in the shape of the bureaucracy—vast powers over individual and property rights.

The ratification of the Sixteenth Amendment to the Constitution in 1913 also affected the size and growth potential of government. It gave Congress the authority to implement a federal income tax to supplement the national treasury and provided a huge infusion of funds to support new federal agencies, services, and programs.

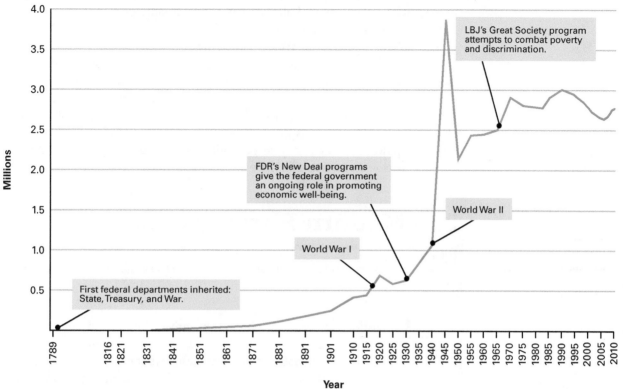

FIGURE 1 HOW MANY EMPLOYEES WORK IN THE FEDERAL EXECUTIVE BRANCH?

The size of the federal executive branch has fluctuated with the needs of the nation. The line graph above tracks these changes from the country's creation to the twenty-first century. Notice the overall growth marked by periods of decline. What events may have caused these fluctuations?

SOURCE: Office of Personnel Management, http://www.opm.gov/feddata/historicaltables/totalgovernmentsince1962.asp.

☐ The World Wars and the Growth of Government

The economy appeared to boom as U.S. involvement in World War I caused an increase in manufacturing, but ominous events loomed just over the horizon. Farmers were in trouble after a series of bad harvests, the nation experienced a severe slump in agricultural prices, the construction industry went into decline, and, throughout the 1920s, bank failures became common. After stock prices crashed in 1929, the nation plunged into the Great Depression. To combat the resultant high unemployment and weak financial markets, President Franklin D. Roosevelt (who was first elected in 1932) created hundreds of new government agencies to regulate business practices and various aspects of the national economy. Roosevelt believed that a national economic depression called for national intervention. Thus, the president proposed, and the Congress enacted, far-ranging economic legislation. The desperate mood of the nation supported these moves, as most Americans began to reconsider their ideas about the proper role of government and the provision of governmental services. Formerly, most Americans had believed in a hands-off approach; now they considered it the federal government's job to get the economy going and get Americans back to work.

World War II also prompted an expansion of the federal bureaucracy. Tax rates were increased to support the war, and they never again fell to prewar levels. After the war, this infusion of new monies and veterans' demands for services led to a variety of new programs and a much bigger government. The G.I. (Government Issue) Bill, for example, provided college loans for returning veterans and reduced mortgage rates to enable them to buy homes. The national government's involvement in these programs not only affected more people but also led to its greater involvement in more regulation. Homes bought with Veterans Housing Authority loans, for example, had to meet certain specifications. With these programs, Americans became increasingly accustomed to the national government's role in entirely new areas, such as affordable middle-class housing and scholarships that allowed lower- and middle-class men who fought in World War II their first opportunities for higher education.

Within two decades after World War II, the civil rights movement and President Lyndon B. Johnson's Great Society program produced additional growth in the bureaucracy. The Civil Rights Act of 1964 brought about creation of the Equal Employment Opportunity Commission (EEOC) in 1965. Congress also created the Departments of Housing and Urban Development (HUD) and Transportation in 1965 and 1966, respectively. These expansions of the bureaucracy corresponded to increases in the president's power and his ability to persuade Congress that new commissions and departments would prove an effective way to solve pressing social problems.

The Modern Bureaucracy

2   Describe modern bureaucrats, and outline the structure of the modern bureaucracy.

The national government differs from private business in numerous ways. Governments exist for the public good, not to make money. Businesses are driven by a profit motive; government leaders, but not bureaucrats, are driven by reelection. Businesses earn their money from customers; the national government raises revenue from taxpayers. Bureaucracies also differ from businesses because it is difficult to determine to whom bureaucracies are responsible. Is it the president? Congress? The people?

The different natures of government and business have a tremendous impact on the way the bureaucracy operates. Because all of the incentive in government "is in the direction of not making mistakes," public employees view risks and rewards very differently from their private-sector counterparts.[4] Government employees have little reason to take risks or go beyond their assigned job tasks. In contrast, private employers are far more likely to reward ambition. One key to understanding the modern bureaucracy is to learn who bureaucrats are, how the bureaucracy is organized, how organization and personnel affect each other, and how bureaucrats act within the political process. It also is important to recognize that government cannot be run entirely like a business. An understanding of these facts and factors can help in the search for ways to motivate positive change in the bureaucracy.

☐ Who Are Bureaucrats?

Federal bureaucrats are career government employees who work in Cabinet-level departments and independent agencies that comprise more than 2,000 bureaus, divisions, branches, offices, services, and other subunits of the federal government. Federal workers number more than 3 million. Over one-quarter of all civilian employees work in the U.S. Postal Service, making it the nation's second largest employer behind Walmart. Small percentages work as legislative and judicial staff. The remaining federal civilian workers are spread out among the various executive departments and agencies throughout the United States. Most of these federal employees are paid according to what is called the "General Schedule" (GS). They advance within fifteen GS grades (as well as steps within those grades), moving into higher GS levels and salaries as their careers progress.

At the lower levels of the U.S. Civil Service, competitive examinations are used to fill most positions. These usually involve a written test. Mid-level to upper ranges of federal positions do not normally require tests; instead, applicants submit résumés online. Personnel departments then evaluate potential candidates and rank them according to how well they fit a particular job opening. The personnel department then forwards to the agency filling the vacancy only the names of those deemed "qualified." This can be a time-consuming process; it often takes six to nine months to fill a position in this manner.

Persons not covered by the civil service system make up the remaining 10 percent of the federal workforce. Their positions generally fall into three categories:

1. *Appointive policy-making positions.* Nearly 3,500 people are presidential appointees. Some of these, including Cabinet secretaries and under- and assistant secretaries, are subject to Senate confirmation. These appointees, in turn, are responsible for appointing high-level policy-making assistants who form the top of the bureaucratic hierarchy. These are called "Schedule C" political appointees.[5]

2. *Independent regulatory commissioners.* Although each president has the authority to appoint as many as one hundred commissioners, they become independent of his direct political influence once they take office.

3. *Low-level, nonpolicy patronage positions.* These types of positions generally concern administrative assistants to policy makers.

More than 15,000 job skills are represented in the federal government. Government employees, whose average age is forty-seven, have a length of service averaging sixteen years. They include forest rangers, FBI agents, foreign service officers, computer programmers, security guards, librarians, administrators, engineers, plumbers, lawyers, doctors, postal carriers, and zoologists, among others. The diversity of jobs in the government mirrors that in the private sector. The federal workforce, itself, is also diverse but underrepresents Hispanics, in particular, and the overall employment of women lags behind that of men. Women make up 64 percent of the lowest GS levels but only 34 percent of the highest GS levels.[6]

About 303,000 federal workers are found in the nation's capital; the rest are located in regional, state, and local offices scattered throughout the country. To enhance efficiency, the United States is divided into ten regions, with most agencies having regional offices in at least one city in that region (see Figure 2). The decentralization of the bureaucracy facilitates accessibility to the public. The Social Security Administration, for example, has numerous offices so that its clients can have a place nearby to take their paperwork, questions, and problems. Decentralization also helps distribute jobs and incomes across the country.

A major concern about the federal workforce is the high rate of turnover in many of the most important positions. This turnover rate has become especially true in the Department of Homeland Security. Many employees of its Transportation Security Administration, for

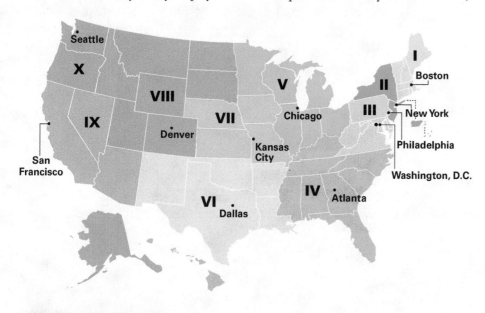

FIGURE 2 WHAT ARE THE FEDERAL AGENCY REGIONS, AND WHERE ARE THEIR HEADQUARTERS LOCATED?

To bring the federal bureaucracy closer to citizens and increase the efficiency of providing government services, the federal agencies maintain an office in Washington, D.C., and in ten other regional locations across the country. These cities are shown on the map above.

SOURCE: Department of Health and Human Services, www.hhs.gov/images/regions.gif.

Who Are Federal Workers?

The federal government employs over 3 million people in a diverse range of jobs, from administrative assistant to scientist. But bureaucrats do not necessarily match the demographics of America. Older Americans and men are overrepresented at the highest levels of the federal workforce, while other groups, such as Hispanics and African Americans, are underrepresented. Examine the demographics of the federal workforce in greater detail in the infographic below.

GENDER TOTAL

56.1%   43.9%

GENDER BY GS GRADE*

35.8%	64.2%	36.9%	63.1%	54.0%	46.0%	65.4%	34.6%
GS 1-4 (lowest pay grade)		**GS 5-8**		**GS 9-12**		**GS 13-15** (highest pay grade)	

RACE / ETHNICITY

White 67.9%

Hispanic 7.5%

African American 17.2%

American Indian 2.1%

Asian and Pacific Island American 5.9%

OTHER CHARACTERISTICS

Disabled 6.8%

College Educated 43.0%

Veteran 21.0%

0   25   50
Percentage

*GS stands for "General Schedule" and indicates the pay scale for U.S. civil service employees

SOURCES: Office of Personnel Management, www.opm.gov; and Equal Employment Opportunity Commission, http://www1.eeoc.gov/eeoc/eeoc/newsroom/release/3-21-12.cfm

CRITICAL THINKING QUESTIONS

1. Compare the male to female ratio at each GS level. How do the percentages change as the GS levels increase? What does this suggest about gender equity in the federal workforce?

2. Which race and ethnicity categories appear to be over- and underrepresented in the federal workforce? Does the federal government appear to be an equal opportunity employer?

3. Why are so many federal workers college educated and veterans? How might these demographic characteristics affect policy outcomes?

example, leave after only a short time on the job for more lucrative careers outside government. At the Department of State, which once boasted many of the most highly coveted jobs in the federal bureaucracy, the dangers associated with postings in Iraq and Afghanistan, as well as elsewhere in the Middle East, are making it harder to find well-qualified people to staff critical positions.[7] Consequently, the military has enlisted private contractors at unprecedented rates to fill many bureaucratic positions in these potentially dangerous sites. Many of these private contractors are former government employees who can make almost twice the amount of money working for private companies.

departments
Major administrative units with responsibility for a broad area of government operations. Departmental status usually indicates a permanent national interest in a particular governmental function, such as defense, commerce, or agriculture.

☐ Formal Organization

At least 1,150 civilian agencies are in existence. But, even experts cannot agree on the exact number of separate governmental agencies, commissions, and departments that make up the federal bureaucracy.[8] A distinctive feature of the executive bureaucracy is its traditional division into areas of specialization. For example, the Occupational Safety and Health Administration (OSHA) handles occupational safety, and the Department of State specializes in foreign affairs. It is normal, however, for more than one agency to be involved in a particular issue or for one agency to be involved in many issues. The largest department, the Department of Homeland Security, with its vast authority and range of activities, is probably the best example of this phenomenon. In fact, numerous agencies often have authority in the same issue areas, making administration even more difficult.

Agencies fall into four general categories: (1) Cabinet departments; (2) government corporations; (3) independent executive agencies; and, (4) independent regulatory commissions.

CABINET DEPARTMENTS The fifteen Cabinet **departments** are major administrative units that have responsibility for conducting broad areas of government operations (see Figure 3). Cabinet departments account for about 60 percent of the federal

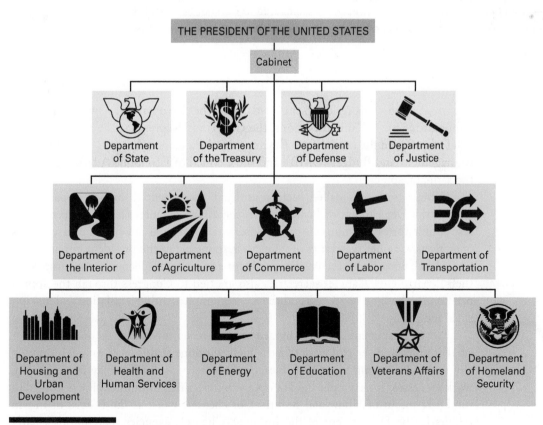

FIGURE 3 WHAT ARE THE CABINET DEPARTMENTS?
Cabinet departments reflect the government's permanent interest in a particular issue area. The modern Cabinet includes fifteen agencies focusing on issues ranging from commerce and foreign affairs to education and health.

The Living Constitution

The President . . . may require the Opinion, in writing, of the principal Officer in each of the executive Departments, upon any subject relating to the Duties of their respective Office. —ARTICLE II, SECTION 2, CLAUSE 1

This clause, along with additional language designating that the president shall be the commander in chief, notes that the heads of departments are to serve as advisers to the president. The Constitution does not directly mention a Cabinet.

This meager language is all that remains of the Framers' initial efforts to create a council to guide the president. Those in attendance at the Constitutional Convention largely favored the idea of a council but could not agree on who should be part of that body. Some actually wanted to follow the British parliamentary model and create the Cabinet from members of the House and Senate, who would rotate into the bureaucracy; most, however, appeared to support the idea of the heads of departments along with the chief justice, who would preside when the president was unavailable. The resulting language above depicts a one-sided arrangement whereby the heads of executive departments must simply answer in writing any questions put to them by the president.

The Cabinet of today differs totally from the structure envisioned by the Framers. George Washington was the first to convene a meeting of what he called his Cabinet. Some presidents have used their Cabinets as trusted advisers; others have used them as a demonstration of their commitment to political, racial, ethnic, or gender diversity, and have relied more on White House aides than particular Cabinet members. Who is included in the Cabinet, as well as how it is used, is solely up to the discretion of the sitting president, with the approval of the U.S. Senate, although both houses of Congress must approve the creation or abolishment of executive departments.

CRITICAL THINKING QUESTIONS

1. What issues arise from requiring senatorial approval for Cabinet positions, and how does the Constitution remedy these issues?

2. Can you think of any new constituencies or issues that are sufficiently important to be elevated to Cabinet-level status?

workforce. The vice president, the heads of all the departments, as well as the U.S. Ambassador to the United Nations, the U.S. Trade Representative, the president's chief of staff, and the heads of the Environmental Protection Agency (EPA), Office of Management and Budget (OMB), and the Council of Economic Advisors make up the formal Cabinet.

Cabinet members called secretaries head the executive branch departments (except the Department of Justice, which the attorney general leads). A secretary is responsible for establishing his or her department's general policy and overseeing its operations. Cabinet secretaries are directly responsible to the president but are often viewed as having two masters—the president and citizens affected by the business of their departments. Cabinet secretaries also are tied to Congress through the appropriations, or budgetary, process and their role in implementing legislation and making rules and policy.

Most departments are subdivided into bureaus, divisions, sections, or other smaller units, and the real work of each agency is done at this level. Subdivision usually takes place along functional lines, but the basis for division may be geography, work processes (for example, the Transportation Security Administration is housed in the Department of Homeland Security), or clientele (such as the Bureau of Indian Affairs in the Department of the Interior). Clientele agencies representing clearly defined interests are particularly subject to outside lobbying. These organized interests are also active at the regional level, where the agencies conduct most of their program implementation.

INDEPENDENT EXECUTIVE AGENCIES **Independent executive agencies** closely resemble Cabinet departments but have narrower areas of responsibility. Generally speaking, independent agencies perform services rather than regulatory functions. The president appoints the heads of these agencies, and they serve, like Cabinet secretaries, at his pleasure.

Independent agencies exist apart from executive departments for practical or symbolic reasons. The National Aeronautics and Space Administration (NASA), for example, could have been placed within the Department of Defense. Such positioning, however, might have conjured up thoughts of a space program dedicated solely to military purposes, rather than to civilian satellite communication or scientific exploration. Similarly, the Department of the Interior could have been home to the Environmental Protection Agency (EPA); instead, Congress created the EPA as an independent agency in 1970 to administer federal programs aimed at controlling pollution and protecting the nation's environment. As an independent agency, the EPA is less indebted to the president on a day-to-day basis than if it were within a Cabinet department, although the president still has the power to appoint its director and often intervenes in high-profile environmental issues and decisions.

INDEPENDENT REGULATORY COMMISSIONS As noted earlier, independent regulatory commissions are agencies created by Congress to exist outside the major departments and regulate a specific economic activity or interest. Because of the complexity of modern economic issues, Congress sought to create commissions that could develop expertise and provide continuity of policy with respect to economic issues because neither Congress nor the courts have the time or specific talents to do so. Examples include the National Labor Relations Board (NLRB), the Federal Reserve Board, the Federal Communications Commission (FCC), and the Securities and Exchange Commission (SEC).[9]

Older boards and commissions, such as the SEC and the Federal Reserve Board, generally are charged with overseeing a certain industry. Most were created specifically to be free from partisan political pressure. Each has five to seven members (always an odd number, to avoid tie votes) selected by the president, and confirmed by the Senate, for fixed, staggered terms to increase the chances of a bipartisan board. Unlike the case of executive department heads, the president cannot easily remove them. In 1935, the U.S. Supreme Court ruled that in creating independent commissions, Congress had intended them to be independent panels of experts sequestered, as far as possible, from immediate political pressures.[10]

Regulatory boards established since the 1960s concern themselves with how the business sector relates to public health and safety. The Occupational Safety and Health Administration (OSHA), for example, promotes job safety. These boards and commissions often lack autonomy and freedom from political pressures; they are generally headed by a single administrator who is subject to removal by the president. Thus, they are far more susceptible to the political wishes of the president who appoints them.[11]

GOVERNMENT CORPORATIONS **Government corporations** are the most recent addition to the bureaucracy. Dating from the early 1930s, they are businesses established by Congress to perform functions that private businesses could provide. Some of the better known government corporations include the United States Postal Service, Amtrak, and the Federal Deposit Insurance Corporation (FDIC). Unlike other governmental agencies, government corporations charge a fee for their services.

The government often forms corporations when the financial incentives for private industry to provide services are minimal. The area served by the TVA demonstrates this point; it was a poor region of Appalachia that had failed to attract private companies. In other cases, Congress intervenes to salvage valuable public assets. For example, when passenger rail service in the United States became unprofitable, Congress stepped in to create Amtrak, nationalizing the passenger-train industry to keep passenger trains running, especially along the Northeast Corridor.

independent executive agencies
Governmental units that closely resemble a Cabinet department but have narrower areas of responsibility and perform services rather than regulatory functions.

government corporations
Businesses established by Congress to perform functions that private businesses could provide.

TABLE 1 WHAT DOES THE LIBERALIZED HATCH ACT STIPULATE?

Federal Employees May	Federal Employees May Not
Be candidates for public office in nonpartisan elections	Use their official authority or influence to interfere with an election
Assist in voter registration drives	Collect political contributions unless both individuals are members of the same federal labor organization or employee organization and the one solicited is not a subordinate employee
Express opinions about candidates and issues	Knowingly solicit or discourage the political activity of any person who has business before the agency
Contribute money to political organizations	Engage in political activity while on duty
Attend political fund-raising functions	Engage in political activity in any government office
Attend and be active at political rallies and meetings	Engage in political activity while wearing an official uniform
Join and be active members of a political party or club	Engage in political activity while using a government vehicle
Sign nominating petitions	Solicit political contributions from the general public
Campaign for or against referendum questions, constitutional amendments, and municipal ordinances	Be candidates for public office in partisan elections
Campaign for or against candidates in partisan elections	
Make campaign speeches for candidates in partisan elections	
Distribute campaign literature in partisan elections	
Hold office in political clubs or parties	

SOURCE: U.S. Special Counsel's Office.

Hatch Act

The 1939 act to prohibit civil servants from taking activist roles in partisan campaigns. This act prohibited federal employees from making political contributions, working for a particular party, or campaigning for a particular candidate.

☐ Government Workers and Political Involvement

As the number of federal employees and agencies grew during the 1930s, many Americans began to fear that members of the civil service would play major roles not only in implementing public policy but also in electing members of Congress and even the president. Consequently, Congress enacted the Political Activities Act of 1939, commonly known as the **Hatch Act.** It prohibited federal employees from becoming directly involved in working for political candidates. Although this act allayed many critics' fears, other people argued that the Hatch Act was too extreme.

In 1993, the Hatch Act was liberalized to allow employees to run for public office in nonpartisan elections, contribute money to political organizations, and campaign for or against candidates in partisan elections. Federal employees still, however, are prohibited from engaging in political activity while on duty, soliciting contributions from the general public, and running for office in partisan elections (see Table 1).

How the Bureaucracy Works

3 Determine how the bureaucracy makes policy.

Explore on MyPoliSciLab Simulation: You Are Head of FEMA

German sociologist Max Weber believed bureaucracies were a rational way for complex societies to organize themselves. Model bureaucracies, said Weber, exhibit certain features, including:

1. A chain of command in which authority flows from top to bottom.
2. A division of labor whereby work is apportioned among specialized workers to increase productivity.
3. Clear lines of authority among workers and their superiors.
4. A goal orientation that determines structure, authority, and rules.

5. Impersonality, whereby all employees are treated fairly based on merit and all clients are served equally, without discrimination, according to established rules.

6. Productivity, whereby all work and actions are evaluated according to established rules.[12]

Clearly, this Weberian idea is somewhat idealistic, and even the best run government agencies do not always work this way, but most try to do so.

When Congress creates any kind of department, agency, or commission, it is actually delegating some of its powers listed in Article I, section 8, of the U.S. Constitution. Therefore, the laws creating departments, agencies, corporations, or commissions carefully describe their purpose and give them the authority to make numerous policy decisions, which have the effect of law. Congress recognizes that it does not have the time, expertise, or ability to involve itself in every detail of every program; therefore, it sets general guidelines for agency action and then allows the agency to work out the details. How agencies execute congressional wishes is called **implementation,** the process by which a law or policy is put into operation.

Historically, in attempting to study how the bureaucracy made policy, political scientists investigated what they termed **iron triangles,** the relatively ironclad relationships and patterns of interaction that occur among federal workers in agencies or departments, interest groups, and relevant congressional committees and subcommittees. Today, iron triangles no longer dominate most policy processes. Some do persist, however, such as the relationships between the Department of Veterans Affairs, the House Committee on Veterans Affairs, and the American Legion and the Veterans of Foreign Wars, the two largest veterans groups (see Figure 4).

Many political scientists who examine external influences on the modern bureaucracy prefer to study **issue networks.** In general, issue networks, like iron triangles, include agency officials, members of Congress (and committee staffers), and interest group lobbyists. But, they also include lawyers, consultants, academics, public relations specialists, and sometimes even the courts. Unlike iron triangles, issue networks constantly are changing as members with technical expertise or newly interested parties become involved in issue areas and others phase out.

implementation
The process by which a law or policy is put into operation.

iron triangles
The relatively ironclad relationships and patterns of interaction that occur among agencies, interest groups, and congressional committees or subcommittees.

issue networks
The loose and informal relationships that exist among a large number of actors who work in broad policy areas.

FIGURE 4 WHAT CONSTITUTES AN IRON TRIANGLE?

Iron triangles are the relatively stable relationships formed between bureaucratic agencies, congressional committees, and interest groups. Cooperation between these three policy actors may make policy making in some issue areas, such as veterans affairs, an insular process confined to a small clientele.

Take a Closer Look

Interagency councils are working groups established to facilitate the coordination of policy making and implementation across a number of agencies. One such group is the U.S. Interagency Council on Homelessness, which was formed in 1987 as a partnership between nearly all of the Cabinet departments and a number of other executive branch agencies, including the Executive Office of the President. The diagram below, taken from the group's "Federal Strategic Plan to Prevent and End Homelessness," shows the interagency scope of the causes and solutions to homelessness in the United States.

The scope and causes, as well as goals and strategies, illustrated in this diagram show the need for multiple agency involvement in addressing the problem of homelessness.

The problem-solving process illustrated in this diagram is typical of policy making in the United States.

The potential solutions to the problem of homelessness involve pooling resources from multiple federal agencies and programs, as well as cooperation from state and local governments.

SOURCE: Input from the New York Stakeholders' Meeting is captured in a graphic format by Art of Hosting volunteer Drew Dernavich, http://www.usich.gov/PDF/OpeningDoors_2010_FSPPreventEndHomeless.pdf.

CRITICAL THINKING QUESTIONS

1. How do the causes, goals, and solutions illustrated in the diagram show the need for interagency cooperation to solve the problem of homelessness?
2. How does this diagram reveal some of the challenges of interagency cooperation?
3. How might similar cooperation help to solve other policy problems facing the United States today? What agencies would you need to bring together to address these problems?

As a result of the increasing complexity of many policy domains, a number of alliances have also arisen within the bureaucracy. One such example is **interagency councils,** working groups established to facilitate the coordination of policy making and implementation across a host of agencies. Depending on the amount of funding these councils receive, they can be the prime movers of administration policy in any area where an interagency council exists. The U.S. Interagency Council on Homelessness, for example, works to coordinate the activities of the more than fifty governmental agencies and programs that work to alleviate homelessness.

In areas marked by extraordinarily complex policy problems, recent presidential administrations have set up **policy coordinating committees** (PCCs) to facilitate interaction among agencies and departments at the subcabinet level. These PCCs gained increasing favor after the September 11, 2001, terrorist attacks.

☐ Making Policy

The main purpose of all of these decision-making bodies is policy making. Policy making and implementation take place on both informal and formal levels. From a practical standpoint, many decisions are left to individual government employees on a day-to-day basis. Department of Justice lawyers, for example, make daily decisions about whether or not to prosecute suspects. Similarly, street-level Internal Revenue Service agents make many decisions during personal audits. These street-level bureaucrats make policy on two levels. First, they exercise broad judgment in decisions concerning citizens with whom they interact. Second, taken together, their individual actions add up to agency behavior.[13] Thus, how bureaucrats interpret and how they apply (or choose not to apply) various policies are equally important parts of the policy-making process.

Administrative discretion, the ability of bureaucrats to make choices concerning the best way to implement congressional or executive intentions, also allows decision makers (whether they are in a Cabinet-level position or at the lowest GS levels) a tremendous amount of leeway. Bureaucrats exercise administrative discretion through two formal procedures: rule making and administrative adjudication.

RULE MAKING **Rule making** is a quasi-legislative process resulting in regulations that have the characteristics of a legislative act. **Regulations** are the rules that govern the operation of all government programs and have the force of law. In essence, then, bureaucratic rule makers often act as lawmakers as well as law enforcers when they make rules or draft regulations to implement various congressional statutes. Some political scientists say that rule making "is the single most important function performed by agencies of government" (see Figure 5).[14]

Because regulations often involve political conflict, the 1946 Administrative Procedures Act established rule-making procedures to give everyone the chance to participate in the process. The act requires that: (1) public notice of the time, place, and nature of the rule-making proceedings be provided in the *Federal Register;* (2) interested parties be given the opportunity to submit written arguments and facts relevant to the rule; and, (3) the statutory purpose and basis of the rule be stated. After rules are published, thirty days generally must elapse before they take effect.

Sometimes the law requires an agency to conduct a formal hearing before issuing rules. A committee helps staffers collect evidence and calls interested parties and interest groups to testify on the issue. The process can take weeks, months, or even years, at the end of which agency administrators must review the entire record and then justify the new rules. Although cumbersome, the process has reduced criticism of some rules and bolstered the deference given by the courts to agency decisions. Many Americans are unaware of their opportunity to influence government through the rule-making process (see Table 2).

ADMINISTRATIVE ADJUDICATION Agencies regularly find that persons or businesses are not in compliance with the federal laws the agencies are charged with enforcing, or that they are in violation of an agency rule or regulation. To force compliance,

interagency councils
Working groups created to facilitate coordination of policy making and implementation across a host of governmental agencies.

policy coordinating committees
Subcabinet-level committees created to facilitate interactions between agencies and departments to handle complex policy problems.

administrative discretion
The ability of bureaucrats to make choices concerning the best way to implement congressional or executive intentions.

rule making
A quasi-legislative process resulting in regulations that have the characteristics of a legislative act.

regulations
Rules governing the operation of all government programs that have the force of law.

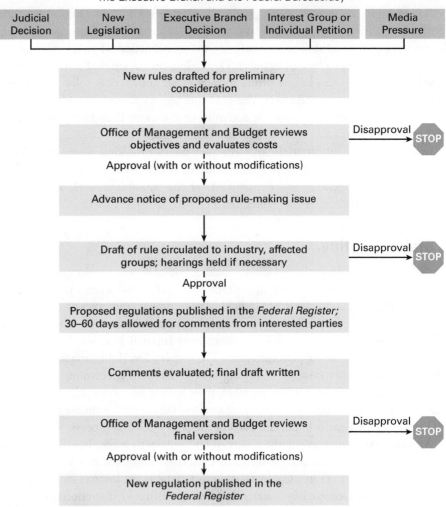

The Executive Branch and the Federal Bureaucracy

| Judicial Decision | New Legislation | Executive Branch Decision | Interest Group or Individual Petition | Media Pressure |

New rules drafted for preliminary consideration

Office of Management and Budget reviews objectives and evaluates costs → **Disapproval** → STOP

Approval (with or without modifications)

Advance notice of proposed rule-making issue

Draft of rule circulated to industry, affected groups; hearings held if necessary → **Disapproval** → STOP

Approval

Proposed regulations published in the *Federal Register;* 30–60 days allowed for comments from interested parties

Comments evaluated; final draft written

Office of Management and Budget reviews final version → **Disapproval** → STOP

Approval (with or without modifications)

New regulation published in the *Federal Register*

FIGURE 5 HOW IS A REGULATION MADE?

The 1946 Administrative Procedures Act spells out a specific process for rule making in the federal bureaucracy. Similar to the process of making legislation, a proposed rule has many opportunities to fail to be implemented. Affected citizens also have a number of opportunities to offer their opinions of a proposed rule.

administrative adjudication

A quasi-judicial process in which a bureaucratic agency settles disputes between two parties in a manner similar to the way courts resolve disputes.

some agencies resort to **administrative adjudication,** a quasi-judicial process in which a bureaucratic agency settles disputes between two parties in a manner similar to the way courts resolve disputes. Administrative adjudication is referred to as quasi-judicial, because adjudication by any body other than the judiciary would be a violation of the constitutional principle of separation of powers.

Several agencies and boards employ administrative law judges to conduct hearings. Although employed by the agencies, these judges are strictly independent and cannot be removed except for gross misconduct. Their actions, however, are reviewable in the federal courts, as are the findings of judges in agencies such as the Equal Employment Opportunity Commission and Social Security Administration.

TABLE 2 HOW MANY COMMENTS DO AGENCIES RECEIVE ON PROPOSED RULES?

Agency	Subject	Comments
Food and Nutrition Service	Nutrition in school lunches	54,468
Federal Motor Carrier Safety Administration	Hours of service for drivers	27,333
Centers for Medicare and Medicaid Services	Physical fee schedule	20,280
National Oceanic and Atmospheric Agency	Annual fish catch limits	14,681
Environmental Protection Agency	Greenhouse gas emissions	5,028

SOURCE: Gregory Korte, "Comments Slow Down Rules Process." *USA Today* (May 25, 2011): A5; and www.regulations.gov.

Explore Your World

A key function of the bureaucracy is to represent the U.S. government to foreign states. One way the Department of State accomplishes this goal is by sending diplomats and bureaucrats to other countries to establish relationships with foreign leaders. Diplomatic offices are of two types: consulates and embassies. Consulates are smaller and are found in large cities that attract tourists; they help U.S. citizens with visas, international law, and identification. Embassies are large, usually located in a foreign capital, and work directly with foreign governments. The structure and functions of an embassy may be telling about the quality of U.S. relations with a particular country. Examine the U.S. embassies shown below and consider the variations in their appearance.

The U.S. Embassy in Paris, France, is the U.S.'s first diplomatic mission. It is located near the Champs-Élysées in the heart of the capital city.

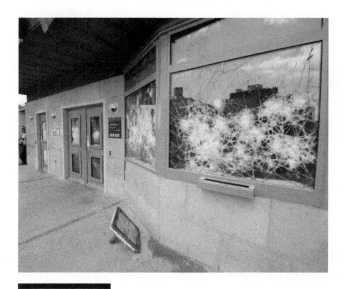

U.S. embassies and consulates are occasionally targets for anti-American sentiment. On September 11, 2012, and for several days thereafter, U.S. diplomatic missions throughout the Muslim world were attacked in a series of protests. This photo shows the embassy in Tunis, Tunisia after these acts of violence. In total, at least 75 people, including the U.S. ambassador to Libya, were killed and hundreds of others were injured.

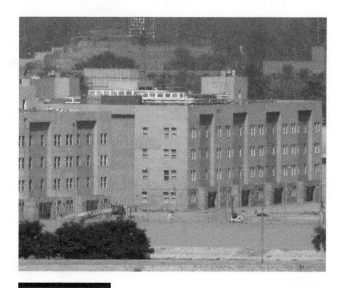

The U.S. Embassy in Iraq was constructed in the past several years. It is the largest, most fortified embassy in the world. It is located in the International (or "Green") Zone of Baghdad.

CRITICAL THINKING QUESTIONS

1. What do these buildings say about the importance of a U.S. embassy in these states?

2. Consider our relationship with each of these governments. Do we maintain strong relationships with these countries, or are we struggling in our efforts to remain friendly? How is the role of an American embassy in an "ally" country different from that of an embassy in a nation where we are constantly in conflict?

3. How do the security and location of embassies vary across states? How might this reflect the quality of a country's relationship with the United States?

Toward Reform: Making Agencies Accountable

4   Evaluate controls designed to make agencies more accountable.

lthough many critics of the bureaucracy argue that federal employees should be responsive to the public interest, the public interest is difficult to define. As it turns out, several factors control the power of the bureaucracy, and to some degree, the same kinds of checks and balances that operate among the three branches of government serve to rein in the bureaucracy (see Table 3).

☐ Executive Control

As the size and scope of the American national government, in general, and of the executive branch and bureaucracy, in particular, have grown, presidents have delegated more and more power to bureaucrats. But, most presidents have continued to try to exercise some control over the bureaucracy. They have often found that task more difficult than first envisioned. President John F. Kennedy, for example, once lamented that to give anyone at the Department of State an instruction was comparable to putting your request in a dead-letter box.[15] No response would ever be forthcoming.

Recognizing these potential problems, presidents try to appoint the best possible people to carry out their wishes and policy preferences. Presidents make hundreds of appointments to the executive branch; in doing so, they have the opportunity to appoint individuals who share their views on a range of policies. Although presidential appointments account for a very small proportion of all federal jobs, presidents or the Cabinet secretaries usually appoint most top policy-making positions.

With the approval of Congress, presidents can reorganize the bureaucracy. They also can make changes in an agency's annual budget requests and ignore legislative initiatives originating within the bureaucracy.

Presidents also can shape policy and provide direction to bureaucrats by issuing executive orders.[16] Executive orders are rules or regulations issued by the president that have the effect of law; the *Federal Register* must publish all executive orders. A president can direct an agency to act, but it may take some time to carry out the order. Given their many jobs, few presidents can ensure that the government will implement all their orders or will like all the rules that have been made, For example, even before Congress acted to protect women from discrimination by the federal government, the

TABLE 3 HOW ARE AGENCIES MADE ACCOUNTABLE?

The President Has the Authority to:	The Congress Has the Authority to:	The Judiciary Has the Authority to:
Appoint and remove agency heads and other top bureaucrats.	Pass legislation that alters the bureaucracy's activities.	Rule on whether bureaucrats have acted within the law and require policy changes to comply with the law.
Reorganize the bureaucracy (with congressional approval).	Abolish existing programs and agencies.	Force agencies to respect the rights of individuals through hearings and other proceedings.
Make changes in an agency's annual budget proposals.	Refuse to appropriate funds for certain programs.	Rule on the constitutionality of all challenged rules and regulations.
Ignore legislative initiatives originating within the bureaucracy.	Investigate agency activities and compel bureaucrats to testify about them.	
Initiate or adjust policies that would, if enacted by Congress, alter the bureaucracy's activities.	Influence presidential appointments of agency heads and other top bureaucratic officials.	
Issue executive orders.	Write legislation to limit bureaucratic discretion.	
Reduce an agency's annual budget.		

National Organization for Women convinced President Lyndon B. Johnson to sign a 1967 executive order that added the category of "gender" to an earlier order prohibiting discrimination on the basis of race, color, religion, or national origin in the awarding of federal contracts. Although the president signed the order, the Office of Federal Contract Compliance, part of the Department of Labor's Employment Standards Administration, failed to draft appropriate guidelines for implementation of the order until several years later.[17]

Congressional Control

Congress can confirm (or reject) nominees to top bureaucratic positions and has also played an important role in checking the power of the bureaucracy. Constitutionally, it possesses the authority to create or abolish departments and agencies. It may also transfer agency functions, and expand or contract bureaucratic discretion, as was the case in the creation of the Department of Homeland Security.

Congress can also use its investigatory powers to conduct program evaluations or hold oversight hearings. It is not at all unusual for a congressional committee or sub-committee to conduct hearings on a particular problem and then direct the relevant agency to study the problem or find ways to remedy it. Representatives of the agencies also appear before these committees on a regular basis to inform members about agency activities, ongoing investigations, and budget requests.

Congress also has the power of the purse. To control the bureaucracy, it can use its abilities to authorize spending and appropriate funds for an agency's activities, much like the proverbial carrot and stick. Money can be a powerful tool to coerce bureaucrats into making particular policies.

Legislators also augment their formal oversight of the executive branch by allowing citizens to appeal adverse bureaucratic decisions to agencies, Congress, and even the courts. Congressional review, a procedure adopted by the 104th Congress, by which joint resolutions of legislative disapproval can nullify agency regulations, is another method of exercising congressional oversight. This form of oversight is discussed in greater detail in our discussion of Congress.

Judicial Control

Whereas the president and Congress have direct ongoing control over the actions of the bureaucracy, the judiciary's oversight function is less apparent, but equally important. Still, federal judges, for example, can issue injunctions or orders to an executive agency even before a rule is publicized, giving the federal judiciary a potent check on the bureaucracy.

The courts also have ruled that agencies must give all affected individuals their due process rights guaranteed by the U.S. Constitution. The Social Security Administration cannot stop a recipient's checks, for example, unless that individual receives reasonable notice and an opportunity for a hearing. These types of cases make up the largest proportion of cases filed in federal district courts.

On a more informal, indirect level, litigation, or even the threat of litigation, often exerts a strong influence on bureaucrats. Injured parties can bring suit against agencies for their failure to enforce a law and can challenge agency interpretations of any law. In general, however, the courts give great weight to the opinions of bureaucrats and usually defer to their expertise.[18]

The development of specialized courts, however, has altered the relationship of some agencies with the federal courts, apparently resulting in less judicial deference to agency rulings. Research by political scientists reveals that specialized courts such as the Court of International Trade, because of its jurists' expertise, defer less to agency decisions than do more generalized federal courts. Conversely, reversal of decisions from executive agencies is more likely than reversal of decisions from more specialized independent regulatory commissions.[19]

What Puts the "Big" in Big Government?

The national government is actually not as big as it once was. Since 1962, the total number of government employees has fallen due to a reduction in the number of military personnel after Vietnam and the Cold War. The number of civilians employed directly by the government has also declined since the 1980s. However, even as the size of government has grown smaller, its spending has increased to the point that one-fourth of the U.S. economy comes from government funded programs, contracts, and benefits.

Size of the Government Workforce*

* In Thousands

	EXECUTIVE	MILITARY	LEGISLATIVE AND JUDICIAL	TOTAL
1962	2,485	2,840	30	5,355
1972	2,823	2,360	42	5,225
1982	2,770	2,147	55	4,972
1992	3,017	1,848	66	4,931
2002	2,630	1,456	66	4,152
2012	2,500	1,602	64	4,166

Government as Percent of GDP

1962
Government consumed just under one-fifth of the total economy and paid for that consumption with income such as taxes.

1%
18%

2012
Government consumed one-fourth of the total economy and paid a larger portion of it by borrowing instead of by taxing.

9%
16%

■ Government Spending Through Taxing
■ Government Spending Through Borrowing

SOURCE: Data from Voteview and U.S. Office of Management and Budget.

Investigate Further

Concept Is the federal government growing larger? The number of federal employees has actually decreased by over one million in a half-century. Since the late 1960s, the main difference in the size of its workforce is due to a smaller military and greater use of outside contractors.

Connection Do fewer federal employees mean smaller government? While the number of employees may be smaller, the federal government's share of the country's gross domestic product has grown every decade since the 1960s.

Cause If the government employs fewer people, how is it "bigger" than it was in 1962? Even with fewer people, the government implements more expensive programs that contribute to the total U.S. economy. Higher salaries, more expensive defense programs, larger entitlement programs, and increased spending to pay for past debt drive up costs.

Review the Chapter

Roots of the Federal Bureaucracy

1 Trace the growth and development of the federal bureaucracy.

The federal bureaucracy has changed dramatically since President George Washington's time, when the executive branch had only three departments—State, War, and Treasury. The size of the federal bureaucracy increased significantly following the Civil War. As employment opportunities within the federal government expanded, a civil service system was created to ensure that more and more jobs were filled according to merit and not by patronage. By the late 1800s, reform efforts led to further growth of the bureaucracy, as independent regulatory commissions came into existence. In the wake of the Great Depression, President Franklin D. Roosevelt's New Deal created many new agencies to get the national economy back on course.

The Modern Bureaucracy

2 Describe modern bureaucrats, and outline the structure of the modern bureaucracy.

The modern bureaucracy has more than 3 million civilian workers from all walks of life. In general, bureaucratic agencies fall into four categories: departments, independent agencies, independent regulatory commissions, and government corporations. The Hatch Act regulates the political activity of employees in the federal government.

How the Bureaucracy Works

3 Determine how the bureaucracy makes policy.

The bureaucracy is responsible for implementing many laws passed by Congress. A variety of formal and informal mechanisms, such as rule making and administrative adjudication, help bureaucrats make policy.

Toward Reform: Making Agencies Accountable

4 Evaluate controls designed to make agencies more accountable.

Agencies enjoy considerable discretion, but they are also subject to many formal controls that help make them more accountable. The president, Congress, and the judiciary all exercise various degrees of control over the bureaucracy through oversight, funding, or litigation.

Learn the Terms

administrative adjudication
administrative discretion
civil service system
departments
federal bureaucracy
government corporations
Hatch Act
implementation

independent executive
   agencies
independent regulatory
   commission
interagency councils
iron triangles
issue networks
merit system

patronage
Pendleton Act
policy coordinating
   committees
regulations
rule making
spoils system

Test Yourself

1. What was the primary goal of the spoils system?

a. To reward political allies for their support

b. To increase pay for certain workers

c. To increase loyalty among members of the opposition party

d. To give soldiers additional food rations

e. To hire federal workers on the basis of their previous experience and credentials

2. Which act of Congress established a merit system of federal employment?

a. Federal Employees Act

b. Pendleton Act

c. Dawes Act

d. Hatch Act

e. Political Activities Act

3. Bureaucratic agencies representing areas of permanent national interest whose heads are appointed directly by the president are known as:

a. government corporations.

b. independent regulatory commissions.

c. independent executive agencies.

d. policy coordinating committees.

e. Cabinet departments.

4. Why did Congress initially create independent regulatory commissions such as the Interstate Commerce Commission?

a. To better address foreign affairs issues

b. To maintain checks and balances in the government

c. To serve the Cabinet departments

d. To regulate specific economic interests

e. To perform functions that could be provided by private businesses

5. The Hatch Act regulates:

a. the creation of federal regulatory commissions.

b. job safety.

c. the use of government contractors.

d. the political activity of government employees.

e. hiring and firing government employees for poor performance.

6. Iron triangles are made up of:

a. the president, Congress, and bureaucrats.

b. interest groups, lobbyists, and bureaucrats.

c. bureaucratic agencies, interest groups, and congressional committees.

d. the vice president, Supreme Court, and Congress.

e. bureaucratic agencies, congressional committees, and the president.

7. Why were interagency councils created?

a. To develop nonpartisan solutions to partisan problems

b. To decrease government spending

c. To give interest groups greater access to the policy-making process

d. To improve relations between the executive and legislative branches

e. To facilitate policy making in complex issue areas

8. Which of the following does the 1946 Administrative Procedures Act NOT require?

a. Giving everyone a chance to participate in the rule-making process

b. Providing public notice of the time, place, and nature of the rule-making proceedings in the *Federal Register*

c. The Office of Management and Budget must review proposed rules.

d. Proposed rules must state the statutory purpose and basis of the provision.

e. The president must sign a rule for it to become law.

9. Which of the following must be published in the *Federal Register* in order to become law?

a. Executive orders

b. Regulations

c. Administrative adjudications

d. Supreme Court decisions

e. Proposed bills

10. The president can check the power of executive branch agencies by:

a. amending the Constitution.

b. issuing executive orders.

c. confirming or rejecting nominees.

d. holding oversight hearings.

e. issuing injunctions before rules are published.

Explore Further

Anderson, James E. *Public Policymaking: An Introduction,* 7th ed. Belmont, CA: Wadsworth Publishing, 2010.

Dolan, Julie A., and David H. Rosenbloom. *Representative Bureaucracy: Classic Readings and Continuing Controversies.* Armonk, NY: M. E. Sharpe, 2003.

Durant, Robert F., ed. *The Oxford Handbook of American Bureaucracy.* New York: Oxford University Press, 2012.

Etzioni-Halevy, Eva. *Bureaucracy and Democracy.* New York: Routledge, 2012.

Gormley, William T., and Steven J. Balla. *Bureaucracy and Democracy: Accountability and Performance,* 3rd ed. Washington, DC: CQ Press, 2012.

Hood, Christopher. *The Blame Game? Spin, Bureaucracy, and Self-Preservation in Government.* Princeton, NJ: Princeton University Press, 2010.

Ingraham, Patricia Wallace, and Laurence E. Lynn Jr. *The Art of Governance: Analyzing Management and Administration.* Washington, DC: Georgetown University Press, 2004.

Kane, John, and Haig Patapan. *The Democratic Leader: How Democracy Defines, Empowers, and Limits Its Leaders.* New York: Oxford University Press, 2012.

Kerwin, Cornelius M., and Scott R. Furlong. *Rulemaking: How Government Agencies Write Law and Make Policy,* 4th ed. Washington, DC: CQ Press, 2010.

Meier, Kenneth J., and Laurence O'Toole. *Bureaucracy in a Democratic State: A Governance Perspective.* Baltimore: Johns Hopkins University Press, 2006.

Nigro, Lloyd G., Felix A. Nigro, and J. Edward Kellough. *The New Public Personnel Administration,* 6th ed. Belmont, CA: Wadsworth, 2006.

Peters, B. Guy. *The Politics of Bureaucracy,* 6th ed. New York: Routledge, 2009.

Stivers, Camilla. *Gender Images in Public Administration: Legitimacy and the Administrative State,* 2nd ed. Thousand Oaks, CA: Sage, 2002.

Twight, Charlotte. *Dependent on DC: The Rise of Federal Control over the Lives of Ordinary Americans.* New York: Palgrave Macmillan, 2002.

Wilson, James Q. *Bureaucracy: What Government Agencies Do and Why They Do It,* reprint ed. New York: Basic Books, 2000.

To learn more about federal employees, go to the Office of Personnel Management Web site at **www.opm.gov** or to the page listing demographic information, **www.opm.gov/feddata/factbook/.**

To learn more about rules, proposed rules, and notices of federal agencies and organizations, go to the Web site of the *Federal Register* at **www.gpoaccess.gov/fr/index.html.**

To view or comment on a proposed regulation, go to **www.regulations.gov.**

To learn more about the Government Accountability Office, go to **www.gao.gov.**

Credits

Answer Key

1. a; 2. b; 3. e; 4. d; 5. d; 6. c; 7. e; 8. e; 9. b; 10. b

Notes

1. Federal Bureau of Investigation, "Most Wanted Terrorist Dead," (May 2, 2011): http://www.fbi.gov/news/stories/2011/may/bin-laden_050211/binladen_050211; Central Intelligence Agency, "Message from the Director: Justice Done," (May 5, 2011): https://www.cia.gov/news-information/press-releases-statements/press-release-2011/justice-done.html; and CBS News, "SEAL's First Hand Account of Bin Laden Killing," (September 9, 2012): http://www.cbsnews.com/8301-18560_162-57508646/seals-first-hand-account-of-bin-laden-killing/?tag=currentVideoInfo;videoMetaInfo.

2. Gallup Poll, July 10–12, 2009.

3. Harold D. Lasswell, *Politics: Who Gets What, When and How* (New York: McGraw-Hill, 1938).

4. David Osborne and Ted Gaebler, *Reinventing Government* (Reading, MA: Addison-Wesley, 1992), 20–21.

5. Al Kamen, "Feingold, McCain Try to Trim Appointees," *Washington Post* (March 9, 2010): B3.

6. Office of Personnel Management, *The Fact Book* (September 27, 2010), www.opm.gov/feddata/factbook/2007/factbook2007.pdf.

7. Barbara Slavin, "State Department Having Staffing Trouble," *USA Today* (November 30, 2005): 10A.

8. "A Century of Government Growth," *Washington Post* (January 3, 2000): A17. On the difficulty of counting the exact number of government agencies, see David Nachmias and David H. Rosenbloom, *Bureaucratic Government: U.S.A.* (New York: St. Martin's Press, 1980).

9. The classic work on regulatory commissions is Marver Bernstein, *Regulating Business by Independent Commission* (Princeton, NJ: Princeton University Press, 1955).

10. *Humphrey's Executor* v. *U.S.,* 295 U.S. 602 (1935).

11. John F. Duffy, "The Death of the Independent Regulatory Commission and the Birth of a New Independence," www.law.georgetown.edu/faculty/documents/duffy_paper.pdf.

12. H. H. Gerth and C. Wright Mills, *From Max Weber* (New York: Oxford University Press, 1958).

13. Michael Lipsky, *Street-Level Bureaucracy: Dilemmas of the Individual in Public Services* (New York: Russell Sage Foundation, 1980).

14. Cornelius M. Kerwin, *Rulemaking: How Government Agencies Write Law and Make Policy,* 2nd ed. (Washington, DC: CQ Press, 1999), xv.

15. Quoted in Arthur Schlesinger Jr., *A Thousand Days* (Greenwich, CT: Fawcett Books, 1967), 377.

16. George A. Krause, "Presidential Use of Executive Orders, 1953–1994," *American Politics Quarterly* 25 (October 1997): 458–81.

17. Irene Murphy, *Public Policy on the Status of Women* (Lexington, MA: Lexington Books, 1974).

18. Rosemary O'Leary, *Environmental Change: Federal Courts and the EPA* (Philadelphia: Temple University Press, 1995).

19. Wendy Hansen, Renee Johnson, and Isaac Unah, "Specialized Courts, Bureaucratic Agencies, and the Politics of U.S. Trade Policy," *American Journal of Political Science* 39 (August 1995): 529–57.

The Judiciary

From Chapter 9 of *Essentials of American Government: Roots and Reform,* 2012 Election Edition. Karen O'Connor. Copyright © 2014 by Pearson Education, Inc. Published by Pearson Education, Inc. All rights reserved.

The Judiciary

I n the summer of 2005, President George W. Bush was given an opportunity to shape the future of the U.S. Supreme Court. The death of Chief Justice William H. Rehnquist, who had presided over the Court for over twenty-five years, left an important vacancy on the high Court. To fill Chief Justice Rehnquist's seat, President Bush nominated an appeals court judge named John Roberts. Roberts's record in the lower courts had been conservative, and observers expected that his ideology would deviate little from that of his predecessor. Less clear was the new chief justice's ability to lead his fellow justices in a similar direction.

Seven years after his nomination, the legacy of the Roberts Court is taking shape. Despite the more recent additions of Justices Sonia Sotomayor and Elena Kagan—both of whom are moderate-to-liberal females appointed by a Democratic president—the Roberts Court is building a reputation as a conservative body dedicated to expanding the institutional power of the Supreme Court.

This legal strategy with an eye toward judicial power has prompted many Court-watchers to draw comparisons between Chief Justice Roberts and one of the Court's most legendary leaders, Chief Justice John Marshall. Chief Justice Marshall, who served on the Court in the early 1800s, is said to have done more for the power and the legacy of the Court and the federal government than any other justice before or since his tenure.

Only time will tell whether the Roberts Court is able to continue on its current trajectory. The personalities and politics of the eight other justices, who are appointed by the president and serve for life terms with good behavior, certainly will play significant roles. But, if recent decisions on health care, criminal rights, and campaign finance, just to name a few, are any indication, the Roberts Court is forming its own identity, one that is quite separate from that of the chief justices who have immediately preceded him.

1	2	3	4	5	6
Trace the development of the federal judiciary and the origins of judicial review.	Explain the organization of the federal court system.	Outline the criteria and process used to select federal court judges.	Evaluate the Supreme Court's process for accepting, hearing, and deciding cases.	Analyze the factors that influence judicial decision making.	Assess the role of the Supreme Court in the policy-making process.

IDEOLOGY ISN'T THE ONLY THING THAT HAS CHANGED Above, members of the liberal Warren Court (1953–1969), which decided a host of civil rights and liberties cases. Below, members of the modern, conservative Roberts Court, which has been especially active in economic and criminal procedure cases.

MyPoliSciLab Videos

1 **The Big Picture** What kinds of cases make it to the Supreme Court? Author Karen O'Connor explains why the Court rarely makes decisions on cases that affect only the parties involved, and discusses why so much attention is paid to the cases that the Supreme Court chooses to rule on.

The Basics Do you have confidence in the U.S. court system? Watch this video to discover what the founders did to make sure the federal judiciary would be independent of political influence. You'll also learn about an important check the Supreme Court has on the other two branches of U.S. government.

How do cases get to the Supreme Court?

3 **In Context** Discover how the Supreme Court gained a check on the other two branches after the U.S. Constitution was written. East Central University political scientist Christine Pappas discusses *Marbury* v. *Madison* (1803) and analyzes how the power of judicial review has impacted campaign finance law.

Thinking Like a Political Scientist Why do legal scholars and political scientists disagree over how judges make decisions? East Central University political scientist Christine Pappas analyzes this and other questions scholars study. She explains how the other branches of government limit the role of the judiciary in public policy making, and discusses research on how public opinion influences the courts.

5 **In the Real World** Should the Supreme Court have the power to knock down popular laws? This segment uses the Supreme Court's decision in *U.S.* v. *Arizona* (2012) to illustrate the tension between protecting the law and having a government that's run by the people.

So What? What is the Supreme Court doing for you? Author Karen O'Connor demonstrates how the Supreme Court's decisions have affected everything from your student newspaper to your birth control, which is why it is important to be engaged and informed about the decisions the courts are making.

In 1787, when writing *The Federalist Papers,* Alexander Hamilton urged support for the U.S. Constitution. He firmly believed that the judiciary would prove to be "the least dangerous" branch of government. The judicial branch seemed so inconsequential that when the young national government made its move to the District of Columbia in 1800, Congress actually forgot to include any space to house the justices of the Supreme Court!

Today, the role of the courts, particularly the Supreme Court of the United States, differs significantly from what the Framers envisioned. The "least dangerous branch" now is perceived by many people as having too much power.

We offer a note on terminology: in referring to the "Supreme Court," the "Court," or the "high Court" here, we always mean the U.S. Supreme Court, which sits at the pinnacle of the federal and state court systems. The Supreme Court is referred to by the name of the chief justice who presided over it during a particular period. For example, the Marshall Court is the Court presided over by John Marshall from 1801 to 1835, and the Roberts Court is the current Court that began in 2005. When we use the term "courts," we refer to all federal or state courts unless otherwise noted.

jurisdiction
Authority vested in a particular court to hear and decide the issues in a particular case.

original jurisdiction
The jurisdiction of courts that hear a case first, usually in a trial. These courts determine the facts of a case.

Roots of the Federal Judiciary

1 Trace the development of the federal judiciary and the origins of judicial review.

The detailed notes James Madison took at the Constitutional Convention in Philadelphia make it clear that the Framers devoted little time to writing Article III, which created the judicial branch of government. The Framers believed that a federal judiciary posed little threat of tyranny. One scholar has even suggested that, for at least some delegates to the Constitutional Convention, "provision for a national judiciary was a matter of theoretical necessity . . . more in deference to the maxim of separation [of powers] than in response to clearly formulated ideas about the role of a national judicial system and its indispensability."[1]

The Framers also debated the need for any federal courts below the Supreme Court. Some argued in favor of deciding all cases in state courts, with only appeals going before the Supreme Court. Others argued for a system of federal courts. A compromise left the final choice to Congress, and Article III, section 1, begins simply by vesting "The judicial Power of the United States . . . in one supreme Court, and in such inferior Courts as the Congress may from time to time ordain and establish."

Article III, section 2, specifies the judicial power of the Supreme Court. It also discusses the types of cases the Court can hear, or its **jurisdiction** (see Table 1). Courts have two types of jurisdiction: original and appellate. **Original jurisdiction** refers to a court's authority to hear disputes as a trial court; these courts determine the facts of a

TABLE 1 WHAT KINDS OF CASES DOES THE U.S. SUPREME COURT HEAR?

The following are the types of cases the Supreme Court was given the jurisdiction to hear as initially specified in Article III, section 2, of the Constitution:

All cases arising under the Constitution and laws or treaties of the United States

All cases of admiralty or maritime jurisdiction

Cases in which the United States is a party

Controversies between a state and citizens of another state (later modified by the Eleventh Amendment)

Controversies between two or more states

Controversies between citizens of different states

Controversies between citizens of the same state claiming lands under grants in different states

Controversies between a state, or the citizens thereof, and foreign states or citizens thereof

All cases affecting ambassadors or other public ministers

case. The Supreme Court has original jurisdiction in cases involving the state governments or public officials. **Appellate jurisdiction** refers to a court's ability to review and/or revise cases already decided by a trial court. The Supreme Court has appellate jurisdiction in all other cases. This section also specifies that all federal crimes, except those involving impeachment, shall be tried by jury in the state in which the crime was committed. The third section of the article defines treason and mandates that at least two witnesses appear in such cases.

Had the Framers viewed the Supreme Court as the potential policy maker it is today, they most likely would not have provided for life tenure with "good behavior" for all federal judges in Article III. The Framers agreed on this feature because they did not want the justices (or any federal judges) subject to the whims of politics, the public, or politicians. Moreover, Alexander Hamilton argued in *Federalist No. 78* that the "independence of judges" was needed "to guard the Constitution and the rights of individuals."

The Constitution nonetheless did include some checks on the power of the judiciary. One such check gives Congress the authority to alter the Court's ability to hear certain kinds of cases. Congress can also propose constitutional amendments that, if ratified, can effectively reverse judicial decisions, and it can impeach and remove federal judges. In one further check, it is the president who, with the "advice and consent" of the Senate, appoints all federal judges.

The Court can, in turn, check the presidency by presiding over presidential impeachment. Article I, section 3, notes in discussing impeachment, "When the President of the United States is tried, the Chief Justice shall preside."

☐ The Judiciary Act of 1789 and the Creation of the Federal Judicial System

In spite of the Framers' intentions, the pervasive role of politics in the judicial branch quickly became evident with the passage of the Judiciary Act of 1789. Congress spent nearly the entire second half of its first session deliberating the various provisions of the act to give form and substance to the federal judiciary.

The **Judiciary Act of 1789** established the basic three-tiered structure of the federal court system. At the bottom were the federal district courts—at least one in each state. If people participating in a lawsuit (called litigants) were unhappy with the district court's verdict, they could appeal their case to the circuit courts, constituting the second tier. Each circuit court, initially created to function as a trial court for important cases, originally comprised one district court judge and two Supreme Court justices who met as a circuit court twice a year. Not until 1891 did circuit courts (or, as we know them today, courts of appeals) take on their exclusively appellate function and begin to focus solely on reviewing the findings of lower courts. The third tier of the federal judicial system defined by the Judiciary Act of 1789 was the Supreme Court of the United States. Although the Constitution mentions "the supreme Court," it did not designate its size. In the Judiciary Act, Congress set the size of the Supreme Court at six—the chief justice plus five associate justices. After being reduced to five members in 1801, Congress expanded and contracted the Court's size until it was fixed at nine in 1869.

When the justices met in their first public session in New York City in 1790, they were garbed magnificently in black and scarlet robes in the English fashion. The elegance of their attire, however, could not compensate for the relative ineffectiveness of the Court. Its first session—presided over by John Jay, who was appointed chief justice of the United States by President George Washington—initially had to be adjourned when fewer than half the justices attended. Later, once a sufficient number of justices assembled, the Court decided only one major case. Moreover, as an indication of its lowly status, one associate justice left the Court to become chief justice of the South Carolina Supreme Court.

In its first decade, the Court took several actions to mold the new nation. First, by declining to give George Washington advice on the legality of some of his actions, the justices attempted to establish the Supreme Court as an independent, nonpolitical branch of government. Second, the early Court also tried to advance principles of nationalism and to maintain the national government's supremacy over the states.

appellate jurisdiction
The power vested in particular courts to review and/or revise the decision of a lower court.

Judiciary Act of 1789
Legislative act that established the basic three-tiered structure of the federal court system.

The Living Constitution

> *The Judges both of the supreme and inferior Courts, shall . . . receive for their services, a compensation, which shall not be diminished during their continuance in office.* —ARTICLE III, SECTION 1

This section of Article III guarantees that the salaries of all federal judges will not be reduced during their service on the bench. At the Constitutional Convention, considerable debate raged over how to treat the payment of federal judges. Some believed that Congress should have an extra check on the judiciary by being able to reduce their salaries. This provision was a compromise after James Madison suggested that Congress have the authority to bar increases as well as decreases in the salaries of these unelected jurists. The delegates recognized that decreases, as well as no opportunity for raises, could negatively affect the perks associated with life tenure.

This clause of the Constitution has not elicited much controversy. When the federal income tax was first enacted, some judges unsuccessfully challenged it as a diminution of their salaries. Much more recently, Chief Justices William H. Rehnquist and John Roberts repeatedly urged Congress to increase salaries for federal judges. As early as 1989, Rehnquist noted that "judicial salaries are the single greatest problem facing the federal judiciary today." Roberts, in his first state of the judiciary message, pointed out that the comparatively low salaries earned by federal judges drive away many well-qualified and diverse lawyers, compromising the independence of the American judiciary.

Increasing numbers of federal judges are leaving the bench for more lucrative private practice. While a salary of $223,500 (for the chief justice) or $213,900 (for the other justices) may sound like a lot to most people, lawyers in large urban practices routinely earn more than double and triple that amount annually. Supreme Court clerks, moreover, now regularly receive $250,000 signing bonuses (in addition to large salaries) from law firms anxious to pay for their expertise.

CRITICAL THINKING QUESTIONS

1. How does prohibiting Congress from diminishing the salaries of judges reduce political influences on the judiciary?

2. How do justices' salaries compare to the average income of a worker in your area? Do you agree with Chief Justice Roberts's contention that judges are underpaid? Why or why not?

The Marshall Court: *Marbury* v. *Madison* (1803) and Judicial Review

judicial review
Power of the courts to review acts of other branches of government and the states.

John Marshall was appointed chief justice in 1800, three years after he declined to accept a nomination as associate justice. An ardent Federalist, Marshall is considered the most important justice to serve on the high Court. Part of his reputation results from the duration of his service and the historical significance of this period in our nation's history.

As chief justice, Marshall helped to establish the role and power of the Court. The Marshall Court, for example, discontinued the practice of *seriatim* (Latin for "in a series") opinions, which was the custom of the King's Bench in Great Britain. Prior to the Marshall Court, the justices delivered their individual opinions in order of seniority. For the Court to take its place as an equal branch of government, Marshall believed, the justices needed to speak as a Court and not as six individuals. In fact, during Marshall's first four years in office, the Court routinely spoke as one, and the chief justice wrote twenty-four of its twenty-six opinions.

The Marshall Court also established the authority of the Supreme Court over the judiciaries of the various states.[2] In addition, the Court established the supremacy of the federal government and Congress over state governments through a broad interpretation of the necessary and proper clause in *McCulloch* v. *Maryland* (1819).[3]

Finally, the Marshall Court claimed the right of **judicial review**, the power of the courts to review acts of other branches of government and of the states. The Supreme Court derives much of its day-to-day power and impact on the policy process from this right. This claim established the Court as the final arbiter of constitutional questions, with the right to declare congressional acts void.[4]

Marbury v. _Madison_ (1803)

Case in which the Supreme Court first asserted the power of judicial review by finding that the congressional statute extending the Court's original jurisdiction was unconstitutional.

trial court

Court of original jurisdiction where cases begin.

appellate court

Court that generally reviews only findings of law made by lower courts.

constitutional courts

Federal courts specifically created by the U.S. Constitution or by Congress pursuant to its authority in Article III.

Alexander Hamilton first publicly endorsed the idea of judicial review in _Federalist No. 78_, noting, "Whenever a particular statute contravenes the Constitution, it will be the duty of the judicial tribunals to adhere to the latter and disregard the former." Nonetheless, because the U.S. Constitution does not mention judicial review, the actual authority of the Supreme Court to review the constitutionality of acts of Congress was an unsettled question. But, in **_Marbury_ v. _Madison_ (1803)**, Chief Justice John Marshall claimed this sweeping authority for the Court by asserting that the Constitution's supremacy clause implies the right of judicial review.[5]

Marbury v. _Madison_ arose amid a sea of political controversy. In the final hours of his administration, John Adams appointed William Marbury as the justice of the peace for the District of Columbia. But, in the confusion of winding up matters, Adams's secretary of state failed to deliver Marbury's commission. Marbury then asked James Madison, Thomas Jefferson's secretary of state, for the commission. Under direct orders from Jefferson, who was irate over the Adams administration's last-minute appointment of several Federalist judges (quickly confirmed by the Federalist Senate), Madison refused to turn over the commission. Marbury and three other Adams appointees who were in the same situation then filed a writ of _mandamus_ (a legal motion) asking the Supreme Court to order Madison to deliver their commissions.

Political tensions ran high as the Court met to hear the case. Jefferson threatened to ignore any order of the Court. Marshall realized that a refusal of the executive branch to comply with the decision could devastate both him and the prestige of the Court. Responding to this challenge, in a brilliant opinion that in many sections reads more like a lecture to Jefferson than a discussion of the merits of Marbury's claim, Marshall concluded that although Marbury and the others were entitled to their commissions, the Court lacked the power to issue the writ sought by Marbury. In _Marbury_ v. _Madison_, Marshall further ruled that those parts of the Judiciary Act of 1789 that extended the original jurisdiction of the Court to allow it to issue writs of _mandamus_ were inconsistent with the Constitution and therefore unconstitutional.

Although the immediate effect of the decision was to deny power to the Court, its long-term effect was to establish the implied power of judicial review. Said Marshall, writing for the Court, "it is emphatically the province and duty of the judicial department to say what the law is." Since _Marbury_, the Court has routinely exercised the power of judicial review to determine the constitutionality of acts of Congress, the executive branch, and the states.

The Federal Court System

2 Explain the organization of the federal court system.

The judicial system in the United States can best be described as a dual system consisting of the federal court system and the judicial systems of the fifty states. Cases may arise in either system. Both systems are basically three-tiered. At the bottom of the system are **trial courts**, where litigation begins. In the middle are **appellate courts**; these courts generally review only findings of law made by trial courts. At the top of both the federal and state court systems sits a court of last resort (see Figure 1). In the federal court system, trial courts are called district courts, appellate courts are termed courts of appeals, and the Supreme Court is the court of last resort.

The federal district courts, courts of appeals, and the Supreme Court are called **constitutional (or Article III) courts** because Article III of the Constitution either established them or authorized Congress to establish them. The president nominates (with the advice and consent of the Senate) judges who preside over these courts, and they serve lifetime terms, as long as they engage in "good behavior."

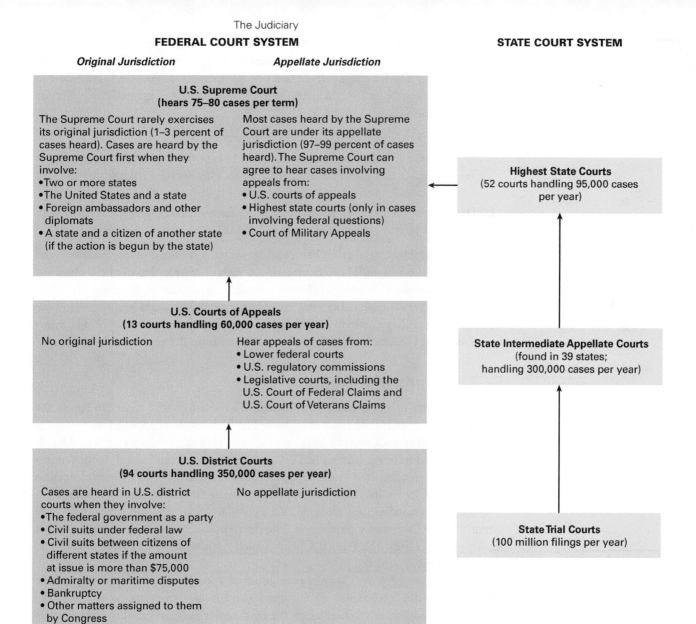

FIGURE 1 HOW IS THE AMERICAN JUDICIAL SYSTEM STRUCTURED?

The American judicial system is a dual system consisting of the federal court system and the judicial systems of the fifty states. In both the federal court system and the judiciaries of most states, there are both trial and appellate courts. The U.S. Supreme Court sits at the top of both court systems and has the power to hear appeals from both federal and state courts as long as they involve a federal question.

In addition to constitutional courts, **legislative courts** are set up by Congress, under its implied powers, generally for special purposes. The U.S. territorial courts (which hear federal cases in the territories) and the U.S. Court of Appeals for Veterans Claims are examples of legislative courts, or what some call Article I courts. The president appoints (subject to Senate confirmation) the judges who preside over these federal courts; they serve fixed, fifteen-year renewable terms.

legislative courts

Courts established by Congress for specialized purposes, such as the Court of Appeals for Veterans Claims.

☐ The District Courts

As we have seen, Congress created U.S. district courts when it enacted the Judiciary Act of 1789. District courts are federal trial courts. Currently, the federal district courts number ninety-four. No district court cuts across state lines. Every state has at least one federal district court, and the most populous states—California, Texas, and New York—each have four.[6]

Federal district courts, in which the bulk of the judicial work takes place in the federal system, have original jurisdiction over only specific types of cases. Although rules governing district court jurisdiction can be complex, cases, which are heard in federal district courts by a single judge (with or without a jury), generally fall into one of three categories:

1. They involve the federal government as a party.

2. They present a federal question based on a claim under the U.S. Constitution, a treaty with another nation, or a federal statute. This is called federal question jurisdiction and it can involve criminal or civil law.

3. They involve civil suits in which citizens are from different states, and the amount of money at issue is more than $75,000.[7]

Each federal judicial district has a U.S. attorney, nominated by the president and confirmed by the Senate. The U.S. attorney in each district is that district's chief law enforcement officer. U.S. attorneys have a considerable amount of discretion regarding whether they pursue criminal or civil investigations or file charges against individuals or corporations. They also have several assistants to help them in their work. The number of assistant U.S. attorneys in each district depends on the amount of litigation.

☐ The Courts of Appeals

The losing party in a case heard and decided in a federal district court can appeal the decision to the appropriate court of appeals. The U.S. courts of appeals (known as the circuit courts of appeals prior to 1948) are the intermediate appellate courts in the federal system and were established in 1789 to hear appeals from federal district courts. Currently, eleven numbered courts of appeals exist. A twelfth, the U.S. Court of Appeals for the D.C. Circuit, handles most appeals involving federal regulatory commissions and agencies, including, for example, the National Labor Relations Board and the Securities and Exchange Commission. The thirteenth federal appeals court is the U.S. Court of Appeals for the Federal Circuit, which deals with patents and contract and financial claims against the federal government.

The number of judges within each court of appeals varies—depending on the workload and the complexity of the cases—and ranges from six to nearly thirty. Supervising each court is a chief judge, the most senior judge in terms of service below the age of sixty-five, who can serve no more than seven years. In deciding cases, judges are divided into rotating three-judge panels, made up of the active judges within the court of appeals, visiting judges (primarily district judges from the same court), and retired judges. In rare cases, all the judges in a court of appeals may choose to sit together (*en banc*) to decide a case of special importance by majority vote.

The courts of appeals have no original jurisdiction. Rather, Congress has granted these courts appellate jurisdiction over two general categories of cases: appeals from criminal and civil cases from the district courts, and appeals from administrative agencies. Criminal and civil case appeals constitute about 90 percent of the workload of the courts of appeals; those from administrative agencies constitute about 10 percent.

In general, courts of appeals try to correct errors of law and procedure that have occurred in lower courts or administrative agencies. Courts of appeals hear no new testimony; instead, lawyers submit written arguments in what is called a **brief** (also submitted in trial courts), and they then appear to present and argue the case orally to the court. Decisions of any court of appeals are binding on only the courts within its geographic confines.

☐ The Supreme Court

The U.S. Supreme Court is often at the center of highly controversial issues that the political process has yet to resolve successfully. It reviews cases from the U.S. courts of appeals and state supreme courts (as well as other courts of last resort) and acts as the final interpreter of the U.S. Constitution.

brief
A document containing the legal written arguments in a case filed with a court by a party prior to a hearing or trial.

Explore Your World

Judiciaries enjoy a unique role in the political systems of many states. They are the ultimate arbiters of the law and the Constitution, and wield significant power in determining innocence, guilt, and liability. Judges also play an important role in maintaining the rule of law and enforcing appropriate punishments for crimes committed. It is only appropriate, then, that judicial officers around the world are outfitted in a way that conveys the honor and responsibility of the position they hold. Most judicial robes are red or black. This tradition may have its roots in the mourning robes worn to pay respect during medieval times.

Judicial dress is a contentious issue in Pakistan. Some Pakistani judges, such as the one shown at right in this photo, dress in the English tradition and wear robes with wigs. Others, especially Muslim judges, choose to wear more traditional Nehru-style jackets with hats.

American Chief Justice William H. Rehnquist, seen here presiding over the 1999 impeachment trial of President Bill Clinton, added embellishments to his traditional black robe in the form of four gold stripes on each sleeve.

Red robes are traditional on the German Federal Constitutional Court. These robes are based on those worn by Italian judges during the Renaissance. Though the hat is officially part of the uniform, it has largely been eliminated in recent years.

CRITICAL THINKING QUESTIONS

1. How does each of these modes of dress reflect the culture and traditions of the countries they represent?

2. How might you expect judges in other countries—for example, Australia or Italy—to dress? What influences your expectation?

3. Does requiring a particular "uniform" accord judges additional power and respect? Should other political leaders, such as members of the legislature, wear uniform dress?

precedent

A prior judicial decision that serves as a rule for settling subsequent cases of a similar nature.

stare decisis

In court rulings, a reliance on past decisions or precedents to formulate decisions in new cases.

Since 1869, the U.S. Supreme Court has consisted of eight associate justices and one chief justice, whom the president nominates specifically for that position. The number nine holds no special significance, and the Constitution does not specify the size of the Court. Between 1789 and 1869, Congress periodically altered the size of the Court. The lowest number of justices on the Court was six; the most, ten. Through December 2012, only 112 justices had served on the Court, with only seventeen chief justices.

Decisions of the U.S. Supreme Court, however, are binding throughout the nation and establish national **precedents**, or rules for settling subsequent cases of similar nature. This reliance on past decisions or precedents to formulate decisions in new cases is called *stare decisis* (a Latin phrase meaning "let the decision stand"). The principle of *stare decisis* allows for continuity and predictability in our judicial system. Although *stare decisis* can be helpful in predicting decisions, at times judges carve out new ground and ignore, decline to follow, or even overrule precedents to reach a different conclusion in a case involving similar circumstances. This is a major reason why so much litigation exists in America today. Parties to a suit know that the outcome of a case is not always predictable; if such prediction were possible, there would be little reason to go to court.

How Federal Court Judges Are Selected

3   Outline the criteria and process used to select federal court judges.

The selection of federal judges is often a highly political process with important political ramifications because the president must nominate judges and the U.S. Senate must confirm them. Presidents, in general, try to select well-qualified men and women for the bench. But, these appointments also provide a president with the opportunity to put his philosophical stamp on the federal courts (see Table 2).

In selecting his nominees, the president may look for guidance from members of Congress, advisers, confidantes, or other high-ranking party officials.[8] The U.S.

TABLE 2 HOW DOES A PRESIDENT AFFECT THE FEDERAL JUDICIARY?

President	Appointed to Supreme Court	Appointed to Courts of Appeals[a]	Appointed to District Courts[b]	Total Appointed	Total Number of Judgeships[c]	Percentage of Judgeships Filled by President
Carter (1977–1981)	0	56	203	259	657	39
Reagan (1981–1989)	3	83	290	376	740	50
Bush (1989–1993)	2	42	148	192	825	22
Clinton (1993–2001)	2	66	305	373	841	44
G.W. Bush (2001–2009)	2	61	261	324	866	37
Obama (2009–)[d]	2	30	130	162	874	19

[a]Does not include the U.S. Court of Appeals for the Federal Circuit.
[b]Includes district courts in the territories.
[c]Total judgeships authorized in president's last year in office.
[d]Barack Obama data through October 2012.

SOURCE: "Imprints on the Bench," *CQ Weekly Report* (January 19, 2001): 173. Reprinted by permission of Copyright Clearance Center on behalf of Congressional Quarterly, Inc. Updated by authors. Obama data from Senate Judiciary Committee, www.judiciary.senate.gov/nominations/112thCongress.cfm and www.judiciary.senate.gov/nominations/111thCongress.cfm.

Constitution, for example, mandates that presidents receive advice and consent from the Senate. Historically, presidents have screened their nominees through a process known as **senatorial courtesy**. This is the process by which presidents generally allow senators from the state in which a judicial vacancy occurs to block a nomination by simply registering their objection. One way senators may voice their opposition is through an informal process known as the "blue slip." When a judicial nomination is forwarded to the Senate Judiciary Committee, senators from the state in which a vacancy occurs are sent a letter, usually printed on light blue paper, asking them to register their support or opposition to a nominee. How seriously senators take the blue slips varies from one Congress to the next.[9]

senatorial courtesy
A process by which presidents generally allow senators from the state in which a judicial vacancy occurs to block a nomination by simply registering their objection.

□ Who Are Federal Judges?

Typically, federal district court judges have held other political offices, such as state court judge or prosecutor. Most have been involved in politics, which is what usually brings them into consideration for a position on the federal bench.

Most recent nominees have had prior judicial experience. White males continue to dominate the federal courts, but since the 1970s, most presidents have pledged (with varying degrees of success) to do their best to appoint more African Americans, Hispanics, women, and other underrepresented groups to the federal bench.

□ Nomination Criteria

Justice Sandra Day O'Connor once remarked that "You have to be lucky" to be appointed to the judiciary.[10] Although luck certainly factors in, over the years a variety of reasons have accounted for nominations to the bench. Depending on the timing of a vacancy, a president may or may not have a list of possible candidates or even a specific individual in mind. Until recently, presidents often looked within their circle of friends or their administration to fill a vacancy. Nevertheless, whether the nominee is a friend or someone known to the president only by reputation, at least six criteria are especially important: experience, ideology or policy preferences, rewards, pursuit of political support, religion, and race and gender.

EXPERIENCE Most nominees have had at least some judicial, legal, or governmental experience. For example, John Jay, the first chief justice, was one of the authors of *The Federalist Papers* and was active in New York politics. In 2012, all nine sitting Supreme Court justices but one—former Solicitor General Elena Kagan—had prior judicial experience (see Table 3).

IDEOLOGY OR POLICY PREFERENCES Most presidents also seek to appoint individuals who share their policy preferences, and almost all have political goals in mind when they appoint a judge or justice. Presidents Franklin D. Roosevelt, Richard M. Nixon, and Ronald Reagan achieved success in molding the federal judiciary to their own political beliefs.

REWARDS Historically, many of those appointed to the judiciary have been personal friends of presidents. Lyndon B. Johnson, for example, appointed his longtime friend Abe Fortas to the bench.

PURSUIT OF POLITICAL SUPPORT During Ronald Reagan's successful campaign for the presidency in 1980, some of his advisers feared that the gender gap would hurt him. Polls repeatedly showed that he was far less popular with female voters than with men. To gain support from women, Reagan announced during his campaign that should he win, he would appoint a woman to fill the first vacancy on the Supreme Court. When Justice Potter Stewart, a moderate, announced his retirement from the bench, under pressure from women's rights groups, President Reagan nominated Sandra Day O'Connor of the Arizona Court of Appeals to fill the vacancy.

TABLE 3 WHO ARE THE JUSTICES OF THE SUPREME COURT IN 2012?

Justices	Year of Birth	Year Appointed	Political Party	Law School	Appointing President	Religion	Prior Judicial Experience	Prior Government Experience
John Roberts	1955	2005	R	Harvard	G. W. Bush	Roman Catholic	U.S. Court of Appeals	Dept. of Justice, associate White House counsel
Antonin Scalia	1936	1986	R	Harvard	Reagan	Roman Catholic	U.S. Court of Appeals	Assistant attorney general, Office of Legal Counsel
Anthony Kennedy	1936	1988	R	Harvard	Reagan	Roman Catholic	U.S. Court of Appeals	None
Clarence Thomas	1948	1991	R	Yale	Bush	Roman Catholic	U.S. Court of Appeals	Chair, Equal Employment Opportunity Commission
Ruth Bader Ginsburg	1933	1993	D	Columbia/ Harvard	Clinton	Jewish	U.S. Court of Appeals	None
Stephen Breyer	1938	1994	D	Harvard	Clinton	Jewish	U.S. Court of Appeals	Chief counsel, Senate Judiciary Committee
Samuel Alito	1950	2006	R	Yale	G. W. Bush	Roman Catholic	U.S. Court of Appeals	Dept. of Justice, U.S. attorney
Sonia Sotomayor	1954	2009	D	Yale	Obama	Roman Catholic	U.S. Court of Appeals	Assistant attorney general, City of New York
Elena Kagan	1960	2010	D	Harvard	Obama	Jewish	None	U.S. solicitor general, associate White House counsel

RELIGION Through late 2012, of the 112 justices who have served on the Court, almost all have been members of traditional Protestant faiths. Only twelve have been Roman Catholic, and only eight have been Jewish.[11] Today, more Catholics—Roberts, Scalia, Kennedy, Thomas, Alito, and Sotomayor—serve on the Court than at any other point in history. Three Jewish justices—Breyer, Ginsburg, and Kagan—round out the Court. At one time, no one could have imagined that Catholics would someday make up a majority of the Court, or that no members of any Protestant faiths would serve.

RACE, ETHNICITY, AND GENDER Through 2012 only two African Americans and four women have served on the Court. Race was undoubtedly a critical issue in the appointment of Clarence Thomas to replace Thurgood Marshall, the first African American justice. But, President George Bush refused to acknowledge his wish to retain a black seat on the Court. Instead, he announced that he was "picking the best man for the job on the merits," a claim that was met with considerable skepticism by many observers.

As the ethnic diversity of the United States has increased, presidents have faced greater pressure to nominate a Hispanic justice to the Supreme Court. Early in his presidency, President Barack Obama fulfilled these expectations by nominating Sonia Sotomayor.

☐ The Confirmation Process

The Constitution gives the Senate the authority to approve all nominees to the federal bench. Ordinarily, nominations are referred to the Senate Judiciary Committee. This committee investigates the nominees, holds hearings, and votes on its recommendation for Senate action. At this stage, the committee may reject a nominee or send the nomination to the full Senate for a vote. The full Senate then deliberates on the nominee before voting. A simple majority vote is required for confirmation.

INVESTIGATION As a president proceeds to narrow the list of possible nominees for a judicial vacancy, White House staff begin an investigation into their personal and

Who Are Federal Judges?

Judicial appointments provide presidents with an opportunity to make a lasting impact on public policy. Recent presidents, including Bill Clinton, George W. Bush, and Barack Obama, have also used them as an opportunity to increase the diversity of individuals serving at the highest levels of the U.S. government and to curry favor with traditionally underrepresented groups. Though a diverse federal judiciary has a definite symbolic effect on American politics, its policy impact is less clear.

Who Presidents NOMINATE

	Obama	W. Bush	Clinton
Female	44%	22%	28%
White	64%	82%	75%
Hispanic	11%	9%	6%
African American	19%	7%	16%
Asian American	6%	1%	1%

The Overall COMPOSITION of the Federal Court

Vacancies 9%

Female 28%
Male 63%

African American 11%
Asian American 2%
Hispanic 8%
White 69%
Vacancies 9%

Vacancies 9%
Democratic Appointee 43%
Republican Appointee 48%

Appointing PRESIDENT

Percent

President	Percent
Previous Presidents	<1%
Carter	1%
Reagan	6%
Bush	7%
Clinton	23%
W. Bush	35%
Obama	18%
Vacancies	9%

SOURCE: Data from Federal Judicial Center, Biographical Directory of Federal Judges

CRITICAL THINKING QUESTIONS

1. Which groups are over- and underrepresented in the federal judiciary?

2. What differences, if any, exist between judges nominated by Republican presidents and those appointed by Democratic presidents?

3. Should gender, race, and ethnicity matter in the federal courts? Why or why not?

professional backgrounds. The Federal Bureau of Investigation also receives names of potential nominees for background checks. After a formal nomination is made and sent to the Senate, the Senate Judiciary Committee embarks on its own investigation.

LOBBYING BY INTEREST GROUPS Many organized interests show keen interest in the nomination process. Interest groups are particularly active in Supreme Court nominations. In 1987, for example, the nomination of Judge Robert H. Bork to the Supreme Court led liberal groups to launch an extensive radio, TV, and print media campaign against the nominee. These interest groups decried Bork's actions as solicitor general, especially his firing of the Watergate special prosecutor at the request of President Richard M. Nixon, as well as his political beliefs.

More and more, interest groups are also involving themselves in district court and court of appeals nominations. They recognize that these appointments often pave the way for future nominees to the Supreme Court.

THE SENATE COMMITTEE HEARINGS AND SENATE VOTE After the conclusion of hearings, the Senate Judiciary Committee usually makes a recommendation to the full Senate. Any rejections of presidential nominees to the Supreme Court generally occur only after the Senate Judiciary Committee has recommended against a nominee's appointment. Few recent confirmations have been close, although current Supreme Court Justices Clarence Thomas and Samuel Alito were confirmed by margins of less than ten votes.

The Supreme Court Today

4   Evaluate the Supreme Court's process for accepting, hearing, and deciding cases.

Explore on
MyPoliSciLab
Simulation: You Are a
Supreme Court Clerk

 iven the judicial system's vast size and substantial, although often indirect, power over so many aspects of our lives, it is surprising that so many Americans know very little about the judicial system in general and the U.S. Supreme Court in particular.

Even after the attention the Court received surrounding many of its recent controversial decisions, two-thirds of those Americans surveyed in 2012 could not name one member of the Court. Virtually no one could name all nine members of the Court. Chief Justice John Roberts was the best-known justice. Still, only about 20 percent of those polled could name him.

While the American public's lack of interest can take the blame for much of this ignorance, the Court has also taken great pains to ensure its privacy and sense of decorum. The Court's rites and rituals contribute to its mystique and encourage a "cult of the robe."[12] Consider, for example, the way the Supreme Court conducts its proceedings. Oral arguments are not televised, and utmost secrecy surrounds deliberations concerning the outcome of cases. In contrast, C-SPAN brings us daily coverage of various congressional hearings and floor debate on bills and important national issues, and CNN and sometimes other networks provide extensive coverage of many important state court trials. The Supreme Court, however, remains adamant in its refusal to televise its proceedings—including public oral arguments, although it now allows the release of same-day audio recordings of oral arguments.

☐ Deciding to Hear a Case

Over 7,250 cases were filed at the Supreme Court during its 2011–12 term; 79 were heard, and 77 decisions were issued. In contrast, from 1790 to 1801, the Court received only 87 total cases under its appellate jurisdiction. In the Court's early years, most of the justices' workload involved their circuit-riding duties.[13] As recently as the

1940s, fewer than 1,000 cases were filed annually. Filings increased at a dramatic rate until the mid-1990s, shot up again in the late 1990s, and generally have now leveled off (see Figure 2).

The content of the Court's docket is every bit as significant as its size. During the 1930s, cases requiring the interpretation of constitutional law began to account for a growing portion of the Court's workload, leading the Court to assume a more important role in the policy-making process. At that time, only 5 percent of the Court's cases involved questions concerning the Bill of Rights. By the late 1950s, one-third of filed cases involved such questions; by the 1960s, half did.[14]

WRITS OF *CERTIORARI* AND THE RULE OF FOUR Since 1988, nearly all appellate cases that have gone to the Supreme Court arrived there on a petition for a **writ of certiorari** (from the Latin "to be informed"), which is a request for the Supreme Court—at its discretion—to order up the records of the lower courts for purposes of review (see Figure 3).

The Supreme Court controls its own caseload through the *certiorari* process, deciding which cases it wants to hear and rejecting most cases that come to it. All petitions, or writs of *certiorari*, must meet two criteria:

1. The case must come from a U.S. court of appeals, a court of military appeals, district court, or a state court of last resort.

2. The case must involve a federal question. Thus, the case must present questions of federal constitutional law or involve a federal statute, action, or treaty. The reasons that the Court should accept the case for review and legal argument supporting that position are set out in the petitioner's writ of *certiorari*.

The clerk of the Court transmits petitions for writs of *certiorari* first to the chief justice's office, where his clerks review the petitions, and then to the individual justices' offices. On the Roberts Court, all of the justices except Justice Samuel Alito (who

writ of *certiorari*
A request for the Supreme Court to order up the records from a lower court to review the case.

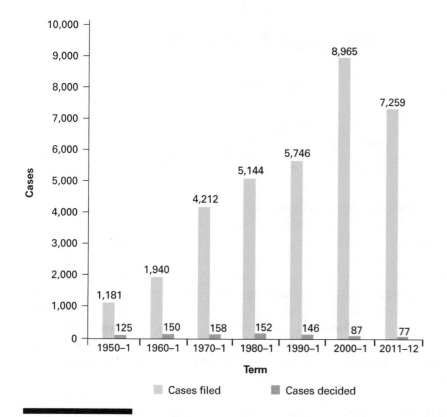

FIGURE 2 HOW MANY CASES DOES THE SUPREME COURT HANDLE?

The modern Supreme Court is asked to hear over 7,000 cases per year (represented by orange bars); of these cases, it reaches a final decision in about 1 percent, or 75 cases (represented by red bars). This is about half of the total number of decisions the Court handed down twenty years ago.

SOURCE: Administrative Office of the Courts; Supreme Court Public Information Office.

Over 100 million cases initially filed in U.S. state and federal trial courts

Federal courts

State courts

Applications for Supreme Court review by appeal or writ of *certiorari* filed by lawyers (7,259 cases in 2011–2012)

Cert pool (Clerks help justices select only most important cases for the discuss list)

Justices decide in conference which cases on discuss list to hear (Rule of Four)

Original jurisdiction (0 cases in 2011–2012)

United States Supreme Court docket (Generally about 33% come from state courts, 66% from federal courts)

Briefs submitted by both sides; *amicus curiae* briefs filed

Oral argument (79 cases in 2011–2012)

Supreme Court justices' conference
 – Cases discussed
 – Votes taken
 – Opinion writing assigned

Opinions drafted and circulated for comment

Final opinion released (77 in 2011–2012)

FIGURE 3 HOW DOES A CASE GET TO THE SUPREME COURT?

This figure illustrates both how cases get on the Court's docket and what happens after a case is accepted for review. A case may take several years to wind its way through the federal judiciary and another year or two to be heard and decided by the Supreme Court, if the justices decide to grant *certiorari*.

Rule of Four

At least four justices of the Supreme Court must vote to consider a case before it can be heard.

allows his clerks great individual authority in selecting the cases for him to review) participate in what is called the *cert* pool. Pool participants review their assigned fraction of petitions and share their notes with each other. Those cases deemed noteworthy by the justices then make it onto what is called the discuss list prepared by the chief justice's clerks and are circulated to the chambers of the other justices. All other petitions are dead listed and go no further. Only about 30 percent of submitted petitions make it to the discuss list. During one of their weekly conference meetings, the justices review the cases on the discuss list. The chief justice speaks first, then the rest of the justices, according to seniority. The decision process ends when the justices vote, and by custom, *certiorari* is granted according to the **Rule of Four**—when at least four justices vote to hear a case.

THE ROLE OF CLERKS As early as 1850, the justices of the Supreme Court beseeched Congress to approve the hiring of a clerk to assist each justice. Congress denied the request, so when Justice Horace Gray hired the first law clerk in 1882, he paid the clerk himself. Justice Gray's clerk was a top graduate of Harvard Law School whose duties included cutting Justice Gray's hair and running personal errands.

Finally, in 1886, Congress authorized each justice to hire a stenographer clerk for $1,600 a year.

Clerks typically are selected from candidates at the top of the graduating classes of prestigious law schools. They perform a variety of tasks, ranging from searching arcane facts to playing tennis or taking walks with the justices. Clerks spend most of their time researching material, reading and summarizing cases, and helping justices write opinions. Clerks also make the first pass through the petitions that come to the Court, undoubtedly influencing which cases get a second look. They often help draft opinions and serve as informal conduits for communication between the justices' chambers. Just how much assistance they provide in the writing of opinions is unknown.[15]

Over time, the number of clerks employed by the justices has increased. Through the 1946 to 1969 terms, most justices employed two clerks. By 1970, most had three clerks, and by 1980, all but three justices had four clerks. In 2010, the nine active justices and three retired justices employed approximately forty clerks. This growth in the number of clerks has had many interesting ramifications for the Court. As the number of clerks has grown, so has the length of the Court's written opinions.[16]

☐ How Does a Case Survive the Process?

It can be difficult to determine why the Court decides to hear a particular case. The Court does not offer reasons, and "the standards by which the justices decide to grant or deny review are highly personalized and necessarily discretionary," noted former Chief Justice Earl Warren.[17] Political scientists nonetheless have attempted to determine the characteristics of the cases the Court accepts. Among the cues are the following:

- The federal government is the party asking for review.
- The case involves conflict among the courts of appeals.
- The case presents a civil rights or civil liberties question.
- The case involves the ideological or policy preferences of the justices.
- The case has significant social or political interest, as evidenced by the presence of interest group *amicus curiae* briefs.

FEDERAL GOVERNMENT One of the most important cues for predicting whether the Court will hear a case is the solicitor general's position. The **solicitor general**, appointed by the president, is the fourth-ranking member of the Department of Justice and is responsible for handling nearly all appeals on behalf of the U.S. government to the Supreme Court. The solicitor's staff resembles a small, specialized law firm within the Department of Justice. But, because this office has such a special relationship with the Supreme Court, even having a suite of offices within the Supreme Court building, the solicitor general often is called the Court's "ninth and a half member."[18] Moreover, the office of the solicitor general, on behalf of the U.S. government, appears as a party or as an *amicus curiae,* or friend of the court, in more than 50 percent of the cases heard by the Court each term. This special relationship helps to explain the overwhelming success the solicitor general's office enjoys before the Supreme Court. The Court generally accepts 70 to 80 percent of cases in which the U.S. government is the petitioning party, compared with about 5 percent of all others.[19]

CONFLICT AMONG THE COURTS OF APPEALS Conflict among the lower courts is another reason justices take cases. When interpretations of constitutional or federal law are involved, justices seem to want consistency throughout the federal court system. Often these conflicts occur when important civil rights or civil liberties questions arise. Political scientists have noted that justices' ideological leanings play a role.[20] It is not uncommon to see conservative justices voting to hear cases to overrule liberal lower court decisions, or vice versa. Justices also take cases when several circuit courts disagree over a main issue.

solicitor general
The fourth-ranking member of the Department of Justice; responsible for handling nearly all appeals on behalf of the U.S. government to the Supreme Court.

amicus curiae
"Friend of the court"; *amici* may file briefs or even appear to argue their interests orally before the court.

INTEREST GROUP PARTICIPATION A quick way for justices to gauge the ideological ramifications of a particular civil rights or liberties case is by the nature and amount of interest group participation. Richard C. Cortner has noted that "Cases do not arrive on the doorstep of the Supreme Court like orphans in the night."[21] Instead, most cases heard by the Supreme Court involve interest group participation. This participation may come in a number of forms.

Well-funded liberal groups, such as the American Civil Liberties Union, People for the American Way, or the NAACP Legal Defense and Educational Fund, and conservative groups, including the Washington Legal Foundation, Concerned Women for America, and the American Center for Law and Justice, routinely sponsor cases before the Supreme Court. Sponsorship implies that a group has helped to devise the legal strategy, pay the costs of litigation, and shepherd the case through the court system. It can be very costly and time-consuming.

Other groups participate as *amicus curiae*, or a friend of the Court. *Amicus* participation has increased dramatically since the 1970s. Because litigation is so expensive, few individuals have the money (or time or interest) to sponsor a case all the way to the U.S. Supreme Court. All sorts of interest groups, then, find that joining ongoing cases through *amicus* briefs is a useful way to advance their policy preferences.

Research by political scientists has found that "not only does [an *amicus*] brief in favor of *certiorari* significantly improve the chances of a case being accepted, but two, three, and four briefs improve the chances even more."[22] Clearly, it's the more the merrier, whether the briefs are filed for or against granting review.

☐ Hearing and Deciding the Case

Once the Court accepts a case for review, a flurry of activity begins. Lawyers on both sides of the case prepare their written arguments for submission to the Court. In these briefs, lawyers cite prior case law and make arguments regarding why the Court should find in favor of their client.

ORAL ARGUMENTS After the Court accepts a case and each side has submitted briefs and *amicus* briefs, oral argument takes place. Generally, only the immediate parties in the case take part in oral argument, although it is not uncommon for the U.S. solicitor general or one of his or her deputies to make an appearance to argue orally as an *amicus curiae*. Oral argument at the Court is fraught with time-honored tradition and ceremony. At precisely ten o'clock every morning when the Court is in session, the Court marshal, dressed in a formal morning coat, emerges to intone "Oyez! Oyez! Oyez!" as the nine justices emerge from behind a reddish-purple velvet curtain to take their places on the raised and slightly angled bench. The chief justice sits in the middle. The remaining justices sit to the left and right, alternating in seniority.

Almost all attorneys are allotted one half-hour to present their cases, including the time required to answer questions from the bench. Although many Court watchers have tried to figure out how a particular justice will vote based on the questioning at oral argument, most researchers find that the nature and number of questions asked do not help much in predicting the outcome of a case.

THE CONFERENCE AND THE VOTE The justices meet in closed conference twice a week when the Court is hearing oral arguments. Since the ascendancy of Chief Justice Roger B. Taney to the Court in 1836, the justices have begun each conference session with a round of handshaking. Once the door to the conference room closes, no others are allowed to enter. The justice with the least seniority acts as the doorkeeper for the other eight, communicating with those waiting outside to fill requests for documents, water, and any other necessities.

Conferences highlight the importance and power of the chief justice, who presides over them and makes the initial presentation of each case. Each individual justice then discusses the case in order of his or her seniority on the Court, with the most senior justice speaking next. Most accounts of the decision-making process

Take a Closer Look

The Supreme Court hears oral argument in most cases in which it reaches a final decision. Scholars have found that oral argument serves a number of important functions. For example, it provides an opportunity for the justices to highlight important case themes and to ask questions about the impact of a case that go beyond what is detailed in the party or *amicus curiae* briefs. Review the illustration of arguments before the Supreme Court during one of the 2012 cases that decided the constitutionality of the health care reform bill.

No cameras are allowed in the Supreme Court during oral arguments. Thus, we have only illustrations of what oral arguments look like in our nation's highest court.

The justices are seated on a curved bench at the front of the courtroom in order of seniority. The chief justice sits in the center, with the most senior associate justice at his right hand side. The second most senior associate justice sits on the chief's left hand side, and so on.

Lawyers are typically allowed to present thirty minutes of oral argument before the Court. However, this time is usually more like a question- and-answer session with the justices than a prepared speech.

CRITICAL THINKING QUESTIONS

1. Why do oral arguments remain important to the Court? How might a discussion between the justices and the parties' attorneys advance and improve judges' decision making?

2. How might the attorney representing a party in a case affect the case's outcome?

3. Should the Supreme Court allow cameras and video recordings in the courtroom? Why or why not?

judicial restraint
A philosophy of judicial decision making that posits courts should allow the decisions of other branches of government to stand, even when they offend a judge's own principles.

judicial activism
A philosophy of judicial decision making that posits judges should use their power broadly to further justice.

reveal that at this point some justices try to change the minds of others, but that most enter the conference room with a clear idea of how they will vote on each case.

WRITING OPINIONS After the Court has reached a decision in conference, the justices must formulate a formal opinion of the Court. If the chief justice is in the majority, he selects the justice who will write the opinion. This privilege enables him to wield tremendous power and is a very important strategic decision; the author of the decision may determine the tone and content of the Court's opinion. If the chief justice is in the minority, the assignment falls to the most senior justice in the majority.

The opinion of the Court can take several different forms. Most decisions are reached by a majority opinion written by one member of the Court to reflect the views of at least five justices. This opinion usually sets out the legal reasoning justifying the decision, and this legal reasoning becomes a precedent for deciding future cases. The reasoning behind any decision is often as important as the outcome. Under the system of *stare decisis*, both are likely to be relied on as precedent later by lower courts confronted with cases involving similar issues.

In the process of creating the final opinion of the Court, informal caucusing and negotiation often take place, as justices may hold out for word changes or other modifications as a condition of their continued support of the majority opinion. This negotiation process can lead to divisions in the Court's majority. When this occurs, the Court may be forced to decide cases by plurality opinions, which attract the support of three or four justices. While these decisions do not have the precedential value of majority opinions, they nonetheless have been used by the Court to decide many major cases. Justices who agree with the outcome of the case, but not with the legal rationale for the decision, may file concurring opinions to express their differing approach.

Justices who do not agree with the outcome of a case file dissenting opinions. Although these opinions have little direct legal value, they can be an important indicator of legal thought on the Court and are an excellent platform for justices to note their personal and legal disagreements with other members of the Court.

Judicial Philosophy and Decision Making

5 Analyze the factors that influence judicial decision making.

Justices do not make decisions in a vacuum. Principles of *stare decisis* dictate that the justices follow the law of previous cases in deciding cases at hand. But, a variety of legal and extra-legal factors have also been found to affect Supreme Court decision making.

☐ Judicial Philosophy, Original Intent, and Ideology

One of the primary issues concerning judicial decision making focuses on judicial philosophy, particularly what is called the activism/restraint debate. Advocates of **judicial restraint** argue that courts should allow the decisions of other branches to stand, even when they offend a judge's own principles. Restraintists defend their position by asserting that unelected judges make up the federal courts, which renders the judicial branch the least democratic branch of government. Consequently, the courts should defer policy making to other branches of government as much as possible.

Restraintists refer to *Roe* v. *Wade* (1973), the case that liberalized abortion laws, as a classic example of **judicial activism** run amok. They maintain that the Court should have deferred policy making on this sensitive issue to the states or to the elected branches of the federal government.

Who Are the Activist Judges?

In practice, an activist judge—liberal or conservative—is one who overturns a law as unconstitutional. Even though the current Roberts Court has handed down fewer decisions than earlier courts, 19 out of 408 decisions declared laws unconstitutional between 2005 and 2010. The data below shows which judges are m[...] responsible for these controversial decisions.

Supreme Court Decisions

In 1986, William Rehnquist was named Chief Justice. Over the next eight years, the number of decisions fell by nearly half.

In 2004, justices were making far fewer decisions than they were in 1984, but their approval ratings by political moderates stayed almost the same.

Supreme Court Approval Rating by Moderates

62%   71%   73%   70%   67%   70%   72%   70%

Judicial Activism on the Roberts Court

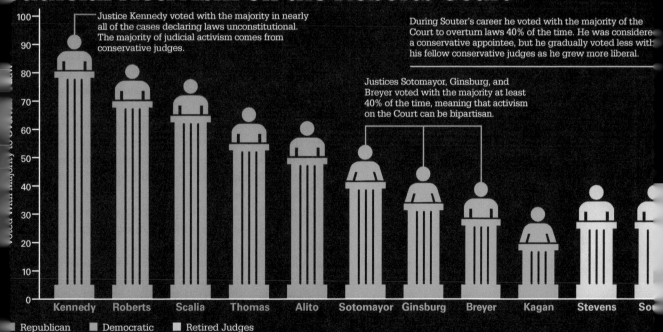

Justice Kennedy voted with the majority in nearly all of the cases declaring laws unconstitutional. The majority of judicial activism comes from conservative judges.

During Souter's career he voted with the majority of the Court to overturn laws 40% of the time. He was considere[...] a conservative appointee, but he gradually voted less wit[...] his fellow conservative judges as he grew more liberal.

Justices Sotomayor, Ginsburg, and Breyer voted with the majority at least 40% of the time, meaning that activism on the Court can be bipartisan.

Kennedy   Roberts   Scalia   Thomas   Alito   Sotomayor   Ginsburg   Breyer   Kagan   Stevens   So[...]

■ Republican   ■ Democratic   ■ Retired Judges

SOURCE: Data from the United States Supreme Court and the General Social Survey, 1980-2010.

Investigate Further

Concept Why is judicial activism controversial? By declaring a law unconstitutional, judicial activism overturns legislation that is a product of the democratic process. It sets precedents for controversial or divisive issues, and it limits future legislation.

Connection Does judicial activism affect public confidence? Over two-thirds of American moderates continued to express confidence in the Court, even as it handed down fewer decisions and became more conservative in the 2000s.

Cause Is judicial activism conservative or liberal? On the Roberts Court, the decisions that overturn laws be bipartisan, but they are usually deci[...] by the conservative justices.

strict constructionist
An approach to constitutional interpretation that emphasizes interpreting the Constitution as it was originally written and intended by the Framers.

Advocates of judicial restraint generally agree that judges should be **strict constructionists**; that is, they should interpret the Constitution as the Framers wrote and originally intended it. They argue that in determining the constitutionality of a statute or policy, the Court should rely on the explicit meanings of the clauses in the document, which can be clarified by looking at founding documents.

Advocates of judicial activism contend that judges should use their power broadly to further justice. Activists argue that it is appropriate for courts to correct injustices committed by other branches of government. Implicit in this argument is the notion that courts need to protect oppressed minorities.[23]

Although judicial activists are often considered politically liberal and restraintists politically conservative, in recent years a new brand of conservative judicial activism has become prevalent. Liberal activist decisions often expanded the rights of political and legal minorities. But, conservative activist judges view their positions as an opportunity to issue broad rulings that impose their own political beliefs and policies on the country at large.

☐ Public Opinion

Many political scientists have examined the role of public opinion in Supreme Court decision making. Not only do the justices read legal briefs and hear oral arguments, but they also read newspapers, watch TV, and have some knowledge of public opinion—especially on controversial issues.

Whether or not public opinion actually influences justices, it can act as a check on the power of the courts. Activist periods on the Supreme Court generally have corresponded to periods of social or economic crisis. For example, in the early, crisis-ridden years of the republic, the Marshall Court supported a strong national government, much to the chagrin of a series of pro-states' rights Democratic-Republican presidents. Similarly, the Court capitulated to political pressures and public opinion when, after 1936, it reversed many of its earlier decisions that had blocked President Franklin D. Roosevelt's New Deal programs.

The courts, especially the Supreme Court, also can be the direct target of public opinion. When *Webster* v. *Reproductive Health Services* (1989) was about to come before the Supreme Court, unprecedented lobbying of the Court took place as groups and individuals on both sides of the abortion issue marched and sent appeals to the Court. Mail at the Court, which usually averaged about 1,000 pieces a day, rose to an astronomical 46,000 pieces per day, virtually paralyzing normal lines of communication.

The Supreme Court also appears to affect public opinion. Political scientists have found that the Court's initial rulings on controversial issues such as abortion or capital punishment positively influence public opinion in the direction of the Court's opinion. However, this research also finds that subsequent decisions have little effect.[24]

The Court also is dependent on the public for its prestige as well as for compliance with its decisions. In times of war and other emergencies, for example, the Court frequently has decided cases in ways that commentators have attributed to the sway of public opinion and political exigencies. In *Korematsu* v. *U.S.* (1944), for example, the high Court upheld the obviously unconstitutional internment of Japanese, Italian, and German American citizens during World War II.[25] Moreover, Chief Justice William H. Rehnquist once suggested that the Court's restriction on presidential authority in *Youngstown Sheet & Tube Co.* v. *Sawyer* (1952), which invalidated President Harry S Truman's seizure of the nation's steel mills, was largely attributable to Truman's unpopularity in light of the Korean War.[26]

Public confidence in the Court, as with other institutions of government, has ebbed and flowed. Public support for the Court was highest after the Court issued *U.S.* v. *Nixon* (1974).[27] At a time when Americans lost faith in the presidency because of the Watergate scandal, they could at least look to the Supreme Court to do the right thing. Although the percentage of Americans with confidence in the courts has fluctuated over time, in 2012, an all-time low of 52 percent of Americans approved of the way the Supreme Court was doing its job.[28]

Toward Reform: Power, Policy Making, and the Court

6   Assess the role of the Supreme Court in the policy-making process.

All judges, whether they recognize it or not, make policy. The decisions of the Supreme Court, in particular, have a tremendous impact on American politics and policy. Over the past 250 years, the justices have helped to codify many of the major rights and liberties guaranteed to the citizens of the United States. Although justices need the cooperation of the executive and legislative branches to implement and enforce a good number of their decisions, it is safe to say that many policies we take for granted in the United States would not have come to fruition without support of the Supreme Court.[29]

Several Courts have played particularly notable roles in the development of the judiciary's policy-making role. As discussed earlier in the chapter, the Marshall Court played an important role establishing the role and power of the Supreme Court, including the power of judicial review in *Marbury* v. *Madison* (1803). The Warren Court decided a number of civil rights cases that broadly expanded civil and political rights. These decisions drew a great deal of criticism but played a major role in broadening public understanding of the Court as a policy maker. The Rehnquist Court made numerous decisions related to federalism, which caused observers to take note of the Court's ability to referee conflicts between the federal government and the states. And, the Roberts Court reversed the general trend of the Court's agreement with executive actions during times of war by finding in 2008 that the Bush administration's denial of *habeas corpus* rights to prisoners being held at Guantanamo Bay was an unconstitutional exercise of presidential power.[30]

☐ Policy Making

One measure of the power of the courts and their ability to make policy is that more than one hundred federal laws have been declared unconstitutional. Although many of these laws have not been particularly significant, others have.

Another measure of the policy-making power of the Supreme Court is its ability to overrule itself. Although the Court generally abides by the informal rule of *stare decisis,* by one count, it has overruled itself in more than 200 cases.[31] Moreover, in the past few years, the Court repeatedly has reversed earlier decisions in the areas of criminal defendants' rights, reproductive rights, and free speech, revealing its powerful role in determining national policy. The modern Supreme Court also handles a number of issues that had been considered political questions more appropriately left to the other branches of government to decide.

☐ Implementing Court Decisions

President Andrew Jackson, annoyed about a particular decision handed down by the Marshall Court, is alleged to have said, "John Marshall has made his decision; now let him enforce it." Jackson's statement raises a question: how do Supreme Court rulings translate into public policy? In fact, although judicial decisions carry legal and even moral authority, all courts must rely on other units of government to carry out their directives. If the president or members of Congress, for example, do not like a particular Supreme Court ruling, they can underfund programs needed to implement a decision or seek only lax enforcement. **Judicial implementation** refers to how and whether judicial decisions are translated into actual public policies affecting more than the immediate parties to the lawsuit.

How well a decision is implemented often depends on how well crafted or popular it is. Hostile reaction in the South to *Brown* v. *Board of Education* (1954) and the absence of precise guidelines to implement the decision meant that the ruling went largely unenforced for years. The *Brown* experience also highlights how much the Supreme Court needs the support of both federal and state courts as well as other governmental agencies to carry out its judgments. For example, you probably graduated from high school after 1992, when the Supreme Court ruled that public middle school and high school graduations could not include a prayer, yet your own commencement ceremony may have included one.[32]

For effective implementation of a judicial decision, the first requirement is for members of the implementing population to show they understand the original decision. For example, the Supreme Court ruled in *Reynolds* v. *Sims* (1964) that every person should have an equally weighted vote in electing governmental representatives.[33] This "one person, one vote" rule might seem simple enough at first glance, but in practice it can be very difficult to understand.

The second requirement is that the implementing population actually must follow Court policy. Thus, when the Court ruled that men could not be denied admission to a state-sponsored nursing school, the implementing population—in this case, university administrators and the state board of regents governing the nursing school—had to enroll qualified male students.[34]

Implementation of judicial decisions is most likely to be smooth if a few highly visible public officials, such as the president or a governor, shoulder the responsibility of seeing to the task. By the same token, these officials also can thwart or impede judicial intentions. Recall, for example, the effect of Governor Orval Faubus's initial refusal to allow black children to attend all-white public schools in Little Rock, Arkansas.

The third requirement for implementation is for the consumer population to be aware of the rights that a decision grants or denies them. Teenagers seeking an abortion, for example, are consumers of the Supreme Court's decisions on abortion and contraception. They need to know that most states require them to inform their parents of their intention to have an abortion or to get parental permission to do so.

Review the Chapter

 Listen to **Chapter** on **MyPoliSciLab**

Roots of the Federal Judiciary

1 Trace the development of the federal judiciary and the origins of judicial review.

Many Framers viewed the judicial branch of government as little more than a minor check on the other two branches, ignoring Anti-Federalist concerns about an unelected judiciary and its potential for tyranny. The Judiciary Act of 1789 established the basic federal court system we have today. It was the Marshall Court (1801–1835), however, that interpreted the Constitution to include the Court's major power, that of judicial review.

The Federal Court System

2 Explain the organization of the federal court system.

The federal court system is made up of constitutional and legislative courts. Federal district courts, courts of appeals, and the Supreme Court are constitutional courts.

How Federal Court Judges Are Selected

3 Outline the criteria and process used to select federal court judges.

District court, court of appeals, and Supreme Court justices are nominated by the president and must also win Senate confirmation. Important criteria for selection include competence, ideology, rewards, pursuit of political support, religion, race, ethnicity, and gender.

The Supreme Court Today

4 Evaluate the Supreme Court's process for accepting, hearing, and deciding cases.

Several factors influence the Court's decision to hear a case. Not only must the Court have jurisdiction, but at least four justices must vote to hear the case. Cases with certain characteristics are most likely to be heard. Once a case is set for review, briefs and *amicus curiae* briefs are filed and oral argument is scheduled. The justices meet in conference after oral argument to discuss the case; votes are taken; and opinions are written, circulated, and then announced.

Judicial Philosophy and Decision Making

5 Analyze the factors that influence judicial decision making.

Judges do not make decisions in a vacuum. In addition to following the law of previous cases, other factors, including personal philosophy and ideology, have an extraordinary impact on how judges decide cases. Public opinion may also play a role in some cases.

Toward Reform: Power, Policy Making, and the Court

6 Assess the role of the Supreme Court in the policy-making process.

The Supreme Court is an important participant in the policy-making process. The power to interpret laws gives the Court a tremendous policy-making power never envisioned by the Framers. However, if the president or members of Congress oppose a particular Supreme Court ruling, they can underfund programs needed to implement a decision or seek only lax enforcement.

Learn the Terms

 Study and **Review** the **Flashcards**

amicus curiae
appellate court
appellate jurisdiction
brief
constitutional courts
judicial activism
judicial implementation
judicial restraint

judicial review
Judiciary Act of 1789
jurisdiction
legislative courts
Marbury v. *Madison* (1803)
original jurisdiction
precedent,
Rule of Four

senatorial courtesy
solicitor general
stare decisis
strict constructionist
trial court
writ of *certiorari*

Test Yourself

1. Which of the following is NOT one of Congress's constitutional powers over the judiciary?

a. Authority to alter the Court's jurisdiction
b. Impeach and remove federal judges
c. Veto a Supreme Court decision
d. Offer advice and consent on presidential appointments
e. Propose constitutional amendments

2. Which of the following paved the way for the courts to become a co-equal branch?

a. Writ of *certiorari*
b. *McCulloch* v. *Maryland* (1819)
c. The Judiciary Act of 1789
d. Judicial review
e. *Federalist No. 78*

3. Courts of original jurisdiction are most often known as:

a. appellate courts.
b. courts of appeals.
c. trial courts.
d. legislative courts.
e. constitutional courts.

4. Which of the following types of courts handles the bulk of the caseload in the federal system?

a. District courts
b. Courts of appeals
c. Special purpose courts
d. Legislative courts
e. Supreme Court

5. Which of the following is NOT true of the courts of appeals?

a. Cases may be heard by multiple judges.
b. Judges try to correct errors in law.
c. They are the highest courts in the federal system.
d. Judges hear no new testimony.
e. Their decisions are binding only within their geographic confines.

6. According to the Constitution, who must offer advice and consent on a presidential appointment to the Supreme Court?

a. Current justices
b. Constituents
c. President
d. Senate
e. House of Representatives

7. All of the following are criteria that would help get a case heard by the Supreme Court EXCEPT:

a. The case presents a civil rights question.
b. The federal government is the party asking for review.
c. The case involves a conflict among the courts of appeals.
d. The case has significant social or political issues.
e. The case presents a lack of evidence.

8. What does it mean if the Court grants a petition for a writ of *certiorari*?

a. They have decided to review a lower court's decision.
b. They are throwing out a case.
c. They have decided that a case is unconstitutional.
d. They have reached a unanimous decision.
e. The court cannot come to a clear decision.

9. Which of the following does NOT appear to affect Supreme Court justices' decisions?

a. *Stare decisis*
b. Political circumstances
c. Judicial philosophy
d. Public opinion
e. Economic impact

10. Which of the following is the best way to measure the power of the courts in policy making?

a. The number of cases heard
b. How many days the court is in session
c. How long justices serve on the court
d. The number of laws declared unconstitutional
e. Popularity of judicial decisions

Explore Further

Baird, Vanessa. *Answering the Call of the Court: How Justices and Litigants Set the Supreme Court Agenda.* Charlottesville: University of Virginia Press, 2008.

Baum, Lawrence. *Judges and Their Audiences: A Perspective on Judicial Behavior.* Princeton, NJ: Princeton University Press, 2005.

Bonneau, Chris W., and Melinda Gann Hall. *In Defense of Judicial Elections.* New York: Routledge, 2009.

Collins, Paul M., Jr. *Friends of the Supreme Court: Interest Groups and Decision Making.* New York: Oxford University Press, 2008.

Epstein, Lee, Jeffrey A. Segal, Harold J. Spaeth, and Thomas G. Walker. *The Supreme Court Compendium: Data, Decisions, and Developments,* 6th ed. Washington, DC: CQ Press, 2012.

Gibson, James L. *Electing Judges: The Surprising Effects of Campaigning on Judicial Legitimacy.* Chicago: University of Chicago Press, 2012.

Greenhouse, Linda. *The U.S. Supreme Court: A Very Short Introduction.* New York: Oxford University Press, 2012.

Hall, Kermit L., ed. *The Oxford Companion to the Supreme Court of the United States,* 2nd ed. New York: Oxford University Press, 2005.

Lazarus, Edward. *Closed Chambers: The First Eyewitness Account of the Epic Struggles Inside the Supreme Court.* New York: Times Books, 1998.

O'Brien, David M. *Storm Center: The Supreme Court in American Politics,* 9th ed. New York: Norton, 2012.

Perry, H. W. *Deciding to Decide: Agenda Setting in the United States Supreme Court,* reprint ed. Cambridge, MA: Harvard University Press, 2005.

Sunstein, Cass R., David Schkade, Lisa M. Ellman, and Andres Sawicki. *Are Judges Political? An Empirical Analysis of the Federal Judiciary.* Washington, DC: Brookings Institution, 2006.

Ward, Artemus, and David L. Weiden. *Sorcerer's Apprentices: 100 Years of Law Clerks at the United States Supreme Court.* New York: New York University Press, 2006.

Whittington, Keith E. *Political Foundations of Judicial Supremacy: The Presidency, the Supreme Court, and Constitutional Leadership in U.S. History.* Princeton, NJ: Princeton University Press, 2007.

Woodward, Bob, and Scott Armstrong. *The Brethren: Inside the Supreme Court,* 2nd reprint ed. New York: Avon, 2005.

To learn more about the U.S. Supreme Court and examine current cases on the Court's docket, go to **www.supremecourt.gov.**

To learn more about the workings of the U.S. justice system, go to the Department of Justice's Web site at **www.usdoj.gov.**

To learn more about the U.S. Senate Judiciary Committee and judicial nominations currently under review, go to the Senate's Web site at **www.senate.gov.**

To learn more about past and current U.S. Supreme Court cases, go to **www.oyez.org** to hear streaming audio of oral arguments before the Court.

Credits

Credits are listed in order of appearance.

Answer Key

1. c; 2. d; 3. c; 4. a; 5. c; 6. d; 7. e; 8. a; 9. e; 10. d

Notes

1. Julius Goebel Jr., *History of the Supreme Court of the United States, vol. 1: Antecedents and Beginnings to 1801* (New York: Macmillan, 1971), 206.

2. *Fletcher* v. *Peck,* 10 U.S. 87 (1810); *Martin* v. *Hunter's Lessee,* 14 U.S. 304 (1816); and *Cohens* v. *Virginia,* 19 U.S. 264 (1821).

3. *McCulloch* v. *Maryland,* 17 U.S. 316 (1819).

4. *Marbury* v. *Madison,* 5 U.S. 137 (1803).

5. *Marbury* v. *Madison,* 5 U.S. 137 (1803).

6. David W. Neubauer, *Judicial Process: Law, Courts, and Politics* (Pacific Grove, CA: Brooks/Cole, 1991), 57.

7. Cases involving citizens from different states can be filed in state or federal court.

8. Sheldon Goldman and Elliot E. Slotnick, "Clinton's First Term Judiciary: Many Bridges to Cross," *Judicature* (May/June 1997): 254–55.

9. Betsy Palmer, "Evolution of the Senate's Role in the Nomination and Confirmation Process." CRS Report RL 31498 (March 29, 2005).

10. Quoted in Lawrence Baum, *The Supreme Court,* 3rd ed. (Washington, DC: CQ Press, 1989), 108.

11. See Barbara A. Perry, *A Representative Supreme Court? The Impact of Race, Religion, and Gender on Appointments* (New York: Greenwood, 1991). Clarence Thomas was raised a Catholic but attended an Episcopalian church at the time of his appointment, having been barred from Catholic sacraments because of his remarriage. He again, however, is attending Roman Catholic services.

12. John Brigham, *The Cult of the Court* (Philadelphia: Temple University Press, 1987).

13. Stephen L. Wasby, *The Supreme Court in the Federal Judicial System,* 4th ed. (Chicago: Nelson-Hall, 1988), 194.

14. Wasby, *The Supreme Court in the Federal Judicial System,* 199. Much of this change occurred as the result of an increase in state criminal cases, of which nearly 100 percent concerned constitutional questions.

15. Paul Wahlbeck, et al., "Ghostwriters on the Court? A Stylistic Analysis of U.S. Supreme Court Opinion Drafts," *American Politics Research* 30 (March 2002): 166–92. Wahlbeck et al. note that "between 1969 and 1972—the period during which the justices each became entitled to a third law clerk . . . the number of opinions increased by about 50 percent and the number of words tripled."

16. Richard A. Posner, *The Federal Courts: Crisis and Reform* (Cambridge, MA: Harvard University Press, 1985), 114.

17. "Retired Chief Justice Warren Attacks Freund Study Group's Composition and Proposal," *American Bar Association Journal* 59 (July 1973): 728.

18. Kathleen Werdegar, "The Solicitor General and Administrative Due Process," *George Washington Law Review* (1967–1968): 482.

19. Rebecca Mae Salokar, *The Solicitor General: The Politics of Law* (Philadelphia: Temple University Press, 1992), 3.

20. See, for example, Lawrence Baum, *The Supreme Court,* 4th ed. (Washington, DC: CQ Press, 1992), 106.

21. Richard C. Cortner, *The Supreme Court and Civil Liberties* (Palo Alto, CA: Mayfield, 1975), vi.

22. Gregory A. Caldeira and John R. Wright, "*Amicus Curiae* Before the Supreme Court: Who Participates, When and How Much?" *Journal of Politics* 52 (August 1990): 803.

23. Donald L. Horowitz, *The Courts and Social Policy* (Washington, DC: Brookings Institution, 1977), 538.

24. Timothy R. Johnson and Andrew D. Martin, "The Public's Conditional Response to Supreme Court Decisions," *American Political Science Review* 92 (June 1998): 299–309.

25. *Korematsu* v. *U.S.,* 323 U.S. 214 (1944).

26. *Youngstown Sheet & Tube Co.* v. *Sawyer,* 343 U.S. 579 (1952). The Supreme Court ruled that President Truman's seizure and operation of U.S. steel mills in the face of a strike threat were unconstitutional, because the Constitution implied no such broad executive power. See Alan Westin, *Anatomy of a Constitutional Law Case* (New York: Macmillan, 1958); and Maeva Marcus, *Truman and the Steel Seizure Case* (New York: Columbia University Press, 1977).

27. *U.S.* v. *Nixon,* 418 U.S. 683 (1974).

28. Pew Research Center for People and the Press, "Supreme Court Favorability Reaches New Low" (May 1, 2012).

29. Alixandra B. Yanus, "Neither Force Nor Will: A Theory of Judicial Power," doctoral dissertation, University of North Carolina, 2010.

30. *Boumediene* v. *Bush,* 553 U.S. 723 (2008).

31. "Supreme Court Cases Overruled by Subsequent Decision," www.gpoaccess.gov/constitution/pdf/con041.pdf.

32. Kevin T. McGuire, "Public Schools, Religious Establishments, and the U.S. Supreme Court: An Examination of Policy Compliance," *American Politics Research,* 37 (2009): 50–74.

33. *Reynolds* v. *Sims,* 377 U.S. 533 (1964).

34. *Mississippi University for Women* v. *Hogan,* 458 U.S. 718 (1982).

GLOSSARY

A

administrative adjudication A quasi-judicial process in which a bureaucratic agency settles disputes between two parties in a manner similar to the way courts resolve disputes.

administrative discretion The ability of bureaucrats to make choices concerning the best way to implement congressional or executive intentions.

affirmative action Policies designed to give special attention or compensatory treatment to members of a previously disadvantaged group.

agenda A set of issues to be discussed or given attention.

agenda setting The process of forming the list of issues to be addressed by government.

American dream An American ideal of a happy, successful life, which often includes wealth, a house, a better life for one's children, and, for some, the opportunity to grow up to be president.

amicus curiae "Friend of the court"; *amici* may file briefs or even appear to argue their interests orally before the court.

Anti-Federalists Those who favored strong state governments and a weak national government; opposed ratification of the U.S. Constitution.

appellate court Court that generally reviews only findings of law made by lower courts.

appellate jurisdiction The power vested in particular courts to review and/or revise the decision of a lower court.

apportionment The process of allotting congressional seats to each state according to its proportion of the population, following the decennial census.

Articles of Confederation The compact between the thirteen original colonies that created a loose league of friendship, with the national government drawing its powers from the states.

B

Barron v. Baltimore **(1833)** The Supreme Court ruled that the due process clause of the Fifth Amendment did not apply to the actions of states. This decision limited the Bill of Rights to the actions of Congress alone.

bicameral legislature A two-house legislature.

bill A proposed law.

bill of attainder A law declaring an act illegal without a judicial trial.

Bill of Rights The first ten amendments to the U.S. Constitution, which largely guarantee specific rights and liberties.

Black Codes Laws denying most legal rights to newly freed slaves; passed by southern states following the Civil War.

block grant A large grant given to a state by the federal government with only general spending guidelines.

Board of Governors In the Federal Reserve System, a seven-member board that makes most economic decisions regarding interest rates and the supply of money.

Bretton Woods System International financial system devised shortly before the end of World War II that created the World Bank and the International Monetary Fund.

brief A document containing the legal written arguments in a case filed with a court by a party prior to a hearing or trial.

Brown v. Board of Education **(1954)** U.S. Supreme Court decision holding that school segregation is inherently unconstitutional because it violates the Fourteenth Amendment's guarantee of equal protection.

budget deficit The economic condition that occurs when expenditures exceed revenues.

C

Cabinet The formal body of presidential advisers who head the fifteen executive departments. Presidents often add others to this body of formal advisers.

campaign consultant A private-sector professional who sells to a candidate the technologies, services, and strategies required to get that candidate elected.

campaign manager The individual who travels with the candidate and coordinates the campaign.

candidate-centered politics Politics that focus on the candidates, their particular issues, and character rather than party affiliation.

categorical grant Grant that appropriates federal funds to states for a specific purpose.

checks and balances A constitutionally mandated structure that gives each of the three branches of government some degree of oversight and control over the actions of the others.

citizen journalists Ordinary individuals who collect, report, and analyze news content.

civic virtue The tendency to form small-scale associations for the public good.

civil liberties The personal guarantees and freedoms that the government cannot abridge by law, constitution, or judicial interpretation.

civil rights The government-protected rights of individuals against arbitrary or discriminatory treatment by governments or individuals.

Civil Rights Act of 1964 Wide-ranging legislation passed by Congress to outlaw segregation in public facilities and discrimination in employment, education, and voting; created the Equal Employment Opportunity Commission.

Civil Rights Cases **(1883)** Name attached to five cases brought under the Civil Rights Act of 1875. In 1883, the Supreme Court decided that discrimination in a variety of public accommodations, including theaters, hotels, and railroads, could not be prohibited by the act because such discrimination was private, not state, discrimination.

civil service system   The merit system by which many federal bureaucrats are selected.

clear and present danger test   Test articulated by the Supreme Court in *Schenck* v. *U.S.* (1919) to draw the line between protected and unprotected speech; the Court looks to see "whether the words used" could "create a clear and present danger that they will bring about substantive evils" that Congress seeks "to prevent."

cloture   Mechanism requiring the vote of sixty senators to cut off debate.

collective good   Something of value that cannot be withheld from a nonmember of a group, for example, a tax write-off or a better environment.

collective security   The idea that an attack on one country is an attack on all countries.

Committees of Correspondence   Organizations in each of the American colonies created to keep colonists abreast of developments with the British; served as powerful molders of public opinion against the British.

communications director   The person who develops the overall media strategy for the candidate.

concurrent powers   Powers shared by the national and state governments.

confederation   Type of government in which the national government derives its powers from the states; a league of independent states.

conference committee   Special joint committee created to reconcile differences in bills passed by the House and Senate.

Congressional Budget Act of 1974   Act that established the congressional budgetary process by laying out a plan for congressional action on the annual budget resolution, appropriations, reconciliation, and any other revenue bills.

congressional review   A process whereby Congress can nullify agency regulations by a joint resolution of legislative disapproval.

conservative   One who favors limited government intervention, particularly in economic affairs.

constitution   A document establishing the structure, functions, and limitations of a government.

constitutional courts   Federal courts specifically created by the U.S. Constitution or by Congress pursuant to its authority in Article III.

containment   U.S. policy of opposing Soviet expansion and communist revolutions around the world with military forces, economic assistance, and political influence.

content regulations   Limitations on the substance of the mass media.

contrast ad   Ad that compares the records and proposals of the candidates, with a bias toward the candidate sponsoring the ad.

cooperative federalism   The intertwined relationship between the national, state, and local governments that began with the New Deal, often referred to as marble-cake federalism.

critical election   An election that signals a party realignment through voter polarization around new issues and personalities.

Cuban Missile Crisis   The 1962 confrontation over the deployment of ballistic missiles in Cuba that nearly escalated into nuclear war between the United States and the Soviet Union.

D

Declaration of Independence   Document drafted largely by Thomas Jefferson in 1776 that proclaimed the right of the American colonies to separate from Great Britain.

deep background   Information provided to a journalist that will not be attributed to any source.

defense policy   Area of policy making that focuses on the strategies that a country uses to protect itself from its enemies.

delegate   Role played by an elected representative who votes the way his or her constituents would want, regardless of personal opinions.

democracy   A system of government that gives power to the people, whether directly or through elected representatives.

democratic enlargement   Policy implemented during the Clinton administration in which the United States would actively promote the expansion of democracy and free markets throughout the world.

Department of Defense   Chief executive branch department responsible for formulation and implementation of U.S. defense and military policy.

Department of Homeland Security   Cabinet department created after the 9/11 terrorist attacks to coordinate domestic security efforts.

Department of State   Chief executive branch department responsible for formulation and implementation of U.S. foreign policy.

departments   Major administrative units with responsibility for a broad area of government operations. Departmental status usually indicates a permanent national interest in a particular governmental function, such as defense, commerce, or agriculture.

détente   The improvement in relations between the United States and the Soviet Union that occurred during the 1970s.

Dillon's Rule   A premise articulated by Judge John F. Dillon in 1868 which states that local governments do not have any inherent sovereignty and instead must be authorized by state governments that can create or abolish them.

direct democracy   A system of government in which members of the polity meet to discuss all policy decisions and then agree to abide by majority rule.

direct incitement test   Test articulated by the Supreme Court in *Brandenburg* v. *Ohio* (1969) holding that the First Amendment protects advocacy of illegal action unless imminent lawless action is intended and likely to occur.

discount rate   The rate of interest at which the Federal Reserve Board lends money to member banks.

disturbance theory   The theory that interest groups form as a result of changes in the political system.

double jeopardy clause   Part of the Fifth Amendment that protects individuals from being tried twice for the same offense in the same jurisdiction.

***Dred Scott* v. *Sandford* (1857)** The Supreme Court concluded that the U.S. Congress lacked the constitutional authority to bar slavery in the territories. This decision narrowed the scope of national power, while it enhanced that of the states.

dual federalism The belief that having separate and equally powerful levels of government is the best arrangement, often referred to as layer-cake federalism.

due process clause Clause contained in the Fifth and Fourteenth Amendments; over the years, it has been construed to guarantee a variety of rights to individuals.

E

economic stability A situation in which there is economic growth, rising national income, high employment, and steadiness in the general level of prices.

Eighth Amendment Part of the Bill of Rights that states: "Excessive bail shall not be required, nor excessive fines imposed, nor cruel and unusual punishments inflicted."

elector Member of the Electoral College.

Electoral College Representatives of each state who cast the final ballots that actually elect a president.

entitlement programs Government benefits that all citizens meeting eligibility criteria—such as age, income level, or unemployment—are legally "entitled" to receive.

enumerated powers The powers of the national government specifically granted to Congress in Article I, section 8 of the Constitution.

Equal Pay Act of 1963 Legislation that requires employers to pay men and women equal pay for equal work.

equal protection clause Section of the Fourteenth Amendment that guarantees all citizens receive "equal protection of the laws."

Equal Rights Amendment Proposed amendment to the Constitution that states "Equality of rights under the law shall not be denied or abridged by the United States or any state on account of sex."

equal time rule The rule that requires broadcast stations to sell air time equally to all candidates in a political campaign if they choose to sell it to any.

establishment clause The first clause of the First Amendment; it directs the national government not to sanction an official religion.

European Union An organization that joins 27 countries in Europe into a union that includes free trade, a central bank, a common currency, ease of immigration, a European Parliament, and other political institutions to govern and administer the organization.

exclusionary rule Judicially created rule that prohibits police from using illegally seized evidence at trial.

executive agreements Formal international agreements entered into by the president that do not require the advice and consent of the U.S. Senate.

Executive Office of the President (EOP) A mini-bureaucracy created in 1939 to help the president oversee the executive branch bureaucracy.

executive order Rule or regulation issued by the president that has the effect of law. All executive orders must be published in the *Federal Register*.

executive privilege An implied presidential power that allows the president to refuse to disclose information regarding confidential conversations or national security to Congress or the judiciary.

exit polls Polls conducted as voters leave selected polling places on Election Day.

***ex post facto* law** Law that makes an act punishable as a crime even if the action was legal at the time it was committed.

extradition clause Part of Article IV of the Constitution that requires states to extradite, or return, criminals to states where they have been convicted or are to stand trial.

F

Farewell Address When President George Washington left office, he wrote a letter, addressed to the People of the United States, warning people of the dangers to avoid in order to preserve the republic.

federal bureaucracy The thousands of federal government agencies and institutions that implement and administer federal laws and programs.

federal system System of government in which the national government and state governments share power and derive all authority from the people.

Federalists Those who favored a stronger national government and supported the proposed U.S. Constitution; later became the first U.S. political party.

Fifteenth Amendment One of the three Civil War Amendments; specifically enfranchised newly freed male slaves.

Fifth Amendment Part of the Bill of Rights that imposes a number of restrictions on the federal government with respect to the rights of persons suspected of committing a crime. It provides for indictment by a grand jury and protection against self-incrimination, and prevents the national government from denying a person life, liberty, or property without the due process of law. It also prevents the national government from taking property without just compensation.

fighting words Words that "by their very utterance inflict injury or tend to incite an immediate breach of peace." Fighting words are not subject to the restrictions of the First Amendment.

filibuster A formal way of halting Senate action on a bill by means of long speeches or unlimited debate.

finance chair The individual who coordinates the financial business of the campaign.

First Amendment Part of the Bill of Rights that imposes a number of restrictions on the federal government with respect to civil liberties, including freedom of religion, speech, press, assembly, and petition.

First Continental Congress Meeting held in Philadelphia from September 5 to October 26, 1774, in which fifty-six delegates (from every colony except Georgia) adopted a resolution in opposition to the Coercive Acts.

fiscal policy The deliberate use of the national government's taxing and spending policies to maintain economic stability.

501(c) groups Interest groups whose primary purpose is not electoral politics.

271

political committee Organizations created with the primary purpose of influencing electoral outcomes; the term is typically applied only to freestanding interest groups that do not explicitly advocate for the election of a candidate.

foreign policy Area of policy making that encompasses how one country builds relationships with other countries in order to safeguard its national interest.

Fourteenth Amendment One of the three Civil War Amendments; guarantees equal protection and due process of the law to all U.S. citizens.

Fourth Amendment Part of the Bill of Rights that reads: "The right of the people to be secure in their persons, houses, papers, and effects, against unreasonable searches and seizures, shall not be violated, and no Warrants shall issue, but upon probable cause, supported by Oath or affirmation, and particularly describing the place to be searched, and the persons or things to be seized."

framing The process by which a news organization defines a political issue and consequently affects opinion about the issue.

free exercise clause The second clause of the First Amendment; it prohibits the U.S. government from interfering with a citizen's right to practice his or her religion.

free rider problem Potential members fail to join a group because they can get the benefit, or collective good, sought by the group without contributing the effort.

free trade system A system of international trade that has limited government interference on the sale of goods and services among countries.

front-loading The tendency of states to choose an early date on the nomination calendar.

full faith and credit clause Section of Article IV of the Constitution that ensures judicial decrees and contracts made in one state will be binding and enforceable in any other state.

fundamental freedoms Those rights defined by the Court as essential to order, liberty, and justice and therefore entitled to the highest standard of review.

G

General Agreement on Tariffs and Trade (GATT) Post–World War II economic development treaty designed to help facilitate international trade negotiations and promote free trade.

general election Election in which voters decide which candidates will actually fill elective public offices.

general election campaign Phase of a political campaign aimed at winning election to office.

gerrymandering The drawing of congressional districts to produce a particular electoral outcome without regard to the shape of the district.

get-out-the-vote (GOTV) A push at the end of a political campaign to encourage supporters to go to the polls.

***Gibbons* v. *Ogden* (1824)** The Supreme Court upheld broad congressional power to regulate interstate commerce. The Court's broad interpretation of the Constitution's commerce clause paved the way for later rulings upholding expansive federal powers.

global war on terrorism An international action, initiated by President George W. Bush after the 9/11 attacks, to weed out terrorist operatives throughout the world.

government The formal vehicle through which policies are made and affairs of state are conducted.

government corporations Businesses established by Congress to perform functions that private businesses could provide.

government The formal vehicle through which policies are made and affairs of state are conducted.

governmental (institutional) agenda Problems to which public officials feel obliged to devote active and serious attention.

grandfather clause Voter qualification provision in many southern states that allowed only those citizens whose grandfathers had voted before Reconstruction to vote unless they passed a wealth or literacy test.

Great Compromise The final decision of the Constitutional Convention to create a two-house legislature, with the lower house elected by the people and with powers divided between the two houses. It also made national law supreme.

gross domestic product (GDP) The total market value of all goods and services produced in an area during a year.

H

Hatch Act The 1939 act to prohibit civil servants from taking activist roles in partisan campaigns. This act prohibited federal employees from making political contributions, working for a particular party, or campaigning for a particular candidate.

hold A procedure by which a senator asks to be informed before a particular bill or nomination is brought to the floor. This request signals leadership that a member may have objections to the bill (or nomination) and should be consulted before further action is taken.

Honest Leadership and Open Government Act of 2007 Lobbying reform banning gifts to members of Congress and their staffs, toughening disclosure requirements, and increasing time limits on moving from the federal government to the private sector.

human rights The protection of people's basic freedoms and needs.

I

impeachment The power delegated to the House of Representatives in the Constitution to charge the president, vice president, or other "civil officers," including federal judges, with "Treason, Bribery, or other high Crimes and Misdemeanors." This is the first step in the constitutional process of removing government officials from office.

implementation The process by which a law or policy is put into operation.

implied powers The powers of the national government derived from the enumerated powers and the necessary and proper clause.

incorporation doctrine An interpretation of the Constitution holding that the due process clause of the Fourteenth Amendment requires state and local governments to guarantee the rights stated in the Bill of Rights.

incumbency Already holding an office.

independent executive agencies Governmental units that closely resemble a Cabinet department but have narrower areas of responsibility and perform services rather than regulatory functions.

independent expenditures Spending for campaign activity that is not coordinated with a candidate's campaign.

independent regulatory commission An entity created by Congress outside a major executive department.

indirect democracy A system of government that gives citizens the opportunity to vote for representatives who work on their behalf.

inflation A rise in the general price levels of an economy.

inherent powers Powers that belong to the president because they can be inferred from the Constitution.

inoculation ad Advertising that attempts to counteract an anticipated attack from the opposition before the attack is launched.

interagency councils Working groups created to facilitate coordination of policy making and implementation across a host of governmental agencies.

interest group A collection of people or organizations that tries to influence public policy.

International Monetary Fund (IMF) International governmental organization designed to stabilize international currency transactions.

interstate compacts Contracts between states that carry the force of law; generally now used as a tool to address multistate policy concerns.

iron triangles The relatively ironclad relationships and patterns of interaction that occur among agencies, interest groups, and congressional committees or subcommittees.

isolationism The U.S. policy of avoiding entangling alliances with European powers.

issue networks The loose and informal relationships that exist among a large number of actors who work in broad policy areas.

J

Jim Crow laws Laws enacted by southern states that required segregation in public schools, theaters, hotels, and other public accommodations.

Joint Chiefs of Staff Military advisory body that includes the Army chief of staff, the Air Force chief of staff, the chief of naval operations, and the Marine commandant.

joint committee Standing committee that includes members from both houses of Congress set up to conduct investigations or special studies.

judicial activism A philosophy of judicial decision making that posits judges should use their power broadly to further justice.

judicial implementation How and whether judicial decisions are translated into actual public policies affecting more than the immediate parties to a lawsuit.

judicial restraint A philosophy of judicial decision making that posits courts should allow the decisions of other branches of government to stand, even when they offend a judge's own principles.

judicial review Power of the courts to review acts of other branches of government and the states.

Judiciary Act of 1789 Legislative act that established the basic three-tiered structure of the federal court system.

jurisdiction Authority vested in a particular court to hear and decide the issues in a particular case.

L

legislative courts Courts established by Congress for specialized purposes, such as the Court of Appeals for Veterans Claims.

***Lemon* test** Three-part test created by the Supreme Court for examining the constitutionality of religious establishment issues.

libel False written statement that defames a person's character.

liberal One who favors greater government intervention, particularly in economic affairs and in the provision of social services.

libertarian One who believes in limited government interference in personal and economic liberties.

lobbying The activities of a group or organization that seek to persuade political leaders to support the group's position.

lobbyist Interest group representative who seeks to influence legislation that will benefit his or her organization or client through political and/or financial persuasion.

logrolling Vote trading; voting to support a colleague's bill in return for a promise of future support.

M

majority leader The head of the party controlling the most seats in the House of Representatives or the Senate; is second in authority to the Speaker of the House and in the Senate is regarded as its most powerful member.

majority party The political party in each house of Congress with the most members.

majority rule The central premise of direct democracy in which only policies that collectively garner the support of a majority of voters will be made into law.

manifest destiny Theory that the United States was divinely supported to expand across North America to the Pacific Ocean.

***Marbury* v. *Madison* (1803)** Case in which the Supreme Court first asserted the power of judicial review by finding that the congressional statute extending the Court's original jurisdiction was unconstitutional.

margin of error A measure of the accuracy of a public opinion poll.

markup A session in which committee members offer changes to a bill before it goes to the floor.

Marshall Plan European collective recovery program, named after Secretary of State George C. Marshall, that provided extensive American aid to Western Europe after World War II.

mass media The entire array of organizations through which information is collected and disseminated to the general public.

...tching funds Donations to presidential campaigns whereby every dollar raised from individuals in amounts less than $251 is matched by the federal treasury.

McCulloch **v.** *Maryland* **(1819)** The Supreme Court upheld the power of the national government and denied the right of a state to tax the federal bank, using the Constitution's supremacy clause. The Court's broad interpretation of the necessary and proper clause paved the way for later rulings upholding expansive federal powers.

means-tested programs Programs that require that beneficiaries have incomes below specified levels to be eligible for benefits. Among these are SSI, TANF, and SNAP.

media effects The influence of news sources on public opinion.

Medicaid A government program that subsidizes medical care for the poor.

Medicare The federal program established during the Lyndon B. Johnson administration that provides medical care to elderly Social Security recipients.

mercantilism An economic theory designed to increase a nation's wealth through the development of commercial industry and a favorable balance of trade.

merit system A system of employment based on qualifications, test scores, and ability, rather than party loyalty.

mid-term election An election that takes place in the middle of a presidential term.

military-industrial complex The network of political and financial relations formed by defense industries, the U.S. armed forces, and Congress.

minority leader The head of the party with the second highest number of elected representatives in the House of Representatives or the Senate.

minority party The political party in each house of Congress with the second most members.

Miranda **rights** Statements required of police that inform a suspect of his or her constitutional rights protected by the Fifth Amendment, including the right to an attorney provided by the court if the suspect cannot afford one.

Miranda **v.** *Arizona* **(1966)** A landmark Supreme Court ruling holding that the Fifth Amendment requires individuals arrested for a crime to be advised of their right to remain silent and to have counsel present.

moderate A person who takes a relatively centrist or middle-of-the-road view on most political issues.

monarchy A form of government in which power is vested in hereditary kings and queens who govern in the interest of all.

monetary policy A form of government regulation in which the nation's money supply and interest rates are controlled.

Monroe Doctrine President James Monroe's 1823 pledge that the United States would oppose attempts by European states to reestablish their political control in the Western Hemisphere.

muckraking A form of journalism, in vogue in the early twentieth century, devoted to exposing misconduct by government, business, and individual politicians.

N

narrowcasting Targeting media programming at specific populations within society.

national convention A party meeting held in the presidential election year for the purposes of nominating a presidential and vice presidential ticket and adopting a platform.

national party platform A statement of the general and specific philosophy and policy goals of a political party, usually promulgated at the national convention.

natural law A doctrine that society should be governed by certain ethical principles that are part of nature and, as such, can be understood by reason.

necessary and proper clause The final paragraph of Article I, section 8, of the Constitution, which gives Congress the authority to pass all laws "necessary and proper" to carry out the enumerated powers specified in the Constitution; also called the elastic clause.

negative ad Advertising on behalf of a candidate that attacks the opponent's character or platform.

New Deal The name given to the program of "Relief, Recovery, Reform" begun by President Franklin D. Roosevelt in 1933 to bring the United States out of the Great Depression.

New Federalism Federal–state relationship proposed by Reagan administration during the 1980s; hallmark is returning administrative powers to the state governments.

New Jersey Plan A framework for the Constitution proposed by a group of small states. Its key points were a one-house legislature with one vote for each state, a Congress with the ability to raise revenue, and a Supreme Court with members appointed for life.

news media Media providing the public with new information about subjects of public interest.

New York Times Co. **v.** *Sullivan* **(1964)** Case in which the Supreme Court concluded that "actual malice" must be proven to support a finding of libel against a public figure.

Nineteenth Amendment Amendment to the Constitution that guaranteed women the right to vote.

Ninth Amendment Part of the Bill of Rights that makes it clear that enumerating rights in the Constitution or Bill of Rights does not mean that others do not exist.

nomination campaign Phase of a political campaign aimed at winning a primary election.

non–means-tested programs Programs that provide cash assistance to qualified beneficiaries, regardless of income. Among these are Social Security and unemployment insurance.

North American Free Trade Agreement (NAFTA) Agreement that promotes free movement of goods and services among Canada, Mexico, and the United States.

North Atlantic Treaty Organization (NATO) The first peacetime military treaty joined by the United States; NATO is a collective security pact that includes the United States, Canada, and Western Europe.

nullification The right of a state to declare void a federal law.

O

off the record Information provided to a journalist that will not be released to the public.

Office of Management and Budget (OMB) The office that prepares the president's annual budget proposal, reviews the budget and programs of the executive departments, supplies economic forecasts, and conducts detailed analyses of proposed bills and agency rules.

oligarchy A form of government in which the right to participate depends on the possession of wealth, social status, military position, or achievement.

on background Information provided to a journalist that will not be attributed to a named source.

on the record Information provided to a journalist that can be released and attributed by name to the source.

open market operations The buying and selling of government securities by the Federal Reserve Bank.

original jurisdiction The jurisdiction of courts that hear a case first, usually in a trial. These courts determine the facts of a case.

P

pardon An executive grant providing restoration of all rights and privileges of citizenship to a specific individual charged or convicted of a crime.

party caucus (or conference) A formal gathering of all party members.

party identification A citizen's personal affinity for a political party, usually expressed by a tendency to vote for the candidates of that party.

party realignment Dramatic shifts in partisan preferences that drastically alter the political landscape.

patron A person who finances a group or individual activity.

patronage Jobs, grants, or other special favors that are given as rewards to friends and political allies for their support.

Pendleton Act Reform measure that established the principle of federal employment on the basis of open, competitive exams and created the Civil Service Commission.

personal liberty A key characteristic of U.S. democracy. Initially meaning freedom *from* governmental interference, today it includes demands for freedom *to* engage in a variety of practices without governmental interference or discrimination.

***Plessy* v. *Ferguson* (1896)** Supreme Court case that challenged a Louisiana statute requiring that railroads provide separate accommodations for blacks and whites. The Court found that separate-but-equal accommodations did not violate the equal protection clause of the Fourteenth Amendment.

pluralist theory The theory that political power is distributed among a wide array of diverse and competing interest groups.

pocket veto If Congress adjourns during the ten days the president has to consider a bill passed by both houses of Congress, the bill is considered vetoed without the president's signature.

polarization The presence of increasingly conflicting and divided viewpoints between the Democratic and Republican Parties.

policy adoption The approval of a policy proposal by people with the requisite authority, such as a legislature.

policy coordinating committees Subcabinet-level committees created to facilitate interactions between agencies and departments to handle complex policy problems.

policy evaluation The process of determining whether a course of action is achieving its intended goals.

policy formulation The crafting of proposed courses of action to resolve public problems.

policy implementation The process of carrying out public policy.

political action committees (PACs) Officially recognized fund-raising organizations that represent interest groups and are allowed by federal law to make contributions directly to candidates' campaigns.

political committee Organizations created with the primary purpose of influencing electoral outcomes; the term is typically applied only to freestanding interest groups that do not explicitly advocate for the election of a candidate.

political culture Commonly shared attitudes, beliefs, and core values about how government should operate.

political equality The principle that all citizens are the same in the eyes of the law.

political ideology The coherent set of values and beliefs about the purpose and scope of government held by groups and individuals.

political machine A party organization that recruits voter loyalty with tangible incentives and is characterized by a high degree of control over member activity.

political party An organized group with shared goals and ideals that joins together to run candidates for office and exercise political and electoral power.

political socialization The process through which individuals acquire their political beliefs and values.

politico An elected representative who acts as a trustee or as a delegate, depending on the issue.

politics The study of who gets what, when, and how—or how policy decisions are made.

pollster A campaign consultant who conducts public opinion surveys.

poll tax A tax levied in many southern states and localities that had to be paid before an eligible voter could cast a ballot.

popular consent The principle that governments must draw their powers from the consent of the governed.

popular sovereignty The notion that the ultimate authority in society rests with the people.

population The entire group of people whose attitudes a researcher wishes to measure.

pork Legislation that allows representatives to bring money and jobs to their districts in the form of public works programs, military bases, or other programs.

itive ad Advertising on behalf of a candidate that stresses the candidate's qualifications, family, and issue positions, with no direct reference to the opponent.

precedent A prior judicial decision that serves as a rule for settling subsequent cases of a similar nature.

preemption A concept that allows the national government to override state or local actions in certain policy areas.

president pro tempore The official chair of the Senate; usually the most senior member of the majority party.

press briefing A relatively restricted session between a press secretary or aide and the press.

press conference An unrestricted session between an elected official and the press.

press release A document offering an official comment or position.

press secretary The individual charged with interacting and communicating with journalists on a daily basis.

primary election Election in which voters decide which of the candidates within a party will represent the party in the general election.

prior restraint Constitutional doctrine that prevents the government from prohibiting speech or publication before the fact; generally held to be in violation of the First Amendment.

privileges and immunities clause Part of Article IV of the Constitution guaranteeing that the citizens of each state are afforded the same rights as citizens of all other states.

programmatic requests Federal funds designated for special projects within a state or congressional district.

progressive federalism A pragmatic approach to federalism that views relations between national and state governments as both coercive and cooperative.

prospective judgment A voter's evaluation of a candidate based on what he or she pledges to do about an issue if elected.

protectionism A trade policy wherein a country takes steps to limit the import of foreign goods through tariffs and subsidies to domestic firms.

public funds Donations from general tax revenues to the campaigns of qualifying presidential candidates.

public opinion What the public thinks about a particular issue or set of issues at any point in time.

public opinion polls Interviews or surveys with samples of citizens that are used to estimate the feelings and beliefs of the entire population.

public policy An intentional course of action or inaction followed by government in dealing with some problem or matter of concern.

push polls Polls taken for the purpose of providing information on an opponent that would lead respondents to vote against that candidate.

R

random sampling A method of poll selection that gives each person in a group the same chance of being selected.

Reagan Doctrine The Reagan administration's commitment to ending communism by providing military assistance to anti-communist groups.

reapportionment The reallocation of the number of seats in the House of Representatives after each decennial census.

recession A decline in the economy that occurs as investment sags, production falls off, and unemployment increases.

reconciliation A procedure that allows consideration of controversial issues affecting the budget by limiting debate to twenty hours, thereby ending threat of a filibuster.

redistricting The process of redrawing congressional districts to reflect increases or decreases in seats allotted to the states, as well as population shifts within a state.

regulations Rules governing the operation of all government programs that have the force of law.

republic A government rooted in the consent of the governed; a representative or indirect democracy.

reserve requirements Government requirements that a portion of member banks' deposits be retained as backing for their loans.

reserved powers Powers reserved to the states by the Tenth Amendment that lie at the foundation of a state's right to legislate for the public health and welfare of its citizens.

retrospective judgment A voter's evaluation of a candidate based on past performance on a particular issue.

right to privacy The right to be left alone; a judicially created principle encompassing a variety of individual actions protected by the penumbras cast by several constitutional amendments, including the First, Third, Fourth, Ninth, and Fourteenth Amendments.

Roe v. Wade (1973) The Supreme Court found that a woman's right to an abortion was protected by the right to privacy that could be implied from specific guarantees found in the Bill of Rights applied to the states through the Fourteenth Amendment.

Roosevelt Corollary Concept developed by President Theodore Roosevelt early in the twentieth century declaring that it was the responsibility of the United States to ensure stability in Latin America and the Caribbean.

rule making A quasi-legislative process resulting in regulations that have the characteristics of a legislative act.

Rule of Four At least four justices of the Supreme Court must vote to consider a case before it can be heard.

S

sample A subset of the whole population selected to be questioned for the purposes of prediction or gauging opinion.

Second Continental Congress Meeting that convened in Philadelphia on May 10, 1775, at which it was decided that an army should be raised and George Washington of Virginia was named commander in chief.

secular realignment The gradual rearrangement of party coalitions, based more on demographic shifts than on shocks to the political system.

select (or special) committee Temporary committee appointed for a specific purpose.

selective incorporation A judicial doctrine whereby most, but not all, protections found in the Bill of Rights are made applicable to the states via the Fourteenth Amendment.

senatorial courtesy A process by which presidents generally allow senators from the state in which a judicial vacancy occurs to block a nomination by simply registering their objection.

seniority Time of continuous service on a committee.

separation of powers A way of dividing the power of government among the legislative, executive, and judicial branches, each staffed separately, with equality and independence of each branch ensured by the Constitution.

Seventeenth Amendment Amendment to the U.S. Constitution that made senators directly elected by the people, removing their selection from state legislatures.

signing statements Occasional written comments attached to a bill signed by the president.

Sixteenth Amendment Amendment to the U.S. Constitution that authorized Congress to enact a national income tax.

Sixth Amendment Part of the Bill of Rights that sets out the basic requirements of procedural due process for federal courts to follow in criminal trials. These include speedy and public trials, impartial juries, trials in the state where the crime was committed, notice of the charges, the right to confront and obtain favorable witnesses, and the right to counsel.

slander Untrue spoken statements that defame the character of a person.

social capital Cooperative relationships that facilitate the resolution of collective problems.

social conservative One who believes that the government should support and further traditional moral teachings.

Social Security Act A 1935 law that established old age insurance; assistance for the needy, aged, blind, and families with dependent children; and unemployment insurance.

solicitor general The fourth-ranking member of the Department of Justice; responsible for handling nearly all appeals on behalf of the U.S. government to the Supreme Court.

Speaker of the House The only officer of the House of Representatives specifically mentioned in the Constitution; the chamber's most powerful position; traditionally a member of the majority party.

spoils system The firing of public-office holders of a defeated political party to replace them with loyalists of the newly elected party.

Stamp Act Congress Meeting of representatives of nine of the thirteen colonies held in New York City in 1765, during which representatives drafted a document to send to the king that listed how their rights had been violated.

standing committee Committee to which proposed bills are referred; continues from one Congress to the next.

stare decisis In court rulings, a reliance on past decisions or precedents to formulate decisions in new cases.

statist One who believes in extensive government control of personal and economic liberties.

strategic trade policy A trade policy wherein governments identify key industries that they wish to see grow and enact policies to support their development and success.

stratified sampling A variation of random sampling; the population is divided into subgroups and weighted based on demographic characteristics of the national population.

straw poll Unscientific survey used to gauge public opinion on a variety of issues and policies.

strict constructionist An approach to constitutional interpretation that emphasizes interpreting the Constitution as it was originally written and intended by the Framers.

strict scrutiny A heightened standard of review used by the Supreme Court to determine the constitutional validity of a challenged practice.

substantive due process Judicial interpretation of the Fifth and Fourteenth Amendments' due process clauses that protects citizens from arbitrary or unjust state or federal laws.

suffrage movement The drive for voting rights for women that took place in the United States from 1890 to 1920.

Super PACs Political action committees established to make independent expenditures.

supremacy clause Portion of Article VI of the Constitution mandating that national law is supreme to (that is, supersedes) all other laws passed by the states or by any other subdivision of government.

suspect classification Category or class, such as race, that triggers the highest standard of scrutiny from the Supreme Court.

symbolic speech Symbols, signs, and other methods of expression generally considered to be protected by the First Amendment.

systemic agenda A discussion agenda; it consists of all public issues that are viewed as requiring governmental attention.

T

Taliban A fundamentalist Islamic group that controlled Afghanistan from 1996 until U.S. military intervention in 2001. The Taliban provided refuge for al-Qaeda, allowing terrorist training camps to operate in the country.

tariffs Taxes on imported goods.

Tenth Amendment The final part of the Bill of Rights that defines the basic principle of American federalism in stating that the powers not delegated to the national government are reserved to the states or to the people.

The Federalist Papers A series of eighty-five political essays written by Alexander Hamilton, James Madison, and John Jay in support of ratification of the U.S. Constitution.

Thirteenth Amendment One of the three Civil War Amendments; specifically bans slavery in the United States.

ee-Fifths Compromise Agreement reached at the Constitutional Convention stipulating that each slave was to be counted as three-fifths of a person for purposes of determining population for representation in the U.S. House of Representatives.

Title IX Provision of the Education Amendments of 1972 that bars educational institutions that receive federal funds from discriminating against female students.

totalitarianism A form of government in which power resides in a leader who rules according to self-interest and without regard for individual rights and liberties.

tracking polls Continuous surveys that enable a campaign or news organization to chart a candidate's daily rise or fall in support.

trade association A group that represents a specific industry.

transactions theory The theory that public policies are the result of narrowly defined exchanges or transactions among political actors.

trial court Court of original jurisdiction where cases begin.

Truman Doctrine U.S. anti-communist policy initiated in 1947 that became the basis of U.S. foreign policy throughout the Cold War.

trustee Role played by an elected representative who listens to constituents' opinions and then uses his or her best judgment to make a final decision.

turnout The proportion of the voting-age public that casts a ballot.

Twenty-Fifth Amendment Adopted in 1967 to establish procedures for filling vacancies in the office of president and vice president as well as providing for procedures to deal with the disability of a president.

Twenty-Second Amendment Adopted in 1951; prevents a president from serving more than two terms, or more than ten years if he came to office via the death, resignation, or impeachment of his predecessor.

U

UN Security Council A principal part of the United Nations, charged with authorizing peacekeeping operations, international sanctions, and military action in order to maintain global peace and security.

unitary system System of government in which the local and regional governments derive all authority from a strong national government.

U.S. v. Nixon (1974) Supreme Court ruling on power of the president, holding that no absolute constitutional executive privilege allows a president to refuse to comply with a court order to produce information needed in a criminal trial.

veto The formal, constitutional authority of the president to reject bills passed by both houses of Congress, thus preventing them from becoming law without further congressional action.

Virginia Plan The first general plan for the Constitution offered in Philadelphia. Its key points were a bicameral legislature, as well as an executive and a judiciary chosen by the national legislature.

voter canvass The process by which a campaign reaches individual voters, either by door-to-door solicitation or by telephone.

W

War Powers Resolution Passed by Congress in 1973; the president is limited in the deployment of troops overseas to a sixty-day period in peacetime (which can be extended for an extra thirty days to permit withdrawal) unless Congress explicitly gives its approval for a longer period.

whip Party leader who keeps close contact with all members of his or her party, takes vote counts on key legislation, prepares summaries of bills, and acts as a communications link within a party.

World Bank International governmental organization created to provide loans for large economic development projects.

World Trade Organization (WTO) An international organization that replaced the GATT in 1995 to supervise and expand international trade.

writ of *certiorari* A request for the Supreme Court to order up the records from a lower court to review the case.

writs of *habeas corpus* Petition requesting that a judge order authorities to prove that a prisoner is being held lawfully and that allows the prisoner to be freed if the government's case does not persuade the judge. *Habeas corpus* rights imply that prisoners have a right to know what charges are being made against them.

yellow journalism A form of newspaper publishing in vogue in the late nineteenth century that featured pictures, comics, color, and sensationalized news coverage.

Index